• Caralan Dams • Adelaide Daniels • Mary Darcy • Cynthia David • se Dawe • Madeline Day • Jessie M. De Both • Elizabeth Delahey • Abbie DeLury • Margaret Demerson • Grace Denison • Rollande Des Bois • Anna Dexter • Thelma Dickman • Edith Emma Dighton • Bert Dodd • Thora Dolan • Ann Donohoe • Elinor Donaldson • Don Douloff • Elizabeth Driver • Judith Drynan • Pierre Dubrulle • Helene Ducie • Elaine Kerr Duffy • Francine Dufresne • Dorothy Duncan • Nancy Durnford • Gertrude Dutton • Eileen Dwillies • Donalda Elder • Greta Elgis • Edith L. Elliott • Eleanor Ellis • Marjorie Ellis • Margaret Bateman Ellison • Patricia Ellison • Marjorie Elwood • Francoise Emard • Margo Embury • Cathy Enright • Nancy Enright • Evelyn Erdman • Mary Evans-Atkinson • Tara Fainstein • Elizabeth Feniak • Carol Ferguson • Dorothy Ferguson • Jeremy Ferguson • Shannon Ferrier • Jack Ferry • Joan Fielden • Betty Fitzsimmons • Marjorie Thompson Flint • Tryphena Flood • Barbara Floyd • Katherine C. Lewis Flynn • Frederique Fournier • Gladys Fraser • Mairi Fraser • Margaret Fraser • Marie Fraser • Ruth Fremes • Jocelyn Frenette • Alison Fryer • Helen Gagen • Mary Jane Gagen • Melvin Gallant • Anne Gardiner • Blanche Pownall Garrett • Nancy George • Gertrude Gerlach • Bruno Gerussi • Josephine Gibson • Janice Murray Gill • Norene Gilletz • Marjorie Gillies • Pearl Gineen • Cecile Girard-Hicks • Margie Glue • Germaine Gloutnez • Marci Goldman-Posluns • Joanne Good • Henrietta Goplen • Jergen Gothe • Sondra Gotlieb • Helen Gougeon • Jennifer Grange • Ethel Green • Barbara Greeno • Brian Greggains • Annie R. Gregory • Francine Grimaldi • Arlene Gryfe • Marjorie J. Guilford • Carol Gulyas • Lillian Gush • Peter Gzowski • Gail Johnston Habs • Gail Hall • Donna-Joy Halliday • Gaye Hansen • Lynne Hansen • Anne Hanson • Claire Hardy • Jeanne Hartley • Helen Hatton • Jan Haworth • Margaret Henderson • Sally Henry • Glenda Hess • Lynn Hestbak • Florence Hilchey • Janet McKenzie Hill • Pamela Hillman • Mary C. Hiltz • Ruth Himmelfarb • Nesta Hinton • Jean Hoare • Joseph Hoare • Sam Hofer • Linda Hogue • Barb Holland • Marie Holmes • Mary Holmes • Shirley Anne Holmes • Betty Holthe • Patricia Holtz • Grace Gordon Hood • Adelaide Hoodless • Jane Hope • Susan Horne • Claire Horsley • Margaret Howard • Frances Hucks • Evelyn Hullah • Hope H. Hunt • Alice Hunter • Juliette Huot • Anita Ivanauskis • Eileen Iwanicki • Ruth Jackson • Patricia Jamieson • Elsa Jenkins • Alice Jenner • Ivan Jesperson • Eve Johnson • Kathy Jupp • Ruby Juss • Marilyn Kaiser • Marion Kane • Lillian Kaplun • Joanne Kates • Francoise Kayler • Gail Keddy • Barbara Kelly • Mary Kelso •

# *A Century of Canadian*

# HOME COOKING

## 1900 THROUGH THE '90s

# A Century of Canadian
# HOME COOKING

## 1900 THROUGH THE '90s

Carol Ferguson

Margaret Fraser

0  57812 53415  5

Prentice Hall Canada Inc., Scarborough, Ontario

**Canadian Cataloguing in Publication Data**

Ferguson, Carol
    A century of Canadian home cooking

Includes bibliographical references and index.
ISBN 0-13-953415-6

1. Cookery, Canadian. 2. Cookery, Canadian - History
- 20th century. I. Fraser, Margaret. II. Title.

TX715.6.F37 1992    641.5971    C92-094671-2

Prentice Hall, Inc., Englewood Cliffs, New Jersey
Prentice-Hall International, Inc., London
Prentice-Hall of Australia, Pty., Ltd., Sydney
Prentice-Hall of India Pvt., Ltd., New Delhi
Prentice-Hall of Japan, Inc., Tokyo
Prentice-Hall of Southeast Asia (Pte.) Ltd., Singapore
Editora Prentice-Hall do Brasil Ltda., Rio de Janeiro
Prentice-Hall Hispanoamericana, S.A., Mexico

Managing editor: Tanya Long
Text editor: Katharine Vanderlinden
Recipe editor: Bev Renahan
Art director: Gail Ferreira Ng-A-Kien
Designer: Aurora Di Ciaula
Composition: Laura Ball
Permissions coordinators: Karen Taylor and Sharon Houston
Food photography: Hal Roth Photography Inc.
Food stylists: Olga Truchan and Jennifer McLagan
Props coordinator: Karen Martin
Recipe testing: Carrie Ross
Nutrition consultant: Denise Beatty

ISBN 0-13-953415-6

Printed and bound in Canada by DW Friesen Printers

1  2  3  4  5  DWF  96  95  94  93  92

# Contents

# Acknowledgements

We gratefully acknowledge all those – associates, consultants, families, friends and strangers – who so generously shared with us their time and advice, cookbook collections, family recipes, archival and reference materials, files, photographs and memories.

We also wish to acknowledge the many professional food "communicators" who over the years have contributed so much to Canadian home cooking. Many of the names that were familiar throughout the decades are listed on the end papers of this book. These include food writers and editors, cookbook authors, nutrition writers, cooking school teachers, radio and television food show hosts and home economists in business.

Thanks, too, to the countless other contributors to the Canadian food scene: chefs and restaurateurs, home economics teachers and professors, test kitchen staffs, food promotion agencies, producer associations and marketing boards, regional home economists, dietitians and nutritionists, food technologists, food photographers and stylists, wine columnists, regional cooks at country inns and bed-and-breakfasts, food historians, food festival organizers, farmers' market vendors, cookbook shops, specialty food and kitchen shops, butchers, bakers, greengrocers, gardeners, farmers, fishermen and women, and all our food producers.

And special thanks to mothers and grandmothers for a legacy of good Canadian home cooking.

# Preface

**C**ome on in! Will you stay for supper? The pot luck offerings of our '90s kitchen may be quite different from what was cooking in 1900, but the welcome is still the same.

The 20th century has brought a multitude of changes to Canadian home cooking. But a tradition of hospitality and sharing has prevailed from the very beginning. At the turn of the century, rural families always had room for another chair around the table and another potato in the stewpot; town folk always invited visitors to stay for tea. The next generations continued that tradition down through the decades, surviving the tough times of the '30s and '40s, celebrating the good times of the '50s and '60s, sampling the latest fashions of the '70s and '80s. And in the 1990s we have come full circle, returning to the simple pleasures of hearth and home, welcoming friends and neighbors into our nests. Vintage recipes are back again as we discover how quick and easy many of them are (our grandmothers were busy, too, out in the fields and factories while keeping the home fires burning).

As we celebrate Canada's 125th birthday and approach not only a new century but a new millenium, it's an appropriate time to look back as well as ahead. One of the best ways to do that is from a culinary perspective. Food, especially home cooking, is a direct reflection of social and cultural history, of regional and family ties and our collective identity as Canadians.

Yet food is largely ignored in the history books, probably because it was long associated with women and domestic life and therefore not considered important. Research into our culinary past is a fairly recent development. Most public archives list little or nothing under "Food." "Cookery" sometimes leads to good collections of vintage cookbooks, but home cooking is otherwise left out. Photo archives are better, often revealing wonderful images of early picnics or pioneer life, but no stories to go with them. And 20th century cooking is usually missing completely.

To document the entire culinary history of this vast country would require many volumes. We chose to start at 1900 for several reasons. First, our pioneering era was mostly over. The 20th century launched the new dominion into her modern history – "Canada's century," as Prime Minister Wilfred Laurier labelled it. The country was completed coast to coast by 1905, with Alberta and Saskatchewan forming the last links in the original chain of provinces. Before 1900, Canada was still a collection of widely separated regions and their culinary history is best looked at individually. By the turn of the century, a gradual blending had produced enough similarities coast to coast to view our cooking nationally.

Another reason to focus on the 20th century is that our pre-1900 food styles have already been documented well in several provinces. Some excellent regional culinary histories have been published by respected researchers, such as Bunny Barss on prairie food. Other authors such as Quebec's Julian Armstrong, Ontario's

Elizabeth Baird, Nova Scotia's Marie Nightingale and P.E.I.'s Julie Watson have contributed notable historical cookbooks. Local and provincial historical societies have also produced valuable studies of pre-1900 cooking.

To document 20th century cooking, we could have chosen any one of many different perspectives. Entire encyclopedias could be written on the history of food products and food companies, developments in agriculture, domestic science education, immigration and ethnic roots, health and nutrition, kitchen equipment, food shops and supermarkets, restaurant trends, media influences, cookbooks. All were important influences on home cooking but they didn't evolve separately. So we've gathered them into a chronological progression, layering decade upon decade, each adding its own blend of new styles and flavors.

Some of the best insights into the past are provided by old cookbooks. As cookbook bibliographer Elizabeth Driver says, "As a direct window into the world of women, cookbooks are an important resource in women's studies. And they often illuminate the local history and ethnic makeup of a particular area." Vintage cookbooks give much more than recipes; they reflect the tastes and attitudes of an era. Many include detailed menus, descriptions of table settings, dining etiquette, instructions on feeding invalids or keeping servants in tow, local advertisements for groceries and new stoves, illustrations of kitchen layouts and photographs of stylish dining rooms.

Tracking recipes through the decades, we also realized that most recipes were a lot older than we thought. Many used in the first half of this century had been simply passed along from earlier generations and adjusted to available ingredients. No really brand-new recipes or methods surfaced until the late '40s and '50s, when postwar technology and affluence launched the "convenience foods" era. Recipe writing styles also showed an interesting evolution, as instructions such as "butter size of an egg," "flour to roll" and "mix as usual" (when it was assumed that anyone with a lick of sense knew what to do) gradually changed to more precise measures in the '20s and metric conversion in the '70s.

Of course many early cookbooks, just like contemporary volumes, represent only the most fashionable cuisine of the day. For a truer look at home cooking, handwritten recipe books are the real treasures of every decade. They are the very best kind of hand-me-downs, culinary family trees that are cherished for generations.

In choosing recipes to represent each decade, we've opted for a sampling of the most typical or popular. Everyone's perspective on food is very personal. We all have our own food memories and favorite dishes. When we asked people what foods they remember from childhood, the answers were as diverse as the families and regions they came from:

"A good mug-up of chowder in Lunenburg"; "Those wonderful wild game recipes of my mother's when we lived at Meadow Lake"; "My Dauphin grandmother's perogies with sour cream"; "Smoking salmon in our back yard in Prince Rupert."

Our food styles vary according to where we came from, when and where we settled in Canada, whether we're rural or urban, rich or poor, live to eat or eat to live. Every community in Canada has its own unique mix of people, all with their own stories to tell, and a collection of personal anecdotes and recipes from across the country would make a very entertaining book. But a comprehensive culinary history must be more than personal nostalgia. Canadian cooking is a complex intermingling of many tastes. Our multicultural cuisine has been compared to a big soup pot where each ingredient complements the others but retains its own identity. Condensing it all into the space of one book was a real challenge (sometimes we felt that we were having to turn that soup into bouillon cubes!).

In the '90s, there is still no easy definition of Canadian cooking. We have always been and probably always will be defined by our diversity.

There's no denying our geography and varied regional histories. But by looking back at the way we were and sampling the flavors of the decades, we can appreciate the combination of influences that has given us all the choices we have today.

We're delighted to share with you our food tour of the 20th century.

Read, cook, eat and enjoy.

# LOOKING BACK

## *Margaret Fraser*

My food memories start in the '30s in Saskatoon, where Mother fed us simply but well – roast beef or chicken for Sunday dinner, shepherd's pie, finnan haddie or mince (a Scottish stew of ground beef served over potatoes) during the week. There was often a big pan of chocolate cake with brown sugar icing or light-as-a-feather scones she cooked on a heavy black griddle. Grandfather Macintosh started life in Canada with a small grocery store in Winnipeg, where he wooed customers with similar scones he made in the back of his store. Bappy, my Dad's mother who made the transition from a Kent County farm in Ontario to the harsh prairies, loved nothing better than afternoon tea with Mother's matrimonial cake or macaroons. I loved it, too.

Family picnics at the Forestry Farm and birthday party wiener roasts at Beaver Creek were special. Christmas was a feast with Dad carving the turkey right at the table, like a surgeon. Mom and her friends in the "circles" at Westminster Church held teas regularly. We lugged our silver candelabra and tea service to the church basement for these occasions, where ladies (always with hats) formally poured tea at either end of the table, others passing plates of fancy sandwiches and "dainties."

I remember feeds of fresh corn-on-the-cob, shelling peas and eating most of them raw, the huge wooden boxes of B.C. apples delivered each winter, and Easter holidays when we kids pulled sprouts from the last of the winter's potatoes in the basement. I hated picking the lamb's quarters that grew along the back fence (it tasted like spinach), but I loved stealing rhubarb and dipping it in sugar to eat raw. A "bun lady" brought warm home-baked white rolls each week to our back door and I rather thought I'd like to do that when I grew up.

Looking back, I realize that in spite of growing up in a city with lots of Ukrainians, Greeks and Chinese, I never once tasted any of their heritage dishes home-cooked. Greek restaurants served steaks and chops and good toasted westerns, and we ate a North American version of chop suey in Chinese cafes, but nary a cabbage roll nor a taste of baklava.

After a home ec degree at the University of Saskatchewan, I opted for hospital dietetics in Toronto, where a whole new world opened up. Ontario seemed magical to me as I walked through the Jewish market (now Kensington) beside Toronto Western hospital, picked cherries at Niagara and watched the tomato harvest near Chatham. Work in the test kitchen at Shirriff's, where the aroma of extracts and marmalade wafted over the neighborhood, seemed very exciting as I created recipes and learned about food photography.

Marriage and a family settled me into a suburban home kitchen for the '60s. I baked cookies for my two girls and a Brownie pack, and free-lanced. Live TV commercials were replaced by film, and package photography was required for the deluge of new mixes, so I concentrated on food styling. Baking 20 or 30 identical layers of cake or 8 cherry pies in a day taught my kids to ask, "Is this for work or for us?" when they opened the refrigerator.

As the Fraser nest emptied in the '80s, food styling and writing for *Canadian Living* took on new meaning, especially at Christmas. Creating holiday cookies with long-distance grandchildren in mind was easy, but we always did Christmas food photography in the heat of summer.

Researching this "decades" book has created new food memories for me. Oatcakes will always be compared to the melt-in-your-mouth kind I ate in Cape Breton. A saskatoon pie (dripping with purple juice) at Riverbend Farm near Saskatoon took me back to berry-picking when I was little. In Yellowknife, the fishing guide panfried our catch over a wood fire, just like we used to cook pickerel on a coal oil stove at Wakaw Lake.

Squid and cod drying on a clothesline down east was new to me. And on our arrival at a St. John's bed and breakfast, the owner announced, "I've just made a half a stone of flour up," so we ate fresh Newfoundland bread. Raspberry sour cream pie in Fredericton brought back memories of sour cream pie my mother baked, only hers had currants.

Along with the food, it's the people I'll remember with love. In a Quebec farm kitchen near Sherbrooke, Marjorie Goodfellow heated homemade soup on a wood stove while her 90-year-old mother told me, "They won't let me have flour anymore . . . I bake too much." And as we stopped for apples at a roadside stand in the Annapolis Valley, the sales gal insisted I "come back to the house and meet Mrs. Inglis. She'll have recipes for you." We drank freshly pressed apple cider and ate homemade ginger cookies, as we pored over a shopping bag full of clippings and handwritten recipes pasted together.

It's hard to believe that hundreds of old recipes are "never-fail," although somehow I trust "Presbyterian Squares" and "Cake That Goes To Church." Of course I have favorite cookbooks: a '40s Purity cookbook with a missing cover; Nabob's *Time-honored Recipes from the West*, full of nostalgia; Lunenburg's *Dutch Oven* book, my first regional cookbook; the *Saskatchewan Homemakers'* book, with prairie memories. And the *Canadian Living Barbecue Cookbook* for year-round use.

I am fiercely Canadian, especially about food, and proud of the differences that make our regional cooking styles unique. And I still love baking cookies.

# LOOKING BACK

## *Carol Ferguson*

The year is about 1905 and I'm a fashionable Edwardian lady – big hat, long skirts, taking tea in the garden or nibbling strawberries from a wicker picnic basket or swooping into an elegant dinner midst potted palms.

Or it's 1915 and I've just baked up an ovenful of "good flaky pies with well-cooked undercrusts" before I march off with Nellie McClung to a suffragist rally. Or it's 1942 and Vera Lynn is singing "I'll be seeing you" as I pack up my best butterless-sugarless-eggless fruitcake for the boys overseas before rushing off to my job as a Bren gun girl.

One of the greatest hazards of researching this book was my inclination to get sidetracked in one decade or another. Never mind if I hadn't actually been around at the time. Interviewing people who remembered it well, and poring over old diaries, letters, vintage photographs and cookbooks has given me a whole new batch of food memories to add to my personal collection.

My favorite decade is the first one, not only for all that lovely upstairs-downstairs stuff (of course I was always "upstairs"), but also for a very personal reason – my own prairie roots. Talking to pioneer prairie women or reading the journals of earlier homesteaders, one can't help but be moved by their constant battles with blizzards, dust storms and loneliness (not to mention their bread-baking, butter-churning and jam-making). Over and over again, they simply say, "It had to be done." Some were luckier (in love or location or both) and rejoiced in the free-spiritedness they felt in their new country; as ranchwoman Moira O'Neill put it, "I like a flannel shirt and liberty."

My grandparents on both sides brought their young families out from Britain to the wild and windy west in the early 1900s, and my mother often talks of her mother and how hard she must have struggled to keep them all fed and happy. But in her big farmhouse in the middle of the empty prairie, my very Scottish granny was soon carrying on the ritual of afternoon tea just like in the old country.

My own childhood memories are filled with aunts and uncles and cousins gathered at that same farm, around the dining room table or at picnics under the trees in the garden. I also remember standing, in a long apron, on a stool in granny's baking pantry, watching her gentle deftness with shortbread and scones.

In another house I sat and watched my mother bake, too. She enjoyed making the lemon tarts, jelly rolls, cream puffs, poppyseed cakes, cinnamon buns and yeast doughnuts (for which she was famous among tea circles, bridge clubs and my high school boyfriends) but was not so crazy about the annual canning of peaches or making jelly out of "those goldarned chokecherries."

The breads, pies and cakes that Mom and her friends regularly turned out were truly an art form, but it was all accompanied by an astonishing modesty, just as it was for the generation of women before them. Any hint of vanity about taken-for-granted skills, or any straying into "fancy" cooking, was seen as "putting on the dog."

My culinary horizons began to expand during university days in late-'50s Winnipeg, mostly via such heady stuff as cherry cheesecake at the Town 'n' Country, steak and salad (choice of dressing!) at Rae and Jerry's and chili dogs at a Pembina Highway take-out.

My first job after graduation was with Sally Henry in Canada Packers' Toronto test kitchen and out on the road doing cooking schools. In an era of innumerable new cake and pastry mixes, we countered with easy "one-bowl" cakes made with Domestic shortening and a "no-fail" pie crust recipe that's still on the lard packages. But at the same time, we shamelessly touted the joys of Polynesian shish kebobs (Klik and pineapple) and chafing-dish wieners in barbecue sauce.

On the other hand, the '60s brought food revelations of the very best kind: my first tastes of fresh lobster in the Maritimes; croissants in Montreal cafés and espresso in Toronto coffee houses; my first encounter with real French cooking when I assisted Dione Lucas at the art gallery cooking show (I'll never forget the *mousse au chocolat* or *filet de sole bonne femme*).

By the '70s, I was battling story deadlines and my kids were decorating the Christmas tree with the same kinds of cookies I'd made at their age. But otherwise they were clearly a different generation. Growing up in an Italian neighborhood, attending a mini-United Nations school and doing a lot of travelling tuned them in very young to a large world of terrific tastes, and they grew up cooking Italian, French and Jamaican.

Looking back at the '80s brings lots of *Canadian Living* memories. Many of my favorite projects involved heritage cooking and digging out our Canadian culinary roots. In one vintage recipe contest, hundreds of readers sent in heart-warming stories along with their treasured family recipes. It was also great fun sleuthing the mysterious origins of Nanaimo Bars with Anne Lindsay and railway cakes with Nancy Millar.

Travelling back and forth across the country turned up lots of interesting cooks to write about and many delicious moments for me: a golden autumn day in the Annapolis Valley, with rum-sauced apple dumplings for lunch; exploring old Quebec with Suzanne Leclerc, a sunset view across the wide St. Lawrence and fresh scallops for supper; munching bake-oven scones and watching the old Red River paddleboats at Lower Fort Garry; gathering oysters in a misty west coast inlet and eating them on the dock at Cortes Bay. I wish every Canadian could do the same; the flavors of our beautiful, bountiful land produce memories to savor forever.

# Introduction

## OUR CULINARY BEGINNINGS: AN UPDATE TO 1900

The pioneering eras of Canada's farflung regions established the diverse culinary roots from which our 20th century cooking evolved. In 1900 Canada was still a very young country, with the West just opening up, while in older regions such as the Maritimes and Quebec, many distinct traditions were already firmly entrenched, some of them going back nearly three centuries.

But despite the differences of time and place, the first settlers of every region faced the same kinds of challenges. In the beginning, life was very hard but defining "Canadian cuisine" was simple: you ate what was put in front of you. For our early pioneers, that meant whatever they could hunt, fish, forage or grow in the wilderness frontiers. They all brought with them the food traditions of their homelands but it took a while for those transplanted roots to take hold. Sharing and learning from each other and from the native peoples, they gradually adapted to new climates and ingredients.  Every region followed a similar pattern of development: as farms improved and gardens grew, steady diets of beans and salt pork were replaced with fresh vegetables and meat; fireplace cooking evolved to woodstoves; better transportation and the first general store brought reliable supplies, better ingredients, kitchen equipment and new gadgets. And eventually, the first cookbooks appeared, adding new recipes to the traditional fare.

Our distinctive Canadian cooking was being born – a product of our many different regions and of the peoples who settled there. Today, Canadians enjoy a taste of the past at restored pioneer villages, historic forts and houses, local heritage museums and countless regional festivals that celebrate our culinary beginnings.

### FIRST PEOPLES

The history of Canadian food begins with the aboriginal peoples who had been here for thousands of years before the first Europeans arrived. The ancestors of our Indian nations migrated from Asia near the end of the last great ice age, at least 12,000 years ago. Crossing the land bridge that is now the Bering Strait, they gradually spread out all over the Americas, evolving into distinct cultures based on available food sources. Most were nomadic hunter–gatherers living on large and small game animals, fish and wild plants. Our present-day Inuit are descended from the Thule culture, a whale-hunting society which spread across the Arctic about a thousand years ago.

By the time the first Europeans arrived in the 15th century, they found many different indigenous societies well adapted to local climates and food supplies: the Micmac fishermen on the east coast; the agricultural Iroquois and Huron nations around the Great Lakes, growing corn, beans and pumpkins; the bison hunters of the great prairie confederations; the caribou-hunters of the north; and complex west coast cultures thriving in a gentle climate with abundant seafood. Native foods like pemmican, corn and dried salmon saved the early explorers and fur traders from starvation, and the first European settlers of every region survived by learning traditional Indian methods of cooking and preservation.

The native cultures, though distinctly diverse, had in common a spirituality bonded with nature. Their beliefs that all living things, plants and animals as well as humans, are related equally in spirit meant intimate ties with the natural world, never dominating, taking only what was needed for food and always putting something back. Only recently has the value of the ancient cultures, with their respect for the land and environment, begun to be recognized by other Canadians.

## NEWFOUNDLAND

The people of Newfoundland and Labrador retain strong links with the past through some of the oldest food traditions in North America.

Viking settlements in the north date back to 1000 A.D., but John Cabot officially "discovered" Newfoundland in 1497. By the early 1500s, ships from England, France, Portugal and Spain were sailing year after year to the great cod-fishing banks. The first official settlement was established by English colonists in 1610 at Conception Bay. During the 17th and 18th centuries, the harbor towns of the Avalon peninsula grew as bases for fishing, whaling, trading and pirating, and outports were settled by English and Irish fishermen. By 1800, St. John's had become a bustling seaport with a population of 5,000 and in 1855, Newfoundland was given full colonial status.

Isolation from the mainland helped maintain a unique culture that is reflected in customs, dialect, folklore, place names and traditional foods. Many of the old favorites are the substantial fare of hard-working seafaring folk and reflect the use of available ingredients. Salt cod, salt beef, fatback salt pork, molasses, root vegetables and dried peas and beans are basic ingredients of the old cooking. Newfoundlanders love a good "scoff" where people socialize and enjoy a hearty meal, often a "Jigg's Dinner" with salt beef and pease pudding. Other traditional favorites include pea soup, fish chowders, fish and brewis with scrunchions, panfried cod tongues, cod au gratin (with cheddar cheese on top) and baked fresh cod or game birds with stuffing (always seasoned with savory). Breads, buns, spicy cakes, cookies and steamed puddings such as figgy duff are often made with pork fat, molasses and raisins. Molasses is used in "lassy" tarts, dumplings, puddings and sauces. Wild berries such as partridgeberries and bakeapples (which look like yellow raspberries) are enjoyed in pies, puddings and preserves.

## THE MARITIMES

The food traditions of the Maritime provinces go back nearly four centuries to the French settlements of Acadia (now regions of Nova Scotia and New Brunswick). In 1605 at Port Royal in the Annapolis Valley, Champlain created North America's first "gourmet club," the Order of Good Cheer, to raise the spirits of his winter-weary troops.

The first Acadian settlers prospered fairly well on their farms and learned the Micmac ways of using wild game, fish, fruit and maple syrup. But life was not stable as the colony passed back and forth from French to English control, and in 1755 the British ordered the expulsion of the Acadians from their homes, scattering families as far south as Louisiana where they came to be called Cajuns. In the 1760s many returned to resettle along maritime shores; much of their new land was poor for farming and many switched by necessity to fishing. Traditional Acadian recipes include many *fricots* (thick soups of potatoes with meat, chicken or seafood), *pâté au râpure* or "rappie pie" made with grated potatoes and chicken or pork, *poutines rapées* (potato dumplings), cod and potato cakes, clam and potato pie and many other fish and meat pies. Favorite desserts are *galettes* (oatmeal, molasses or sugar cookies), sugar pies and steamed or baked fruit puddings (*poutines*).

By the mid 1700s, the garrison town of Halifax had become a centre of British social life, with the governor and his lady setting the pace with elegant banquets.

German farmers settled at Lunenburg, producing many well-known regional dishes such as Dutch Mess (codfish and potatoes), Solomon Gundy (pickled herring), Kohl Slaw, homemade sausages and sauerkraut. Following the American Revolution, 30,000 Loyalists moved north to the Maritimes, instilling the flavors of New England and some southern states into the region. Loyalists founded the city of Saint John, which soon became a thriving ship-building centre with an active cultural life. A large number of blacks arrived in Nova Scotia at this time, though more came during the war of 1812.

The early 1800s brought waves of Irish and Scottish immigration to all three provinces and Lebanese to Prince Edward Island. Many Scots settled in the highlands of Cape Breton where their beloved oatcakes, scones and shortbread remained favorite fare.

The mid to late 1800s were a prosperous age in the Maritimes. Logging, shipbuilding, farming and fishing flourished; lobster and oyster production peaked. But even as the economy slowed near the turn of the century, the region retained a solid identity with traditions (many of them culinary) that down-homers still celebrate proudly.

## QUEBEC

New France was claimed by Jacques Cartier in 1534 and the first French colony was founded by Champlain at Quebec in 1608. Louis Hébert was the first Frenchman to cultivate land in the new colony in 1617. Along the St. Lawrence, land was divided by the old seigneurial system with habitant families farming long narrow strips stretching back from the river.

Most of the early settlers came from northwestern France, a hardy rural background that served them well in their new world of long winters and severe food shortages. They learned to use wild game, fish and berries, adopted Indian methods of tapping maple trees, and gradually adapted many old-country dishes to available ingredients. Pork provided the basis of many traditional favorites such as *tourtières*, *cretons*, baked beans, hearty soups and *ragoûts* that simmered all day in cast-iron pots on the hearth.

After the British conquest at Quebec in 1759, Scottish and Irish immigrants introduced their favorite ingredients such as oatmeal and potatoes to local cooking, but the greatest influx of non-French stock came after the American Revolution when large groups of Loyalists settled in the Eastern Townships.

Meanwhile, the cities were growing rapidly. Quebec was well established with fine stone buildings and the fragrance of French cooking wafting through the narrow streets of the upper and lower towns. Montreal gradually pulled ahead in both population and commercial importance. The port was the entry point of European immigrants, and the many who stayed, including Scottish, Irish and Jewish, gave Montreal a cosmopolitan mix of classes and all manner of food styles – from the rough tavern food of the waterfront to the old-country fare of working class neighborhoods and the classic bourgeois cuisine of private clubs and mansions.

By the time of Confederation, settlements along the river were getting crowded, land was scarce and people began to venture to new homesteads in other parts of Quebec. Many distinctly regional cooking styles developed as settlers adapted to local conditions, especially in the remote "kingdom of the Saguenay" and around Lac St-Jean. Abundant blueberries were used in *tartes aux bleuets* and other desserts; local beans called *gourganes* produced a unique soup; and hefty *tourtières* were made in deep casseroles.

The first domestic science school in Quebec was begun by the nuns at Roberval on Lac St-Jean in 1882, and the second at St-Pascal de Kamouraska in 1905. Teaching girls to become skilled homemakers continued a tradition begun by Mère Bourgeois in the 1600s and played an important part in preserving the rural culinary heritage. The traditional fare of old Quebec has always been beloved to its people and has remained entrenched, especially for special occasions such as Reveillon on Christmas Eve.

## ONTARIO

The first settlers in what is now Ontario were the 10,000 United Empire Loyalists who arrived in the 1780s. They were mostly of British stock but also included German and other European ancestries and Six Nations Indians. Some blacks came as Loyalist servants; slavery was abolished in Upper Canada in the1790s and the region had many black pioneers long before those who arrived on the Underground Railway in the 1850s. The Loyalists settled first along the St. Lawrence, around the Bay of Quinte and in the Niagara region, clearing the bush to establish farms, and founding the first small towns including Kingston and Niagara-on-the-Lake.

After the war of 1812, a great influx of British immigrants began settling along the rivers and lakes, gradually establishing the agricultural heartland of southern Ontario. Scottish highlanders farmed Glengarry Country and worked as loggers in the Ottawa valley. German-speaking Mennonites ("Pennsylvania Dutch") settled in Waterloo County, adding new flavors that eventually intermingled with the British styles.

One of the earliest farmers, John McIntosh of Dundas county, developed the seedlings that produced the famous apples now bearing his name.

By 1840 when Upper Canada became Canada West, colonists living on prosperous farms or in market towns enjoyed an abundance of foods. In larger centres, a variety of shops supplied every need and the gentry were dining on multi-course dinners topped off with cakes and ale. In stark contrast, those still roughing it in backwoods settlements had to make do with meagre supplies. But everywhere, British culinary traditions remained strong and were combined with native ingredients used by Indians and Loyalists – corn, beans, pumpkin, squash, turkeys, wild rice and maple syrup. Rural social life revolved around barn-raisings, ploughing bees, logging bees and picnics, all with large quantities of food. Cooking was simple and seasonal, with much preserving for the winter.

By Confederation, Ontario had developed into a prosperous rural society. Most of the available land had been cleared and settled. Improved roads, canals, railroads and new farm machinery provided abundant food supplies.

The last half of the century marked a transition to more refined foods and the beginnings of food processing industries; in the 1880s shoppers could buy packaged yeast, imported marmalades, bottled pickles and ketchup. The large cities had evolved into bustling commercial and industrial centres, and southern Ontario was rapidly shifting from a rural to an urban society. In northern Ontario, the first large grain elevators were built when the CPR came through the lakehead in the1880s, leading to booming industries and new waves of immigration at the turn of the century.

## THE PRAIRIES

The exploration of the prairies began with the fur traders of the Hudson's Bay Company and the rival North West Company. The hardy brigades of voyageurs survived on whatever foods were available, mainly dried buffalo meat, pemmican, salt pork and wild rice, supplemented by any fish or game they caught on the way. Both companies established a vast network of posts and forts, amalgamating in 1821 with their major base at Fort Garry. At the outlying posts, conditions were spartan and food shortages common, but the larger posts such as Fort Edmonton had an abundance of food from their own gardens and cattle herds. Buffalo, supplied mainly by Indian and Métis hunters, provided a mainstay of the diet as well as meat for making pemmican.

The first true settlement on the prairies was established in 1812 by Lord Selkirk who brought a group of displaced Scottish crofters to the Red River valley (where they struggled on diets of oatmeal and little else). Nearby, the Métis population followed food styles from both their Indian and French-Canadian heritage. In 1870 the government of Canada purchased the huge area then known as Rupert's Land from the Hudson's Bay Company, and created the province of Manitoba from the Red River colony. Some of the Métis of the region, threatened both by the influx of settlement and the demise of the great buffalo herds, moved farther west to stake out farms along the Saskatchewan River, but discontent eventually led to uprisings that erupted in the Riel Rebellion of 1885.

Meanwhile, in order to populate the vast empty prairies, the government passed the Dominion Lands Act in 1872, offering homesteads of 160 acres for 10 dollars to settlers who would break the land and live on it for a specified time. German-speaking Mennonites established settlements on the Manitoba plains and Icelanders at Gimli on Lake Winnipeg. Scandinavian farmers began to move north from the Dakotas, and American ranchers into the foothills of southern Alberta where at first the grasslands were one big open range, with chuckwagons following the cattle roundups to feed the cowboys on steak, beans, bannock, sourdough flap-jacks and raisin pies.

But the true opening up of the western interior came after the vigorous immigration promotions set up in 1896 by the Minister of the Interior, Clifford Sifton. Great waves of settlers from all over Europe, the northern states and eastern Canada moved onto homesteads and into the towns that sprang up along the rail lines. In just a few years at the turn of the century, more than a million newcomers poured through Winnipeg, "the gateway to the West."

## BRITISH COLUMBIA

The white-sailed ships of Spanish and British explorers first appeared on the west coast in the 1700s, with Captain James Cook reaching Nootka Sound on Vancouver Island and Captain George Vancouver charting coastal waters. Mackenzie, Fraser and Thompson reached the Pacific from inland, and forts and trading posts were built along the main routes. Vancouver Island became a crown colony in 1849, and by the mid '60s Victoria had burgeoned into a bustling port of 6,000 people and a centre of genteel English society with garden parties and fancy dress dinners amidst an often raucous frontier mix of merchants, sailors, fortune-seekers and countless saloons. The food of the west coast, even in the earliest years, showed different influences than the rest of Canada; proximity to California and the Pacific brought many products such as citrus fruit and tins of Oriental tea as well as Chinese cooks to Victorian kitchens.

The mainland became the colony of British Columbia in 1858 when the discovery of gold in the Cariboo brought thousands of fortune-seekers to the Interior. As the famous Cariboo wagon road snaked north, roadhouses were built every few miles as stopping places where travellers could enjoy a hearty meal of beef stew or baked beans and stock up on flour, coffee, beans and bacon for the next trek. Many prospectors lived from the packs on their backs, with a gold pan often doubling as a frying pan. As the gold rush slowed down, the first big ranches were established in the Cariboo and new communities grew up along the Fraser and Thompson Rivers. In the Okanagan Valley, a missionary named Father Pandosy planted the seeds that founded the first orchards. Agriculture was flourishing in lower Fraser Valley, with homesteading encouraged at first to protect British interests before the 49th parallel boundary was declared in 1846, and later to supply provisions for the gold rush. Well into the 1900s, paddle-wheelers plied the river, bringing fresh vegetables and dairy products from the south shore across to New Westminster and other town markets. Along the coast, commercial logging and fishing industries were booming. Railway building brought thousands of Chinese workers in addition to those who had come during the gold rush. The first Japanese arrived in the 1890s, entering the fishing industry in considerable numbers.

The colonies of Vancouver Island and British Columbia joined Canada as one province in 1871, and the completion of the transcontinental railway came in 1885. The next year, the city of Vancouver was incorporated from Hastings Township (now known as Gastown) and began its rapid growth into a modern centre of commerce.

## THE NORTH

The vast expanse of the Yukon and Northwest Territories encompass one-third of Canada's land mass, with a population still sparse in numbers but with special ties

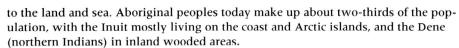

to the land and sea. Aboriginal peoples today make up about two-thirds of the population, with the Inuit mostly living on the coast and Arctic islands, and the Dene (northern Indians) in inland wooded areas.

For countless generations, the native cultures followed the seasonal cycles of nature, regularly moving camp to hunting grounds and available food sources. These lifestyles have been in transition ever since the first European fur traders and whalers introduced the trading goods – blankets, guns, metal axes, knives and cooking pots – and the ways of the outside world. Over time, traditional native ways of life were eroded as seasonal hunting patterns and skills declined, settlement clustered around trading posts and dependence on southern goods increased. The Hudson's Bay Company was closely associated with northern development and every community had its HBC store. The introduction of white bread, sugar, canned and packaged foods drastically changed native diets through the years. Traditional "country" foods such as caribou, muskox, moose, muktuk (whale skin), seal, fish and wild birds such as ptarmigan remained staples in remote areas, but elsewhere, a mixed diet of country foods and southern foods became common and remains so today.

The course of northern history took a dramatic turn with the discovery of gold in the Klondike in 1896. The famous gold rush brought a stampede of ill-equipped prospectors up the tortuous trails of mountain passes into the Yukon River valley. Food shortages were so severe that the North West Mounted Police refused entry to anyone not toting a year's supply (about one ton) of food. Sourdough was the standby for bread, biscuits and pancakes and to this day remains synonomous with the gold rush era. By 1898 more than 30,000 newcomers had arrived in Dawson City where the saloons, dance halls and hot meals were welcome diversions from the rigors of prospecting.

The Yukon Territory was established in 1898, and as the gold rush faded, Dawson dwindled into a more staid existence. The non-native population of the North remained very small until the mid 20th century when Whitehorse and Yellowknife became territorial capitals with large numbers of outsiders arriving to work in government and business.

# The FIRST DECADE
## 1900–1909

# A CENTURY OF CANADIAN HOME COOKING

*In the early 1900s the social event of the year was the community picnic on the First of July.... When it was time for the picnic lunch, tablecloths and blankets were spread under the trees and the homemade specialties were displayed. Everyone filled a plate with cold baked ham, fried chicken, jellied chicken, potato salad, coleslaw, jellied fruit, chutney, beet pickles, buttered buns, fudge layer cake, sponge cake, ginger cake, jelly roll, rhubarb pie, pumpkin pie, date cookies and lemonade.*

*– Bunny Barss*
*Come 'n Get It*

The turn of the century ushered in the Edwardian era – often called the age of abundance – and bountiful meals were a hallmark of the times.

In every region, picnics were a favorite form of socializing in the summer, and food was always the star attraction. At country church picnics, families from miles around gathered for wheelbarrow races and pie-eating contests before settling in to potluck feasts.

In well-established towns like Victoria and Fredericton, genteel folk played croquet on manicured lawns or watched cricket matches while nibbling potted shrimp and fresh strawberries from wicker hampers. In the Alberta foothills, gentlemen ranchers hosted horse races, hunts and gymkhanas (games played on horseback), all embellished with great spreads of food.

Throughout the year, everywhere in rural Canada, neighbors brought food to schoolhouse dances, all kinds of "bees" from sewing to barn-raising, and to shivarees at the homes of newlyweds. At box socials, the women packed fancy lunches into decorated boxes to be auctioned off to the highest male bidder (thus igniting many a romance).

In the cities, the rich often dined in extravagant style. "Lady Gay," a social columnist for Toronto's *Saturday Night* magazine, described a 14-course banquet that began with oysters, progressed through fish and meat dishes and ended with three desserts plus liqueurs. Sumptuous luncheons and afternoon teas were also de rigueur for the urban elite.

Even in Dawson City (dubbed the Paris of the North during the gold rush), social events proceeded in grand Edwardian style. In *I Married The Klondike,* Laura Beatrice Berton recalls a reception at Government House in 1907. "We took tea, poured into delicate porcelain cups from an elaborate silver service by the town's two leading socialites... seated regally at a lace-covered table dominated by tall candles and bouquets... fashionable women [glided] through the crowd passing those refreshments which the local social rules decreed must be served at such gatherings: salted almonds, stuffed olives, home-made Turkish delight, fudge and maple creams and pineapple sherbert."

*Family gatherings in King's County, Nova Scotia at the turn of the century meant wicker baskets filled with homemade favorites.*

*Picnic suppers like this one at Rutherford's Grove, Saskatchewan were major social events in a prairie summer.*

Public Archives of Nova Scotia/J.A. Irvine Collection, Album 35, Item 64, Neg. N5620

Saskatchewan Archives Board, Regina/#R-A17989

On pages 2 – 3:   A turn-of-the- century Edwardian picnic: Veal and Ham Pie, Mustard Pickles, Raspberry Vinegar, Butter Tarts, Shortbread and Ginger Cookies.

## HEADLINES

1900    Meat-packing, butter and cheese processing, bread-baking, sugar refining listed in top ten Canadian industries.

1900    IODE organized in Montreal.

1900    Canadian troops see action in Boer War.

1900    Wilfrid Laurier re-elected prime minister.

1901    Canada's population: 5,371,315.

1901    Canada Fruit Marks Act is first Canadian food grading.

1901    May 24 declared public holiday honoring Queen Victoria.

1901    First refrigerator rail cars transport perishable food.

1902    First gasoline-powered tractors on farms.

1903    Mountain slide buries town of Frank, Alberta.

1904    Charles E. Saunders develops rust-resistant Marquis wheat.

1905    Alberta and Saskatchewan join Confederation.

1906    Canada's Reginald Fessenden transmits world's first radio message.

1907    Toronto pharmacist invents Canada Dry Ginger Ale.

1907    Meat Inspection and Canned Food Act implemented for factories.

1908    Boy Scouts of Canada organized.

1908    Quebec City's 300th birthday.

1909    Canada's first airplane flight at Baddeck, Nova Scotia.

Many Canadian homes observed the English tradition of "tea" at supper time, having served a hot dinner at noon. In Prince Edward Island, L.M. Montgomery was writing her Anne of Green Gables books, and in one chapter Anne describes a typically substantial tea: "We had cold tongue and chicken and strawberry preserves, lemon pie and tarts and chocolate cake and raisin cookies and pound cake and fruit cake and a few other things...."

Such abundance was still a dream, however, for the pioneers pushing onward to the wilderness frontiers of the West and North – where the nearest lemon could be two days away by ox-cart. Life was harsh and dinner was whatever was available. "Rabbit and prairie chicken, and sometimes beef... plenty of oatmeal... and beans" recalled a prairie homesteader in Barry Broadfoot's *The Pioneer Years*. In *The Last Best West,* Eliane Leslau Silverman quotes an early

Albertan. "I came out here as a person who was used to fresh meat, fresh milk, fresh butter. All I had here was canned stuff, eggs maybe one month old.... I talked my husband into letting me have a few hens so we could have fresh eggs. Later we could have a fresh chicken once a week.... In the winter there was moose and deer meat. As soon as I could, I put in a vegetable garden."

For the many thousands of immigrants who arrived on the prairies with "ten dollars and a dream," a vision of the first bountiful harvest was what kept them going – through dust storms, blizzards, prairie fires, grasshopper plagues, the loneliness of isolation and monotony of oatmeal and beans. Many tales are told of the bachelor home-steaders, in particular, who in their lonely shacks subsisted solely on porridge or pancakes.

More than a million newcomers came to "the last best west" between 1896 and 1913 in the final and greatest wave of North

*Posters urged British, east Europeans and Americans to settle on the prairies.*

National Archives of Canada/#C-30624

*Mrs. Biggs churned butter out-of-doors when the weather was fine, in Alberta 1908.*

Glenbow Archives, Calgary/#NC-43-12

American migration. During the first decade of the 20th century, the most recent arrivals were still riding westward in Red River carts and covered wagons. Others were living in tents or "soddies" (houses built of tough prairie sod) or building their first wooden dwelling, ploughing a firebreak and starting a garden.

However, some were well enough established to have large spreads and the bumper harvests that made all the hard work worthwhile. Everyone looked forward to the arrival of the big noisy threshing machines and their crews who travelled from farm to farm. "It was the best time of the year," recalls a homesteader's daughter. "The women cooked all day long, and I helped my mother and the others. The men worked hard, maybe 16 hours a day, and boy, could they eat. Three big meals plus an afternoon lunch that I took out to the field. Way before daylight, we'd be making breakfast for 15 or 20 men. Big platters piled with pancakes, fried eggs and bacon and potatoes, stacks of toast and sometimes even pie, with coffee and tea by the gallon. Dinner at noon was roast beef or pork or ham with vegetables and more pies or big puddings with cream."

The Edwardian era, the decade following Queen Victoria's death in 1901, had begun with a self-assurance typified by the extravagant new king, Edward VII. The shrouds of the Victorian age were gone, confidence in the Empire was high, and the new century was heralded as a time of optimism and growth. In Canada, the decade marked a turning point from colonialism toward a new nationalism, and from a rigid class system to more flexible social patterns.

In 1900, Canada was still very conservative, and old traditions were strong. The Church stood guard over morals and education. Canadians were divided by region, class, religion and education. Farmers and townspeople, rich and poor, lived in different worlds.

The wealthy lived in mansions with fancy turrets, ballrooms, conservatories and large staffs of servants. In most cities and towns,

*Prairie women served mammoth threshers' dinners – hot and hearty – right in the field.*

Glenbow Archives, Calgary/#NA-2284-15

## LOOKING BACK

*From* Come 'n Get It *(1983) by Bunny Barss.*

*Annie McKinnon Fuller recalls her childhood on the L K Ranch in Alberta:*

There were always extra people dropping in for a meal. Planks were added to the end of the dining room table until it became so long it extended right into the kitchen. Meals were informal, the food hearty and healthy. Nothing was wasted. A bone was turned into soup, with even the beef marrow eaten. Extra milk made cheese; doughnuts were made with extra lard; dried bread was the basis for a bread pudding.

We drove to town two or three times a year and loaded up on supplies: one hundred pounds of honey; cases of dried fruit; five barrels of apples every fall; one-hundred-pound bags of sugar and flour, each in five-bag lots.

Most of the food came from the ranch itself. A cow and a pig were butchered and the meat put up for later use as corned beef, canned beef, hams, bacon, sausages. Chickens were raised for eggs and Sunday dinner. The vegetable garden provided fresh greens all summer and enough potatoes, turnips, and carrots to store in the root house for winter use.

Wild berries, saskatoons, chokecherries, and gooseberries were made into jam and preserves. Milk was separated, the cream used for butter and baking, the milk for drinking and puddings.

There was fun as well as work. We had taffy pulls and hymn singing on Sunday nights. There were summer picnics and parties to which everyone went – children, parents, and the hired help.

prosperous households had electric lights, running water, iceboxes, gas ranges, washing machines and a "hired girl" who lived in. But many homes still had kerosene lamps, a backyard pump for water and a washboard for laundry; the children were bathed in a tub near the kitchen woodstove, where their mother baked all the bread and boiled gallons of preserves.

Farm families worked from dawn to dark, raised their own cows and chickens, grew their own fruits and vegetables, churned butter and baked bread. They came to town by horse and buggy on Saturday to buy oatmeal, sugar, molasses, beans and prunes (called CPR strawberries in the West), maybe some candy for the kids and a bolt of cloth for a new dress.

Rural Canadians in both west and east often lived miles from their nearest neighbor, so visitors were always welcomed and offered something to eat. The first thing said was, "Will you stay for supper?" There was always room for another chair around the table and another potato in the pot. Rural cooks also developed a vast repertoire of baking to go with coffee and tea. Fruitcake, gingerbread or spicy cookies were always in a tin in the pantry. Daintier sweets – tarts, scones and small cakes – were prepared when the Ladies Aid met or the preacher came to call. Heartier fare – muffins, raisin cookies, hefty spice cakes – was carried out to the men in the fields.

The decade brought growth and change on every front. Western immigration was altering the face of Canada. By the end of the first decade, the Prairie population had leapt to more than 1.2 million, 60,000 born outside Canada. Ukrainians (at that time called Galicians and Ruthenians), Czechs, Slovaks, Poles, Hungarians, Serbs and Croats added to earlier immigrations of Germans, Mennonites, Scandinavians, Icelanders, European Jews, Chinese and

*Fancy meals also meant plenty of "washing-up" afterwards.*

Vancouver Public Library/Photo #2266

*Children learned to cook from their mothers, and everyone pitched in with chores like shelling peas.*

Public Archives of Nova Scotia/J.A. Irvine Collection, Album #17, Neg.#N699

## NUTRITION

- Nutrition recognized for first time as independent, scientific discipline.

- By turn of century, calories, protein, fat, carbohydrates and minerals identified. Last four plus water the five "principles" believed essential for health. Vitamins unknown.

- Later in decade, animal-feeding experiments began to challenge "five principles" theory, suggesting that other still unidentified dietary factors must also be necessary for health.

- Food and nutrition viewed mainly as treatment or cure. Their role in promoting health and preventing disease not widely recognized or understood.

- Nearly every cookbook included section on "invalid" or "sickroom" cookery.

- Strong suspicions arose that diseases such as scurvy and rickets had something to do with diet, but no real connection made between diet and health.

- 1906: First graduates in nutrition and dietetics received degrees from University of Toronto.

- 1906: Method found for determining caloric value of foods, a procedure still used today.

Americans. Immigrants were also pouring into northern Ontario, where workers were needed in lumbering and railroad construction. Large numbers of Scandinavians, Italians, Germans, Russians and Ukrainians settled in the Port Arthur-Fort William region, and by 1910 the population had shifted from predominantly British to an ethnic diversity that remains today. Canadians whose origins were other than British and French began to build the foundations of a multicultural society.

All groups in the great mosaic preserved something of their homeland cultures, especially the food. Traditional old-country dishes were adapted to new ingredients in a new land, and favorite foods from around the world have flavored Canadian cooking ever since.

Homeland traditions were especially cherished at Christmas. As author Rose Murray comments in *The Christmas Cookbook* (1979): "By baking a plum pudding or stuffing a goose, British settlers could forget, at least a short time, that they were thousands of miles from their homes and families. For the same reason Ukrainian families would spend weeks preparing the twelve lenten dishes for their Svyata Vechera (holy supper), and Icelandic children would be introduced to the delights of Vinaterta." An exchange of traditions among different ethnic groups led to a typical Canadian Christmas mix that might include shortbread, mincemeat pie, spiced beef, eggnog and elaborate German and Scandinavian cookies and breads.

In northern Ontario, industry was thriving. The world's largest grain elevators were rising at the Lakehead; coal docks, sawmills, steel foundries and shipbuilding were being established. Mining was booming. The discovery of silver at Cobalt in 1903 and gold at Porcupine in 1909 brought thousands of fortune-seekers. Cobalt grew to 30,000, Haileybury became home to millionaires, and burgeoning towns opened up the vast Canadian Shield.

*A familiar sight outside general stores in Newfoundland was delivery of beef and pork in barrels.*

Provincial Archives of Newfoundland/Photo: W. Bowman store c.1900

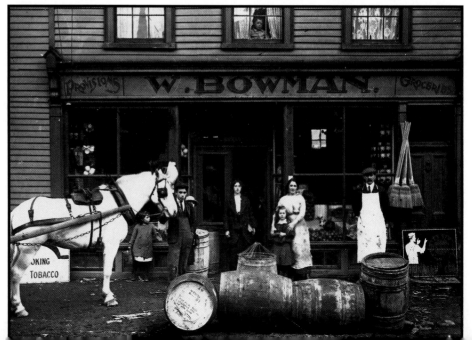

The growth of lumbering and mining in the early 1900s created one of the era's culinary footnotes. The camps were temporary homes to large numbers of workers, all demanding rib-sticking food and plenty of it. Hard-working camp cooks who could satisfy the men's huge appetites became justly renowned for their hearty, home-style cooking.

Mining and lumber camps also dotted the wilds of northern British Columbia, with logging expanding into the Interior and remote coastal inlets. Along the coast, huge salmon runs made fish canning big business. Mixed farming brought the big interior valleys into cultivation and great orchards spread through the Okanagan. The southern part of the province was already well-established, with suburbs beginning to cluster around Vancouver and urbanization creeping up the Fraser Valley.

Canadian business was flourishing. Canada had become the fastest-growing country in the world, and the world's largest exporter of wheat. The money from wheat poured energy into the economy, fuelling industry in the East and ending unemployment as easterners headed west on trains called harvester's specials. The wheatlands of the western plains swept for a thousand miles and Canadian wheat was considered the finest in the world, winning gold medals at the 1904 St. Louis World's Fair.

The face of the countryside was transformed as railroad stations and grain elevators sprang up. By 1904, Winnipeg's railway yards were the largest in the world. By 1908, more than 22,000 miles (35,000 kilometres) of track, including a second transcontinental, spread across the country. Settlers pushed farther north, into Peace River country. Towns sprouted along the rail lines and each new community both needed and supplied goods and services. The railways erected palatial hotels in major cities – the Empress in Victoria,

*Many brand names popular in the first decade are still favorites in the '90s.*

Courtesy of Best Foods Canada Inc.

*This outdoor bake oven in Quebec is just one of many styles common across the country.*

National Archives of Canada/#C-21266

the Hotel Vancouver, Winnipeg's Fort Garry, Toronto's King Edward, Quebec's Château Frontenac.

The cities were growing rapidly. By the end of the decade, Ontario and Quebec had become mainly urban. Winnipeg, third largest city after Montreal and Toronto, was burgeoning as the gateway to the West. Vancouver's population increased to more than 100,000. The provinces of Alberta and Saskatchewan had been formed out of the Northwest Territories in 1905, and Edmonton, Calgary, Regina and Saskatoon were creations of the period. The urbanization of the Maritimes was less rapid, but the cities experienced steady growth as the rural population decreased.

Investment was pouring into Canada from the United States and Britain. Demand for Canadian agriculture and fisheries products, such as Okanagan fruit and Malpeque oysters, became worldwide. Food processing prospered and grew. Many of Canada's large food processing companies (such as Canadian Canners and B.C. Packers) were created from the amalgamation of several smaller operations. And many famous brand-name products, including Heinz pickles and ketchup, Salada tea, MacLaren's cheese and Burns meats, were launched in this era.

It was the new age of capitalism, in which the working class and employing class were assumed to occupy two different worlds. However, by decade's end, the role of the working class was changing. Increased mechanization created greater efficiency. Better productivity meant that workers could be paid higher wages and thus be able to buy more products themselves. The availability of mass-produced goods, including food, introduced a new era of consumerism. New products called for new sales techniques, and modern advertising was born.

*Weeks of planning and anticipation culminated in Christmas dinner in a Manitoba home (1908).*

Provincial Archives of Manitoba (Lindsay #43)

*Canned food labels were works of art in early years.*

Courtesy of the Ontario Agricultural Museum

*Markets like this one in Hamilton (1909) meant fresh seasonal produce as well as social visits.*

Courtesy City of Toronto Archives - SC 244-640 (James #9011)

# Cookbook Sampler

## THE 1ST DECADE

For more cookbooks of the decade, see Bibliography p. 232.

# FRENCH CANADIAN PEA SOUP

*Newfoundland Pea Soup is very similar, but usually includes more vegetables, such as diced turnips and carrots, and is often topped with small dumplings. This soup is very good reheated.*

| | | |
|---|---|---|
| 1 lb | dried peas | 500 g |
| 8 cups | water | 2 L |
| 1/2 lb | salt pork (in one piece) | 250 g |
| 1 | large onion, chopped | 1 |
| 1/2 cup | chopped celery | 125 mL |
| 1/4 cup | grated carrots | 50 mL |
| 1/4 cup | chopped fresh parsley | 50 mL |
| 1 | small bay leaf | 1 |
| 1 tsp | dried savory | 5 mL |
| | Salt and pepper | |

Wash and sort peas; soak in cold water overnight. Drain and place in large pot; add water, salt pork, onion, celery, carrots, parsley, bay leaf, savory and 1 tsp (5 mL) salt. Bring to boil; reduce heat, cover and simmer until peas are very tender, about 2 hours, adding more water if needed. Remove salt pork; chop and return to soup. Discard bay leaf. Season to taste with salt and pepper. Makes 8 servings.

The most authentic versions of Quebec's famous *soupe aux pois* use whole yellow peas, with salt pork and herbs for flavor. After cooking, the pork is usually chopped and returned to the soup, or sometimes removed to slice thinly and serve separately. Instead of fresh or dried herbs, *herbes salées* (herbs preserved with salt) are often used; they are available commercially or are made at home.

Pea soup remains a popular dish in restaurants where tourists enjoy a true taste of old Quebec. In some variations, a little garlic, leeks, other vegetables or a ham bone are added for flavor. For a thicker consistency (though this is not traditional), a cup or two of the cooked peas can be puréed then returned to the soup.

# WELSH RAREBIT

*Some recipes today simply add cheese to a white sauce made with flour, but earlier recipes used an egg for thickening. Other versions added tomato juice or stewed tomatoes for a **Tomato Rarebit**. **Crab Rabbit** (creamed crabmeat with a little cheese) was a variation in Mrs. Flynn's Cookbook (Prince Edward Island, 1930).*

| | | |
|---|---|---|
| 2 cups | shredded old Cheddar cheese | 500 mL |
| 1 tbsp | butter | 15 mL |
| 1/2 tsp | dry mustard | 2 mL |
| Pinch | cayenne pepper | Pinch |
| Pinch | salt | Pinch |
| 1/4 cup | milk or beer | 50 mL |
| 1 | egg, beaten | 1 |
| | Toast | |

In double boiler, chafing dish over hot water or heavy saucepan over low heat, combine cheese, butter, mustard, cayenne, salt and milk; cook, stirring, until smooth. Add a little to beaten egg; return to pan and cook, stirring, about 1 minute or until slightly thickened. Serve over toast. Makes 2 or 3 servings.

Most early cookbooks (from the late 1800s to the 1930s) included a section on Luncheon Dishes, many of which could be served in chafing dishes. Welsh rarebit was a favorite and was served on toast squares or fried bread rounds. The 1905 Ogilvie Flour Mills cookbook cautioned, "A chafing dish needs to be watched carefully from a chair with a high seat to make its use comfortable."

# VEAL AND HAM PIE

*Not for the novice cook or prairie settler, this was the kind of dish packed for the Edwardian upper-class city folk for a country picnic. (More than likely "cook" made the pie.)*

| | | |
|---|---|---|
| 3/4 lb | ground veal | 375 g |
| 3/4 lb | ground pork | 375 g |
| 1/2 lb | ham, cubed | 250 g |
| 1/4 lb | ground pork fat | 125 g |
| 1/3 cup | sliced green onions | 75 mL |
| 1 tbsp | each chopped fresh tarragon, sage and basil (or 1 tsp/5 mL dry) | 15 mL |
| 3 | juniper berries, ground (optional) | 3 |
| 2 | cloves garlic, minced | 2 |
| 1 tsp | salt | 5 mL |
| 1/2 tsp | pepper | 2 mL |
| 2 | eggs, beaten | 2 |
| | **Hot Water Pastry** | |
| 1 | egg yolk, lightly beaten | 1 |
| *Aspic:* | | |
| 2 cups | chicken stock | 500 mL |
| 1/4 cup | sherry | 50 mL |
| 1-1/2 | pkg unflavored gelatin | 1-1/2 |
| 1 tbsp | white wine vinegar | 15 mL |
| 2 | egg whites (with shells) | 2 |

Mix together veal, pork, ham, pork fat and green onions. Combine tarragon, sage, basil, juniper berries, garlic, salt and pepper; blend into meat mixture along with 2 eggs, mixing well with hands.

On floured surface, roll out 2/3 pastry; fit into terrine dish or 9- x 5-inch (2 L) loaf pan, leaving 1/2-inch (2 cm) overhang. Spoon in filling; tap pan on counter to release air pockets. Roll out remaining pastry. Brush edges of bottom pastry with water; top with pastry, sealing and crimping edges. Cut three 1/2-inch (2 cm) holes in top.

Mix yolk with 2 tsp (10 mL) water; brush over pastry. Insert pie birds or funnel-shaped foil tubes in holes to catch bubbling juices. Bake in 400°F (200°C) oven for 15 minutes. Reduce heat to 350°F (180°C) and bake for 1-1/4 hours. Cool on rack to room temperature.

Aspic: Combine stock, sherry, gelatin, vinegar, egg whites and crumbled shells; bring to boil, stirring constantly. Reduce heat to medium-low and simmer, uncovered, without stirring, for 5 minutes. Strain through cheesecloth-lined sieve. Let cool until syrupy. Using funnel, pour a little at a time through holes in pastry, chilling between additions, until aspic fills gap under pastry. Chill for 24 hours before serving in slices. Makes 12 servings.

**HOT WATER PASTRY:**

| | | |
|---|---|---|
| 2-1/2 cups | all-purpose flour | 625 mL |
| 1/2 tsp | salt | 2 mL |
| 3/4 cup | boiling water | 175 mL |
| 1/3 cup | shortening, melted | 75 mL |
| 1 | egg yolk, beaten | 1 |

Stir flour with salt. Combine water and shortening; pour over flour mixture and mix well with fork. Blend in egg yolk; form into ball. Knead gently on floured surface. Cover and let stand at room temperature for 30 minutes before rolling out.

Savoury pies were as common as sweet pies in early years. Double-crust pies were usually made with a flaky pastry (see p. 21). "Raised" pies baked in fancy moulds or terrines were unmoulded and served cold. Deep dish pies with pastry or mashed potatoes on top were also favorites.

Meat pies were served hot or cold. Along with combinations of veal and ham, beefsteak, mutton, game and rabbit were popular. Chicken, pigeon and game birds, as well as fish pies of cod or "salt fish" (salted cod), oysters, or any fresh boneless fish in a rich sauce were served.

# BAKED STUFFED FISH

*From* Muskie Jones's Northwoods Cookery, *a word of advice: "Above all, don't overcook any fish. Nature made 'em mighty sweet morsels, quick cooking and dee – licious! If you take an old codger's advice, you'll aim to keep 'em that way!"*

| | | |
|---|---|---|
| 1/2 cup | cracker or dry bread crumbs | 125 mL |
| 1 cup | fresh bread crumbs | 250 mL |
| 3 tbsp | butter, melted | 50 mL |
| 1/2 tsp | salt | 2 mL |
| Pinch | white pepper | Pinch |
| 1 tbsp | chopped fresh parsley | 15 mL |
| 1 tsp | chopped pickle | 5 mL |
| | Cream or lemon juice | |
| 2 to 3 lb | pickerel, whitefish, salmon, etc., cleaned | 1 to 1.5 kg |
| | Melted butter | |

Combine dry and fresh crumbs, butter, salt, pepper, parsley and pickle. If too dry, moisten with cream. Sprinkle insides of fish with salt. Stuff and fasten with toothpicks. Basting often with butter, bake in 450°F (230°C) oven for 10 minutes per inch (2.5 cm) of thickest part of fish or until fish flakes easily when tested with fork. Makes 4 servings.

**Egg Sauce** (optional): In saucepan melt 2 tbsp (125 mL) butter over medium heat. Whisk in 2 tbsp (25 mL) all-purpose flour; cook for 1 minute without browning. Whisk in 1 cup (250 mL) hot milk; bring to boil, stirring constantly. Reduce heat; cook for 2 to 3 minutes. Season to taste with salt and pepper. Add 1 or 2 chopped, hard-cooked eggs and 2 tbsp (25 mL) chopped parsley, if desired. Serve with fish. Makes 1 cup (250 mL).

Whole fish were often served "planked." *A Treasury of Nova Scotia Heirloom Recipes* outlines the method still used in Queen's County: "Have a clean hardwood plank, 3 feet long and 14 inches wide. Make a good hardwood fire. Clean salmon (freshly caught) and split through back, removing backbone. With large-headed roofing nails, fasten salmon to plank, flesh side out. Stand fish before hot coals and 'plank' (cook) until done. The time depends on size of fish and amount of heat. When fish will flake off readily with a fork, remove from heat, spread with butter, season with salt and pepper, and serve hot."

Another version of "planked fish," appearing in many cookbooks, baked or broiled the fish on a hardwood board in the oven, then piped mashed potatoes around the fish.

West Coast Indians cooked salmon skewered to willow branches and facing the campfires.

# CORNED BEEF HASH

*One way to preserve meat for the summer was to "corn" it, i.e. salt it or pack it in brine in barrels. Once the beef had been used for **Boiled Dinner** in the Maritimes or **Jigg's Dinner** (called "cooking the pot" in Newfoundland), the leftovers had to be dealt with.*

| 1-1/2 cups | shredded or chopped corned beef (or 1 can 14 oz/340 g) | 375 mL |
|---|---|---|
| 1-1/2 cups | mashed potatoes | 375 mL |
| 1 | small onion, chopped | 1 |
| 2 tbsp | milk or cream | 25 mL |
| 1 | egg | 1 |
| | Salt and pepper | |
| | Butter | |

Mix together corned beef, potatoes, onion, milk, egg, and salt and pepper to taste. Melt butter in medium-hot skillet; pack corned beef mixture onto bottom of pan. Cook, turning once, until heated through and crusty on both sides. Makes 4 servings.

World War I veterans came home from years in the trenches with an unexplained fondness for canned "bully-beef" (corned beef), often the only meat in their mess tins for months on end.

By 1958 a new version called **Red Flannel Hash** (because of added diced cooked beets) was a great hit demonstrated at Toronto's Canadian National Exhibition Kitchen Theatre in August of that year.

By 1972, the hash recipe in Margo Oliver's *Weekend Magazine Cookbook* was served with a poached egg on top.

Recipe books of the '70s and '80s from Labrador refer to **Ringalls**: chopped caribou or venison, fatback pork, potatoes and onion mixed with just enough flour and water to make into cakes and fry.

# PUMPKIN PRESERVES

*While "preserve" covers a multitude of tastes and textures, this pumpkin recipe is really for a conserve or jam. In earlier days, jams and jellies were ladled into jelly glasses and sealed with paraffin. Today's jars have a sealing compound on the lids, making paraffin melting a thing of the past.*

| 8 cups | cubed (1/2-inch/ 2 cm) peeled pumpkin | 2 L |
|---|---|---|
| 4 cups | granulated sugar | 1 L |
| 1 | lemon | 1 |
| 5 | whole cloves | 5 |

Layer pumpkin with sugar in large bowl. Cover and let stand overnight at room temperature, stirring once or twice.

Drain off juice into saucepan; boil 10 minutes. Add pumpkin, grated rind and chopped pulp of lemon (white pith removed) and cheesecloth-tied cloves. Boil for 40 minutes or until pumpkin is clear and mixture sheets from spoon (jelly test). Remove cloves. Pour into hot sterilized jars and seal. Makes 4 cups (1 L).

In the early years, settlers made good use of anything edible by preserving for the long winter. Rose Hip Jam, Mountain Ash Jelly, Wild Strawberry Jam, Rhubarb Preserves, Apple Butter and Crabapple Jelly were all "put down" or "put up" when in season. Berries, from foxberries (partridgeberries in Newfoundland, red berries in Labrador) to serviceberries (saskatoons on the Prairies), to chokecherries and bakeapples were preserved. Pumpkin and vegetable marrow could be cooked into a decent conserve, with the addition of orange or lemon rind and a bit of citrus juice for flavor. Rhubarb was another pioneer favorite for jams. The tendency in early decades was to make these spreads extremely sweet; today's tastes are for less sweet preserves.

## Mustard Pickles

*As well as mustard pickles, mustard relishes were served with ham and other cold meats and are popular with hot dogs and hamburgers today.*

| | | |
|---|---|---|
| 8 cups | chunks (unpeeled) pickling cucumbers | 2 L |
| 4 cups | cauliflower florets | 1 L |
| 2 cups | peeled pearl onions | 500 mL |
| 1 cup | pickling salt (coarse) | 250 mL |
| 1 cup | water | 250 mL |
| 3 cups | cider vinegar | 750 mL |
| 1-1/4 cups | granulated sugar | 300 mL |
| 1/4 cup | all-purpose flour | 50 mL |
| 1 tbsp | dry mustard | 15 mL |
| 1 tsp | each turmeric, mustard seed and celery seed | 5 mL |

Mix together cucumbers, cauliflower and onions; sprinkle with salt. Add water, cover and let stand overnight, stirring occasionally.

Next day, bring just to boil. Remove from heat immediately; drain and set aside. In same pot, combine vinegar, sugar, flour, mustard, turmeric, mustard seed and celery seed; bring to boil, stirring until thickened. Add vegetables and return to boil, partially covered; simmer for 10 minutes or until tender-crisp.

Fill sterilized canning jars with vegetables. Add mustard sauce to within 1/2 inch (2 cm) of tops. Seal and process in boiling water bath for 10 minutes. Makes 9 cups (2.25 L).

---

**VARIATION:**

**Sour Mustard Pickles:** Reduce sugar to 3/4 cup (175 mL).

All through New Brunswick, tourist shops sell Lady Ashburnham's Mustard Pickles. It seems that this fashionable Fredericton matron was renowned for her entertaining. Always included on the menu, given as gifts or donated to charitable functions were her mustard pickles. However, it was really Lady A's sister Lucy who made these famous pickles.

Mustard seed is a major crop in Canada, and Saskatchewan is known as the mustard capital of the world.

Even though we export mustard seed to England and France for their well-known versions, we now have cottage industries producing fine mustard blends for Canadian tables, and for export as well.

Mustard pickles are made coast to coast in Canada, often with carrot, zucchini or sweet peppers, or with cucumber, cauliflower, onion and peppers and sometimes called **Thousand Island Pickles**.

# CORN PUDDING

*Succotash, made with beans and corn, was fast supper fare, but this pudding (especially if rich farm cream was used instead of milk) made a tasty side dish.*

| 2 tbsp | chopped onion | 25 mL |
|---|---|---|
| 2 tbsp | butter | 25 mL |
| 2 tbsp | all-purpose flour | 25 mL |
| 1 tsp | granulated sugar | 5 mL |
| 1/2 tsp | salt | 2 mL |
| 1 cup | milk | 250 mL |
| 3 | eggs, beaten | 3 |
| 2 cups | corn kernels | 500 mL |

Cook onion in butter until softened. In bowl, combine flour, sugar and salt; stir in milk, eggs, corn and onion. Pour into greased 6-cup (1.5 L) casserole. Set in slightly larger pan; add boiling water to come 1 inch (2.5 cm) up sides. Bake in 325°F (160°C) oven for 50 to 60 minutes or until just set in centre. Makes 4 servings.

## VARIATION:

**Corn and Cheese:** Add 1 cup (250 mL) shredded sharp Cheddar cheese.

Vegetables for the supper table varied from season to season. Year-round standbys included potatoes, onions, carrots and turnips (rutabagas today), as well as the dozens of jars of preserved vegetables like green beans, beets and peas. Late-summer gardens yielded rows of corn, including early varieties. By the '30s and '40s, Golden Bantam was a favorite, while the '80s brought a variety called Peaches and Cream (or Bread and Butter, Gold and Silver). Now we are so used to a tender, sweet corn-on-the-cob that we wouldn't likely care for Golden Bantam anymore.

# SOURDOUGH WHOLE WHEAT BREAD

*Prospectors during the gold rush carried yeast starter for breads as part of their supplies, earning the men the name "sourdoughs." Flapjacks and biscuits, scones and coffeecakes were most commonly made with this starter even before the turn of the century. On the Prairies and in areas without stores, starter was made with homemade yeast, usually prepared by fermenting potatoes with sugar and flour.*

| 1 cup | sourdough starter | 250 mL |
|---|---|---|
| 1-1/2 cups | warm water | 375 mL |
| 2 cups | all-purpose flour | 500 mL |
| 5 cups | (approx) whole wheat flour | 1.25 L |
| 1/2 cup | warm milk | 125 mL |
| 1/4 cup | honey or maple syrup | 50 mL |
| 1-1/2 tsp | salt | 7 mL |
| 2 tbsp | butter, melted | 25 mL |

Mix together starter, water and all-purpose flour until smooth. Cover and let stand in warm place for 12 hours.

In large bowl, mix batter with 1 cup (250 mL) whole wheat flour. Stir in milk, honey, salt and butter. Mix in remaining flour, 1 cup (250 mL) at a time, until too stiff to stir. (You may need up to 6 cups/1.5 L flour.)

Knead on floured surface until smooth and elastic. Form into loaves; place in two greased 9- x 5-inch (2 L) loaf pans. Cover and let rise in warm place until doubled in bulk, 2 to 3 hours. Bake in 375°F (190°C) oven for 40 to 50 minutes or until loaves sound hollow when tapped. Remove from pans; cool on rack. Makes 2 loaves.

**SOURDOUGH STARTER:**

| 1 tsp | sugar | 5 mL |
|---|---|---|
| 2 cups | lukewarm water | 500 mL |
| 1 | pkg active dry yeast | 1 |
| 2 cups | all-purpose flour | 500 mL |

In very large nonmetallic bowl, dissolve sugar in 1/2 cup (125 mL) water. Sprinkle in yeast; let stand 10 minutes or until frothy. Gradually stir in 1/2 cup (125 mL) water and 1 cup (250 mL) flour. Cover and store at room temperature for 24 hours. Add remaining flour and water; store 24 hours more or until bubbly and sour smelling.

To feed starter: To each 1 cup (250 mL) leftover starter, add 1 cup (250 mL) each warm water and all-purpose flour; mix well. Refrigerate for several days in large glass jar, leaving room for mixture to rise. Let stand at room temperature for 24 hours before using.

# BANNOCK

*Bannock, a simple type of scone, was cooked in pioneer days over open fires. Variations in flours and additions of dried or fresh fruit make this bread the simple choice of Canadian campers even today.*

*Oven-baking has become an acceptable alternate to the cast-iron frypan.*

*McKelvie's restaurant in Halifax serves an oatmeal version similar to this one. For plain bannock, omit rolled oats and increase all-purpose flour to 1 cup (250 mL).*

| 1 cup | whole wheat flour | 250 mL |
|-------|-------------------|--------|
| 1/2 cup | all-purpose flour | 125 mL |
| 1/2 cup | rolled oats | 125 mL |
| 2 tbsp | granulated sugar | 25 mL |
| 2 tsp | baking powder | 10 mL |
| 1/2 tsp | salt | 2 mL |
| 2 tbsp | melted butter | 25 mL |
| 1/3 cup | raisins (optional) | 75 mL |
| 3/4 cup | (approx) water | 175 mL |

Stir together flours, oats, sugar, baking powder and salt. Add melted butter, raisins (if using) and water, adding more water if needed to make sticky dough. With floured hands, pat into greased pie plate. Bake in 400°F (200°C) oven for 20 to 25 minutes or until browned and tester comes out clean. Cut into wedges. Makes 6 servings.

### VARIATIONS:

In place of raisins, add chopped dried apricots or fresh berries.

One of the earliest quick breads, bannock was as simple as flour, salt, a bit of fat (often bacon grease) and water. In gold rush days, dough was mixed right in the prospector's flour bag and cooked in a frypan over an open fire.

Indians wrapped a similar dough around sticks driven into the ground beside their camp fire, baking it along with freshly caught fish. Today's native **Fried Bread** is like bannock and cooked in a skillet.

Newfoundlanders' **Damper Dogs** are small rounds of dough cooked on the stove's dampers, while **Toutens** are similar bits of the dough deep-fried. At a promotional luncheon for the 1992 Inuit Circumpolar Conference, Eskimo Doughnuts, deep-fried rings of bannock dough, were served. It is said that Inuit children prefer these "doughnuts" to sweet cookies.

Red River settlers from Scotland made a frugal bannock with lots of flour, little sugar and drippings or lard. Now this same bread plays a prominent part in Winnipeg's own Folklorama Festival.

At Expo '86 in Vancouver, buffalo on bannock buns was a popular item at the North West Territories' restaurant. In many regions of Canada today, whole wheat flour or wheat germ replaces part of the flour, and cranberries or blueberries are sometimes added. A Saskatchewan firm markets a bannock mix, and recipe books from coast to coast upgrade bannock with butter, oatmeal, raisins, cornmeal and dried fruits.

# Cape Breton Oatcakes

*This is a sweet version. If desired, process oats in food processor for 10 seconds to get finer texture.*

| | | |
|---|---|---|
| 2 cups | all-purpose flour | 500 mL |
| 2 cups | rolled oats | 500 mL |
| 1 cup | packed brown sugar | 250 mL |
| 2 tsp | baking powder | 10 mL |
| 1/2 tsp | salt | 2 mL |
| 1 cup | shortening | 250 mL |
| 1/2 cup | cold water | 125 mL |

Stir together flour, oats, sugar, baking powder and salt; rub in shortening with fingertips. Mix in water with fork until ball forms; divide in half.

On floured surface, roll out each half to 1/4-inch (5 mm) thickness. Cut into 2-1/2-inch (6 cm) squares, then into triangles. Bake on lightly greased baking sheets in 350°F (180°C) oven for 15 minutes or until lightly browned. Transfer to racks to cool. Makes 60.

## VARIATION:

**Oatcakes** (to serve with cheese): Mix 2 cups (500 mL) Scotch-type oatmeal, 1 cup (250 mL) all-purpose flour, 2 tsp (10 mL) each granulated sugar and baking powder, and 1/4 tsp (1 mL) salt. Work in 1/3 cup (75 mL) shortening, lard or bacon fat. Add 1/4 cup (50 mL) cold water. Proceed as above.

The original recipe for oatcakes likely arrived with Scottish settlers to Nova Scotia. Fine oatmeal ground in the pioneers' gristmills, a little fat worked in with fingertips, and perhaps a touch of sugar, made a crisply baked "cake" to eat with cheese or jam. Over the years, Cape Bretoners (and eventually cooks all across Canada) used rolled oats and more sugar to make a cookie-like oatcake. The Glenghorm Resort at Ingonish, Nova Scotia, prints a recipe for these regional favorites on its postcards. **Trilbys**, a British version, richer and filled with a cooked date mixture before baking, led to the **Date Sandwich Cookies** so popular in Canada over the years. (See Date Filling recipe p. 90.)

# Buttermilk Flapjacks

*The tradition of serving pancakes on Shrove Tuesday (pancake day or Mardi Gras) was continued by European immigrants to Canada.*

| | | |
|---|---|---|
| 2 cups | all-purpose flour | 500 mL |
| 2 tbsp | granulated sugar | 25 mL |
| 2 tsp | baking powder | 10 mL |
| 1 tsp | baking soda | 5 mL |
| 1/2 tsp | salt | 2 mL |
| 2 | eggs, lightly beaten | 2 |
| 2 cups | buttermilk | 500 mL |
| 1/4 cup | butter, melted | 50 mL |

In bowl, combine flour, sugar, baking powder, baking soda and salt. Beat together eggs, buttermilk and butter; stir into dry ingredients until almost smooth.

Pour 1/4 cup (50 mL) for each flapjack onto medium-hot greased skillet or griddle. (If batter becomes too thick, add a little water.) Cook until browned underneath and bubbly on top, about 2 minutes; turn and brown other side. Makes 12 flapjacks.

## VARIATIONS:

**Blueberry:** Gently stir 3/4 cup (175 mL) blueberries into batter, or dot with berries before turning.
**Raisin:** Stir 3/4 cup (175 mL) raisins into batter.
**Buckwheat:** Substitute buckwheat flour for half of the flour.
**Apple:** Stir 3/4 cup (175 mL) coarsely chopped apples into batter, or top with thin slices apple before turning.
**Sweet Milk:** Use regular milk instead of buttermilk; omit baking soda and use 1 tbsp (15 mL) baking powder.

Pancakes, also called hot cakes and griddle cakes, were flapjacks to the chuckwagon cooks of Alberta, who prided themselves on flipping the cakes high in the air when turning them. To early western settlers (especially bachelors who were often as short on cooking skills as groceries), rib-sticking pancakes were often the staple fare not only for breakfast but also for dinner and supper.

For farm women, most of whom made their own butter, there was always buttermilk to use up. Pancakes usually were topped with corn syrup, and every prairie household had large pails of Roger's Golden Corn Syrup. (When empty, these made perfectly good school lunch pails.)

Pancakes in eastern Canada were smothered in maple syrup, when available. Later came fruit syrups and other toppings.

# GREEN TOMATO MINCEMEAT

*Chopped or grated peeled apple stretches mincemeat and cuts the sweet, strong flavor.*

| 8 cups | chopped (unpeeled) green tomatoes (about 20 medium) | 2 L |
|---|---|---|
| 4 cups | finely chopped peeled apples | 1 L |
| 3 cups | raisins | 750 mL |
| 1/2 cup | chopped mixed peel or citron | 125 mL |
| 1/4 cup | chopped candied orange peel | 50 mL |
| 1 tsp | salt | 5 mL |
| 2 tsp | cinnamon | 10 mL |
| 1 tsp | ground cloves | 5 mL |
| 1/2 tsp | allspice | 2 mL |
| 1 cup | packed brown sugar | 250 mL |
| 1-1/2 cups | granulated sugar | 375 mL |
| 1/3 cup | cider vinegar | 75 mL |
| 2 tbsp | lemon juice | 25 mL |
| 1 cup | apple juice or water | 250 mL |
| 1/2 cup | brandy | 125 mL |

In large heavy saucepan, combine tomatoes, apples, raisins, peels, salt, cinnamon, cloves, allspice, sugars, vinegar, lemon juice and apple juice; bring to boil over medium-high heat. Reduce heat and simmer (just boil lightly) 1-1/2 hours, stirring often.

Remove from heat; add brandy. Ladle into hot sterilized canning jars. Process in boiling water bath for 15 minutes. Makes about 7 cups (1.75 L).

**MINCEMEAT PIE:**

For each double-crust 9-inch (23 cm) pie, mix 2 cups (500 mL) mincemeat with 2 cups (500 mL) chopped apple. Cut steam vents in top and bake in 425°F (220°C) oven for 15 minutes; reduce heat to 350°F (180°C) and bake 30 minutes or until pastry is browned.

Turn-of-the-century baking supplies included everything necessary for homemade mincemeat, an English tradition: raisins, currants, spices, brown sugar and, in those days, meat, which was usually beef but sometimes venison or moose. Perhaps the spices and sugar were necessary to mask the poor flavor of the meat. In any case, there were two schools of thought about making good mincemeat. One cooked the meat and ground it before adding the other ingredients, the second started with raw meat and let it cook with the seasonings. If supplies couldn't be spared, there would be no meat at all and often an overabundance of green tomatoes was used. Ordering enough spirits in time for making mincemeat and fruitcakes was important to the well-to-do.

# SQUASH PIE

*Maritimers and Newfoundlanders still prefer evaporated milk in this recipe. Serve with sweetened whipped cream.*

| 1-1/4 cups | mashed cooked squash or pumpkin (canned if desired) | 300 mL |
|---|---|---|
| 2/3 cup | packed brown sugar | 150 mL |
| 1/2 tsp | salt | 2 mL |
| 1/2 tsp | cinnamon | 2 mL |
| 1/4 tsp | each ginger and nutmeg | 1 mL |
| 1 | egg, beaten | 1 |
| 1 cup | milk | 250 mL |
| 1 | 9-inch (23 cm) unbaked pie shell | 1 |

Beat together squash, sugar, salt, cinnamon, ginger, nutmeg, egg and milk; pour into pie shell. Bake in 425°F (220°C) oven for 15 minutes. Reduce heat to 350°F (180°C); bake 30 to 35 minutes longer or until knife inserted in centre comes out clean.

The native peoples were growing squash and pumpkins in Canada long before Europeans arrived. Mashed cooked squash, pumpkin and vegetable marrow have been used with ingenuity by cooks over the years. **Pumpkin Pie** is a tradition for Canadian Thanksgiving, family reunions or local church harvest-home suppers. Pumpkin is also a favorite flavor for muffins, breads, cheesecake and cookies.

# BUTTER TARTS

*These tarts were the basis for **Butter Tart Pie** and **Butter Tart Squares**, which appeared in later decades. Another variation uses maple syrup instead of corn syrup.*

| | | |
|---|---|---|
| 1/4 cup | butter | 50 mL |
| 1/2 cup | packed brown sugar | 125 mL |
| 1/2 tsp | vanilla | 2 mL |
| 1 | egg | 1 |
| 1/2 cup | corn syrup | 125 mL |
| 1/2 cup | raisins or currants | 125 mL |
| 12 | pastry-lined tart shells | 12 |

In bowl, cream together butter, sugar and vanilla. Beat in egg and corn syrup. Spoon raisins into tart shells; pour in filling, two-thirds full. Bake in 375°F (190°C) oven for 15 to 18 minutes or until lightly browned. Makes 12 tarts.

Butter Tarts are uniquely Canadian. There are theories about their origin and whether they were adapted from southern pecan pie, old-fashioned sugar pies, or maple syrup, backwoods or vinegar pies. Squabbles arise about whether the tarts should be runny or not, and just how runny. Opinions differ about the use of syrup or sugar only, eggs beaten or not, currants or raisins, and how full tart pans should be filled.

# FLAKY PASTRY

*Pastry was traditionally made with lard or shortening in most Canadian kitchens. Another favorite was a never-fail pastry made with an egg and a little vinegar, still printed on many lard packages today. In later decades, a pastry made with oil and rolled out between sheets of waxed paper was promoted as easy to make and low in cholesterol.*

| | | |
|---|---|---|
| 1-3/4 cups | all-purpose flour (or 2 cups/ 500 mL cake-and-pastry flour) | 425 mL |
| 1 tsp | salt | 5 mL |
| 3/4 cup | shortening (part butter or lard, if desired) | 175 mL |
| 6 tbsp | (approx) ice cold water | 75 mL |

Mix together flour and salt. With pastry blender or two knives, cut in shortening until mixture has texture of coarse meal with a few large pieces.

Add cold water gradually, using slightly less or more, to make dough that clings together and leaves side of bowl. Form into ball. Makes enough for 9-inch (23 cm) double-crust pie or 18 large tart shells.

Instructions for making pastry at the turn of the century were quaint, like these from the 1905 Blue Ribbon cookbook: "In baking, have the oven hot with strong underheat first." The rules were in place and correct: cold ingredients, quick, light handling; roll from centre to edges. Then "...trim off edge with a sharp knife or pastry jagger, which trims and flutes at the same time...."

A later Ogilvie Four Mills book states, "The digestibility of pies has been called into question, but when properly made, pies are as easily digested as anything else."

Elsewhere there were good pie-making instructions, including placing a small funnel-shaped piece of paper in "an incision in top crust" for juicy fruit pies. And in the first decade, reference was made to pie tins, likely made by the local tinsmith or sold to the women from the travelling tinkers' wagons. Aluminum cookware, new to kitchens in the early 1900s, was also referred to as tin.

# APPLE DUMPLINGS

*Apple dumplings are simply sugared apples, whole or sliced, wrapped in Flaky Pastry (p. 21) or this biscuitlike covering.*

| 2 cups | all-purpose flour | 500mL |
|---|---|---|
| 2 tsp | baking powder | 10 mL |
| 1/2 tsp | salt | 2 mL |
| 1/2 cup | shortening (part butter) | 125 mL |
| 1/2 cup | milk | 125 mL |
| *Filling:* | | |
| 4 | apples, peeled and sliced | 4 |
| 1/3 cup | raisins | 75 mL |
| 3 tbsp | packed brown sugar | 50 mL |
| 1 tsp | cinnamon | 5 mL |
| *Sauce:* | | |
| 1 cup | water | 250 mL |
| 1 cup | packed brown sugar | 250 mL |
| 2 tbsp | butter | 25 mL |

In bowl, mix together flour, baking powder and salt; cut in shortening until mixture resembles coarse crumbs. Stir in milk with fork to form soft dough. On floured surface, roll out dough to 1/4-inch (5 mm) thickness; cut into six 6-inch (15 cm) squares.

Filling: Divide apples among pastry squares; top with raisins, brown sugar and cinnamon. Moisten pastry edges with milk; bring corners together at top, pinching edges closed. Place in baking dish just large enough to hold them with sides barely touching.

Sauce: Mix together water, brown sugar and butter; bring just to boil and pour over apples. Bake in 425°F (220°C) oven for 25 to 30 minutes or until apples are tender and pastry is golden, basting twice during baking. Makes 6 servings.

Baked fruit desserts, topped with crumbs, biscuits or rolled up in pastry, have been a Canadian favorite through the decades. As well, apples in pie or sauce and plenty of dried fruits like figs, prunes and sliced apples (called *schnitz* by those of German ancestry) appear in cookbooks.

**Cobblers, Buckles** and **Grunts** (particularly common in Maritime cookbooks) are baked with a sweet biscuit dough dropped onto hot bubbling fruit, usually apples, peaches or plums, blueberries or cranberries. **Roly-Poly** is a biscuit dough rolled around sliced apples, sprinkled with sugar and cinnamon, then baked or steamed. And all manner of crumbles, crisps and Bettys were popular: fruit layered or topped with crumblike mixtures of butter, brown sugar and rolled oats or bread crumbs.

Many of the old favorite varieties of apple trees have disappeared. Farmers in apple-growing regions reminisce about varieties like Melbas, Yellow Transparents, St. Lawrence, Snows, Famus, Cox and Pippens.

# MARMALADE STEAMED PUDDING

*You can serve this pudding with Custard Sauce (p. 47).*

| 1/2 cup | orange or lemon marmalade | 125 mL |
|---|---|---|
| 1/2 cup | butter | 125 mL |
| 1/2 cup | granulated sugar | 125 mL |
| 2 | eggs | 2 |
| 1-1/2 cups | all-purpose flour | 375 mL |
| 1-1/2 tsp | baking powder | 7 mL |
| Pinch | salt | Pinch |
| 2 tbsp | orange juice | 25 mL |

Butter 5-cup (1.25 L) mould or pudding dish; sprinkle with granulated sugar. Spoon marmalade into mould; set aside.

In bowl, cream butter with sugar until light; beat in eggs, one at a time. Combine flour, baking powder and salt; add to creamed mixture along with orange juice, beating well. Spread evenly over marmalade. Cover with greased lid or greased foil tied tightly with string.

Place on rack or trivet in large saucepan; add boiling water to come halfway up sides. Cover and steam for 1-1/4 to 1-1/2 hours until cake tester comes out clean, keeping water at simmer and adding more if necessary. Unmould. Makes 6 to 8 servings.

Steamed puddings, done in a basin or mould, were good solid dessert fare. The suet or pork fat used in early years was later replaced by shortening or butter.

Molasses and currants or raisins turn a plain pudding into a Maritimer's **Lassy Duff** or **Hunter's Pudding**. Fruit-filled puddings (fig, date, apple, cranberries, partridgeberries) are all variations. **Plum Pudding** contained no plums, but lots of raisins, currants, spices and nuts made it heavier than a duff. In Newfoundland today, you can still buy traditional pudding bags to steam **Figgy Duff**, a simple biscuit dough or bread crumb mixture studded with raisins and full of spices.

# GINGER COOKIES

*For crisp cookies, roll dough as thin as possible. One vintage cookbook says, "Roll out as thin as brown paper."*

| 1/4 cup | molasses | 50 mL |
|---------|----------|-------|
| 1/4 cup | corn syrup | 50 mL |
| 1/2 cup | butter | 125 mL |
| 2/3 cup | packed brown sugar | 150 mL |
| 1 | egg, lightly beaten | 1 |
| 3 cups | all-purpose flour | 750 mL |
| 1 tbsp | ginger | 15 mL |
| 1 tsp | baking soda | 5 mL |
| 1/2 tsp | cinnamon | 2 mL |
| 1/4 tsp | ground cloves | 1 mL |
| 1/4 tsp | salt | 1 mL |

Heat molasses, corn syrup, butter and sugar over medium heat just until boiling; transfer to bowl and let cool to room temperature. Blend in egg.

Stir together flour, ginger, baking soda, cinnamon, cloves and salt; gradually add to bowl, mixing thoroughly after each addition. Cover and refrigerate for 3 hours or until firm enough to handle.

On well-floured surface, roll dough, half at a time, as thin as possible, about 1/16-inch (2 mm) thickness. Cut into desired shapes; place on well-greased baking sheets. Bake in 375°F (190°C) oven for 7 to 9 minutes until firm to the touch. Remove immediately to racks. Makes 60 to 70 cookies.

### VARIATION:

For softer cookies: Cream together molasses, syrup, butter, sugar and egg. Combine dry ingredients; gradually blend into creamed mixture. Form small balls; roll in granulated sugar. Flatten on well-greased baking sheet with fork or sugar-dipped glass and bake.

Ginger was a primary spice at the beginning of the century and for many years after. **Gingerbread Boys** iced to hang on the Christmas tree and **Gingersnaps** with crinkled sugary tops are longtime Canadian traditions.

In Quebec's Laurentian district, you can still buy big soft ginger cookies at Paget's bakery in St. Sauveur.

In *A Treasury of Nova Scotia Heirloom Recipes*, one ginger cookie recipe is called **Fat Archies**, presumably because Archie is a popular name in Cape Breton. **Boularderie Biscuits**, typical of another area in Cape Breton, were thick. **Long Johns** were thin, and a thin batter baked in a sheet and cut in squares when cool were called **Boot Heels**.

A Nabob Foods cookbook from the Canadian west calls thin, crisp cookies **Granny Herman's Shin-Plasters** after the paper money of early days.

# SHORTBREAD

*Classic shortbread, brought by our Scottish ancestors to Canada, is a rich, buttery cookie that melts in your mouth. The recipe is as simple as 1, 2, 4: one part sugar, two parts butter, four parts flour.*

| 1/2 cup | granulated sugar | 125 mL |
|---------|------------------|--------|
| 1 cup | butter | 250 mL |
| 2 cups | all-purpose flour | 500 mL |

In bowl, cream sugar into butter. With wooden spoon, gradually mix in flour to make dough that can be gathered into ball. Knead gently on lightly floured surface until smooth. Pat or roll into 3/4-inch (2 cm) thick round. Place on ungreased baking sheet; prick all over and crimp edges. Chill for at least 1 hour.

Bake in 275°F (140°C) oven for 40 to 45 minutes or until lightly browned. When warm, score into wedges to cut later. Makes 12 wedges.

### VARIATION:

**Shortbread Squares:** Pat dough into 8-inch (2 L) square baking pan. Bake and score into squares.

Traditionally shaped into a round, scored with a fork or patterned with a wooden mould, shortbread comes in many versions. Rice flour, icing sugar or cornstarch are often added. Whipped shortbread is a lighter version. Brown sugar or the addition of rolled oats give a flavor change. In recent years, chopped hazelnuts or macadamia nuts, white or dark chocolate chunks have been added, and some recipes call for unsalted butter – enough to make a Scottish granny turn over in her grave!

# GINGERBREAD

*Served warm with a hot lemon sauce or whipped cream, this was a favorite on a cold Canadian winter night. The cake tester in early years was usually a straw from the kitchen broom.*

| | | |
|---|---|---|
| 1 tsp | baking soda | 5 mL |
| 1 cup | boiling water | 250 mL |
| 1 cup | molasses | 250 mL |
| 1/4 cup | butter, melted | 50 mL |
| 1/2 cup | packed brown sugar | 125 mL |
| 1 | egg | 1 |
| 2-1/2 cups | all-purpose flour | 625 mL |
| 1 tsp | ginger | 5 mL |
| 1/4 tsp | each cinnamon, nutmeg, cloves and allspice | 1 mL |

Dissolve baking soda in boiling water; stir in molasses. Set aside to cool.

In bowl, cream butter with sugar until smooth; beat in egg. Combine flour, ginger, cinnamon, nutmeg, cloves and allspice. Add to creamed mixture alternately with molasses mixture, beating until smooth.

Pour into greased 9-inch (2.5 L) square pan. Bake in 350°F (180°C) oven for 40 to 50 minutes or until cake tester inserted in centre comes out clean.

---

## VARIATION:

**Maple Gingerbread:** Substitute maple syrup for molasses.

**Lemon Sauce:** In small saucepan mix together 1/2 cup (125 mL) granulated sugar, 2 tbsp (25 mL) cornstarch, 1 cup (250 mL) water, 1/4 cup (50 mL) lemon juice and 1 tsp (5 mL) grated lemon rind. Bring to boil over medium heat, stirring constantly until thickened and clear. Blend in 2 tbsp (25 mL) butter. Makes 1-1/2 cups (375 mL).

Many recipes for a cakelike gingerbread have appeared in cookbooks over the years. One old handwritten recipe for Soft Ginger Bread went like this: "Half cup yellow sugar filled up with molasses, one teaspoon ginger, a piece of butter the size of a walnut, one teacup boiling water, dissolve in it one heaping teaspoon soda, flour to mix." Period. No mixing instructions, no pan size, no oven temperature or time.

# RASPBERRY VINEGAR

*Summer coolers for picnic fare or simply sipping on the front porch were often fruit flavored. Well worth a trip to today's pick-your-own raspberry farms, this concentrate provides a sip of the past. To serve, pour 1/4 cup (50 mL) over ice cubes in glass and fill with cold water.*

| 10 cups | raspberries | 2.5 L |
|---------|-------------|-------|
| 2 cups | white vinegar | 500 mL |
| | Granulated sugar | |

In nonmetallic bowl, gently stir raspberries with vinegar; cover and let stand 4 days. Let drip overnight through sieve lined with several layers of cheesecloth.

Measure juice; add equal volume sugar. Bring to boil; simmer for 20 minutes. Pour into hot sterilized jars; seal. Makes 2 cups (500 mL).

From *Canada's Favorite Cook Book* by Annie R. Gregory: "Fill a stone jar that is not glazed with raspberries. Pour vinegar over them till jar is full. Let it stand 9 days, stirring every day. Strain it off and to every pint of juice add 3/4 lb white sugar. Boil it as long as any scum rises and bottle for use. A dessert-spoonful of this in a glassful of water will prove a refreshing drink."

**Ginger Cordial, Rhubarb Wine,** bubbly phosphates and sharp and tangy acids were refreshing fruit drinks for hot summer days. Iced buttermilk quenched the thirst as well.

Today at Marshland's Inn in New Brunswick, **Foxberry Cocktail** is served in season.

# PULLED TAFFY

*An ad for the Regina Public Library's Prairie Room mentions pulled taffy in early days. Peanut brittle, brown sugar fudge and molasses candy were favorites. In Newfoundland, this same candy was called **Molasses Knobs**. And by 1915, the Moffat cookbook (from the stove company) had a recipe for **Humbugs** that used much the same method. Quebec and New Brunswick, with access to plenty of maple syrup, make a maple version of this candy.*

| 2 cups | packed brown sugar | 550 mL |
|--------|--------------------|--------|
| 1/2 cup | molasses | 125 mL |
| 1/3 cup | water | 75 mL |
| 1/4 tsp | cream of tartar | 1 mL |
| 2 tbsp | butter | 25 mL |
| 1/2 tsp | vanilla | 2 mL |

Bring sugar, molasses and water to boil; add cream of tartar. Boil, without stirring, to hard-crack (brittle) stage, 300°F (150°C) on candy thermometer. Add butter and vanilla; immediately pour into well-greased pie plate.

As candy starts to firm, pull outside edges toward centre. When cool enough to handle, gather candy into ball with buttered hands. Pull taffy repeatedly until straw color. Form into twisted ropes about 1/2-inch (2 cm) thick. Cut into pieces.

All across Canada, pull taffy was a treat. French-Canadian children traditionally made *tire au sucre* or *tire à la mélasse* on November 25, *la Ste. Catherine*. This was also the day when unmarried young women of 25 were expected to don the starched white cap of the spinster. The cap has long since disappeared, but the pull taffy remains.

Candy making with the children was a good way to pass long wintry days.

At Christmas, barley sugar toys were made for children in special heavy tin moulds. Naturally yellow, the candy was often tinted with red food coloring.

# The 2ND DECADE
## 1910 – 1919

# A CENTURY OF CANADIAN HOME COOKING

*I got more comfort that day out of my cooking spree than I did from either my philosophy or my religion....No woman can turn out an oven full of good flaky pies with well-cooked undercrusts and not find peace for her troubled soul.*

*– Nellie McClung*
*The Stream Runs Fast*

Even the feisty Nellie, who fought for women's rights and helped win them the vote in 1916, sought solace in cooking the day she lost an election by a mere 60 votes. The pleasures of hearth and home were an important part of family life in her day, and good cooking was much admired. Even in the midst of wartime and social upheaval, women kept the home fires burning and the oven full of fine baking.

Life at the beginning of this decade moved at a gentle pace, with most Canadians feeling secure, comfortable and optimistic.

The population was beginning to shift from rural to urban. City streets were being paved and lit by electricity, and the daring dodged the tram traffic in their "merry Oldsmobiles." At Eaton's, Simpson's, Woodward's and the Hudson's Bay stores, men's celluloid shirt collars and women's high-laced boots were fashionable. Stylish dressmakers copied the Gibson Girl look, and huge-brimmed hats were all the rage for garden parties.

Most of the big department stores had groceterias that sold fancy packages of imported goods, along with Canadian-made Kellogg's Cornflakes and All-Bran, and even Triscuits from the makers of Shredded Wheat. Food supplies were unlimited at most grocery stores, at Saturday morning farmers' markets and big public markets in cities such as Montreal, Saint John, Ottawa (Byward) and Toronto (St. Lawrence and Kensington).

Prices for food, clothing and furniture were reasonable –

Edmonton stores were featuring coffee at 40 cents a pound, stewing beef at six cents, canned apples for 35 cents a gallon. Barter was common in many areas. A local history of Huntsville, Ontario, notes that farm women brought in their butter and eggs to trade for the groceries they needed, and "if there was any money coming to the lady after the groceries were deducted, she took that cash home and put it in her cookie jar, that is if her husband wasn't a boozer."

Cooking was largely seasonal, making use of locally grown ingredients, though some food supplies were transported by railroad coast to coast. Steamships in British Columbia carried passengers and freight to the most isolated settlements. Newfoundland outports also relied on supply boats.

The flood of immigration to the Prairies continued, spreading to the northern parklands and reaching a peak in 1913. But more and more newcomers to

*A peaceful picnic on a prairie summer day.*

Saskatchewan Archives Board, Regina/Ref #R-A23721

On pages 26 – 27:   The art of home baking: Boiled Raisin Cake, Jumbo Raisin Cookies, Potato Scones, Graham Gems and Maple Syrup Pie.

*Annie McElrea (now Mrs. Goodfellow) of Quebec's Eastern Townships stands with pride by her new wood stove in 1914.*

Courtesy of Marjorie Goodfellow

*Many immigrants passed through the rail station at Quebec City, like this German family in 1911.*

National Archives of Canada/#PA-10254

## HEADLINES

1910 Heinz ketchup production begins at Leamington, Ontario.

1910 Royal Canadian Navy formed.

1911 Gold found at Kirkland Lake, Ontario.

1911 Canada's population: 7,207,838.

1912 Titanic sinks after hitting iceberg.

1912 Manitoba, Ontario and Quebec borders extended north to Hudson's Bay.

1913 Immigration at all-time high: 400,000 newcomers arrive.

1914 Canada enters First World War.

1914 Panama Canal opens.

1915 Workmen's Compensation Act passed.

1916 National Research Council established.

1916 Edmonton's Emily Murphy first woman magistrate in British Empire.

1917 Vimy Ridge taken by Canadians.

1917 Parliament buildings destroyed by fire.

1917 Federal Income Tax introduced as temporary wartime measure.

1918 Federal vote granted to women.

1918 Canned Fruit and Vegetable Act introduces grading.

1918 First airmail flight takes 6 hours Montreal to Toronto.

1918 Armistice ends war at 11th hour, 11th day, 11th month.

1919 Winnipeg General Strike paralyzes city.

1919 Group of Seven formed.

Canada began to choose the city life over homesteading. Of the 500,000 who arrived in Winnipeg in this decade, one in 10 went no further.

In northern British Columbia, Prince George and Prince Rupert were born as the railway pushed through the Yellowhead Pass to the ocean, opening up the timber lands and rich fishing grounds. Vancouver's population was growing at the rate of a thousand per month, and B.C. Electric's tramways went all the way to Chilliwack. Electric streetcars serviced cities from Victoria to Halifax.

Leisure activities ranged from simple to extravagant. Steamboats took the well-to-do on excursions from Vancouver to Bowen Island, from Halifax to McNab's Island, from Murray Bay along the St. Lawrence and up the Saguenay, and on Lake Ontario to Niagara or the Thousand Islands. In Ontario's Muskoka Lake country, the *Seguin* brought city people to fashion-

able resorts and summer homes. Torontonians packed picnics for Centre Island and band concerts, or dressed for opening night concerts of the Mendelssohn choir. Military balls, social debuts and private soirées meant fancy dinners with fancy food. Enthusiastic crowds flooded to sporting events – lacrosse, golf, the Queen's Plate horse races, Grey Cup football games and Stanley Cup hockey playoffs.

By contrast, rural leisure centred around the one-room schoolhouse or the church. All community activities – picnics, softball games, curling, Christmas concerts, dances, sleighrides and sugaring-off parties – were for the whole family and included plenty of home-cooked food.

Summer and fall fairs were annual highlights in small towns and big cities alike. The year 1912 marked the beginning of the famous Calgary Stampede.

The Canadian National Exhibition and Royal Winter Fair

*The lunch counter at the Saint John Exhibition in 1912 offered 5¢ coffee, 5¢ sandwiches and 2¢ doughnuts.*

Wilson Studio, St. John, New Brunswick

*From* Madame Benoit Cooks at Home *(1978). Mme Jehane Benoit fondly recalls her Quebec childhood:*

In those days, women took great pride in preserving the traditions of the past. The eldest daughter (which I was) was the one who had the almost sacred duty of carrying them to the next generation. I remember how I followed handwritten recipes on yellowed pages of an old notebook written by my grandmother, aunts I had never known, and friends of our family. Many years ago I wrote a book called *Les Secrets du Cahier de ma Grand'mère*. It was filled with the treasured recipes I found in that little black book, worn out and dog-eared at the corners because *grand'mère* usually kept it in the big flour bin, in a wax paper bag. Why there? Because she was an excellent baker and her favorite bread recipes were in that little book. It also contained the recipes for her justly famous baked beans, which my mother used to prepare the same way. I can never forget those hot baked beans. They had spent the whole night in the big brick oven of our local baker, two blocks away, and were enjoyed at Friday's breakfast. . . . Oh, those winter breakfasts of my youth: creamy porridge, simmered all night at the back of the wood stove and eaten with freshly-shaved maple sugar and thick cream; the stacks of piping hot homemade bread, sliced and toasted on the wood stove, a taste I have never lost; freshly churned, unsalted butter; and buckwheat honey that was cut in slices like the dark brown cheese that we always bought from our neighborhood Scottish cheeseman.

brought a taste of the country to Torontonians. And all across the land, Victoria Day and Dominion Day were occasions for patriotic celebrations with parades and picnics.

In many ways it was an energetic and buoyant decade. Steam powered not only trains and boats, but also tractors, threshing machines, steam rollers, saws and fire engine pumpers. New telephones, telegraph and newspaper wire services brought the world closer. New art galleries, public libraries and universities sprang up across the country.

But conflicts were simmering: regional inequities, labor unrest, the fight for women's rights, ethnic and religious discrimination, and especially the gap between wealthy and poor were all explosive issues. On the Prairies, bumper harvests meant wealth for mill and railroad companies, but for the homesteader only hard work and no pay. In British Columbia, northern Ontario and Quebec, profits soared in lumbering, pulp and paper, and mining, while underpaid workers struggled to survive. In Winnipeg, discrimination pushed thousands of immigrants – Ukrainian, German, Polish and Jewish – into crowded North-End slums, while the establishment on the other side of town danced the turkey trot and dined at midnight suppers tended by servants. In Nova Scotia, steel and coal barons made fortunes while the Cape Breton miner's family lived on baked beans. Especially neglected were native people – stripped of their land and livelihood, they were relegated to reserves or city streets.

The sexes were as segregated as the classes. Woman's place was in the home, and her work was never done. With or without servants, she was responsible for running the household – cooking, cleaning, laundry – as well as for child care and tending the sick. On the farm she still split kindling, banked fires, took out ashes and polished the black iron stove. Washing dishes meant pumping water and emptying dishpans. Cream and butter went into a dugout in the floor, out to the ice house or

*Volunteers distributed baskets of food to the urban needy.*

The United Church of Canada/Victoria University Archives, Toronto

*Garden parties for the social set, like this one in Winnipeg, meant elegant finery and fancy food.*

National Archives of Canada

## LOOKING BACK

*From* Raincoast Chronicles *(1976) edited by Howard White. In the early years, the coastal communities of British Columbia were linked only by the supply boats of the CPR and Union Steamship Lines. Al Lloyd, a Pender Harbour storekeeper for many years, remembers "boat day":*

Timing was important as there was not much use going on other than a "boat day" for anything but staples. You tried to arrive long enough before the boat so that you could have a good visit with other customers before the freight got to the store . . . .

Despite the long delays everyone was quite cheerful and the store would be the scene of endless discussions on the topics of the day.

Selection was not quite what it is today. Tea was Nabob green label in one or half pound packages, coffee the same, take it or leave it. Fruit was apples, oranges and bananas and very rarely grapes. Vegetables were spuds, onions, cabbage, turnips and carrots. Tomatoes, lettuce, celery , etc. were only for special occasions like Christmas, and you had to order ahead. . . .

Your shopping completed and final good-byes said to friends you were faced with getting the groceries, packed in boxes tied with string . . . down to the boat and home . . . before the gulls got into them, or they dissolved into the bilge. One note of caution, "Watch the bottom of the box." Many a load of groceries went into the chuck at the home float, twixt boat and float.

down the well. City women were slightly better off with iceboxes and sinks, electric lights and gas stoves.

Work for domestics in private homes was pure drudgery – long hours, low pay and no privacy. So when factories and offices began to spring up, many servants turned in their aprons. But their new jobs were limited and also poorly paid. The professions, such as medicine, were largely out of bounds for women. "Nice" girls stayed home with their parents until a husband came along.

However, the foundations of feminism were being built. Determined women in every province were fighting for the vote. Prairie women, especially, were among the world's most outspoken campaigners for women's rights. Nellie McClung spearheaded both the suffrage and temperance movements, first in Manitoba as leader of the Winnipeg Women's Press Club and later in Edmonton where she was eventually elected to the

Alberta legislature. The spirited campaigns of McClung, Emily Murphy ("Janey Canuck") and many others finally won the vote provincially, first in the Prairie provinces in 1916 and 1917, and federally in 1918. By 1919, women could vote in every province but Quebec, where they waited until 1940.

The temperance movement urged everyone to "Sign the Pledge" and waged a "Banish the Bar" campaign, which succeeded in closing the bars in Saskatchewan on July 1, 1915. (Drinkers found this a less than ideal way to celebrate Dominion Day.) Other provinces followed suit until prohibition was in effect coast to coast by 1919.

This was also a decade of great expansion in the formation of Women's Institutes, which promoted the education of women and the welfare of the family. The organization had been founded in 1897 in Stoney Creek, Ontario, by Adelaide Hoodless (following the death of

*Prairie chickens and other wild game were readily available to good shots like Mrs. Denning. (c.1917)*

Glenbow Archives, Calgary/#NA-2574-17

*A scene at Grand Manan, New Brunswick fish market, before the fire of 1912.*

Provincial Archives of New Brunswick/Ref.#P8/71

## NUTRITION

- Nutrition still meant little more than a full belly.
- Hospital dietitians lamented that people believed toast and coffee an adequate breakfast.
- 1912: Scientists labelled unidentified factors in food "vitamines." In 1920, spelling changed to vitamins.
- Six dietary essentials now recognized: protein, carbohydrates, fat, minerals, water and vitamins. List remains unchanged today.
- 1913: Vitamin A, originally called the milk factor, identified.
- Dietitians, recognized primarily as providers of good-quality food, were greatly in demand in department store and office cafeterias.
- During First World War, getting enough to eat the major concern. Department of Fisheries actively promoted fish, but more for health of economy than health of public.
- Dietary notions of the day:
  - Irregular mealtimes cause disordered digestion.
  - Rest after meals essential to digestion.
  - Condiments suitable only for those over age 14.
  - Bananas poorly digested so should not be eaten by children or "delicate" adults.
  - Gas in soft drinks aids digestion.
  - Alcohol should be avoided in the interest of health and "Imperial stability."

her son from contaminated milk) and quickly became a strong force. By 1915 there were branches in every province, and in 1919 the Federated Women's Institutes of Canada was in place. Along with similar groups (Homemakers' Clubs in Saskatchewan, Cercles des Fermières in Quebec), the WI worked to improve the quality of country life and provided a forum for rural women. Meetings tackled a range of subjects, from "Hygiene in the Home" and "Motherhood – its Relation to Our Country and the Empire" to pastry-making demonstrations. For years the work continued, a cooperative venture between the Department of Agriculture, which provided the information, and the WI, which made sure the information got out.

New cookbooks also helped homemakers cope. *The Real Home Keeper for the Vancouver Bride* (1913) offered recipes for everything from Emergency Soup and Good Cheap Cake to rarebits made in chafing dishes. Ingredients included local produce such as shad and butternuts. Cookbooks from the Naval Service in Ottawa gave fish recipes, and the Department of Agriculture explained fireless cookery (food was heated to boiling, placed in a homemade insulated container and left to cook in its own heat). Life insurance companies offered booklets with tips for healthy eating and food preparation.

Home economics education was also expanding. The teaching of domestic science had begun in Quebec in the 1880s and in a few public schools in Ontario and Nova Scotia in the late 1890s. Teacher training was offered at Normal Schools soon after the turn of the century. The first university to establish a degree program in household science was Victoria College, University of Toronto in 1902, followed by Manitoba in 1915, and both Macdonald College (McGill) and Alberta in 1918.

Homesteading in the West slowed during the decade, and crops were poor in 1917 and 1918. Still, Canadian wheat flour had established its supremacy, and home baking was a regular routine in

*A 1910 class of domestic science students in Ontario.*

Special Collections, Hamilton Public Library

Canadian kitchens. The milling companies promoted Five Roses, Purity and Ogilvy's Royal Household flours with cookbooks that would be treasured and passed down through generations. The Moffat Stove Company printed a cookbook with ads showing stoves to suit any lifestyle.

But in 1914, World War I arrived to overshadow all else. This was Canada's first real encounter with war, and patriotism sent thousands of ill-prepared soldiers off to answer Britain's call. However inexperienced, the Canucks became the heroes of many now-famous battles, braving hellish conditions with little to cheer them except parcels from home.

On the home front, volunteer land armies produced food for both "the boys over there" and the people of war-ravaged Europe. Victory gardens flourished. "War bread" made from inferior wheat flour (the best went to Europe) became acceptable at home. Social events revolved around dances and card parties to raise money for cigarettes and candy to send overseas. In every province, the Imperial Order Daughters of the Empire (IODE) produced cookbooks to raise money for servicemen's families.

Women met to pack ditty bags, roll bandages or knit socks in khaki or navy wool. Thousands of women also went out to work for the first time, filling jobs in munitions plants and offices (for less pay than men got, of course). Fashion reflected the somewhat freer times with hemlines shortened a bit and a touch of lipstick in evidence.

Despite the patriotic deeds on the home front, the war remained rather remote for most Canadians. Everyday life went on, even in Halifax where convoys formed and German U-boats lurked. In 1917, however, the explosion of a munitions vessel in Halifax harbor devastated the city and brought the grim realities of wartime to our doorstep.

*The first kitchen space savers (sometimes known as hoosiers) included a flour bin, bread box, plate rail, cutting board and pull-out enamel table top.*

*Canadians were encouraged to use other grains as wartime shipments of wheat and flour went to Europe.*

Courtesy of Maple Leaf Foods

When the Great War finally ended, it had taken a heavy toll: 60,000 Canadians did not return. And when the rest came marching home again, some with British war brides in tow, they found a different Canada. Veterans faced inflation and unemployment, housing shortages and high rents. There were lots of cars and no bars.

The end of the war, however, also brought a renewed optimism – the euphoria of regained peacetime, of pride in Canada's contribution to the war and enhanced image abroad. For women, the future looked especially bright. The war had emancipated them: they had the vote and new roles as wage-earners; one in seven was in the labor force. Canada's adolescence was over, and for women a new world of choices was just around the corner.

*Many cookbooks of the era included lovely soft-toned illustrations.*

Courtesy of Robin Hood Multifoods Inc.

*The women's Land Army marched to the fields, replacing harvest hands during wartime.*

Courtesy City of Toronto Archives - SC 244-1220 (James #640)

*Patriotism inspired many food ads during WW I.*

Courtesy of Cadbury Beverages Canada Inc.

*War work for women included "putting down" vast quantities of preserves, often outdoors or in summer kitchens.*

Provincial Archives of New Brunswick/Ref# P153/63

# Cookbook Sampler
## THE 2ND DECADE

For more cookbooks of the decade, see Bibliography p. 232-233.

# BORSCHT

*For a creamy version, stir in some heavy cream just before serving.*

| | | |
|---|---|---|
| 1 lb | meaty soup bone | 500 g |
| 1/4 lb | smoked pork or bacon | 125 g |
| 8 cups | cold water | 2 L |
| 1 tsp | salt | 5 mL |
| 1 | large onion, chopped | 1 |
| 4 to 6 | beets, peeled diced or grated | 4 to 6 |
| 1 | large carrot, diced | 1 |
| 1 | large potato, diced | 1 |
| 1/2 cup | diced celery | 125 mL |
| 2 cups | finely shredded cabbage | 500 mL |
| 3/4 cup | chopped canned tomatoes | 175 mL |
| 1 | clove garlic, crushed | 1 |
| 1/4 cup | (approx) lemon juice | 50 mL |
| | Salt and pepper | |
| | Chopped fresh dill | |
| | Sour cream | |

Cover soup bone and pork with water; add salt and bring slowly to boil. Skim; simmer, partially covered, for 1-1/2 hours. Remove meat and bone; dice meat and set aside. Discard bone.

Add onion and beets; cook 10 to 15 minutes or until beets are nearly tender. Add carrot, potato and celery; cook 10 minutes. Add cabbage; cook until tender but not over-cooked. Add tomato juice and garlic. Add enough lemon juice to make soup pleasantly tart but not sour. Season to taste with salt and pepper. Heat just to boiling; add dill. Return meat to soup; heat through. Dollop or swirl sour cream through each serving. Makes 8 servings.

Lured to this country by cheap, abundant farmland and the hope of religious freedom, 170,000 Ukrainians settled in Canada between 1891 and 1914. Most were hard-working peasants who toiled to open up the Prairies. They brought their love of such simple fare as borscht, their national soup, with all its regional differences, to Canada. Variations of this soup are endless, depending on the season, religious tradition (meatless versions often served during Lent) and choice of ingredient to add tartness. Some used beet *kvass* (fermented beets), some a rye *kvass* (fermented yeast/rye flour mixture), some just added lemon or rhubarb juice, vinegar or slightly acidic sorrel leaves.

While most of the recipes recorded by families of Ukrainian descent start with a piece of meat, lots of water and only two or three beets, over the years, we've become used to a heartier borscht with a lot more beets. If meat is used in this soup, it is either taken out and served as a separate course, or a few slices are added to each bowl. Central Ukrainians like extra cabbage, few beets; those from western regions prefer more beets. Doukhobors settling in British Columbia, vegetarians by choice, made a meatless version.

A Polish version (*barszcz*), often adding Polish sausage, *kielbasa*, as well as German and other European versions appear in regional Canadian cookbooks.

# RAGOÛT DE BOULETTES

*The traditional rib-sticking stews of old Quebec, rich in flavor and color despite their humble ingredients, are still very satisfying fare on cold winter nights. Serve this with small boiled potatoes.*

| | | |
|---|---|---|
| 1 lb | ground pork | 500 g |
| 1/2 lb | ground veal or beef | 250 g |
| 2 oz | ground salt pork (optional) | 60 g |
| 1 | small onion, minced | 1 |
| 1 | clove garlic, minced | 1 |
| 1/4 tsp | each cinnamon and allspice | 1 mL |
| 2 | slices bread, crumbled and soaked in 1/2 cup (125 mL) milk | 2 |
| | Salt and pepper | |
| 2 tbsp | shortening or vegetable oil | 25 mL |
| 3 cups | water or pork stock* | 750 mL |
| 1/4 cup | browned all-purpose flour | 50 mL |
| 1/2 cup | water | 125 mL |

Combine ground meats, onion, garlic, cinnamon, allspice, soaked bread, and salt and pepper to taste. Shape into 1-1/2-inch (4 cm) balls. In casserole, brown meat balls in shortening; add water, cover and simmer for 30 minutes. Mix flour with 1/2 cup (125 mL) water until smooth; stir into pan and cook, stirring, until thickened. Makes 6 servings.

*\* To make pork stock, cover about 1-1/2 lb (750 g) pork hocks or meaty bones with water; add quartered onion, carrot, celery stalk, bay leaf, 2 whole cloves, salt and pepper; simmer about 2 hours and strain.*

*Ragoût de boulettes* (meatball stew) and *ragoût de pattes* (pork hock stew) are sometimes combined into one dish *(ragoût de boulettes et de pattes)* by browning the hocks first and then simmering for hours to make a dark stock. With meatballs alone, browned flour is used for color, flavor and thickening. To make browned flour, spread a thin layer of flour in a heavy pan and place over moderate heat or in oven until a dark golden color, stirring occasionally.

# LAMB CURRY

*This curry would have been served with a chutney like Rhubarb Chutney (p. 40) or a well-seasoned pickle. Serve over steamed rice sprinkled with coconut and raisins.*

| | | |
|---|---|---|
| 1 | onion, chopped | 1 |
| 1 | apple, peeled and chopped | 1 |
| 1 tbsp | butter | 15 mL |
| 2 tbsp | all-purpose flour | 25 mL |
| 1 tbsp | packed brown sugar | 15 mL |
| 1 tbsp | curry powder | 15 mL |
| 2 cups | milk or canned tomatoes, chopped | 500 mL |
| 1/2 tsp | salt | 2 mL |
| 1 tbsp | vinegar | 15 mL |
| 3 cups | diced cooked lamb, veal or chicken | 750 mL |

In saucepan, sauté onion and apple in butter over medium heat until soft. Blend in flour, sugar and curry powder; cook for 1 minute. Gradually add milk; cook, stirring, until boiling and thickened. Blend in salt and vinegar. Add meat; reduce heat and simmer 10 minutes or until heated through. Makes 4 servings.

Whether a carryover from British tastes acquired in India or a result of the coast-to-coast availability of a vast array of spices, curried veal, lamb and chicken were popular dishes. In early days, Blue Ribbon, Gold Medal, Barbour in the Maritimes and Nabob in the West were familiar brands of spices.

The curries of this era were usually mild in flavor and used up leftover meat. By the '70s, Canadians were expanding their international tastes to include spicier curries with more authentic seasonings. Also, a wide selection of condiments accompanied the curry.

# TOURTIÈRE

*Traditionally, the filling is quite shallow. This recipe may be baked in two smaller pie plates if desired. Tourtière is served with homemade preserves such as pickled beets, green tomato ketchup and other relishes.*

| | | |
|---|---|---|
| 1-1/2 lb | ground pork | 750 g |
| 1 | onion, chopped | 1 |
| 1/4 cup | finely chopped celery | 50 mL |
| 2 | cloves garlic, minced | 2 |
| 1 tsp | salt | 5 mL |
| 1/2 tsp | ground savory | 2 mL |
| 1/4 tsp | pepper | 1 mL |
| 1/4 tsp | ground allspice or cloves | 1 mL |
| 1 | bay leaf | 1 |
| 3/4 cup | water | 175 mL |
| 1 | small potato, boiled and mashed (optional) | 1 |
| | Pastry for 10-inch (25 cm) double-crust pie | |
| 1 | egg yolk | 1 |
| 1 tbsp | milk | 15 mL |

In heavy saucepan, cook pork until no longer pink, breaking up meat; drain off any fat. Add onion, celery, garlic, salt, savory, pepper, allspice, bay leaf and water. Cover and simmer for 15 minutes, stirring occasionally; simmer, uncovered, 5 minutes longer or until most liquid is absorbed but mixture is still very moist. Stir in potato (if using). Remove bay leaf. Let cool to lukewarm.

Pour into pastry-lined plate; cover with top crust. Seal and crimp edges; cut vents in top. Combine egg yolk with milk; brush over pastry. Bake in 425°F (220°C) oven for 30 minutes or until golden. Makes 6 to 8 servings.

The traditional tourtières of Quebec vary according to each region of the province, and there are as many recipes as there are cooks (each of whom is sure her recipe is the right one). Julian Armstrong's book, *A Taste of Quebec*, gives eight different regional tourtière recipes (not counting those made with fish).

Many of the most popular tourtières are the simplest – a filling of ground pork simmered with onion, celery and seasonings (usually savory and cloves or allspice) baked in a pastry crust. These pies can be thin or thick, and with or without diced potatoes or a little mashed potato for thickening the filling.

Some versions use a mixture of ground pork and beef. Similar pies with fairly shallow fillings from Saguenay-Lac St. Jean are often called **Pâté à la viande**. Other tourtières from Saguenay and Charlevoix are made with pork, beef and potatoes, all cut in small cubes.

Also found in these regions as well as the Côte du Sud (the south shore of the St. Lawrence between Quebec City and Gaspé) are the thick layered pies called *cipâte* or *cipaille*. The old-time versions were made with three layers of cubed meat (traditionally game such as venison, rabbit, partridge or pheasant, or if game was unavailable, a mixture of chicken, beef or pork) with a layer of pastry on top of each meat layer. More recent variations are made in a deep dish, with pastry on top and bottom only.

# SAVORY SHORTRIBS

*Similar recipes are found in many early western cookbooks and are still popular today. The canned tomato sauce in this recipe replaces the canned tomatoes or tomato soup, stock or water called for in earlier recipes. Worcestershire sauce also adds more flavor.*

| | | |
|---|---|---|
| 1/4 cup | all-purpose flour | 50 mL |
| 1 tsp | salt | 5 mL |
| 1/4 tsp | pepper | 1 mL |
| 1/4 tsp | paprika | 1 mL |
| 3 lb | shortribs of beef or moose cut in 3-inch (8 cm) pieces | 1.5 kg |
| 2 tbsp | vegetable oil | 25 mL |
| 1 | onion, chopped | 1 |
| 1/2 cup | diced celery | 125 mL |
| 1/4 cup | cider vinegar | 50 mL |
| 2 tbsp | packed brown sugar | 25 mL |
| 2 tbsp | Worcestershire sauce | 25 mL |
| 1 cup | canned tomato sauce | 250 mL |

Combine flour, salt, pepper and paprika; add meat and toss. In skillet, brown ribs well in oil; transfer to casserole. To skillet, add onion; cook until softened. Add celery, vinegar, sugar, Worcestershire and tomato sauce; bring to boil. Pour over ribs. Cover and bake in 325°F (160°C) oven for 2 hours or until very tender. Makes 4 servings.

This recipe is adapted from one called **Cariboo Shortribs,** found in the *British Columbia Women's Institute Cookbook* (1958), which tells the early history of each region of the province. The rugged Cariboo country of the interior was a region of big appetites, from the earliest gold rush years through the era of the first homesteads and ranches, which were stopping places for wagon trains. Hearty supper dishes like this one, with its satisfying sweet-and-sour flavor, made use of whatever meat was available from hunting or farms.

# FISH CAKES

*This recipe is still a great way to use up leftovers.*

| | | |
|---|---|---|
| 1 lb | salt cod (or 2 cups/500 mL cooked fish) | 500 g |
| 2 cups | mashed potatoes | 500 mL |
| 1 | egg | 1 |
| 1 | small onion, chopped | 1 |
| 1/4 cup | chopped fresh parsley | 50 mL |
| | Salt and pepper | |
| | Fine dry bread crumbs | |
| | Vegetable oil or butter | |

If using salt cod, soak in cold water overnight; drain. In skillet, cover cod with fresh water; simmer until it flakes easily with fork; drain.

With fork, flake cooked fish. Combine with potatoes, egg, onion, parsley, and salt and pepper to taste. Form into patties; coat lightly with bread crumbs. In skillet, fry in liberal amount of oil over medium-high heat for 2 to 3 minutes on each side until crisp and golden. Makes 4 to 6 servings.

Old-fashioned fish cakes, crispy and golden, economical and simple to make, were popular in every region in the early decades. Salt cod is the traditional ingredient on the East Coast, but fresh cod or other fish, especially salmon (cooked or canned), make delicious fish cakes, too. In Newfoundland today, many people still like their fish cakes fried in a generous amount of lard instead of oil.

# TOMATO MARMALADE

*An abundance of tomatoes, from coast to coast but especially in Kent County in Ontario, made this recipe popular.*

| 2 | oranges | 2 |
|---|---|---|
| 1 | lemon | 1 |
| 4 cups | chopped seeded peeled ripe tomatoes | 1 L |
| 4 cups | granulated sugar | 1 L |

Remove rind from oranges and lemon. Remove white pith; cut rind into thin slivers. Cut pulp into chunks; set aside.

In saucepan, cover rind with 1 cup (250 mL) water; boil for 5 minutes. Drain. In large pot, combine rind, tomatoes, orange and lemon pulp and sugar. Bring to boil; boil hard for 30 minutes or until jam stage. Pour into hot sterilized jars and seal. Makes 4 cups (1 L).

Preservation was a necessity in early days. Everyone had pint and quart sealers – glass jars that required rubber rings (hard to get in wartime) and a glass lid with a metal screw-ring to hold the whole thing in place. The old copper boiler used on wash days doubled as a suitable boiling water bath container.

Whatever grew in abundance was preserved, enough to last until the next season. Besides fruits and vegetables, pickles and jams, frugal kitchens turned out a year's supply of canned chicken, meat and fish.

# RHUBARB CHUTNEY

*Since curries were popular during this decade, chutney recipes appear in early cookbooks. Often made with apples and tomatoes, chutneys were sometimes called* **India Pickle.** *This recipe shows the ingenuity of using available produce. Green ginger was mentioned in an early recipe, presumably referring to fresh gingerroot.*

| 6 cups | sliced rhubarb (2 lb/1 kg) | 1.5 L |
|---|---|---|
| 5 cups | chopped peeled apples | 1.25 L |
| 4 cups | packed brown sugar | 1 L |
| 1 tsp | whole cloves | 5 mL |
| 1 tbsp | grated gingerroot (or 1/4 cup/50 mL minced preserved ginger) | 15 mL |
| 1 | clove garlic, chopped (optional) | 1 |
| 1 cup | raisins | 250 mL |
| 1 tsp | salt | 5 mL |
| 1 tsp | cinnamon | 5 mL |
| 1-1/2 cups | vinegar | 375 mL |
| 1/2 cup | water | 125 mL |

In large heavy saucepan, combine rhubarb, apples and sugar. Tie cloves in cheesecloth; add to fruit along with ginger, garlic, raisins, salt, cinnamon, vinegar and water. Bring to boil and boil gently, stirring often, until thickened, about 1 hour. Remove spice bag. Pour into sterilized canning jars. Seal and process in boiling water bath for 10 minutes. Makes 9 cups (2.25 L).

In early days, rhubarb was known as "pie plant," and delicious pies it certainly made. Most farms had great clumps of rhubarb, and children soon learned that, although it was sour, fresh rhubarb was delicious when dipped into a small fistful of sugar.

Rhubarb was featured in everything from drinks to desserts: rhubarb wine, crisps, cobblers, tea breads, coffeecakes, upside-down cakes, in jams or spreads, or mixed with strawberries, raisins or apples in pies. The simplest treat was a **Rhubarb Compote** (stewed rhubarb) made by cooking rhubarb until barely tender with just enough water to prevent burning, and enough sugar to sweeten. Served by itself or over hand-cranked ice cream, it was an early summer treat.

# GRAHAM GEMS

*Gems were often made with molasses; however this version uses brown sugar. For a variation, add 1 cup (250 mL) fresh or frozen blueberries. Graham flour is whole wheat flour that is coarser than the regular grind.*

| 1 cup | graham or whole wheat flour | 250 mL |
|---|---|---|
| 1 cup | all-purpose flour | 250 mL |
| 1/4 cup | packed brown sugar | 50 mL |
| 1 tsp | baking soda | 5 mL |
| 1/2 tsp | salt | 2 mL |
| 1 cup | soured milk* or buttermilk | 250 mL |
| 1 | egg, lightly beaten | 1 |
| 3 tbsp | butter, melted | 50 mL |

In bowl, combine flours, sugar, soda and salt. Beat together soured milk, egg and butter; pour all at once into flour mixture. Stir with fork just until blended. (Do not overmix.)

Spoon into 12 greased muffin tins; bake in 400°F (200°C) oven for 20 minutes or until tops are firm to the touch. Makes 12.

* To sour milk: In measure, combine 1 tsp (5 mL) lemon juice or vinegar with enough milk to make 1 cup (250 mL). Let stand 10 minutes; stir.

Muffins were often referred to as gems and baked in special pans called gem pans. Recipes often called for heating baking pans before filling. An old recipe book says, "Bake in hissing-hot" gem pans. Cereals, such as cream of wheat, and whole wheat flour sometimes replaced part of the flour.

# POTATO SCONES

*Potato scones reflect the influence of the Scottish in the Maritimes and their adaptability in using the famous P.E.I. potato.*

| 1-1/2 cups | all-purpose flour | 375 mL |
|---|---|---|
| 1/4 cup | (approx) granulated sugar | 50 mL |
| 1 tbsp | baking powder | 15 mL |
| 1 tsp | salt | 5 mL |
| 2 tbsp | butter or shortening | 25 mL |
| 1/4 cup | currants | 50 mL |
| 2 | eggs | 2 |
| 1/3 cup | milk | 75 mL |
| 3/4 cup | mashed potatoes | 175 mL |

In bowl, combine flour, sugar, baking powder and salt; cut in butter until mixture resembles coarse meal. Stir in currants. Beat eggs lightly; reserve 1 tbsp (15 mL). With fork, stir into dry ingredients along with milk and potatoes until well moistened.

Knead gently on lightly floured surface about 20 times. Roll or pat into circle 1/2 inch (1 cm) thick. Place on ungreased baking sheet; brush with reserved egg yolk and sprinkle with more sugar. Cut into 16 wedges, separating slightly. Bake in 425°F (220°C) oven for 12 to 15 minutes or until lightly browned. Makes 16 scones.

## VARIATIONS:

**Raisin Scones:** Add 3/4 cup (175 mL) raisins with dry ingredients.
**Oat Scones:** Use 1/2 cup (125 mL) rolled oats in place of 1/2 cup (125 mL) flour.

Scones were a favorite Scottish tradition. According to *A Treasury of Nova Scotia Heirloom Recipes*, "the difference between a bannock and a scone (which the Scots rhyme with 'on,' not 'bone') is that the bannock is a rather large, round cake, and the scone is a smaller triangle, or 'farl,'... But local and personal usages vary considerably, Scots being strong individualists."

A similar recipe for **German Buns** appears in an Ontario cookbook from the Kitchener area, where German settlers were predominant.

When Their Majesties King George VI and Queen Elizabeth visited Government House in Halifax on June 15, 1939, scones were served. And Canadian Brits gathered for "tea at the Empress" in Victoria for scones and jam.

By the '40s and '50s when biscuit mixes made life simpler, recipes for scones were temporarily moved to the back of the recipe box. In the '80s and '90s, the comfort food craze returned them once more to their rightful place at the front.

# STEAMED BROWN BREAD

*One old recipe states that "a five-pound lard pail answers the purpose of the mould."*

| | | |
|---|---|---|
| 2 cups | graham or whole wheat flour | 500 mL |
| 1 cup | cornmeal | 250 mL |
| 2 tbsp | packed brown sugar | 25 mL |
| 2 tsp | baking soda | 10 mL |
| 1 tsp | salt | 5 mL |
| 1 cup | raisins (optional) | 250 mL |
| 3/4 cup | molasses | 175 mL |
| 1-1/2 cups | buttermilk or soured milk* | 375 mL |
| 2 tbsp | shortening, melted | 25 mL |

In bowl, combine flour, cornmeal, sugar, baking soda, salt, and raisins (if using). Add molasses, buttermilk and shortening all at once; stir just until completely moistened. Pour batter into well-greased cans (two 28 oz/796 mL or three 19 oz/540mL), filling cans about three-quarters full. Cover with foil; tie with string.

Place on rack in large saucepan; pour in boiling water to come halfway up sides. Cover and steam over simmering, not boiling, water for 2-1/2 hours until cake tester comes out clean. Let stand for 10 minutes; turn out of cans and cool on rack. Makes 2 or 3 loaves.

* To sour milk: Place 2 tsp (10 mL) lemon juice or vinegar in measure; pour in enough milk to make 1-1/2 cups (375 mL). Let stand for 10 minutes; stir.

A Maritime tradition served with baked beans, this bread was part of the Saturday Night Special. Since an oven was not needed, it was easily steamed over an open fire or on the stove.

Sometimes known as **Boston Brown Bread,** this was also called **Indian Bread** since cornmeal was known as Indian meal.

Cornmeal was a staple in early households, and a popular dessert was **Indian Pudding** made with molasses, cornmeal and lots of milk.

# JUMBO RAISIN COOKIES

*During the Depression, an even firmer version of these cookies were jokingly called "door stoppers."*

| | | |
|---|---|---|
| 2 cups | raisins | 500 mL |
| 1 cup | water | 250 mL |
| 1 cup | shortening | 250 mL |
| 2 cups | granulated sugar | 500 mL |
| 3 | eggs | 3 |
| 1 tsp | vanilla | 5 mL |
| 4 cups | all-purpose flour | 1 L |
| 1 tsp | baking powder | 5 mL |
| 1 tsp | baking soda | 5 mL |
| 1 tsp | salt | 5 mL |
| 1-1/2 tsp | cinnamon | 7 mL |
| 1/4 tsp | each nutmeg and allspice | 1 mL |
| 1 cup | chopped nuts (optional) | 250 mL |

Boil raisins in water 5 minutes; let cool. (There should be about 1/4 cup/50 mL liquid.)

In bowl, cream shortening with sugar; beat in eggs, one at a time, then vanilla. Add cooled raisin mixture. Stir together flour, baking powder, baking soda, salt, cinnamon, nutmeg and allspice; gradually blend into creamed mixture. Add nuts (if using).

Drop rounded teaspoonfuls onto greased baking sheet, allowing space for spreading. Bake in 375°F (190°C) oven for 12 to 15 minutes or until set and browned. Transfer to racks to cool. Makes about 6 dozen cookies.

Big, soft cookies were easy and fast to make. During World War I, the recipe was revised to make firmer cookies that travelled well and improved with age, called **Cookies for Soldiers** or **Miners Cookies.** Later versions, called **Rocks** and **Hermits,** eliminated boiling the raisins. As times improved, a rich fruit-filled version became **Fruit Drops. Ranger Cookies** were similar, but had rolled oats, Rice Krispies, and Grapenut Flakes or coconut instead of raisins or dates. Rolled in balls then flattened with a fork or glass, these were popular in the '50s.

# ALMOST A POUND CAKE

*This version of pound cake is more like a rich loaf cake with baking powder added, and could be called Half-Pound Cake.*

| 1/2 cup | butter | 125 mL |
|---------|--------|--------|
| 1 cup | granulated sugar | 250 mL |
| 2 | eggs | 2 |
| 1-1/2 cups | all-purpose flour | 375 mL |
| 1 tsp | baking powder | 5 mL |
| 1/4 tsp | salt | 1 mL |
| 1/2 cup | milk | 125 mL |
| 1 tsp | vanilla | 5 mL |

In bowl, cream together butter, sugar and eggs until light. Combine flour, baking powder and salt; add to creamed mixture alternately with milk. Blend in vanilla. Pour into greased and floured 8- x 4-inch (1.5 L) loaf pan. Bake in 350°F (180°C) oven for 50 to 60 minutes or until cake tester comes out clean.

## VARIATIONS:

**Lemon Loaf:** Add grated rind of one lemon. Before removing from pan, pour glaze made with 1/4 cup (50 mL) granulated sugar mixed with juice of one lemon over hot cake.

**Orange Loaf:** Use orange rind and juice instead of lemon in the Lemon Loaf.

**Seed Loaf Cake:** Add 1 tbsp (15 mL) caraway seeds.

**Cherry Loaf:** Add 1 cup (250 mL) halved candied cherries tossed with 2 tbsp (25 mL) all-purpose flour. Use 9- x 5-inch (2 L) loaf pan.

**Raisin and Currant Loaf:** Add 1 cup (250 mL) raisins and 1/2 cup (125 mL) currants (rinsed in hot water) tossed with 2 tbsp (25 mL) all-purpose flour. Use 9- x 5-inch (2 L) loaf pan.

**Nut Loaf Cake:** Add 1 cup (250 mL) chopped nuts. Use 9- x 5-inch (2 L) loaf pan.

**Ginger Loaf Cake:** Add 1/2 cup (125 mL) currants and 1/2 cup (125 mL) chopped candied ginger tossed with 2 tbsp (25 mL) all-purpose flour. Use 9- x 5-inch (2 L) loaf pan.

True pound cake was made with a pound each of sugar, butter, eggs and flour. The texture of the cake depends on the beating. One cookbook cautioned, "Beat thoroughly as each ingredient is added as upon this depends the quality of the cake." No electric mixers then. It usually took two pairs of hands: one to beat and one to sift flour and add eggs as necessary. Full marks go to the arm that beat this much batter. Flours have changed considerably and sifting is a thing of the past today.

Early versions suggested placing several scented geranium leaves (rose or lemon were favorites) in the bottom of the greased loaf pan before adding the batter. Turned out, the cake had a leafy pattern on top and just a hint of their flavor.

# BOILED RAISIN CAKE

*Today's cooks replace the lard used originally with shortening or butter, and some recipes add eggs.*

| | | |
|---|---|---|
| 1 cup | water | 250 mL |
| 1 cup | packed brown sugar | 250 mL |
| 1-1/2 cups | raisins | 375 mL |
| 1/2 cup | shortening | 125 mL |
| 1 tsp | cinnamon | 5 mL |
| 1/2 tsp | nutmeg | 2 mL |
| 1/4 tsp | each allspice and cloves | 1 mL |

| | | |
|---|---|---|
| 1-3/4 cups | all-purpose flour | 425 mL |
| 1 tsp | baking soda | 5 mL |
| | Icing sugar | |

In saucepan combine water, sugar, raisins, shortening, cinnamon, nutmeg, allspice and cloves; bring to boil, stirring constantly. Let cool to lukewarm.

Mix flour with baking soda; blend into cooled mixture. Pour into greased and floured 8-inch (2 L) square cake pan. Bake in 350°F (180°C) oven for 45 minutes or until top is firm to the touch. Let cool in pan. Sprinkle with icing sugar.

**Eggless, Butterless, Milkless Cake** or just simply **War Cake** (and in one book **Blitzkrieg Cake**), this was a good keeper and easily packed for shipping. Its popularity continued through World War II. The '40s also produced **Miracle Chocolate Cake,** which replaced eggs and butter with Miracle Whip salad dressing.

# CAKE DOUGHNUTS

*Doughnut recipes (beignes in French Canada) abound in old cookbooks. Yeast made "raised" doughnuts; cake doughnuts were often called **Fried Cakes**; potato doughnuts were **Spudnuts**. There was no end to fat for frying (fall butchering produced lots of it for rendering). Deep-frying also meant **Corn Fritters**, served with maple syrup, **Funnel Cakes** of Mennonite fame (made by pouring batter through a funnel into the hot fat) and **Rosettes** made with fancy-shaped irons dipped into batter then into hot oil. If desired, roll warm doughnuts in icing sugar or a mixture of 1/4 cup (50 mL) granulated sugar and 1/2 tsp (2 mL) cinnamon.*

| | | |
|---|---|---|
| 2-3/4 cups | all-purpose flour | 675 mL |
| 2/3 cup | granulated sugar | 150 mL |
| 1 tsp | baking soda | 5 mL |
| 1/2 tsp | salt | 2 mL |
| 1/2 tsp | nutmeg | 2 mL |
| 1/2 cup | sour milk | 125 mL |
| 3 tbsp | butter, melted | 50 mL |
| 2 | eggs, lightly beaten | 2 |

Mix together flour, sugar, baking soda, salt and nutmeg. Blend milk and butter into eggs; gradually add dry ingredients to make soft, not sticky, dough. Chill 1 hour.

On floured board, roll dough to 1/4-inch (5 mm) thickness. With floured doughnut cutter, cut out and fry in 375°F (190°C) oil for 1 to 2 minutes per side or until golden brown. Drain on paper towels. Makes about 1-1/2 dozen.

Prize Doughnuts
One cup sugar, one cup milk
Two eggs beaten fine as silk
Salt and nutmeg (lemon'll do)
Of baking powder, teaspoons two.
Lightly stir the flour in,
Roll on pie board not too thin,
Cut in diamonds, twists or rings,
Drop with care the doughy things
Into fat that briskly swells
Evenly the spongy cells.
Watch with care the time for turning;
Fry them brown – just short of burning.
Roll in sugar, serve when cool
Price – a quarter for this rule.
– *The War Time Cook Book: For the benefit of our Soldiers and Sailors,* by the Daughters of the Empire

# Basic vanilla ice cream

*Usually called **Philadelphia Ice Cream** in old cookbooks, this smooth ice cream is a good base for fruit variations. Other vanilla ice creams started with a custard base. You can halve or double the recipe.*

| | | |
|---|---|---|
| 4 cups | light cream | 1 L |
| 1 cup | granulated sugar | 250 mL |
| 1/8 tsp | salt | 0.5 mL |
| 1 tbsp | pure vanilla | 15 mL |

In heavy saucepan, heat cream, sugar and salt just until sugar is dissolved. Remove from heat; add vanilla. Cover and chill. Freeze. Makes about 8 cups (2 L).

### VARIATIONS:

**Strawberry, Raspberry, Peach** or other **Fruit:** When ice cream is half frozen, stir in 2 cups (500 mL) crushed fruit, sweetened to taste.

**Chocolate:** Add 4 oz (125 g) unsweetened chocolate to cream mixture in saucepan; gently melt and beat smooth.

**Coffee:** Heat half the cream almost to boiling; add 1/4 cup (50 mL) ground coffee and steep 10 minutes over low heat; strain. Add remaining cream and continue with recipe.

**Ginger:** To cream mixture, add 3/4 cup (175 mL) chopped preserved ginger (preserved in syrup) and 2 tbsp (25 mL) of the syrup.

**French Vanilla** (Custard Ice Cream): Beat 4 egg yolks with 3/4 cup (175 mL) granulated sugar until thick and pale yellow; stir in 2 cups (500 mL) scalded light cream. Cook in double boiler or heavy saucepan over low heat, stirring often, until mixture thickens enough to coat a spoon. Remove from heat; add 1 tbsp (15 mL) vanilla and 2 cups (500 mL) whipping cream. Cover and chill thoroughly. Freeze. Makes about 6 cups (1.5 L).

In the good old summertime, the highlight of big holiday picnics in the park or clan gatherings at Grandmother's house was always the ritual of ice cream making. Longtime Eastern Township residents remember ice stored under the barn being brought out at ice cream time. They nearly always made strawberry ice cream by putting a jar of homemade strawberry jam in with cream or sometimes with custard. Everyone took turns at cranking the big old hand-cranked ice cream freezer, until the very last person (who had to work the hardest) got to lift the lid and the dasher for the first lick of the delectable frosty cream.

Ice cream was a rare treat before the days of refrigeration, and the favorite flavors of the time are just as irresistible today. The recipes, which have been adapted to today's creams, work just as well in our ice cream machines (follow manufacturers' directions) as they did in the old hand-cranked models. If you've inherited one, use it to conjure up the good old days.

# Maple syrup pie
## (Tarte au sirop d'érable)

*This classic sweet of old Quebec has a smooth, rich filling, typically shallow and very sweet. Variations of the traditional recipes are still popular in Quebec.*

| | | |
|---|---|---|
| 1/2 cup | cold water | 125 mL |
| 1/4 cup | all-purpose flour | 50 mL |
| 1 cup | pure maple syrup | 250 mL |
| 1 | egg, lightly beaten | 1 |
| 2 tbsp | butter | 25 mL |
| | 8-inch (20 cm) baked pie shell | |

Whisk water with flour until smooth; stir into syrup in small heavy saucepan. Stir in egg; cook over medium-low heat, stirring, until thick, about 7 minutes. Stir in butter until melted. Pour into pie shell. Let cool.

Syrup, sugar or molasses pies of all kinds were made in every region in pioneer days. In Quebec, **Maple Syrup Pie** *(tarte au sirop d'érable)* and **Sugar Pie** *(tarte au sucre)* made use of local maple syrup and maple sugar when available, or brown sugar for economy.

**Backwoods Pie,** using brown sugar plus maple or corn syrup, appears in early Nova Scotia cookbooks as well as national books such as the *Five Roses Cookbook* (1915). **Molasses Pie** *(tarte à la ferlouche* or *tarte à la mélasse* in Quebec and **Lassy Tart** in Newfoundland) was usually lightly spiced and thickened with bread crumbs. **Shoofly Pie,** most common in Mennonite areas, had a molasses and brown sugar filling with crumbs on top. In the early years when ingredients were scarce, molasses was a standby everywhere.

# Coconut macaroons

*Served with afternoon tea, these originally required a double boiler. When sweetened condensed milk appeared on the market, the initial cooking was eliminated.*

| | | |
|---|---|---|
| 3 | egg whites | 3 |
| 1 cup | granulated sugar | 250 mL |
| 1 tbsp | cornstarch | 15 mL |
| 1-1/2 cups | shredded coconut | 375 mL |
| 1 tsp | vanilla | 5 mL |

Beat egg whites until stiff peaks form. Combine sugar and cornstarch; gradually stir into egg whites. Fold in coconut. In double boiler, cook mixture over gently boiling water, stirring once or twice, for 15 minutes or until slightly crusty around edges. Remove from heat; add vanilla.

Drop teaspoonfuls onto brown-paper-lined or greased baking sheet. Bake in 275°F (140°C) oven for 25 to 30 minutes or until lightly browned. Makes about 3 dozen.

Other meringue-based cookies have evolved since coconut macaroons appeared. Hard **Meringues** (plain or colored and later with chocolate chips or toasted almonds added) were often called **Kisses. Forgotten Cookies** were simply meringues that were left overnight in the oven to dry out. **Ragged Robins** were meringues with various additions such as chopped cherries, nuts and/or Corn Flakes.

# LEMON SNOW WITH CUSTARD SAUCE

*Cold desserts ranged from simple **Junket** (a milk-based dessert, coagulated by rennet) to puddings like **Blanc Mange** (cornstarch pudding) to moulded fancy desserts. **Snows, Fools and Whips** were fruit-flavored. **Apple Snow** and **Prune Whip** were simply sweetened, cooked fruit, sieved and folded into egg whites. Fools started out the same, but the fruit purée was folded into whipped cream.*

| | | |
|---|---|---|
| 1 tbsp | grated lemon rind | 15 mL |
| 1/4 cup | cornstarch | 50 mL |
| 1/2 cup | granulated sugar | 125 mL |
| 1/2 tsp | salt | 2 mL |
| 2 cups | boiling water | 500 mL |
| 1/4 cup | lemon juice | 50 mL |
| 2 | egg whites | 2 |
| | Custard Sauce | |

In saucepan, combine lemon rind, cornstarch, sugar and salt; gradually stir in water. Cook over medium heat, stirring, until thickened and clear. Remove from heat; add lemon juice.

Beat egg whites until stiff but not dry. Fold in lemon mixture. Pour into 6 rinsed 1/2 cup (125 mL) moulds. Refrigerate until firm, about 4 hours. Unmould; serve with sauce. Makes 6 servings.

### CUSTARD SAUCE:

| | | |
|---|---|---|
| 4 | egg yolks | 4 |
| 1/4 cup | granulated sugar | 50 mL |
| 1/4 tsp | salt | 1 mL |
| 2 cups | scalded milk or light cream | 500 mL |
| 1 tsp | vanilla | 5 mL |

In double boiler, beat egg yolks lightly; add sugar and salt. Gradually stir in milk. Cook, stirring, over simmering water until slightly thickened. Remove from heat; add vanilla. Serve cold. Makes 2 cups (500 mL).

**Baked Custard:** Lightly beat 3 eggs with 1/3 cup (75 mL) granulated sugar and 1/4 tsp (1 mL) salt. Gradually stir in 2 cups (500 mL) scalded milk and 1/2 tsp (2 mL) vanilla. Pour into 6 custard cups; sprinkle with nutmeg and set in pan of hot water. Bake in 350°F (180°C) oven for 40 minutes or until knife inserted in centre comes out clean. Serve warm or chilled. Makes 6 servings.

**Trifle:** Sprinkle chunks of Sponge Cake (recipe p. 63) with orange juice or sherry; spread with raspberry jam and top with Custard Sauce. Repeat layers. Top with sweetened whipped cream, slivered cherries or angelica, toasted almonds, or chocolate shavings.

**Floating Island:** Beat 3 egg whites until foamy; gradually beat in 1/3 cup (75 mL) granulated sugar until stiff peaks form. Drop by rounded tablespoons onto 3 cups (750 mL) scalding milk; poach for 4 minutes, turning once. Lift out onto towel. Use 2 cups (500 mL) of this milk to make Custard Sauce. Float meringues on top. Makes 6 servings.

# MAPLE CREAM FUDGE

*Fudges – chocolate, maple cream or penuche/pinoche – filled with walnuts, dates or raisins, or fondants were popular.*

| | | |
|---|---|---|
| 2 cups | packed brown sugar | 500 mL |
| 1/2 cup | 18% cream | 125 mL |
| 2 tbsp | butter | 25 mL |
| 1 tsp | vanilla | 5 mL |
| 1 cup | chopped nuts | 250 mL |

In saucepan, bring sugar and cream just to boil, stirring. Boil, without stirring, for 5 minutes (or to 236°F/113°C). Remove from heat; add butter and vanilla. Let cool just to lukewarm. Beat for 2 to 3 minutes or until thick and sheen just starts to disappear. Quickly stir in nuts. Pour into buttered pan. Score; cut when cool.

### VARIATIONS:

**Sucre à la crème:** Substitute 1 cup (250 mL) brown and 1 cup (250 mL) granulated sugar (or maple sugar if available) for the brown sugar.

**Penuche Icing:** Boil 1 cup (250 mL) brown sugar, 1/4 cup (50 mL) cream, and 2 tbsp (25 mL) butter for 3 minutes; add 1 tsp (5 mL) vanilla. Cool slightly; add 1 cup (250 mL) sifted icing sugar; beat until spreadable.

One of the simple pleasures in kitchens then, as now, was candy making. Chocolate and cocoa were readily available, along with brown sugar, maple sugar and corn or maple syrups. Candy thermometers were nonexistent, so home candy-makers relied on cold-water tests.

In New Brunswick and Prince Edward Island, uncooked fudge using mashed potatoes was innovative and delicious.

The
TWENTIES
1920    1929

# A CENTURY OF CANADIAN HOME COOKING

*[Even] after Mother bobbed her hair and one terrible day gave up baking bread…she continued to bake the world's best apple pies and bran muffins.*

– Jeanne Scargall
*The Canadian Homestead Cookbook*

The "new woman" of the Roaring Twenties may have bobbed her hair, shortened her skirts and even gone out to work, but at home her life went on much as before.

The '20s images that spring to mind – flappers and the Charleston, bathtub gin and "twenty-three skidoo" – belonged mainly to the sophisticated "fast" set in the cities. Most Canadians who were young at the time recall an era of simpler pleasures, with lots of picnics and dances, crazy songs like "Yes, We Have No Bananas," and evenings at the movies, watching Rudolph

Valentino and Mary Pickford on the silent screen.

Many of the new ideas and much of the fun of the '20s didn't surface until the middle of the decade. Although usually thought of as a prosperous time, the '20s actually began with four hard years. The euphoria produced by the end of the First World War soon gave way to a postwar slump as war industries shut down and the Prairies suffered a series of poor crops. Across the country, and especially in the Maritimes, unemployment brought tough times.

Some Canadians found a lucrative and sporting answer in rum-running across the border to the United States, where Prohibition continued longer than in Canada. But even when the economy picked up in 1925 and the Jazz Age invaded the land, the lives of most Canadians are best described not as wild but as contented and secure, with

jobs for everyone. Men carried lunch pails to work, women baked for church bazaars, children did their homework, and Sunday always brought a roast beef or chicken dinner. In winter there were hockey games and curling on outdoor rinks; in summer, softball and berry-picking and picnics.

The food of the decade was plentiful and mostly familiar. A few new fads – drug-store soda fountains, cocktail parties and other American creations – caught on in the cities. And some interesting new regional dishes emerged, especially in the menus of the Canadian Pacific Railway grand hotels. *A Taste of Banff* by Douglas Leighton (1985) recalls the era: "The Roaring Twenties really roared into the resorts of the Rockies. At the Banff Springs and the Château Lake Louise, the carefree mood of the times reached extravagant heights. Their dining rooms were filled

---

*A commemorative plate from Nabisco portrays idyllic family life.*

On pages 48 – 49:   A dainty luncheon: Chicken Salad, Tomato Aspic, Deviled Eggs, Tea Biscuits, Lemon Curd Tarts and Jelly Roll slices.

*Dining cars resplendent with silver and linens served regional foods to cross-Canada travellers.*

with 'everybody who's anybody' sipping champagne and enjoying such specialties as Slice of Sirloin 'Bow Valley,' Julienne of Sole 'Mount Victoria' and Eggs 'Lac Miroir' created by top European chefs and served with impeccable style. With their outrageously elegant decor and palatial settings, these CPR dining rooms, in this golden age of rarified exclusiveness, were truly bastions of unabashed snobbery."

Also served in the elegant dining cars of the transcontinental trains, Canadian railway cuisine had become world-famous. The best of regional products – succulent spring lamb chops, fine Alberta beef steaks, fresh blueberry pies, Lake Superior whitefish, Oka and cheddar cheeses – were available en route. Train travel gave many people their first taste of delicacies such as Lake Winnipeg goldeye. This famous specialty is said to have been invented accidentally in the 1880s when a Manitoban tried smoking his fish lightly over a

wood fire, in the traditional Indian manner, and absentmindedly left it much longer than intended, only to discover the heavily smoked fish was not only fully cooked but even more delicious than ever.

Regional specialties gradually began to make their way into home kitchens across the country. But on most family supper tables of the '20s, the baked ham, scalloped potatoes, apple pie and other familiar fare came from Mom's repertoire of old family favorites. Everyone loved her hearty stews and pot roasts, steak-and-kidney pie, sausages with fried tomatoes, roast beef with Yorkshire pudding, fresh-baked biscuits and breads. Most of these recipes she summoned up from memory as needed; others, especially for fancier baking, were quickly retrieved from a kitchen drawerful of clippings and scribblings, a handwritten notebook or from the well-splattered pages of cookbooks passed down from her mother and grandmother.

*A pretty table and polite manners were part of pleasant family meals.*

Courtesy of J.R. Ouimet, Ville d'Anjou, Quebec

*Summer meant strawberries to these 1920 berry-pickers on Vancouver Island.*

British Columbia Archives and Records Service/Ref #96191

# A CENTURY OF CANADIAN HOME COOKING

Along the way she had probably added a few recipe books from outside sources, such as local church and charity fund-raisers, and some of the booklets – on canning, flour, yeast, gelatin and other products – published in the '20s by food companies.

Until the mid-'20s, the typical Canadian kitchen did not include a large, all-purpose cookbook. Most homemakers felt no need for the basics until new theories about "scientific cookery" were widely publicized that decade. The so-called rational school of domestic science had got its start in the late 1890s with *The Boston Cooking-School Cook Book* by Fannie Merritt Farmer, who earnestly championed the cause: "I certainly feel that the time is not far distant when a knowledge of the principles of diet will be an essential part of one's education. Then mankind will eat to live, will be able to do better mental and physical work, and disease will be less frequent."

A revised edition of her book was published in Boston in 1923 and in Toronto by McClelland and Stewart in 1924. This and many other books by reformers entranced with the science of nutrition and "laboratory cookery" have been lauded by many for their substance and accuracy, and decried by others as responsible for over-standardization and over-sanitization of the North American diet. This decade has been referred to as the white era: the ideal kitchen was overwhelmingly white, as was much of the food. Traditional ethnic dishes were largely ignored by domestic science teachers, most of whom were simply unaware of them.

In Canada, the *Canadian Cook Book* by Nellie Lyle Pattinson, published in 1923, was the first to set new standards for accurate measurements and recipe-writing. Pattinson, a graduate of the Lillian Massey School of Household Science, was a key figure in introducing domestic science into schools. She and her colleagues at Toronto's Central Technical School produced the book as a text for their students, but over

*The poultry class at Olds College in Alberta, 1921, began with the basics: plucking and cleaning the birds.*

Glenbow Archives, Calgary/#ND-932

## LOOKING BACK

*Judy Ross recounts cottage life in the '20s when Muskoka lured visitors from all over Canada and the United States. Many journeyed with their wicker baskets, leather satchels and steamer trunks by train from Toronto to Gravenhurst wharf and then by steamboat to summer homes.*

For wealthy summer cottagers, the Roaring Twenties was a time of fancy dress balls, dance parties and formal dinners served in large cottage dining rooms with fine china and silver. In areas like Beaumaris on Lake Muskoka the summer household often included a retinue of servants who, among other chores, prepared and served the food. They worked in cavernous kitchens with large wood-burning stoves, handpumps to draw water from the lake, coal oil lamps for light and an icehouse out back where perishable foods were kept in sawdust-coated blocks of ice.

At the beginning of the summer, crates of food staples arrived by steamboat from the T. Eaton Company. This was supplemented by the weekly arrival of the supply boat, a floating store which was often less amply supplied than its name would suggest. Chicken, eggs and meat came from local farmers and a famous treat in those days was Muskoka lamb which appeared on menus in fancy New York restaurants. Fish was plentiful in the lakes and since most of the men's time was spent fishing, daily fare included pan fried lake trout and pickerel. Berries were another staple. A favorite afternoon outing was berry picking, and the baskets of blueberries, huckleberries and blackberries were turned into homemade pies.

the years and through many revisions up to 1947 it became a standard for homemakers. After her death in 1953, the book was revised in several editions by Helen Wattie and Elinor Donaldson Whyte.

The new domestic efficiency was widely supported by women's groups such as the Women's Institutes and church and service clubs. Cooking demonstrations and courses were eagerly attended. Government departments of agriculture, flour and appliance companies, newspaper and magazine food pages all reflected the general enthusiasm.

The federal Department of Agriculture produced many booklets on home preserving. The Little Blue Books Home Series from the Department of Health advised on healthy eating. And as electricity and natural gas began to replace coal stoves, the utilities got into consumer education in most provinces. Alberta Power's 60th anniversary cook-

book, *Diamond Dishes* (1987), recalls the period: "On September 28, 1928, Alberta Power brought round-the-clock electricity to Grande Prairie for the first time. The local bridge club, accustomed to playing until the lights went out at midnight, didn't realize they were up past their usual hour until about two in the morning." In 1929, just seven years after Canadian Western first brought natural gas to southern Alberta kitchens, the company established its first home service department, conducting cooking schools and appliance demonstrations throughout the region. Over the next decades, their Blue Flame Kitchens cooking programs expanded to radio and television, and their 50th anniversary cookbook, *Western Favourites* (1979), featured recipes through the years, from '30s crumb cakes and porcupine meatballs to '70s beef Wellington and barbecued trout.

In Vancouver in 1928, a notice for a new school for cookery,

*Proper attire was essential for home economics students as shown in a 1929 Sask. Dept. of Education recipe pamphlet.*

Courtesy of Saskatchewan Department of Education, Instructional Resources Branch

*Porridge for breakfast in the '20s often started with cooking the night before.*

National Archives of Canada

opening on Alder Street under the auspices of Queen Mary Coronation Hostel, announced: "There has been a wide demand in Vancouver for a school of this description. Their membership is open to anyone wishing to acquire a thorough knowledge of general and high class cookery. We have been fortunate in acquiring the services of a highly trained graduate of The Edinburgh School of Cookery and Domestic Economy."

The flour companies continued to publish new editions of their popular cookbooks, and Maple Leaf Milling offered several editions of a 20-lesson cooking course, "Cookery Arts and Kitchen Management," to homemakers enrolled in its Maple Leaf Club.

In 1923, food guru Kate Aitken began her 30-year association with the Canadian National Exhibition, offering cooking demonstrations as part of her "Country Kitchen" exhibit. By 1927, enthusiastic audiences filled the Women's Building for every show. "Mrs. A." went on to become Director of Women's Activities for the CNE from 1938 to 1952.

In 1924, a collection of *Montreal Star* columnist Margaret Currie's earnest "chats" about domestic life was published, including recipes ranging from oyster soup to charlotte russe.

In 1922, the *Grain Grower's Guide* magazine, published in Winnipeg, produced *The Country Homemaker*, a book of articles on labor-saving kitchens, fireless cookers, hot school lunches and feeding the threshers. The *Western Producer*, a newspaper owned by prairie farmers who were members of the Wheat Pool, began a publishing venture in 1923. For many generations to follow, its food pages became a forum for rural homemakers.

For most women life was easier in many ways than it had been for their mothers. The new efficient kitchens boasted Hoosier cabinets, enamelled tabletops, cereal cookers, food choppers with numerous attachments, Pyrex oven glass, stamped tinware and white enamelware.

*The 1926 Nova Scotia Provincial Exhibition displayed this up-to-date kitchen.*

Courtesy of the Women's Institutes of Nova Scotia

The latest layer-cake pans (sometimes called jelly cake plates) had a "jigger" to loosen the cake for removal.

For those who could afford them, new electric appliances such as refrigerators, wringer washers, hot-water heaters, toasters and vacuum cleaners were revolutionary labor-savers after ice boxes and scrub boards. Rural electrification, however, was very slow in coming, and the great majority of farm women still had to cope with wood stoves, wells and no indoor plumbing.

Food shopping in small towns was done at local grocers or the general store, probably with a stop at the butcher's shop with its wooden blocks and saw-dust on the floor, or maybe at the baker's for a Melton Mowbray pork pie or for hot cross buns at Easter time. But in larger centres, grocery chains such as Safeway, Red and White, Steinberg's and Loblaws were expanding.

Women's work was still centred mainly in the home, with extensions into the community; women baked for bazaars and catered countless turkey dinners for their churches and fund-raiser banquets for men's service clubs, participating through women's auxiliaries. Those who sought paid work had few "suitable" choices, mainly nursing, teaching and typing. Women who became store clerks or factory workers were paid much less than the men.

But times were changing. The '20s marked the beginning of an emerging new world for women. The war had opened a few doors and enlarged perspectives. Women were beginning to make an impact in politics and in journalism. More women were working outside the home, and new women's issues were evolving.

Even those who remained homemakers applied a new freedom of thought to child-rearing, housekeeping and cooking. By the late '20s, magazines began to reflect their readers' wider interests. The first issues of *Chatelaine*

*Always a Canadian favorite, loose tea was sold in packs under many popular labels.*

Courtesy of G.E. Barbour Inc., Sussex, New Brunswick

*This 1919 store in Toronto was one of the first self-service grocery stores.*

Courtesy City of Toronto Archives - SC 244-9011 (James #12220)

in 1928 were clearly aimed at the "new woman," even in articles about food preparation.

In the late '20s, *Chatelaine* discussed such modern topics as "part-time housekeeping" (time-saving meal plans for women working at full-time or part-time jobs). Frigidaire ads touted new frozen desserts, and "waterless cooking" reflected receptiveness to new ideas. An article titled "Who Wants to Cook in August?" featured a simplified one-plate luncheon with a moulded salad, jellied veal, potato salad and garnishes.

Articles on home entertaining included some surprising new ideas: a progressive dinner (each course served at a different home) and Chinese dishes to make at home. Other food features, more traditional, were still of interest: canapes for wedding receptions, fish recipes for Friday and Lent, a 75-cent menu for a church supper.

By the second half of the decade, with the economy on the upswing, life improved for most Canadians. Ontario and Quebec experienced rapid industrial growth, the Prairies enjoyed bumper crops, and mining and lumbering boomed in other provinces.

The '20s were roaring at last – more jobs, more security, more money, more everything. The '20s brought new radios, telephones, roads, fancy new cars, the first electric appliances and the first talkies in movie theatres.

Everyone wanted to be a millionaire – investing, borrowing, taking a chance, living it up. But the roller coaster that had briefly shot up was poised for another downswing. Paper profits and too much wheat finally ended it all on Black Thursday at the Winnipeg Grain Exchange, followed by the New York stock market crash five days later, on October 29, 1929.

*One 1920s cookbook states: "...it lies within the reach of each and every hostess to paint upon the canvas of the table a gleaming picture of loveliness."*

Courtesy of Specialty Brands

*Silent movies and variety shows added to the gaiety of the '20s.*

Courtesy of The Imperial Order of the Daughters of the Empire, Toronto

# Cookbook Sampler

## THE TWENTIES

For more cookbooks of the decade, see Bibliography p. 233.

# MARITIME FISH CHOWDER

*If a thicker consistency is desired, stir in 3 tbsp (50 mL) flour along with the potatoes. Crushed soda crackers will also thicken the broth.*

| | | |
|---|---|---|
| 2 tbsp | butter | 25 mL |
| 1 cup | chopped onion | 250 mL |
| 1/4 cup | chopped celery | 50 mL |
| 2 cups | diced peeled potatoes | 500 mL |
| | Salt and pepper | |
| 2 cups | water | 500 mL |
| 1 lb | cod or other fillets, cut in pieces | 500 g |
| 1 cup | milk | 250 mL |
| 1 cup | light cream | 250 mL |
| | Chopped fresh parsley or paprika | |

In large heavy saucepan, melt butter; cook onion and celery until softened. Add potatoes, and salt and pepper to taste. Add water and bring to boil; reduce heat, cover and simmer for 10 minutes or until potatoes are just tender.

Add fish, cover and simmer for 5 to 10 minutes or just until fish flakes easily with fork. Add milk and cream. Heat gently until very hot; do not boil. Add salt and pepper to taste. Sprinkle each serving with parsley. Makes 4 or 5 servings.

## VARIATIONS:

**Salmon Chowder:** Use fresh or frozen salmon instead of cod; or break canned salmon into chunks and stir in gently with milk.

**Scallop, Lobster** or **Mixed Seafood Chowder:** Use 2 cups (500 mL) cooked bite-size seafood instead of cod; add along with milk.

**Clam Chowder:** Use 2 cups (500 mL) cooked or 2 cans (5 oz/142 g each) clams instead of cod; add along with milk. Replace part of the water with the drained clam juice.

Old-fashioned chowders of the Atlantic provinces are at their best using the simplest ingredients – fish, onions and potatoes in a creamy broth (often with evaporated milk or cream for richness).

Chopped celery or carrots are common additions, and a pinch of savory or thyme is optional. Rendered salt pork, a favorite in Newfoundland, is often used instead of butter.

Oysters, especially at Christmas and for '20s entertaining, were cooked in many ways, but the most preferred was **Oyster Stew**. To make it, simmer 1 pint (500 mL) shucked fresh oysters in their liquor along with 1/4 cup (50 mL) butter just until edges begin to curl. Heat 2 cups (500 mL) light cream and 1 cup (250 mL) milk almost to boiling; add oysters. Season with salt, pepper and optional pinch of nutmeg; sprinkle with paprika. Makes 6 to 8 servings.

# Scotch Eggs

*Picnic fare in earlier decades, these sausage-wrapped eggs are great for today's outdoor parties or out-of-hand suppers. Originally deep-fried, this version is oven-baked, adapted from a method used by Jan Main, a versatile Toronto caterer.*

| 6 | hard-cooked eggs | 6 |
|---|---|---|
| 1 lb | bulk sausage meat | 500 g |
| 1 cup | dry bread or cracker crumbs | 250 mL |
| 1/3 cup | finely chopped fresh parsley | 75 mL |
| 1/4 tsp | (approx) each pepper, dried sage, savory and thyme | 1 mL |

Wrap each egg in meat, encasing evenly. Combine crumbs, parsley, pepper, sage, savory and thyme, adding more seasonings to taste; completely coat eggs in mixture. Bake on ungreased baking sheet in 375°F (190°C) oven for 30 to 35 minutes, turning several times, or until crisp and browned. Serve hot or cold. Makes 6 lunch or 24 appetizer servings, cut in wedges.

From cocktail parties for the flapper set to church basement receptions for the new preacher, '20s entertaining usually involved large trays of hors d'oeuvres. All were tasty but simple to assemble, using fairly familiar ingredients. Along with fancy sandwiches, such as pinwheels and checkerboards filled with ham and walnut, chicken and almond, or cream cheese and pimiento fillings, there might be this assortment:

**Pigs in Blankets:** Cooked breakfast sausages wrapped in flaky pastry.
**Asparagus Rolls:** Cooked asparagus spears rolled in buttered white bread.
**Angels on Horseback:** Broiled bacon-wrapped oysters.
**Solomon Gundy:** Marinated herring and raw onion on crackers.
**Digby Chicks:** Smoked fillets of herring on toast.

# Yorkshire Pudding

*You can make individual puddings by baking this in 12 very generously greased muffin tins for about 25 minutes. Many recipes say to let the batter stand for an hour or so, but it doesn't seem necessary.*

| 2 | eggs | 2 |
|---|---|---|
| 1 cup | milk | 250 mL |
| 3/4 cup | all-purpose flour | 175 mL |
| 1/2 tsp | salt | 2 mL |
| 1/4 cup | (approx) fat drippings | 50 mL |

In bowl, beat eggs with milk. Add flour and salt; beat for 2 minutes with electric mixer. Pour fat into 9-inch (2.5 L) square or 12- x 8-inch (3 L) metal pan. Heat in 425°F (220°C) oven for 2 to 3 minutes until very hot. Without removing pan from oven, quickly pour in batter. Bake for 30 minutes or until puffed, browned and with high crusty edges and soft centre. Cut into squares. Makes 6 servings.

### VARIATION:

**Toad in the Hole:** Pour batter over 1 lb (500 g) cooked breakfast sausages; bake as in Yorkshire Pudding.

For Canadians of British descent, Sunday dinner was often roast beef, and Yorkshire pudding was a must, along with gravy and roast potatoes.

Traditional Yorkshire pudding used the drippings from the roast and was baked in the roasting pan or a separate pan. In early days, the Sunday roast was large and liberally marbled with fat, producing lots of drippings for the pudding as well as for roast potatoes and gravy. Today's leaner roasts (except perhaps prime rib) are likely to be short on drippings. You can ask for extra fat to place on top of the roast; otherwise use whatever fat you can skim from the surface of the pan drippings and make up the difference with melted shortening or lard.

# SCALLOPED POTATOES WITH HAM

*For plain scalloped potatoes, omit the ham. Sometimes a sauce was made with the butter, flour and milk, then poured over the potato-onion layers.*

| | | |
|---|---|---|
| 6 | potatoes, peeled and thinly sliced | 6 |
| 1 | onion, chopped | 1 |
| 2 tbsp | butter, in bits | 25 mL |
| 2 tbsp | all-purpose flour | 25 mL |
| | Salt and pepper | |
| 2 cups | (approx) milk, heated | 500 mL |
| 1 lb | ham, thickly sliced | 500 g |

In buttered 8-cup (2 L) casserole, layer one-third each potatoes, onion, butter, flour, and salt and pepper to taste. Repeat layers twice.

Pour enough milk over top to just be able to see it through slices. Bake, covered, in 350°F (180°C) oven for 45 minutes. Uncover and bake 30 minutes. Top with ham; bake for 15 minutes. Makes 6 servings.

### VARIATIONS:

Cheese Topping: Sprinkle with 1 cup (250 mL) shredded sharp Cheddar cheese 30 minutes before baking is finished.

Herb-Crumb Topping: Sprinkle with 1/2 cup (125 mL) dry bread crumbs mixed with 1 tbsp (15 mL) chopped fresh parsley, 1/2 tsp (2 mL) crumbled dried rosemary and 3 tbsp (50 mL) melted butter before baking.

Whole hams, pickled or brined in the fall and smoked in the spring, were boiled to cook the meat and remove a lot of the salt. The traditional finish was a baked-on crust of crumbs. Later, a brown sugar/mustard/vinegar glaze was spooned over a scored and clove-studded ham and cooked until glazed.

Fruit, like pineapple rings, was an even later addition.

A tasty way to serve ham the second or third time around was baked with scalloped potatoes. If the ham was in nice slices, it was on top; if slivered or diced, it was buried in the potatoes.

# Steak and Kidney Pie

*Instead of pastry, this stew can be topped with Dumplings (p. 82) or Tea Biscuits (p.62).*

| | | |
|---|---|---|
| 1 lb | round steak | 500 g |
| 1/2 lb | kidney (beef, pork or lamb) | 250 g |
| 1 | large onion, chopped | 1 |
| 2 tbsp | shortening, lard or vegetable oil | 25 mL |
| 1-3/4 cups | beef broth | 425 mL |
| 1 tsp | salt | 5 mL |
| 1 | bay leaf | 1 |
| | Pepper | |
| 1/2 tsp | dried thyme or savory | 2 mL |
| 3 tbsp | all-purpose flour | 50 mL |
| 1 cup | peas | 250 mL |

**Flaky Pastry
(recipe p. 21)**

Cut steak into 3/4-inch (2 cm) cubes. Trim kidney; cut into 1/2-inch (1 cm) pieces. In skillet, sauté onion in shortening until softened. Add steak and kidney; brown on all sides. Add broth, salt, bay leaf, pepper to taste, and thyme; simmer until meat is tender, about 45 minutes.

Mix flour with 1/4 cup (50 mL) cold water; add to pan and cook, stirring, until thickened. Add peas. Remove bay leaf. Pour into greased deep pie plate or shallow casserole. Top with pastry. Bake in 425°F (220°C) oven for 20 minutes or until crust is golden. Makes 6 servings.

Imaginative cooks had to use creative means to dress up tough meats. In Newfoundland and Labrador, the Territories, northern Ontario and the Prairies, the meat was often moose, muskox, caribou or venison instead of beef. Herbs for seasoning also changed according to region, savory being the choice of Newfoundlanders. Back then, peas were likely canned or cooked leftovers. Today, frozen peas or frozen mixed vegetables are popular for their brighter color.

Newfoundlanders render salt pork for drippings to brown the meat and add the remaining cracklings, called scrunchions, to the pie.

After the '20s, a couple of teaspoons of Worcestershire sauce added flavor, and beef broth or stock became readily available in dry and liquid forms.

# Perfection Salad

*Let the jelly set in four 3/4 cup (175 mL) individual moulds, if desired. Rinse moulds with cold water first, but don't dry them, to ensure ease in unmoulding. Serve on lettuce-lined plates.*

| | | |
|---|---|---|
| 1 | pkg unflavored gelatin | 1 |
| 2 cups | cold water | 500 mL |
| 2 tbsp | granulated sugar | 25 mL |
| 2 tbsp | vinegar | 25 mL |
| 1 tbsp | lemon juice | 15 mL |
| 1 tsp | salt | 5 mL |
| | Pepper | |
| 1/3 cup | finely shredded cabbage | 75 mL |
| 1/4 cup | chopped celery | 50 mL |
| 1/4 cup | chopped pimiento or sweet green pepper | 50 mL |

Soak gelatin in 1/2 cup (125 mL) of the cold water. In saucepan, combine remaining water, sugar, vinegar, lemon juice, salt, and pepper to taste; bring to boil. Stir in gelatin until dissolved. Chill until slightly thickened. Fold in cabbage, celery and pimiento. Pour into rinsed 3-cup (750 mL) mould. Chill until set. Makes 4 servings.

### VARIATIONS:

**Tomato Aspic:** Substitute tomato juice for water. Vegetables are optional.
**Jellied Beef, Chicken** or **Tongue:** Omit cabbage; add 1-1/2 cups (375 mL) diced or shredded cooked beef, chicken or tongue.

Although jelly powders were available in the '20s, cookbooks had many recipes for "from scratch" jellied salads. Perfection Salad and aspics to coat or garnish meats were popular. A tomato jelly, made by stewing tomatoes with a gelatin mixture then straining out the seeds and seasonings, was likely the original **Tomato Aspic**. Jellied tongue, chicken and ham (or even moose in the Yukon) were all '20s style. Some earlier recipes without added gelatin were still popular; calves'-foot jelly, jellied pork hocks and head cheese all gelled naturally.

# COOKED SALAD DRESSING

*Often called Boiled Dressing, this was the most popular salad dressing until commercial varieties appeared. It was used for all kinds of salads from chicken to apple, and to moisten sandwich fillings as well. Eventually, bottled salad dressings arrived at the corner grocer's, then jars of mayonnaise, unfamiliar to most Canadians and hard to make at home with a Dover (rotary/hand) egg beater.*

*Likely made in a double boiler in the '20s, we now cook this dressing carefully in heavy-bottomed saucepans over medium-low heat, or quickly in the microwave.*

| | | |
|---|---|---|
| 2 tbsp | all-purpose flour | 25 mL |
| 2 tbsp | granulated sugar | 25 mL |
| 1 tsp | salt | 5 mL |
| 1-1/2 tsp | dry mustard | 7 mL |
| 1 cup | milk | 250 mL |
| 1 | egg, beaten | 1 |
| 2 tbsp | butter | 25 mL |
| 1/3 cup | cider vinegar | 75 mL |

In saucepan, combine flour, sugar, salt and mustard; gradually blend in milk. Cook, stirring, until boiling. Add a little hot mixture to egg; stir back into saucepan. Cook over low heat, stirring, for 2 to 3 minutes or until thick and creamy.

Remove from heat; stir in butter until melted. Gradually add vinegar, stirring constantly. Cool, tightly cover and refrigerate for up to 3 weeks. Makes 2 cups (500 mL).

**Waldorf Salad:** Toss diced unpeeled apples with a little lemon juice, celery, walnuts, cooked dressing to moisten, and salt to taste.
**Chicken Salad:** Mix cubed cooked chicken with chopped celery and onion, cooked dressing to moisten, and salt, pepper and curry powder to taste.
**Potato Salad:** Mix diced cooked potatoes with sliced green onions, chopped hard-cooked eggs and sliced radishes. Blend dry mustard (to taste) into enough cooked salad dressing to moisten potato mixture. Season with salt and pepper.
**Deviled Eggs:** Mash yolks of halved hard-cooked eggs with a little mustard, and salt, pepper and cooked dressing to taste. Spoon back into whites. Sprinkle with paprika, chopped parsley or chives.

# TEA BISCUITS

*One of the first recipes taught in domestic science classes, this was also called Baking Powder Biscuits.*

| | | |
|---|---|---|
| 2 cups | all-purpose flour | 500 mL |
| 4 tsp | baking powder | 20 mL |
| 1 tsp | salt | 5 mL |
| 1/2 cup | shortening (part butter if desired) | 125 mL |
| 3/4 cup | milk | 175 mL |

In bowl, combine flour, baking powder and salt; cut in shortening until mixture resembles coarse crumbs. Add milk all at once, stirring with fork to make soft, slightly sticky dough.

Gently knead on lightly floured surface 10 times. Roll out to 1/2-inch (1 cm) thickness; cut into 2- to 3-inch (5 to 7 cm) rounds. Place on ungreased baking sheet, slightly apart for crusty biscuits or touching for pull-apart biscuits. Bake in 425°F (220°C) oven for 10 to 12 minutes or until lightly browned. Makes about 12.

### VARIATIONS:

**Cheese:** Add 1 cup (250 mL) shredded Cheddar before adding milk.
**Whole Wheat:** Replace 1 cup (250 mL) of the all-purpose flour with whole wheat flour.
**Herbed:** Add 1 tbsp (15 mL) chopped fresh parsley or dill, or 1/2 tsp (2 mL) each dried thyme and sage.
**Buttermilk:** Instead of 4 tsp (20 mL) baking powder, use 1 tbsp (15 mL) baking powder and 1/2 tsp (2 mL) baking soda. Use 3/4 cup (175 mL) buttermilk instead of milk.
**Strawberry Shortcake:** Add 1 tbsp (15 mL) granulated sugar with dry ingredients.

In Newfoundland, **Pork Buns** were made by using finely chopped salt pork for half the shortening. A few scrunchions (crisp pork bits left after rendering fat) were added before kneading, if desired.

An early *Chatelaine* magazine column called "Bride's Progress" printed a cooking lesson for Tea Biscuits in response to a reader's request: "I was at a bridge luncheon the other day and ate the most delicious cheese biscuits. I was wondering if I might learn to make them."

One-hundred-year-old Mrs. Margaret MacDonnell, who taught WW I war brides about Canadian cooking, remembered teaching young girls all over rural Saskatchewan to make these biscuits with quick hands and a light touch.

# DATE NUT LOAF

*Sweet quick breads such as this, also called* ***Date Nut Bread****, were great favorites, thinly sliced and buttered, for tea time, lunch boxes and bazaar bake tables.*

| | | |
|---|---|---|
| 1 cup | packed chopped dates | 250 mL |
| 1 tsp | baking soda | 5 mL |
| 1 cup | boiling water | 250 mL |
| 1 cup | packed brown sugar | 250 mL |
| 1/4 cup | butter, melted | 50 mL |
| 1 | egg, beaten | 1 |
| 1 tsp | vanilla | 5 mL |

| | | |
|---|---|---|
| 1-1/2 cups | all-purpose flour | 375 mL |
| 1 tsp | baking powder | 5 mL |
| 1/2 tsp | salt | 2 mL |
| 3/4 cup | chopped walnuts | 175 mL |

In bowl, combine dates and baking soda; stir in boiling water. Let cool. Mix in sugar, butter, egg and vanilla. Combine flour, baking powder and salt; stir into date mixture along with nuts. Turn into greased and floured 9- x 5-inch (2 L) loaf pan. Bake in 325°F (160°C) oven for 1 hour or until tester comes out clean. Cool 10 minutes in pan; turn out onto rack. Makes 1 loaf.

Dried fruits such as dates and raisins were staple ingredients from the earliest years.

Other favorite loaves found in almost every recipe collection included **Orange Raisin**, which was made with orange rind put through a food grinder or thinly sliced and boiled to soften. **Apricot Bread** used dried apricots instead of dates.

# SPONGE CAKE

*True sponge cake has no added fat or leavening; the eggs do all the work, so thorough beating is necessary, and today we use an electric mixer. Many sponge cake recipes call for whole eggs, others have you beat the whites separately with part of the sugar to make the cake a little more foolproof.*

*For this old recipe, sometimes called* ***Hot Water Sponge Cake****, some people used hot milk instead, and others flavored it with grated lemon rind. It makes a good moist cake to serve plain or as a base for strawberry shortcake and trifle. It also adapts well to tube cake or jelly roll pans.*

*Newfoundland shortcake is often sponge cake with "scald cream" (like Devonshire cream) or Nestle's canned cream, chilled, instead of whipped cream.*

| | | |
|---|---|---|
| 4 | eggs, separated | 4 |
| 3/4 cup | granulated sugar | 175 mL |
| 1/4 cup | hot water | 50 mL |
| 1 tsp | vanilla | 5 mL |
| 1 cup | sifted cake-and-pastry flour | 250 mL |
| Pinch | salt | Pinch |

In bowl, beat egg yolks with 1/2 cup (125 mL) sugar until thick and pale; beat in water and vanilla. Fold in flour and salt. Beat egg whites to soft peaks; gradually beat in remaining sugar to stiff peaks. Fold in yolk mixture. Pour into greased and floured 9-inch (2.5 L) square cake pan or tube pan. Bake in 350°F (180°C) oven for 40 to 45 minutes or until centre springs back when touched lightly. Invert pan to cool. Loosen and remove cake.

**Jelly Roll** was a standard in many homes for decades. Jam fillings were most common but Lemon Curd (recipe p. 65) or flavored whipped cream was also used. Spread sponge cake batter in 15- x 10-inch (40 x 25 cm) jelly roll pan lined with buttered waxed paper. Bake 15 to 20 minutes. Invert pan onto tea towel dusted with icing sugar, remove pan and peel off paper. Beginning at narrow end, roll warm cake in towel; let cool completely. Unroll and spread with jelly or jam; roll again and dust with icing sugar.

**Chocolate Roll** was a special treat for dessert or decorated as a **Yule Log** at Christmas, especially in Quebec (**Bûche de Noël**). Sift 1/4 cup (50 mL) cocoa with the flour and bake as for jelly roll.

**Calla Lilies** were another treat made from a similar batter, which was spooned into small rounds on baking sheets, baked briefly and rolled up into cone shapes. The "lilies" were popular at Easter, filled with whipped cream and a dab of jelly or orange peel in the centre. A version in the *The CanLit Foodbook* comes from Margaret Atwood's mother.

# BASIC WHITE CAKE

*This excellent basic cake is moist, tender, fine-textured and has many uses. Good plain or frosted, it adapts to different pan sizes for birthday cakes, mocha cakes or upside-down cakes and makes a great dessert topped with strawberries and whipped cream.*

| | | |
|---|---|---|
| 1/2 cup | butter | 125 mL |
| 1 cup | granulated sugar | 250 mL |
| 2 | eggs | 2 |
| 1 tsp | vanilla | 5 mL |
| 2 cups | sifted cake-and-pastry flour (or 1-3/4 cups/425 mL all-purpose flour) | 500 mL |
| 2-1/2 tsp | baking powder | 12 mL |
| 1/4 tsp | salt | 1 mL |
| 1 cup | milk | 250 mL |

In bowl, cream butter with sugar; beat in eggs one at a time, then vanilla. Sift together flour, baking powder and salt; blend into creamed mixture alternately with milk. Pour into greased and floured 9-inch (2.5 L) square cake pan or two 8-inch (1.2 L) round cake pans. Bake in 350°F (180°C) oven for 40 to 45 minutes for square, 25 to 30 minutes for layers, or until tester comes out clean.

## VARIATIONS:

**Cupcakes:** Bake in 18 large greased or paper-lined baking cups in 375°F (190°C) oven for 20 minutes.
**Devil's Food Cake:** Replace 1/2 cup (125 mL) flour with sifted cocoa.

**Pineapple Upside-Down Cake:** In deep 9-inch (2.5 L) square or 10-cup (2.5 L) round pan, melt 3 tbsp (50 mL) butter; sprinkle with 3/4 cup (175 mL) brown sugar. Arrange pineapple rings or tidbits on top, adding pecan halves or maraschino cherries if desired. Pour batter on top. Bake, let cool slightly, then invert onto plate. Sliced peaches, apples or apricot halves may replace pineapple.

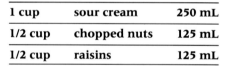

# HONEY CAKE

*Called* medivnyk *by Ukrainians,* piernik *by the Polish, this cake is but one of many versions.*

| | | |
|---|---|---|
| 1 cup | honey (preferably buckwheat) | 250 mL |
| 1/2 cup | butter | 125 mL |
| 1 cup | packed brown sugar | 250 mL |
| 4 | eggs, separated | 4 |
| 3 cups | all-purpose flour | 750 mL |
| 2 tsp | baking soda | 10 mL |
| 1 tsp | baking powder | 5 mL |
| 2 tsp | ginger | 10 mL |
| 1/2 tsp | salt | 2 mL |
| 1 cup | sour cream | 250 mL |
| 1/2 cup | chopped nuts | 125 mL |
| 1/2 cup | raisins | 125 mL |

Bring honey to boil; cool to room temperature. In bowl, cream butter with sugar; beat in egg yolks, one at a time, then honey. Combine flour, baking soda and powder, ginger and salt, blend into creamed mixture alternately with sour cream. Stir in nuts and raisins. Beat egg whites until stiff; fold into batter.

Bake in greased 10-inch (4 L) tube pan in 325°F (160°C) oven for 1 hour or until tester comes out clean. Cool in pan 10 minutes; turn out onto rack. When cooled, wrap to keep moist.

The need for diversification on the Prairies saw an increase in honey production, until today, all three provinces are renowned for high-quality honey. Honey blends (mixing honeys with fruits to make a spread) are full-scale businesses.

In early years, Ukrainian settlers used honey in much of their baking. Their traditional Christmas cake and sour cream cakes filled with either walnuts or almonds are even better with the aromatic flavor of buckwheat honey. Bars, squares and cookies (*medivnychky*) are also made with honey. Honey cake changes with the addition of yeast to make a delicious sweet bread with a cakelike texure.

Savella Stechishin, who was the first Ukrainian woman to graduate from the University of Saskatchewan, organized the Ukrainian Women's Association in 1923 to encourage pride in their heritage. She wrote *Traditional Ukrainian Cookery* in 1957.

## CAKES AND MORE CAKES

Pages and pages of cake recipes in cookbooks of the '20s reflected the popularity of sweets for all occasions and purposes, from fancy tea tables to harvesters' lunch pails.

Most books included all the standard cakes, although similar recipes often had different names; others with the same name were completely different. Royal names were among the most popular. **Prince of Wales Cake**, a spice cake containing molasses and coffee, appeared in cookbooks from High River, Alberta, about the time that Edward, Prince of Wales, purchased the nearby E.P. Ranch (which was owned by the royal family from 1919 to 1962). In the 1980s, the current owners opened a teahouse on the ranch and served another version of Prince of Wales Cake, a Boiled Raisin Cake (p. 44) with a brown sugar icing (see Penuche Icing, p. 47).

A Nova Scotia book refers to an earlier Prince of Wales (who became Edward Vll in 1901) visiting Halifax in 1860 and gives a recipe for a cake with two spicy and two white layers, similar to Ribbon Cake. In *The Old Ontario Cookbook*, Prince of Wales Cake also has dark and light layers. In the 1923 *Purity Cookbook*, it's a layer cake made with grated chocolate (similar to **Princess May Cake** in the 1898 *Galt Cookbook*).

**Prince Albert Cake**, in the 1926 *Moffat Cookbook*, is a spice cake made with sour milk and raisins; a similar recipe from the *Chatelaine* centennial collection says the recipe was named in 1850 after Queen Victoria's husband.

**King Edward Cake** in the 1915 *Five Roses Cookbook* is similar to the Prince Albert cakes, and to **King George Cake** in a 1930 book from St. Luke's Church, Winnipeg.

Other interesting cake names:
**Ribbon Cake** appears in many old family recipe collections as well as the *Five Roses Cookbook* (1915) and *Purity* cookbooks (1917 and 1923). It's usually two white layers with a dark layer (spices, molasses, raisins) in between.

**Minnehaha Cake**, with various spellings in the 1898 *Galt* and 1926 *Moffat* cookbooks and in Crisco advertisements featuring "Miss Allen's Tested Recipes," was a white layer cake with a filling similar to boiled frosting with raisins added.

**Watermelon Cake**, in many books including *Five Roses, Purity* and *Moffat*, was created by adding raisins to a dark pink cake batter, baked in a round pan, then frosted with green icing.

**Scripture Cake** gave a list of Bible verses representing each ingredient, such as 2 cups Jeremiah 6:20 (sugar), to produce a light fruit cake that was popular for church bazaars.

**Railway or Railroad Cake** recipes ranged from pound cakes with raisins (or caraway seeds and candied peel, as in the 1915 *Five Roses Cookbook*) to spiced versions similar to Prince of Wales or Boiled Raisin cakes. The origin of the name is debated, but most were very sturdy cakes, which supports the theory of a stationmaster's wife who said that railway cake was any cake heavy enough to stand up to the thumping of passing trains (and not fall as it baked). Another explanation is that when the coming of the railroad brought fancier ingredients to the early settlers, they began to bake "railroad cakes." Nellie McClung's autobiography, *Clearing In The West*, mentions a railroad cake along with other foods taken to an 1892 Manitoba picnic.

# LEMON CURD

*Known as **Lemon Cheese, Lemon Butter** or just **Lemon Filling**, a small crock of this was usually kept in the icebox for tiny tea-time tarts, cake filling or for a spread on toast. **Apple Butter**, popular in earlier decades, still is a favorite in apple country and in cottage industries. Other versions of fruit curds and butters used mashed cooked dried apricots, fresh strawberries or pears.*

| | | |
|---|---|---|
| 3 | eggs, beaten | 3 |
| 1 cup | granulated sugar | 250 mL |
| 1/2 cup | lemon juice | 125 mL |
| 1 tbsp | grated lemon rind | 15 mL |
| 1/4 cup | butter | 50 mL |

In small heavy saucepan, combine eggs, sugar, lemon juice, rind and butter. Cook over low heat, stirring, until thick enough to thickly coat spoon, about 15 minutes. (Mixture will thicken when cold.) Let cool and refrigerate. Makes 1-1/2 cups (375 mL).

**Lemon Meringue Pie:** In heavy saucepan, combine 1-1/4 cups (300 mL) granulated sugar, 6 tbsp (100 mL) cornstarch and 1/2 tsp (2 mL) salt; gradually stir in 2 cups (500 mL) water. Bring to boil; boil gently for 3 minutes, stirring constantly. Whisk small amount into 3 lightly beaten egg yolks; return to saucepan and cook over medium heat, stirring, for 2 minutes. Blend in 3 tbsp (50 mL) butter, 1/2 cup (125 mL) lemon juice and 1 tbsp (15 mL) grated lemon rind. Let cool slightly; pour into baked 9-inch (23 cm) pie crust.

Beat 3 egg whites with 1/4 tsp (1 mL) cream of tartar; gradually beat in 1/3 cup (75 mL) sugar. Spread meringue over filling; bake in 350°F (180°C) oven for 12 to 15 minutes. Cool.

# FLAPPER PIE

*In eastern Canada, this recipe was usually called* **Graham Wafer Cream Pie,** *but westerners knew it as Flapper Pie.*

| | | |
|---|---|---|
| 1-1/4 cups | graham wafer crumbs | 300 mL |
| 1/4 cup | granulated sugar | 50 mL |
| 1/2 tsp | cinnamon | 2 mL |
| 1/4 cup | butter, melted | 50 mL |
| *Filling:* | | |
| 1/4 cup | granulated sugar | 50 mL |
| 3 tbsp | cornstarch | 50 mL |
| 2 cups | milk | 500 mL |
| 2 | egg yolks, lightly beaten | 2 |
| 1 tsp | vanilla | 5 mL |
| *Meringue:* | | |
| 2 | egg whites | 2 |
| 1/4 tsp | cream of tartar | 1 mL |
| 2 tbsp | granulated sugar | 25 mL |

Combine crumbs, sugar and cinnamon; blend in butter. Set 1/4 cup (50 mL) aside. Press remainder onto bottom and sides of 9-inch (23 cm) pie plate. Bake in 375°F (190°C) oven for 8 minutes. Cool.

Filling: In saucepan, mix sugar with cornstarch; blend in milk. Cook over medium heat, stirring, until boiling; stir a little into yolks, then return to saucepan. Cook over low heat, stirring, for 2 minutes or until thickened. Remove from heat; add vanilla and cool slightly. Pour into pie crust.

Meringue: Beat egg whites with cream of tartar until soft peaks form; gradually beat in sugar until stiff peaks form. Spread over filling, sealing to crust. Top with reserved crumbs. Bake in 400°F (200°C) oven for 5 minutes or until lightly browned. Cool to room temperature, about 4 hours.

Cream pies like butterscotch, banana cream and coconut cream were favorites of this decade, and restaurants (called cafés in small towns in the West and usually run by Chinese cook/owners) always had cream pies on their menus.

**Banana Cream Pie:** Into baked pie shell, slice 2 bananas. Pour Flapper Pie filling over top. Top with meringue or whipped cream.
**Coconut Cream Pie:** Add 1 cup (250 mL) shredded coconut to Flapper Pie filling. Pour into baked pie shell. Top with meringue or whipped cream.

# CREAM PUFFS

*Lighter than air, crispy puffs filled with whipped cream and sprinkled with icing sugar were the pride of '20s hostesses and remained popular for many decades of teas and bridge parties. These can also be filled with custard and/or sliced fruit, or made in miniature for savory fillings.*

| 1 cup | water | 250 mL |
|-------|-------|--------|
| 1/2 cup | butter | 125 mL |
| 1 cup | all-purpose flour | 250 mL |
| 1/4 tsp | salt | 1 mL |
| 4 | eggs | 4 |

In small heavy saucepan, combine water and butter; bring to full boil. Reduce heat; add flour and salt all at once, stirring vigorously with wooden spoon until in smooth ball that leaves side of pan. Remove from heat. Add eggs, one at a time, beating vigorously after each. Beat until smooth and shiny (with electric mixer if desired). Chill a few minutes.

Drop by large spoonfuls onto lightly greased baking sheet, mounding each in centre. Bake in 425°F (220°C) oven for 15 minutes; bake in 350°F (180°C) oven for 20 to 30 minutes longer or until puffed and golden. Cool thoroughly. Slice tops from each puff; remove any moist dough inside. Fill as desired. Makes 12 medium or 8 large puffs.

Cream puff dough is called *choux* paste and is also used for many French pastries such as éclairs. With the addition of cheese, they become cheese puffs or **Gougères**. In later decades ('80s), it was stylish to serve the impressive **Croquembouche**, a pyramid of tiny filled cream puffs, drizzled with caramel and spun sugar.

### VARIATIONS:

**Chocolate Éclairs:** Bake cream puff batter in elongated shapes. Fill with whipped cream or custard filling; spread tops with thin chocolate icing.

**Cheese Puffs:** After beating in eggs in cream puff batter, beat in 1/2 tsp (2 mL) dry mustard and 1 cup (250 mL) shredded Cheddar or Swiss cheese. Drop by small spoonfuls and bake for 15 to 20 minutes. Fill with savory fillings.

# RICE PUDDING

*Old-fashioned rice pudding brings out two schools of thought. For some, it's a baked pudding with a hint of nutmeg or cinnamon and a crusty brown top. To others, it's a softer, slowly cooked, creamy pudding done on top of the stove. Served warm or chilled, either is delicious. Danish settlers added the traditional one whole almond to the pudding and served it with a red currant sauce.*

| 1/4 cup | rice (preferably short-grain) | 50 mL |
|---------|-------------------------------|-------|
| 4 cups | milk, scalded | 1 L |
| 1/3 cup | packed brown or granulated sugar | 75 mL |
| 1/4 tsp | salt | 1 mL |
| 1/4 tsp | cinnamon or nutmeg | 1 mL |
| 1/4 cup | raisins | 50 mL |

In 8-cup (2 L) buttered casserole, combine rice, milk, sugar, salt, cinnamon and raisins. Bake in 300°F (150°C) oven for 2 hours, stirring occasionally during first hour. (The mixture should not boil.) Makes 6 servings.

### VARIATION:

**Stovetop Rice Pudding:** In double boiler, heat milk; add rice, sugar, salt and cinnamon. Cook over simmering water, partly covered, for 1-1/2 hours, stirring occasionally. Add raisins; cook, uncovered, for 15 minutes. Add a little hot mixture to 1 lightly beaten egg. Return to pan and cook 15 minutes, stirring every 5 minutes. Makes 6 servings.

Rice, tapioca and sago were the basis of some mighty good desserts in the '20s. The instant, Minute, Converted and parboiled types of rice hadn't arrived on the scene, and long slow cooking was in order. To many kids, tapioca pudding was "fish eyes and glue." But it filled you up.

By the '50s and '60s, we made **Heavenly Hash** and **Glorified Rice** with precooked rice – fast and simple. Marshmallows, crushed pineapple and often coconut and toasted slivered almonds gave the rice an elegant status it hadn't had before, and it was considered very clever and a snap to make.

In the '80s, the Olympic chefs team from Saskatchewan presented a Wild Rice Pudding at the match in Frankfurt.

# SPANISH CREAM

*Many old recipes do not chill the custard before folding in the whites. This results in a pudding with a layer of clear jelly on top when unmoulded, which is the way many people remember and prefer it. Serve this plain or with whipped cream, chocolate sauce, sliced fruit or fruit purée such as raspberry.*

| 1 | pkg unflavored gelatin | 1 |
|---|---|---|
| 1/4 cup | cold water | 50 mL |
| 2 | eggs, separated | 2 |
| 1/3 cup | granulated sugar | 75 mL |
| 1-3/4 cups | hot milk | 425 mL |
| 1 tsp | vanilla | 5 mL |

Sprinkle gelatin into water; let stand 5 minutes. In double boiler, beat egg yolks with sugar until creamy; stir in hot milk and softened gelatin. Cook, stirring often, until slightly thickened. Add vanilla. Chill, stirring occasionally, until consistency of raw egg white. Beat egg whites until stiff; fold into custard. Pour into rinsed 4-cup (1 L) mould or individual moulds; chill until firm, 2 to 3 hours. Unmould. Makes 8 servings.

## VARIATIONS:

**Charlotte Russe:** Prepare same as Spanish Cream but omit egg whites and fold in 1 cup (250 mL) whipping cream, whipped. Pour into 5-cup (1.25 L) mould lined with ladyfingers.
**Vanilla Bavarian:** Prepare same as Spanish Cream but reduce milk to 1-1/4 cups (300 mL). Fold in 1 cup (250 mL) whipping cream, whipped, along with egg whites. Serve with chocolate or fruit sauce.

Charlotte Russe

**Raspberry Bavarian:** Prepare same as Spanish Cream but instead of milk, use 1 cup (250 mL) water and 1/2 cup (125 mL) raspberry purée; increase sugar to 2/3 cup (150 mL). Fold in 1 cup (250 mL) whipping cream, whipped, along with egg whites. (Delete egg yolks, if desired.)

Many attractively moulded desserts graced the dinner tables of the '20s. Cookbooks offered countless variations of classic creams, whips and russes. Even basic recipes varied for each type, but generally both Spanish Cream and **Russian Cream** were made with egg whites folded into a cooked custard, **Charlotte Russe** had whipping cream but no whites, and **Bavarians** used both. Later books added fruit-flavored creams similar to today's fruit mousses.

# CHINESE CHEWS

*Often served at church teas in the '20s, '30s and '40s, these appeared as balls or tiny log shapes rolled in sugar.*

| | | |
|---|---|---|
| 1 cup | chopped walnuts | 250 mL |
| 1 cup | finely chopped dates | 250 mL |
| 2 tbsp | chopped candied ginger | 25 mL |
| 1 cup | (approx) granulated sugar | 250 mL |
| 3/4 cup | all-purpose flour | 175 mL |
| 1 tsp | baking powder | 5 mL |
| 1/4 tsp | salt | 1 mL |
| 2 | eggs, beaten | 2 |
| 2 tbsp | butter, melted | 25 mL |

In bowl, combine walnuts, dates, ginger and 1 cup (250 mL) sugar. Combine flour, baking powder and salt; add to nut mixture. Blend in eggs and butter thoroughly.

Spread into greased 8-inch (2 L) square pan. Bake in 325°F (160°C) oven for 25 minutes. While still warm, cut into small squares and shape each into log or ball. Roll in sugar. Let cool. Makes about 30.

Alongside the Chinese Chews on the cookie plates of the '20s would be an assortment of other dainties: meringues and macaroons, **Empire Cookies** (jam-filled thin shortbread rounds, iced), **Petit Fours** or **Mocha Cakes** (small cake squares dipped in icing and rolled in chopped nuts), **Maid of Honour Tarts** (tiny sweet tart shells with jam and cake filling), **Melting Moments** (small very short drop cookies), **Almond Crescents** and **Pecan Snowballs** (often called **Mexican Wedding Cakes**) and an assortment of sugar cookies.

# DIVINITY FUDGE

*A popular pure white treat that often included candied cherries as well as nuts, this candy is frequently called **Christmas Puffs** or **Heavenly Bliss**. Have all ingredients ready before starting to cook. A heavy electric mixer is a necessity today.*

| | | |
|---|---|---|
| 2 cups | granulated sugar | 500 mL |
| 1/2 cup | corn syrup | 125 mL |
| 1/2 cup | boiling water | 125 mL |
| 2 | egg whites | 2 |
| 1 tsp | vanilla (or 1/2 tsp/ 2 mL almond extract) | 5 mL |
| 1/2 cup | chopped nuts | 125 mL |

In saucepan, slowly heat sugar, syrup and water, stirring, until sugar is dissolved. Boil, without stirring, to 254°F (123°C), hard-ball stage; remove from heat. Beat egg whites to soft peaks; gradually add hot syrup, beating constantly until mixture begins to thicken and lose its gloss. Add vanilla and nuts. Pour into buttered pan and score into squares while soft or drop by teaspoonfuls onto waxed paper and swirl tops.

Patience was a virtue in making these candies in the '20s, without today's candy thermometers. Divinity Fudge beaten by hand required a strong arm. Often the sugar syrup was added in two stages, with one half taken to a slightly higher temperature.

Molasses candies, caramels (toffees) and fudge were popular in the '20s. **Peanut Brittle**, **Pralines** and **Butterscotch** were hard candies made by pouring the hot mixture onto a plate, then breaking the candy into pieces when cool. **Turkish Delight** was a fruit jelly cut in pieces and rolled in a mixture of icing sugar and cornstarch.

# The THIRTIES
## 1930 - 1939

*My mother was a virtuoso at "making do." She performed endless sleights of hand with bleached Robin Hood flour sacks…turning them into dresses, dish towels, pillow cases and opaque windows for chicken coops. She used Squirrel Peanut Butter pails for lunch buckets, Empress jam tins for flowerpots and leftover baked beans for succulent sandwiches.*

– Robert Collins
*Butter Down the Well*

It was a decade of "use it up, wear it out, make it do, or do without." For most Canadians, the Depression meant ingenuity in the kitchen and belt-tightening, or a lot of baked beans and bread pudding, at the table. For families with a steady income, however meagre, the times were difficult but not really desperate.

For many others, though, the '30s meant unemployment and destitution, soup kitchens, bread lines and relief vouchers: thousands in the cities were on the dole, or pogey. From St. John's to Victoria, the unemployed lined up for starvation-wage jobs or rode the rails across the country in search of work. Fishing and farming families struggled to make ends meet as markets for their products dried up. The Prairies were dealt a double blow – the Hungry Thirties became the Dirty Thirties as drought turned "the bread basket of the world" into a dust bowl. Many had to abandon their farms, though greener pastures were hard to find.

But hard times also bred good times. Resilient Canadians made their own fun. They gathered in each other's homes to sing around the piano, "I found a million dollar baby in a five and ten cent store" and "I can't give you anything but love," played contract bridge and Monopoly at the kitchen table and rolled up the rugs to dance to the radio music of Mart Kenny or Guy Lombardo and his Royal Canadians.

Radio was the panacea of the decade. The console in the corner of the living room brought a happier world into bleak lives. The whole family gathered in the evening to laugh at the gags of Jack Benny or Amos 'n' Andy (many family mealtimes were juggled around favorite programs) and Saturday night was always Hockey Night in Canada. Daytime radio brought "The Happy Gang" and the first soap operas to brighten up tedious washdays. Down-to-earth household tips and cooking advice came courtesy of the kindly Kate Aitken.

Women's magazines of the '30s occasionally presented money-saving ideas in their food articles and advertising, but most tended to ignore the Depression and instead offered cheery domestic advice, menus for entertaining, and glamorous escape stories. *Canadian Home Journal* leaned heavily to fiction and happy home-life features.

An issue of *Chatelaine* in 1931 included food budget advice from Nellie L. Pattinson as well as an

*Picking wild berries (probably saskatoons or chokecherries) was a summer ritual on the prairies.*
Saskatchewan Archives Board, Regina/Ref# R-A6230

On pages 70 – 71:   A cheap and cheerful supper: Chicken and Dumplings, coleslaw, celery and olives, Rice Pudding and Matrimonial Cake.

*Freshwater fish was free for the catching in local lakes and streams.*
C.M. Johnston/National Archives of Canada/PA-57794

*Electric refrigerators began to replace old-fashioned ice-boxes.*
Courtesy of WCI Canada Inc.

ad for Crown Brand corn syrup offering a 10-cent recipe booklet, "Feed the Family for Less." But the main features presented menus for a Valentine party (jellied chicken with pimiento, ice cream hearts and angel food cake) and a trousseau tea (strawberry bavarian, frozen lemon marlow and macaroons) and photographs of the new *Chatelaine* test kitchen. A 1935 issue featured ideas for a Jubilee party to celebrate the 25th anniversary of the reign of George V and Queen Mary.

Newspaper food pages often focused on local food prices and seasonal specials. The *Kitchener-Waterloo Record* urged housewives to use plentiful, cheap tomatoes, red or green, in "piquant sauces" to stretch the winter meals ahead. Schell Bros. grocery store advertised vinegar at 50 cents a gallon, Crown fruit jars at 98 cents a dozen, and orange pekoe tea for 50 cents a pound with a china cup and saucer as a premium.

The daily challenge to find one more way to disguise what

little she had taxed the best of cooks. Cookbooks featured lots of economical "luncheon and supper dishes," often making them sound more exotic than they really were – Spanish Rice, English Monkey, Heavenly Hash. Sunday dinner was always special: roast chicken or roast beef if possible. Monday began the round of leftovers: shepherd's pie or chicken and dumplings (heavy on the dumplings). Friday was fish day – finnan haddie or salmon loaf. An ongoing pot of soup could be extended with potatoes or barley.

Economy was the watchword in almost every household, but especially for those families who had to trade relief vouchers for groceries. Winnipeg relief in 1931 gave a family of four a weekly allowance of seven quarts and seven pints of milk, seven loaves of bread, 65 cents for meat and $2.38 for other groceries. Newfoundland vouchers were for beans, peas, molasses, pork fat-back and a coarse, forti-

*Grocery stores serviced relief vouchers according to price schedules such as these from the City of Toronto, May 1933.*

Courtesy of Metropolitan Toronto Archives. Photographer: John McNeill.

### STANDARD ORDERS

**No. 1 — Total Order Price — $1.07**
**Calling for:**

| | | |
|---|---|---|
| 1 | lb. | Rolled Wheat |
| 2 | lbs. | Granulated Sugar |
| 1½ | lbs. | Flour |
| ½ | lb. | Tea |
| ½ | lb. | Cheese |
| 1 | tin | Applesauce |
| ½ | lb. | Prunes |
| ¼ | lb. | Peanut Butter |
| 1 | bar | Soap |
| 1 | tin | Pineapple |
| ¼ | lb. | Salt |
| ¼ | lb. | Cocoa |
| 1 | cake | Toilet Soap |
| 1 | lb. | Sunera |
| 3 | oz. | Baking Powder |
| 1 | tin | Salmon |
| 1 | tin | Tomatoes |
| ½ | lb. | Beans |
| ½ | lb. | Bacon |

*During the Depression, life to many meant a hand-to-mouth struggle from day to day.*

Felix H. Man/National Archives of Canada/#PA-145949

## LOOKING BACK

*Adapted from* Home on the Range *(1982) by Calgary writer Nancy Millar, who grew up in the Peace River country of northern Alberta.*

Community dances were a little bit of dancing, a little bit of communing and a whole lot of fun. The ladies brought sandwiches, cookies and cake. Around 11:30 they would make the coffee, set out the food, dust out the cups and wait for the supper waltz. It was the married women who made all these preparations, since the supper waltz was more or less decided for them . . . what else did you have a husband for? But the single girls couldn't begin to think of anything so mundane until somebody asked them for the supper waltz. It was always sweet agony waiting for those sensitive arrangements to be completed. Thus, for the singles, the food was an anticlimax. Not so for people like Uncle Carl who batched and definitely preferred someone else's cooking to his own.

Sandwiches were more often than not bologna but on homemade bread that tasted pretty good. The coffee was made by dumping coffee into a boilerful of cold water, bringing it to a rolling boil, then letting the grounds settle. Finest kind, people remember today.

Cakes were pretty standard in the early days too. Dad still likes to whip up his favorite boiled raisin cake that he learned to make in the '30s. When slightly better times came along, Mom branched out into more complicated cakes. She never could go beyond one cup of shortening and two cups of sugar however. Her depression memories were just too close for comfort. Even now if a recipe calls for two cups of raisins, she cuts the amount by at least half a cup. Her kids sometimes go to the other extreme. Only slightly extravagant though . . . we are our mother's daughters!

fied flour that was loathed for the dark, heavy bread it produced. The destitute Prairies received some shipments of food from other provinces: the carloads of apples from Nova Scotia were welcomed gratefully, but the dried salt cod inspired a lot of joking – no one knew what to do with it except maybe shingle the roof. Roasted barley and wheat were often used as coffee substitutes.

Rural life was pretty grim, even on the best farms (and in the small towns that depended on rural business). In many areas, the economic woes came from too much production and too few markets. Ontario farmers got four cents or less a pound for cattle. In Prince Edward Island, bumper potato crops were dumped before they rotted. In British Columbia, tons of tomatoes were ploughed under. But eastern farmers at least had some crop diversity; the Prairies depended on a single crop: wheat. At the mercy of nature, crops were wiped out by drought, wind, grasshoppers, Russian thistle, hail and rust.

Many a farm woman was still living a life of endless labor, with no electricity or running water, no cash, no escape. At the crack of dawn she lit the fire under the porridge, fed the chickens and milked the cows. She made butter, baked bread, pumped water, tended a vegetable garden, pickled and preserved. She packed syrup pails with school lunches and cared for the sick. Often the "head of the household" was off looking for work that paid in hard cash. Yet nowhere in Canada, farm or city, did anyone refuse to "set an extra place." Hand-outs at the back door for drifters and down-and-outers were the norm as single young men roamed the country in search of work. As author Max Braithwaite once said, "At least when we were poor, everybody was poor and that made it easier to take."

Rural isolation, only somewhat eased by telephones, still meant any social contact became an occasion. Just to have visitors drop by, or neighbors in for whist or euchre, called for at least a cup of tea and a

*Extension departments such as at the University of Saskatchewan in 1935 offered farm women an opportunity to learn the latest techniques.*

Gibson's Photo/University of Saskatchewan Archives A-1326

LOOKING BACK

*From* Nova Scotia Down-Home Cooking *(1978) by Janice Murray Gill.*

November was a dull, dark month, and everyone was much occupied with preparations for the winter. Any house that did not possess a heating system was banked to keep out the cold drafts. A popular dish of salt cod and potatoes was called "house banking," possibly referring to the fact that many people ordered dried salt cod in sufficient quantities to serve that purpose. Salt cod was certainly common winter fare; but, when properly treated, it was amazingly good too, and every housewife had a repertoire of dishes based upon it – everything from codfish balls to a delectable concoction in which the fish was mixed with eggs and cream and poured over thick slices of toasted, home-made bread. . . .

The ingredients for the orgy of Christmas baking also had to be collected. November saw the compounding of the two great Christmas cakes, one dark and one light, and an enormous stone crock of mincemeat. Peel was candied for the cakes, and pounds of raisins and currants had to be picked over. . . . Gingerbread cookies, which needed to ripen, and brandy snaps, which kept well, were also made in November. . . .

While all this baking was going on, the everyday meals still had to be prepared. Since the kitchen stove now burned all day there was, at all times, a slow oven available to give the bean crock the long day's cooking required. It was a time too for pot roasts and braised meats, heavy steamed puddings and suet dumplings. After supper, we would settle down to long evenings of monopoly and cro-quinole, while our mothers and aunts knitted and crocheted furiously against the approaching Christmas season.

cookie, or lemonade in the summer heat. Drudgery was temporarily forgotten at church picnics and weddings. Newfoundlanders had a "time" when neighbors gathered. Box socials and schoolhouse dances on the Prairies, strawberry socials in Ontario, lobster suppers in Prince Edward Island all featured home-style food. And from coast to coast, fund-raising "fowl suppers" or sports banquets for curling or softball teams meant homecooking. Despite the hard times, women cooked their hearts out for the annual Harvest Home suppers at Thanksgiving. Social events written up in the newspapers always ended with "Refreshments were served."

In *No Place Like Home* (a 1988 collection of the diaries and letters of Nova Scotia women from 1771 to 1938), the journals of Laura Kaulback Slauenwhite give an evocative account of life during the Depression years when

she worked as a housekeeper in the village of New Germany:

*Nov. 28 [1936]....I baked brown bread, two pumpkin pies and marble cake and did the usual work and cleaning in kitchen and pantry....Made macaroni & tomato for supper at Gordon's request. Flue caught fire as we were eating supper. Quite a commotion for a while....*

*Dec. 11. I made date cookies and cleaned upstairs this forenoon....We heard the late King Edward's farewell speech at 6 this evening. It was very touching. I had to cry....*

*Dec. 12. I made pies, a cake, beans and bread and had roast spare ribs for dinner....Listened to the radio broadcast of the proclamation of the new King George VI. It was very thrilling as it came right from London and was real clear.*

Besides having the radio as a constant companion, Laura was a member of the Women's Insitute and the Rebecca Lodge (a women's auxiliary to the

*Hudson's Bay Company stores were often the only source of supplies in settlements like Port Burwell, N.W.T.*

Saskatchewan Archives Board, Regina/ Ref #R-B1452-5

*Sales were brisk for commemorative memorabilia – cups, candy boxes, plates – for the 1936 coronation and the 1939 royal tour.*

Courtesy of the Taylor family

## NUTRITION

- Food in short supply, many people on relief food allowances. Key nutrition advice urged budgeting to stretch food dollar.

- Dominion government organized Council on Nutrition to survey national nutrition status and uncover common "dietary mistakes." Poor diets blamed on ignorance of nutrition; generally believed that adequate diets possible if mothers were "clever in buying and cooking."

- Some larger communities had pasteurized milk; health professionals began to push for Canada-wide pasteurization.

- Eggs highly valued. People on relief allowed to buy eggs only when ill.

- Nutritionists advocated use of whole grain or lightly milled flours instead of highly refined flours.

- In early '30s, lemons, bananas and oranges were luxury items used mostly for flavoring.

- In Toronto, dietitians calculated cost of adequate, "appetizing and not monotonous" diet for family of five at $7.65 per week.

- Dietary notions of the day:
  - Bread burns up unwanted fat.
  - Cheese is constipating.
  - Alkaline foods prevent "acidosis."

Independent Order of Odd Fellows) and maintained an active social life typical of the time:

*Mar. 8 [1938]. Here I am just setting sponge for bread. Just got home from an Institute meeting....Yesterday in the evening I was up to the Oddfellows feed. Ham & corn chowders and all kinds of cake and then band music, speeches & toasts. It was 12 when I got home some unholy hours for an old Grandma. But I sure enjoyed it.*

And later that year,

*Mrs. Wes Hamm called up for me to come over and help decorate the Hall for our Halloween Tea Monday....Lottie went down to the Parish Hall to an afternoon tea and Pantry Sale....Thursday night the United people from here and 5 or 6 different parts of the Circuit had a cabbage supper in the Hall.*

A woman's pride was involved in setting a good table, even in a Depression. Dr. Edith Simpson, former dean of home economics at the University of Saskatchewan, recalls travelling the province giving talks and demonstrations to Homemakers' Clubs. "At the end of meetings, people always served lunch, usually a cake with icing. Only once did I get to a home, in Porcupine Hills I think it was, where the woman served a big pan of fresh-baked whole wheat muffins made from her own ground wheat – and was embarrassed to have nothing else to offer."

Food writer Marie Nightingale of Halifax recalls the shame that Maritime kids felt when they had to take lobster sandwiches to school (lobster was what you got when there wasn't anything "better"). But she also remembers the little flourishes women like her grandmother added to even the simplest fare. "Her date and nut loaf, served when the ladies came for afternoon bridge, would be fanned out in a circle on the plate."

*Charming illustrations in cookbooks such as this one, Robin Hood's* Baking Made Easy, *depicted happiness in the kitchen.*

Courtesy of Robin Hood Multifoods Inc.

Competition often crept into cooking. To be famous for her sour cream pie was a feather in a woman's cap. Threshing gangs often rated farmers by the kind and amount of food served. Regional fairs also gave rise to competitions of all kinds and the fiercest battles took place in the home-baking arena. From the CNE (Canadian National Exhibition) in Toronto to the PNE (Pacific National Exhibition) in Vancouver and at every small-town fair, contestants took great pride in turning out the best butter tarts, apple pies or sponge cakes in the country.

In most cities and towns, life was easier than in rural areas. Some who had steady jobs were actually better off than before the Depression. Rents were cheap and so were groceries (eggs at 10 cents a dozen, a whole chicken for 25 cents and butter for 10 cents a pound). A round of golf cost 50 cents, movies were a dime. Most ordinary homes were equipped with electricity, water came from taps, Congoleum covered wooden floors.

As the Depression eased by 1936, labor-saving appliances appeared in modern kitchens. New stoves were electric or gas; refrigerators ended the era of iceboxes; porcelain sinks with drainboards made dishwashing easier; built-in cupboards and countertops replaced freestanding Hoosiers.

Meanwhile, the rich carried on much as always. For wealthy matrons, who were clients of such carriage-trade purveyors as Dionne's or Morgan's in Montreal, hard times may have simply meant reducing the household staff to one less cook or maid.

Even during the worst years (1930-36), resorts flourished across Canada. In Muskoka's posh summer homes, holiday fun continued. Posters advertised glorious times at St. Andrews-by-the-Sea in New Brunswick, Château Lake Louise in the Rockies, and Manoir Richelieu and the Seigneury Club in

*Cooking schools featuring visiting experts were enormously popular with homemakers.*

The Vancouver Sun

*A 1931 gas company's home service department tested Girl Guides for their Cook's Badges.*

Consumers Gas Archives

Quebec. Grand dining rooms offered lavish meals, and afternoon tea was still in vogue at the Empress Hotel in Victoria. Railway excursions across the country or steamship cruises to Alaska or Europe meant fine cuisine with white linen tablecloths, silver serving dishes and masses of flowers.

At home, service with a smile continued, and not just for the rich. Horsedrawn wagons or small trucks brought to the door the milkman, breadman, coal and ice man. Other peddlars, such as the Rawleighs or Watkins salesmen with their array of seasonings and extracts, sold anything and everything door to door.

Bartering thrived in farmers' and city markets. In some areas, grocery chain stores and groceterias in department stores had trouble competing with the corner store. Many women preferred to shop often, carry smaller bags of groceries or have them delivered and run up a tab with the

local grocer. Credit in some locations, like the outports of Newfoundland, was a necessity; fishermen swapped their catch for nets, gas and food.

Independent grocers were still served by travelling salesmen with sample cases and order books in hand. But choice expanded as refrigerated boxcars now brought out-of-season and exotic foods from thousands of miles away: boxes of B.C. apples were familiar on the Prairies, and Japanese mandarin oranges were tucked into the toes of Christmas stockings.

In most Canadian kitchens, the British influence still persisted, as it did in most aspects of Canadian life. Canada remained staunchly loyal to the Empire even after gaining independence from Britain through the Statute of Westminster in 1931. In 1939, Canadians cheered King George VI and Queen Elizabeth during their Royal Tour across the country. They celebrated Dominion Day

and Victoria Day with flags, parades and picnics. Ethnic differences, Old World tastes and traditions were largely ignored. Schoolteachers were mainly of British heritage, and home economics classes taught familiar, not "foreign," cooking. In Saskatchewan, extension workers were even teaching Doukhobors who had been vegetarians for generations the proper way to cook meats.

Domestic science courses, Women's Institutes, Homemakers' Clubs on the Prairies and 4-H groups in Ontario all continued to stress standardization in home cooking. In 1931, the *Toronto Star Weekly*'s food pages headlined a column by Mairi Fraser: "On the level, cookie, do you use level measurements?"

By the late '30s, developments in science and technology were expanding rapidly. Out of the Depression came agricultural advances aimed at ensuring future crops. Research in animal and field husbandry helped farm-

*Elegance and romance in cookbooks and ads took our minds off the Depression.*

Courtesy of Specialty Brands

*The favorite recipes of socialites in this booklet came from their personal cooks or caterers.*

Courtesy of Nestlé Canada Inc.

*Specialty food stores in large cities sold fresh local produce alongside fancy imported goods.*

ers and industry market large-scale production of poultry, pigs and calves and to control soils and crops with fertilizers and pesticides. Synthetic materials such as nylon, rayon and imitation rubber were perfected.

Improvements in communications and transportation were shrinking the country. In 1936, the Canadian Broadcasting Corporation was born. We immediately knew when the Dionne quintuplets arrived; J. Frank Willis took us to the edge of a Nova Scotia mine disaster. Faster cars and better roads expanded travel. Bush pilots opened new frontiers in the North. Now Robin Hood products were sold as far north as Churchill and Frobisher Bay. In 1939, Trans-Canada Airlines began flying passengers across the country.

Change was brewing on the home front, too. More women were in the labor force than ever before. They smoked in public. The divorce rate was up. As the economy improved, fashion became fun again. Hats with veils, very high heels, gloves and nail polish showed that a little indulgence was okay.

Busier days for working women meant less time to spend in the kitchen. The '30s brought us Kraft Dinner, Miracle Whip, pudding mixes, Worcestershire sauce, sliced bread and canned cream of mushroom soup from both Campbell's and Aylmer.

In 1939, though a million Canadians were still on relief, plenty of food, improved health and the best crop in eleven years made spirits soar. The Prairie drought was over. Eastern manufacturers were eager to sell new farm machinery, stoves and refrigerators. Even the ominous rumblings coming from Europe and Japan didn't dampen the general good mood. But as the crops were being harvested that fall, Germany invaded Poland, and Canada was once again formally at war.

*Grocery prices reflected hard times.*
North Bay Nugget

*Developed by physicians at Toronto's Hospital for Sick Children, Pablum was the world's first pre-cooked fortified cereal for infants.*
Courtesy of Mead Johnson Canada

*Great excitement surrounded the birth of Canada's famous Dionne Quintuplet in 1934.*
Courtesy of Best Foods Canada Inc.

*Baking utensils in the '30s were simple, utilitarian and colorful.*
Courtesy of Kellogg Canada Inc.

# Cookbook Sampler

## THE THIRTIES

For more cookbooks of the decade, see Bibliography p. 233-234.

# VEGETABLE, BEEF AND BARLEY SOUP

*Browning the soup bones makes a rich-colored stock. As in pioneer days, use whatever vegetables you have on hand (turnip, parsnips or leftover cooked peas or corn) to suit your taste. Slightly overripe or canned tomatoes add extra flavor.*

| | | |
|---|---|---|
| 3 lb | meaty beef soup bones | 1.5 kg |
| | Vegetable oil | |
| 2 | onions, cut in wedges | 2 |
| 2 | carrots, sliced | 2 |
| 2 | stalks celery, chopped | 2 |
| 12 cups | water | 3 L |
| 1 | bay leaf | 1 |
| 9 | peppercorns | 9 |
| 1 tsp | salt | 5 mL |
| 2 tbsp | butter | 25 mL |

| | | |
|---|---|---|
| 1 | large onion, chopped | 1 |
| 2 | potatoes, peeled and diced | 2 |
| 2 | carrots, chopped | 2 |
| 1/2 cup | pearl or pot barley | 125 mL |
| | Salt and pepper | |

Brown bones in oil on stove top or in oven. In large soup pot or Dutch oven, combine bones, onions, carrots, celery, water, bay leaf, peppercorns and salt. Bring to boil; cover and simmer for 2 hours or until meat nearly falls off bones. Strain and refrigerate stock overnight; remove solidified fats. Cut beef from bones; chop and refrigerate.

In soup pot, melt butter; simmer onion, potatoes and carrots for 15 minutes or until softened. Add reserved beef stock, barley and beef; simmer for 45 minutes or until barley is tender. Season to taste with salt and pepper. Makes 8 servings.

In the '30s in rural Canada, beef was still slaughtered right on the farm, so access to meaty bones and tough cuts of meat suitable for stewing and soup making was good. "Beef rings"– groups of farmers who butchered and shared meat in a rotating fashion – were neighborly and necessary. They continued even when people got freezers and food lockers. In the city, butchers kept the choicest soup bones for regular customers.

Soup has always been a good way to make a little serve a lot. Soups were extended with barley, rice, macaroni, potatoes and other vegetables. Often the soup started with a turkey carcass or ham bone, and the stock was bolstered with liquid from cooking vegetables or corned beef. **Lob Scouce** is a Newfoundland soup of vegetables and salt meat.

# SHEPHERD'S PIE

*For today's tastes, add 2 cloves garlic, minced with the onion. Before baking, brush potatoes with lightly beaten egg or sprinkle with 1 cup (250 mL) shredded Cheddar cheese.*

| | | |
|---|---|---|
| 1-1/2 lb | lean ground beef | 750 g |
| 1 cup | chopped onion | 250 mL |
| 1/2 tsp | dried thyme | 2 mL |
| 1/4 cup | all-purpose flour | 50 mL |
| 2 cups | beef stock | 500 mL |
| 1 tbsp | Worcestershire sauce | 15 mL |
| 1 cup | cooked, canned or frozen vegetables (peas, corn, diced carrots) | 250 mL |

| | | |
|---|---|---|
| | Salt and pepper | |
| 2 to 3 cups | mashed potatoes | 500 to 750 mL |

In large heavy saucepan, brown beef lightly, stirring to break up; drain off excess fat. Add onion; cook until softened. Add thyme; stir in flour. Add stock and Worcestershire sauce; simmer, stirring often, until thickened. Add vegetables, and salt and pepper to taste.

Spread in 10-cup (2.5 L) baking dish; let cool a few minutes. Spread potatoes over meat. Bake in 400°F (200°C) oven for 20 minutes or until bubbling and golden. Makes 6 servings.

Popular for using up leftovers, this potato-topped meat pie was often made with chopped or ground roast beef (every kitchen had a hand-cranked meat grinder that attached to the edge of the table) moistened with gravy and mixed with cooked or canned vegetables. Another version starts with fresh ground beef and is often more practical today when we don't have so much leftover roast beef. Variations in later decades included **Hamburger Pie** and **Cheeseburger Pie** baked in pie plates.

*Pâté chinois* is the French-Canadian name for shepherd's pie. It is still made often by Quebecers, who usually add canned peas or niblet corn (or creamed corn in a layer between meat and potatoes).

# CHICKEN AND DUMPLINGS

*Stews were well-known ways to stretch food to feed more mouths. The simple addition of more potatoes or extra bread to mop up the gravy was the ticket. Topped with dumplings, Tea Biscuits (p. 62) or Flaky Pastry (p. 21), leftovers were easily reheated and extended once again.*

| 1/4 cup | butter | 50 mL |
|---|---|---|
| 1 | onion, chopped | 1 |
| 1/2 tsp | each dried thyme or savory and sage | 2 mL |
| 1/3 cup | all-purpose flour | 75 mL |
| 2 1/2 cups | chicken stock | 625 mL |
| 1 cup | light cream or milk | 250 mL |
| 2 | cooked carrots, sliced | 2 |
| 4 | cooked onions, quartered | 4 |
| 1 cup | frozen peas | 250 mL |
| 1/2 cup | cooked sliced celery | 125 mL |
| | Salt and pepper | |
| | Dumplings | |
| Stock: | | |
| 1 | chicken or stewing hen (4 to 5 lb/2 to 2.2 kg), cut in pieces | 1 |
| 6 cups | water | 1.5 L |
| 1 | large onion, sliced | 1 |
| 2 | carrots, chopped | 2 |
| | Celery tops (optional) | |
| 1-1/2 tsp | salt | 7 mL |

Stock: In large saucepan, combine chicken, water, onion, carrots, celery tops (if using) and salt; bring to boil. Reduce heat, cover and simmer for 45 to 60 minutes, or up to 2 hours for stewing hen, or until chicken is tender. Let cool; remove chicken and refrigerate. Strain and refrigerate stock; remove solidified fat.

In large saucepan, melt half the butter; cook onion until tender. With slotted spoon, transfer to 12-cup (3 L) flameproof casserole. Add remaining butter, thyme and sage to saucepan; cook for 1 minute. Stir in flour; cook for 2 minutes, stirring constantly.

Stir in 2-1/2 cups (625 mL) stock and cream; cook until thickened and smooth. Pour into casserole. Remove chicken meat from bones and add to casserole. Add carrots, onions, peas, celery, and salt and pepper to taste. Bring to boil, stirring gently. Top with Dumplings. Makes 8 servings.

### DUMPLINGS:

| 1-1/2 cups | all-purpose flour | 375 mL |
|---|---|---|
| 2 tsp | baking powder | 10 mL |
| 1/4 tsp | salt | 1 mL |
| 2 tbsp | shortening | 25 mL |
| 3/4 cup | milk | 175 mL |

In bowl, combine flour, baking powder and salt; cut in shortening until like crumbs. Add milk all at once, stirring with fork only until moistened. Drop by spoonfuls onto boiling stew. Cover and simmer for 10 minutes.

Dumplings were called doughboys in some Canadian households. In northern cookbooks, Bannock Dumplings top Rabbit (Arctic Hare) Stew.

Over the years, the chicken and dumplings of the '30s has taken on fashionable new tastes. In the '60s, we added a bay leaf and whole peppercorns when stewing the chicken and sautéed mushrooms with the onions. The dumplings might have chopped parsley in them. In the late '70s and early '80s, we made the sauce richer and added sherry or vermouth. Toppings became innovative, from Sour Cream Biscuits to Corn Dumplings to Cheese Pastry. By the late '80s, we used leeks in place of some of the onions, cooked the vegetables tender-crisp and reduced the amount of butter and cream. (No doubt the chicken was free-range as well.)

**Chicken fricot** is an Acadian stew made with fowl and salt pork. **Rabbit Stew** was made the same way using rabbit instead of chicken. Old recipes simmered fowl for hours to make it tender. Today's supermarket chickens, unless labelled fowl or stewing chicken, require less cooking.

# MOCK DUCK

*Today, a nonstick heavy frypan works well, but just as in the '30s, a black cast iron one is great, too. Thicken the gravy with flour if desired.*

| | | |
|---|---|---|
| 1 | onion, chopped | 1 |
| 1/4 cup | chopped celery | 50 mL |
| 1/2 cup | chopped mushrooms | 125 mL |
| 1 tbsp | butter | 15 mL |
| 3/4 cup | dry bread crumbs | 175 mL |
| 1/2 tsp | dried savory | 2 mL |
| 1/4 tsp | dried thyme | 1 mL |
| | Salt and pepper | |
| 1 lb | round steak | 500 g |
| 1 tbsp | vegetable oil | 15 mL |
| 3/4 cup | beef stock | 175 mL |

In skillet, cook onion, celery and mushrooms in butter until softened. Remove from heat; stir in bread crumbs, savory, thyme, salt and pepper to taste and just enough water or stock to moisten.

Pound meat to 1/4-inch (5 mm) thickness. Cut into 4 or 5 serving pieces; spread with stuffing almost to edges. Roll up each from widest side; secure with string. In skillet, brown rolls in oil. Add stock; cover and simmer for 1 hour, turning and basting occasionally, or bake in 325°F (160°C) oven for 1 hour. Makes 4 or 5 servings.

With the prairie sloughs dried up, no rain and little snow in the winter, there were very few wild birds in the worst years of the '30s. Stuffed, thinly pounded less-tender cuts of beef made an adequate substitute. Some books called for flank steak, others for round steak. **Veal Birds** are similar. **Rouladen**, a German dish, is made with meat spread with mustard and wrapped around dill pickle spears. And in many regions of Canada, venison, moose and caribou were used in place of beef. In Newfoundland, savory seasons the stuffing and salt pork tops the meat rolls.

# MACARONI AND CHEESE

*Some '30s versions were pretty skimpy on the cheese and butter, or used stewed tomatoes instead of cheese sauce. Buttered bread crumbs topped the casserole for company or Sunday supper.*

| | | |
|---|---|---|
| 2 cups | elbow macaroni | 500 mL |
| 3 tbsp | butter | 50 mL |
| 3 tbsp | all-purpose flour | 50 mL |
| 1-1/2 cups | milk | 375 mL |
| | Salt and pepper | |
| 1/2 tsp | dry mustard | 2 mL |
| 3 cups | shredded sharp Cheddar cheese | 750 mL |
| 2 tbsp | dry bread crumbs | 25 mL |
| 1 tbsp | butter, melted | 15 mL |
| 2 tbsp | chopped fresh parsley or chives | 25 mL |

Cook macaroni in boiling salted water until tender but firm. In heavy saucepan, melt butter; blend in flour and cook until bubbly. Gradually add milk, stirring until thickened and boiling. Season to taste with salt and pepper; blend in mustard and half the cheese.

In casserole, layer one-third macaroni, one-third sauce and 1/2 cup (125 mL) cheese. Repeat twice. Top with crumbs mixed with butter and parsley. Bake in 350°F (180°C) oven for 30 minutes or until bubbly. Makes 6 servings.

The elbow macaroni in this recipe, along with spaghetti and alphabet shapes for soup, were the familiar pastas of the '30s.

In 1937, Kraft Dinner, often referred to as seven-minute dinner, hit the market. Canadians of all ages, especially young families and college kids were, and are, hooked on "KD." By the '80s, "from scratch" macaroni and cheese was back and updated with variations such as Macaroni with Four Cheeses.

# FISH AND BREWIS

*Fish and brewis (pronounced "brews") is one of the oldest traditional dishes of Newfoundland.*

| | | |
|---|---|---|
| 1 lb | salt cod | 500 g |
| 2 | cakes hardbread | 2 |
| 1 cup | diced salt pork | 250 mL |

Cut cod into serving-size pieces. Soak cod and hardbread separately in cold water for 8 hours or overnight. Drain fish. In saucepan, cover fish with cold water. Heat to boiling and boil gently for 15 to 20 minutes or until tender; drain.

Meanwhile, in skillet, fry salt pork until golden. Drain bread and place in saucepan; cover with salted water and bring to full boil. Drain immediately and serve with fish on warm plates. Sprinkle with scrunchions. Makes 4 servings.

The fish in Fish and Brewis is salt cod, and the brewis is made from hardtack or hardbread, which is available everywhere in Newfoundland and in specialized grocery stores across the country. The dish is always sprinkled with scrunchions, crisp-fried bits of salt pork. **Fisherman's Brewis** is sometimes the same as Fish and Brewis, but often the fish and bread are chopped while hot and mixed together, or fresh cod is used instead of salt cod.

# CREAMED ONIONS

*This remains a traditional favorite, often on Christmas menus.*

| | | |
|---|---|---|
| 20 | small onions, peeled | 20 |
| 1/4 cup | butter | 50 mL |
| 1/4 cup | all-purpose flour | 50 mL |
| 1-1/2 cups | light cream | 375 mL |
| | Salt and pepper | |
| | Nutmeg or cayenne (optional) | |

In saucepan of boiling water, cook onions until barely tender; drain, reserving 1/2 cup (125 mL) liquid.

In heavy saucepan, melt butter; blend in flour and cook until bubbly. Gradually add cream, stirring constantly; cook until boiling. Blend in enough reserved liquid to give desired consistency. Season to taste with salt, pepper, and nutmeg (if using). Add onions; heat through. Makes 4 to 6 servings.

VARIATIONS:

**Crumb-Topped Onions:** In shallow casserole, sprinkle creamed onions with 1/2 cup (125 mL) fine fresh bread crumbs tossed with 2 tbsp (25 mL) melted butter. Broil until crumbs are toasted.

**Cheese-Topped Onions:** Make Crumb-Topped Onions, adding 1 cup (250 mL) shredded Cheddar cheese to crumb mixture.

All year round, Canadians relied on root vegetables: potatoes, carrots, onions, rutabaga. As a result, home cooks soon learned dozens of ways to present them at family meals. Onions flavored all savory dishes from soups to stews and performed yeoman duty as side vegetables or in salads. Whole onions were glazed with molasses, maple syrup or honey; stuffed with stewed tomatoes, crumbs and sometimes cheese; sliced and marinated in vinegars or sour cream. There were onion pies, fried onions, onion soups and onion relishes.

At the same time, there was what was commonly called the "library paste school of cooking," where everything was served in a thick white sauce. Gravies were also often made with milk.

# BAKED BEANS

*Dried beans, molasses and pork were around long before the turn of the century and were staple foods of pioneers in all regions. Depression days made good use of these economical staples.*

| 4 cups | white pea (navy) beans | 1 L |
|--------|------------------------|-----|
| 1/2 cup | packed brown sugar | 125 mL |
| 1/2 cup | molasses | 125 mL |
| 1/2 cup | ketchup | 125 mL |
| 1 tsp | each salt and dry mustard | 5 mL |
| 1 | large onion | 1 |
| 4 | whole cloves | 4 |
| 1/2 lb | lean salt pork | 250 g |

Soak beans overnight or by quick-soak method*; drain. Cover beans with fresh water; bring to boil. Reduce heat and simmer, covered, for 1 hour. Drain, reserving liquid. Place beans in 12-cup (3 L) bean pot or casserole.

Combine sugar, molasses, ketchup, salt and mustard. Mix with beans, adding enough reserved liquid to cover beans. Stud onion with cloves; bury in beans. Push salt pork into beans, leaving just rind exposed.

Cover and bake in 250°F (120°C) oven for 6 hours, adding enough reserved liquid, when necessary, to keep beans from drying out. Uncover and bake for 1 hour longer or until beans are tender. Makes 10 servings.

*Quick-Soak Method: Place beans in sieve; wash thoroughly. Discard any discolored beans. In large pot, cover beans with 3 times their volume of cold water. Bring to boil; boil for 2 minutes. Remove from heat; cover and let stand for 1 hour.

In Quebec, **Feves au lard** were made with maple syrup if available, and even today in sugaring-off season, the dwindling number of sugar shacks list this familiar dish on their menus. If maple syrup is in short supply, molasses is used.

In both Quebec and Newfoundland, salt pork was in the top and bottom of the pot. In Quebec, baked beans were often baked all night for Friday breakfast. And everywhere else, preparation for baked beans (the Saturday Night Special) began on Friday with the bean-soaking overnight. Revised and updated versions over the years have added chunks of ham and apple wedges to dress up the beans. In the 90s as legumes and fibre are promoted for healthy eating, mixtures of various dried beans and lentils are baked together and are back in vogue, usually less sweet and without the salt pork.

# ROLLED OATS BREAD

*This version makes a soft dough that is kneaded briefly to produce a moist, flavorful bread. In the Atlantic provinces, the dough is often shaped into four balls, with two balls placed side by side in each pan. If desired, before baking, brush tops of loaves with egg wash (1 egg beaten with 1 tbsp/ 15 mL water) and sprinkle with oats (large flake or regular).*

| | | |
|---|---|---|
| 1 cup | rolled oats | 250 mL |
| 2 cups | boiling water | 500 mL |
| 2 tbsp | butter | 25 mL |
| 1-1/2 tsp | salt | 7 mL |
| 1 tsp | granulated sugar | 5 mL |
| 1/2 cup | warm water | 125 mL |
| 1 | pkg active dry yeast | 1 |
| 1/2 cup | molasses | 125 mL |
| 5 cups | (approx) all-purpose flour | 1.25 L |

In large bowl, combine oats, boiling water, butter and salt; let stand until lukewarm. Dissolve sugar in warm water; sprinkle yeast into water and let stand 10 minutes or until frothy. Add to oat mixture along with molasses and 1 cup (250 mL) flour. Beat 2 minutes with mixer or vigorously by hand.

Gradually add remaining flour, mixing first with wooden spoon then hands to make soft dough. Knead on lightly floured board about 5 minutes until smooth and springy. Place in large greased bowl, turning to grease all over. Cover and let rise until doubled, about 1-1/2 hours.

Punch dough down. Cut in half and shape into 2 loaves. Place in two greased 8-1/2- x 4-1/2-inch (1.5 L) loaf pans. Let rise until doubled, about 1 hour. Bake in 375°F (190°C) oven for 50 minutes or until hollow sounding when tapped. Remove from pans; cool on racks. Makes 2 loaves.

Also called **Oatmeal Bread** or **Porridge Bread**, this was a favorite during hard times because it was made with leftover porridge. Fresh (compressed) yeast cakes or dry yeast cakes (apparently half the strength of fresh) were commonly used to make bread in the '30s. Dry yeast cakes kept better but had to be dissolved and took a long time to start working.

Many old recipes used a no-knead method, which was popular with novice cooks but required long rising times. Some books say, "Let rise overnight," or "Start first thing in the morning and let rise all day."

Maritime recipes generally called for Scotch-type fine oatmeal instead of rolled oats, and in other regions, cooked cereals such as Red River cereal were used in similar breads. At about this time, cooks also used Dr. Jackson's Roman Meal and Shredded Wheat in bread making.

# BANANA BREAD

*The riper the bananas, the better this bread seems to be. Overripe bananas may be stored in the freezer; they will blacken but still make good banana bread.*

| | | |
|---|---|---|
| 1/3 cup | butter | 75 mL |
| 3/4 cup | granulated sugar | 175 mL |
| 1 cup | mashed bananas (2 large) | 250 mL |
| 2 | eggs, beaten | 2 |
| 2 cups | all-purpose flour | 500 mL |
| 1 tsp | baking powder | 5 mL |
| 1 tsp | baking soda | 5 mL |
| 1/4 tsp | salt | 1 mL |
| 1/2 cup | sour milk or buttermilk | 125 mL |

In bowl, cream together butter and sugar. Beat in bananas; add eggs and beat well. Stir together flour, baking powder, soda and salt. Add to creamed mixture alternately with sour milk, stirring well after each addition.

Pour batter into greased 9- x 5-inch (2 L) loaf pan. Bake in 350°F (180°C) oven for 50 to 60 minutes or until cake tester inserted in centre comes out clean. Let cool for 10 minutes; remove to rack to cool completely.

### VARIATIONS:

**Banana Muffins:** Spoon batter into 14 large greased muffin pans, filling two-thirds full. Bake in 375°F (190°C) oven for 18 to 20 minutes or until firm to the touch.

Some '30s church cookbooks included as many as a dozen different banana bread or cake recipes. Many of these recipes were so familiar to most cooks that the list of ingredients was often followed simply by "Bake as usual." In the health-conscious '80s, many recipes replaced white flour with whole wheat or added oat bran.

This banana bread recipe can be varied by adding: 1/2 cup (125 mL) chopped walnuts or pecans; or 1 cup (250 mL) shredded coconut; or 1/2 cup (125 mL) raisins. A Labrador cookbook adds 3/4 cup (175 mL) redberries (partridgeberries), fresh or frozen.

# DAFFODIL CAKE

*Usually served plain, dusted with icing sugar or drizzled with a simple glaze, this is also delicious with a Lemon (p. 24) or Custard Sauce (p. 47).*

| | | |
|---|---|---|
| 1 cup | egg whites (about 8) | 250 mL |
| 1 tsp | cream of tartar | 5 mL |
| 1 tsp | vanilla | 5 mL |
| 1/2 tsp | salt | 2 mL |
| 1-2/3 cups | granulated sugar | 400 mL |
| 1-1/4 cups | sifted cake-and-pastry flour | 300 mL |
| 4 | egg yolks | 4 |
| 2 tbsp | orange or lemon juice | 25 mL |
| 2 tsp | grated orange or lemon rind | 10 mL |

In large bowl, beat egg whites with cream of tartar, vanilla and salt until soft peaks form. Gradually beat in 1 cup (250 mL) sugar until stiff peaks form. Combine flour with 1/3 cup (75 mL) sugar; fold into egg whites.

In small bowl, beat egg yolks, remaining 1/3 cup (75 mL) sugar, orange juice and rind until thick and pale; fold in one-third of the egg white mixture.

Spoon alternate mounds of white and yellow batters into ungreased 10-inch (4 L) tube pan. Gently run spatula through batter for marbled effect. Bake in 375°F (190°C) oven for 35 minutes or until cake springs back when lightly touched. Invert in pan until cool.

**Vanilla Glaze:** Melt 1/4 cup (50 mL) butter; blend in 2 cups (500 mL) sifted icing sugar and 1 tsp (5 mL) vanilla. Gradually blend in 2 to 4 tbsp (25 to 50 mL) hot water, a spoonful at a time, until glaze is proper consistency to drizzle over top and down sides of cake.

**Citrus Glaze:** Add 1/2 tsp (2 mL) grated lemon or orange rind to melted butter; use lemon or orange juice in place of vanilla and water.

Even before the '30s, making beautiful and tasty cakes was considered an art. To be known for making the "best" of any type of cake in town was a great compliment. Ever-popular angel food cakes were made with lots of egg whites for leavening, hence lots of beating (at a time when electric mixers were unheard of). Daffodil cake is similar, but with egg yolks folded into part of the batter to produce a light yellow and white cake. **Sunshine Cake** was also light and airy, baked in a tube pan, but a sugar syrup was usually beaten into the egg whites, then the yolks and dry ingredients folded in.

# CRUMB CAKE

*The crumb topping takes the place of icing.*

| | | |
|---|---|---|
| 1-3/4 cups | all-purpose flour | 425 mL |
| 1 cup | packed brown sugar | 250 mL |
| 3/4 cup | butter | 175 mL |
| 1 tsp | cinnamon | 5 mL |
| 1/4 tsp | each nutmeg, cloves and salt | 1 mL |
| 1 tsp | baking soda | 5 mL |
| 1/2 tsp | baking powder | 2 mL |
| 3/4 cup | buttermilk or soured milk | 175 mL |
| 1 | egg, beaten | 1 |
| 1 cup | raisins tossed with 1 tbsp (15 mL) flour | 250 mL |

In bowl, combine flour and sugar; cut in butter until in fine crumbs. Set 3/4 cup (175 mL) aside. To bowl, add cinnamon, nutmeg, cloves, salt, baking soda and baking powder; mix well. Add buttermilk and egg, beat for 1 minute or until smooth. Stir in floured raisins.

Spread in greased 9-inch (2.5 L) square cake pan. Sprinkle with reserved crumbs. Bake in 350°F (180°C) oven for 40 to 45 minutes or until tester comes out clean.

An old favorite for coffee time, lunch boxes and carrying out to the harvesters in the field, this is fast and easy, moist and flavorful. Frugal cooks often made this recipe to use up soured milk.

For a plain crumb cake, spices and raisins were omitted.

# VINARTERTA

*Bake these cakes in stages if you have only two pans. If desired, the cake may be frosted with a very thin butter icing.*

| | | |
|---|---|---|
| 1 cup | butter | 250 mL |
| 1-1/2 cups | granulated sugar | 375 mL |
| 2 | eggs | 2 |
| 2 tbsp | light cream | 25 mL |
| 1 tsp | almond extract | 5 mL |
| 4 cups | all-purpose flour | 1 L |
| 1 tsp | baking powder | 5 mL |
| 1/4 tsp | salt | 1 mL |
| *Prune Filling:* | | |
| 1 lb | pitted prunes | 500 g |
| 1 cup | granulated sugar | 250 mL |
| 1 tsp | cinnamon | 5 mL |
| 1/2 tsp | ground cardamom | 2 mL |
| 1 tsp | vanilla | 5 mL |

In bowl, cream butter with sugar; beat in eggs, one at a time. Blend in cream and almond extract. Combine flour, baking powder and salt; gradually blend into creamed mixture. Divide into six parts.

Cut waxed paper circles to fit bottoms of six 9-inch (1.5 L) round cake pans. Roll or pat dough evenly to edges of paper; set into greased pans. Bake in 350°F (180°C) oven for 10 to 15 minutes or until very lightly browned. Let cool.

Prune Filling: In saucepan, cover prunes with water; simmer until tender. Let cool and drain, reserving liquid; chop prunes. In heavy saucepan, combine prunes, sugar, cinnamon, cardamom, and 1/2 cup (125 mL) reserved liquid; simmer until thickened, about 15 minutes, adding more liquid if needed. Add vanilla. Let cool.

Spread five cakes with filling; stack and place remaining layer on top, smooth side up. Store in covered container for a few days to soften. To serve, cut into long strips; cut each strip into 2-inch (5 cm) pieces.

The first annual Icelandic Festival at Gimli, Man., was held in the '30s. Vinarterta, a traditional Icelandic cake composed of many thin layers which makes it attractively striped when sliced, is still one of the most famous treats served at such festivities all over the Prairies. The recipe was brought to Manitoba with the first Icelanders who settled in the Gimli area in the 1870s. With them came the spice cardamom, a favorite in their baking.

The name Vinarterta is said to mean Viennese torte. Some sources claim that Icelandic students used to go to the Continent to study and the cake was named for an opera playing in Vienna. Canadian recipe books use a variety of spellings; an old Fort William newspaper called it "wine tart."

# SOUR CREAM RAISIN PIE

*Winter baking in the '30s often meant making good use of dried fruit. Raisins and dates were most commonly used, but compotes of dried prunes, figs and apricots made simple, self-sweetened desserts.*

*With either raisins or currants, the sour cream pie in the '30s would be made with thick cream that had gone sour. Today's commercial sour cream, even the light versions, works just as well.*

| 1 cup | packed brown sugar | 250 mL |
|---|---|---|
| 3/4 tsp | cinnamon | 4 mL |
| 3 | eggs, separated | 3 |
| 1 tbsp | vinegar | 15 mL |
| 1 cup | sour cream | 250 mL |
| 1 cup | raisins or currants | 250 mL |
| 1 tbsp | all-purpose flour | 15 mL |
| | Unbaked 9-inch (23 cm) pastry shell | |

In bowl, combine 2/3 cup (150 mL) of the sugar, 1/2 tsp (2 mL) of the cinnamon and egg yolks. Blend vinegar into sour cream; stir into sugar mixture. Stir raisins with flour; stir into sugar mixture. Pour into pastry shell.

Bake in 350°F (180°C) oven for 30 minutes.

Beat egg whites, remaining sugar and cinnamon to stiff peaks. Spread over hot filling and bake 15 to 20 minutes or until golden.

**Raisin Pie:** In saucepan heat 2 cups (500 mL) raisins and 2 cups (500 mL) water to boiling; simmer 5 minutes. Mix together 1/2 cup (125 mL) granulated or brown sugar and 2 tbsp (25 mL) all-purpose flour; stir into raisin mixture. Cook over medium heat, stirring constantly, until mixture thickens and boils. Remove from heat; stir in 1 tsp (5 mL) lemon rind and 3 tbsp (50 mL) lemon juice and 1 tbsp (15 mL) butter. Cool slightly.

Pour cooled filling into pastry-lined 9-inch (23 cm) pie plate. Cover with top crust; seal, flute and cut slits for steam to escape. Bake in 425°F (220°C) oven for 10 minutes; reduce heat to 375°F (190°C) and bake 25 to 30 minutes longer or until crust is brown.

# MOCK APPLE PIE

*Serve this pie warm, with vanilla ice cream, whipped cream or Custard Sauce (p. 47).*

| | | |
|---|---|---|
| 1 cup | crumbled Ritz crackers (about 25 crackers) | 250 mL |
| 1/2 cup | packed brown sugar | 125 mL |
| 1/3 cup | butter or margarine, melted | 75 mL |
| 1/2 tsp | cinnamon | 2 mL |
| 1 | unbaked 9-inch (23 cm) pastry shell | 1 |
| *Filling:* | | |
| 2 cups | water | 500 mL |
| 1/4 cup | granulated sugar | 50 mL |
| 2 tsp | cream of tartar | 10 mL |
| 30 | Ritz crackers | 30 |
| 1 tbsp | lemon juice | 15 mL |
| 1 tsp | cinnamon | 5 mL |

Combine cracker crumbs, sugar, butter and cinnamon; set aside.

Filling: In saucepan, combine water, sugar and cream of tartar; bring to boil. Stir in whole crackers. Reduce heat to medium-low and simmer 5 minutes. Let cool 5 minutes. Pour into pie crust; sprinkle with lemon juice and cinnamon. Sprinkle with crumb topping. Bake in 400°F (200°C) oven for 15 minutes. Bake in 350°F (180°C) oven 15 to 20 minutes longer or until pastry is golden.

Unchanged since the '30s, this recipe is so popular that Nabisco has put it back on its '90s Ritz packages. Depression-weary housewifes were delighted to learn that crackers retain their shape when moistened and taste like apple pie filling when combined with cinnamon and sugar.

In *Canada's Prize Recipes*, a book compiled by The Canada Starch Co. in 1930, a recipe for **Boy's Favourite Pie** is made with bread crumbs, Corn Flakes and corn syrup. An earlier recipe for **Mock Mince Pie** combines "Boston crackers" with molasses, raisins, vinegar and spices.

# MATRIMONIAL CAKE

*This recipe in some old cookbooks is called Date Sandwich Cake. Other variations are Raisin Squares or Fig Squares.*

| | | |
|---|---|---|
| 1-1/2 cups | all-purpose flour | 375 mL |
| 1-1/2 cups | rolled oats | 375 mL |
| 1 cup | packed brown sugar | 250 mL |
| 1/2 tsp | baking soda | 2 mL |
| 1/4 tsp | salt | 1 mL |
| 3/4 cup | butter, softened | 175 mL |
| *Filling:* | | |
| 2 cups | chopped pitted dates (1/2 lb/ 250 g) | 500 mL |
| 1/2 cup | granulated sugar | 125 mL |
| 1 tsp | lemon juice | 5 mL |
| 3/4 cup | boiling water | 175 mL |

Filling: In saucepan, cook dates, sugar, lemon juice and water over medium heat, stirring often, until dates are soft, about 15 minutes. Let cool.

In bowl, combine flour, rolled oats, sugar, baking soda and salt; blend in butter until mixture is crumbly. Pat half onto bottom of 9-inch (2.5 L) square pan. Spread filling evenly over top. Sprinkle with remaining flour mixture, patting lightly. Bake in 350°F (180°C) oven for 30 to 35 minutes or until nicely browned. Let cool; cut into 36 squares.

### VARIATION:

**Mincemeat Squares:** Use 2 cups (500 mL) mincemeat instead of date filling.

**Date Squares** (Matrimonial Cake, if you come from the West) are a real nostalgic treat. The filling in '30s recipes was extremely sweet. Today's versions reduce the sugar in the filling, since dates are sweet enough, and are often microwaved. **Raisin Puff,** an old favorite in P.E.I., is somewhat similar, with raisin filling sandwiched between layers of soft cookie dough instead of an oatmeal mixture.

# BREAD PUDDING

*Use rather dry, firm, homemade-style bread. About five slices should be enough for this recipe, which makes a soft pudding with slightly crusty sides. For a more custardy pudding, place baking dish in larger pan filled with hot water to come halfway up sides and bake about 1 hour.*

| 3 | eggs | 3 |
|---|---|---|
| 1/3 cup | granulated sugar | 75 mL |
| 1 tbsp | butter, melted | 15 mL |
| 1 tsp | vanilla | 5 mL |
| 1/4 tsp | each nutmeg and salt | 1 mL |
| 2 cups | hot milk | 500 mL |
| 3 cups | cubed bread | 750 mL |
| 1/3 cup | raisins | 75 mL |

In bowl, beat eggs with sugar until foamy. Add butter, vanilla, nutmeg and salt. Stir in milk, bread and raisins. Turn into buttered 6-cup (1.5 L) baking dish. Bake in 350°F (180°C) oven for 50 to 60 minutes or until set. Let stand for about 1 hour before serving. Makes 4 to 6 servings.

## VARIATIONS:

**Bread and Butter Pudding:** Instead of bread cubes, remove crusts from 4 large slices bread. Spread with butter; cut in strips or squares. Place half in baking dish and sprinkle with raisins; pour in half of custard mixture. Repeat layers.

**Queen of Puddings:** Instead of 3 eggs, use 2 eggs and 2 yolks. After baking, spread top of pudding with tart jelly or jam. Beat 2 egg whites to soft peaks; gradually beat in 1/4 cup (50 mL) granulated sugar to stiff peaks. Spread over hot pudding. Return to oven for 8 minutes or until lightly browned.

A dessert of lowly beginnings, designed to use up stale bread during hard times, this has lived on as delicious comfort food. Bread puddings in early cookbooks are often made with bread crumbs instead of cubes, giving a more custardy pudding, and are sometimes called **Custard Bread Pudding.** Another popular variation was **Bread and Butter Pudding. Queen of Puddings** is a dressed-up version with meringue. *Boomtown's Cookbook* from the Western Development Museum in Saskatoon has a bread pudding recipe called **Hudson's Bay Pudding.**

# THIMBLE COOKIES

*Swedish Cookies or Jelly Dimples, Thumbprint or Thimble Cookies – the name depended on where you lived and how you made these morsels. Bachelor Buttons was one name for these cookies as well as for many other kinds.*

| 1 cup | butter | 250 mL |
|---|---|---|
| 1/2 cup | granulated sugar | 125 mL |
| 2 | eggs, separated | 2 |
| 2 tsp | vanilla | 10 mL |
| 2 cups | all-purpose flour | 500 mL |
| | Finely chopped nuts or flaked coconut | |
| | Jam, jelly or halved glacé cherries | |

In bowl, cream butter with sugar; beat in egg yolks and vanilla. Blend in flour. Shape into small balls. Dip into unbeaten egg whites; roll in nuts.

Place on lightly greased baking sheets; make depression in centre of each, using thimble or fingertip. Bake in 325°F (160°C) oven for 12 to 15 minutes or just until firm; do not overbake. Let cool. Fill centres with jam at serving time. (Stored filled cookies will be soggy.) Makes about 5 dozen.

In earlier decades, a thimble was used to make the depressions in the centres of these cookies. At Christmas, a half red or green candied or maraschino cherry was often placed in the centre instead of jam (do this after five minutes of baking). A good tart jelly, like black or red currant, or strawberry or raspberry jam made tasty fillings. If nuts or coconut were hard to come by, crushed corn flakes were often used instead.

# HASTY PUDDING

*Easy to make, this was often a favorite on washday. It was considered rush-hour cooking in those days, although not very hasty by today's standards.*

| | | |
|---|---|---|
| 1 cup | all-purpose flour | 250 mL |
| 1/3 cup | packed brown or granulated sugar | 75 mL |
| 2 tsp | baking powder | 10 mL |
| 1/4 tsp | salt | 1 mL |
| 3/4 cup | raisins | 175 mL |
| 1/2 cup | milk | 125 mL |
| 2 tbsp | butter, melted | 25 mL |
| *Sauce:* | | |
| 1 cup | packed brown sugar | 250 mL |
| 1 tbsp | all-purpose flour | 15 mL |
| 1 tbsp | butter | 15 mL |
| 2 cups | boiling water | 500 mL |
| 2 tsp | vanilla | 10 mL |

Mix together flour, sugar, baking powder, salt, raisins, milk and butter; spread in buttered 8-inch (2 L) square baking dish.

Sauce: In bowl, mix sugar with flour; blend in butter, boiling water and vanilla. Carefully pour over batter. Bake in 350°F (180°C) oven for 30 minutes or until tester inserted in cake comes out clean. Makes 6 servings.

---

## VARIATIONS:

**Chocolate Hasty Pudding:** Add 2 tbsp (25 mL) cocoa to batter; add 1/4 cup (50 mL) cocoa to sauce. Omit raisins, if desired.

**Hasty Pudding with Fruit:** Instead of raisins, add blueberries or chopped cherries. Or top batter with thinly sliced apples or peaches before adding sauce. Increase baking time to 40 minutes.

Hasty Pudding, **Half-Hour Pudding, Ten-Cent Pudding, Pudding-Cake, Hard Times Pudding** or **Self-Saucing Pudding,** as well as Quebec's **Pouding du chômeur** (unemployed person's pudding), are in all the old cookbooks. A simple cake batter is topped with sugar and boiling water, and as it bakes, cake forms on top, sauce underneath. In parts of Quebec and the Maritimes, the batter is spooned on top of the sauce.

**Liberal Pudding with Tory Sauce** (or vice versa if your family argues about puddings as well as politics) was the name of a spicy raisin version, so named, the story goes, because it was served at so many political convention dinners in Halifax. In Nova Scotia, there is also a **Poor Man's Pudding** with coconut sprinkled on top. And a New Brunswick book titled this same recipe "Buick Pudding with Gasoline Sauce."

## OLD-FASHIONED LEMONADE CONCENTRATE

*This concentrate is also good made with leftover cold tea instead of water. Both citric and tartaric acid are available at drug stores.*

| 3/4 cup | fresh lemon juice | 175 mL |
| 2 tbsp | grated lemon rind | 25 mL |
| 3 cups | granulated sugar | 750 mL |
| 2 tbsp | citric acid | 25 mL |
| 1 tbsp | tartaric acid | 15 mL |
| 2 cups | boiling water | 500 mL |

Combine lemon juice and rind, sugar, citric and tartaric acid and water; stir until dissolved. Refrigerate in jar with tight lid. For each serving, mix 2 to 4 tbsp (25 to 50 mL) concentrate with 3/4 cup (175 mL) water. Makes 4 cups (1 L) concentrate.

VARIATIONS:

**Orange Drink Concentrate:** Prepare as for Lemonade Concentrate using 1 cup (250 mL) orange juice and 1/4 cup (50 mL) lemon juice instead of 3/4 cup (175 mL) lemon juice; use 2 tbsp (25 mL) grated orange rind in place of lemon rind.

**Strawberry Drink Concentrate:** Omit lemon juice, rind and tartaric acid. Combine 4 cups (1 L) strawberries (sliced), 1 oz (30 g) citric acid, 2 cups (500 mL) cold water, 2-1/2 cups (625 mL) sugar. Bring to boil; boil 3 minutes. Strain into jar. Use 1/4 cup (50 mL) concentrate with 3/4 cup (175 mL) soda water or cold water. Makes about 2-1/2 cups (625 mL) concentrate.

The old icebox always had a jar of this concentrate for a quick-to-mix thirst quencher. Variations, including Epsom salts, can be found in many old-time church cookbooks.

Frosty pitchers of lemonade or iced tea were popular choices for picnics on hot summer days. And for parched throats there were drinks like root beer, ginger beer, raspberry or currant shrubs, real apple cider or dandelion wine. Old-timers still sat in the shade on the verandah with an ice-cold glass of sasparilla, claret cup, or tall drinks made with mint syrup or lime juice.

## PINEAPPLE MILK SHERBET

*This recipe doesn't require an ice cream machine, but the use of one will give a smoother texture.*

| 1/2 cup | undrained crushed pineapple | 125 mL |
| 2/3 cup | granulated sugar | 150 mL |
| 1 tsp | grated lemon rind | 5 mL |
| 1 tbsp | lemon juice | 15 mL |
| 2 cups | milk | 500 mL |
| 1/2 cup | 10% cream | 125 mL |

In saucepan, heat pineapple and sugar over low heat until sugar dissolves. Stir in lemon rind and juice, milk and cream. Pour into 8-inch (2 L) square pan. Freeze until mushy but not quite frozen. Spoon into bowl; beat well with mixer. Return to pan; freeze until firm. Makes 8 servings.

VARIATION:

**Lemon Milk Sherbet:** Use 1/3 cup (75 mL) lemon juice in place of pineapple. Increase sugar to 1-1/2 cups (375 mL).

This frozen treat would have been made in a handcranked ice-cream maker before refrigerators with freezers came into vogue. The 1932 version of Lake of the Woods Mills' *A Guide to Good Cooking* (known forever as the *Five Roses Cookbook*) simply states, "Freeze in the usual way."

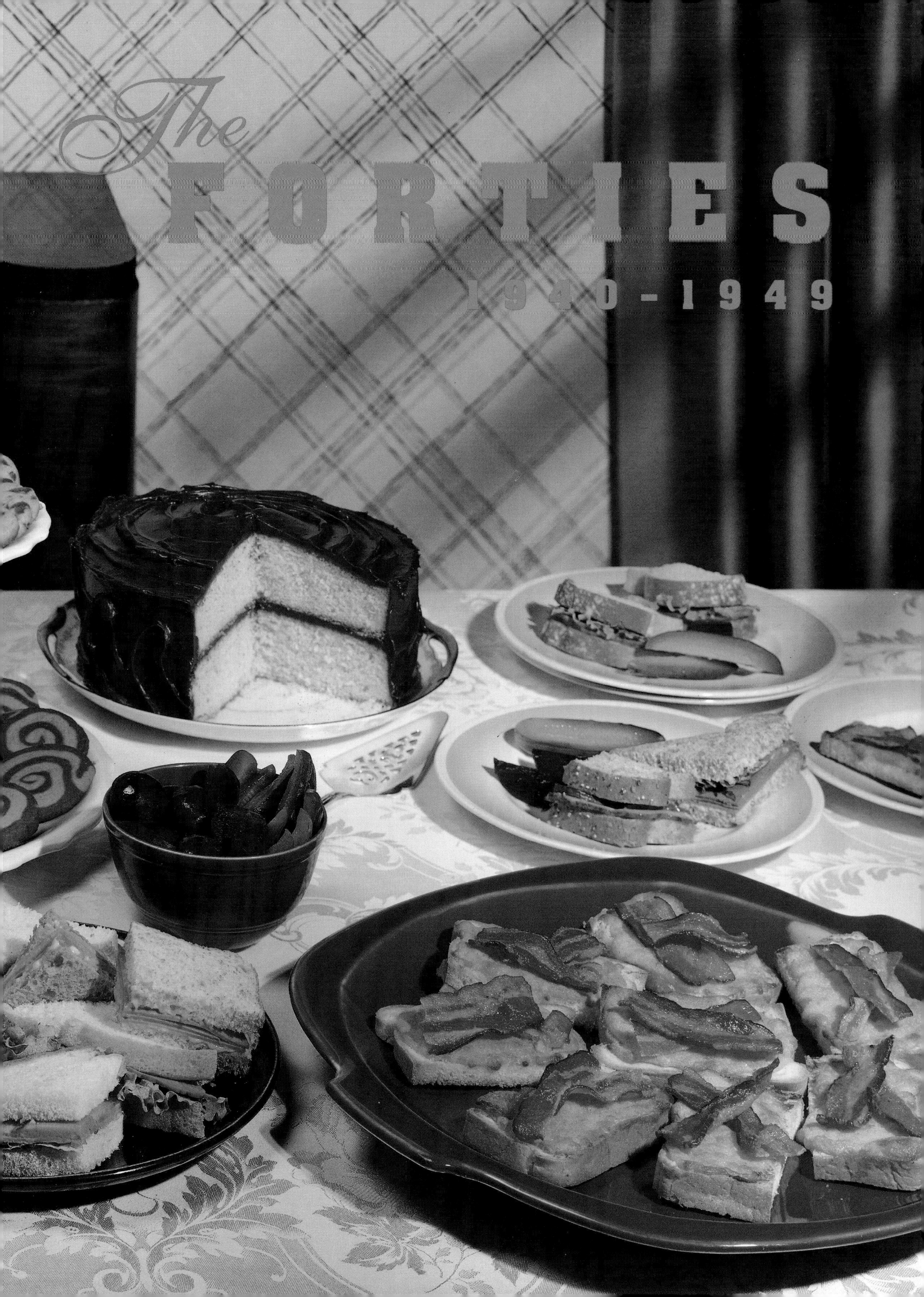

The
FORTIES
1940-1949

*Soldiers of the Kitchen Front! ...Like many a private detailed to kitchen police, a homemaker occasionally feels that she is doing a strange kind of fighting....Saving a teaspoonful of sugar or using no more canned beans seems far removed from what son Johnny in Britain or Ned in Italy is doing. But there's nothing insignificant about the total result.*

– The T. Eaton Co. Limited
Ad in the *Victory Cook Book*

As Canadian troops went marching into the Second World War, Canadians on the home front rallied to the cause. "Back them up to bring them back" was the goal, and food was often the means. In "Food for Freedom" campaigns all across the country, Canadians packed thousands of overseas parcel for soldiers, collected tons of food for Britain, planted enormous Victory gardens and coped cheerfully with food ration coupons.

Faraway sugar and coffee supplies were cut off; fats got diverted into bombs instead of cakes, and metals into tanks instead of cookstoves. Canadian cooks returned to making do or doing without.

Patriotic slogans on billboards and posters, in magazine ads and in newspaper cooking columns constantly reminded Canadian households to do their bit: "Saving bones is a terrible chore, but better than the War at your door"..."Fats in the garbage won't win the War"..."Loyal citizens do not hoard"..."A food stamp a day will keep Hitler away."

Along with kitchen economy, good citizens were encouraged to be generous with their savings ("Your dollar is better in a tank than in a bank; Buy Victory Bonds"), their blood donations ("Johnny is risking his life for you; be a Red Cross blood donor") and their spare bedrooms ( "Hospitality is not rationed. Don't forget to share your home

with the armed forces. Overnight and weekend accommodation is greatly appreciated by members of all the Services").

It was a time of sacrifice and sharing, of sad partings and joyful reunions, of tragedy and triumph. Along with the shortages and anxieties of the war years, the '40s brought a new prosperity to Canada. Following a decade of depression and unemployment, jobs were suddenly plentiful, and the economy got a kick-start from the industries of war.

Canada supplied the war effort with astonishing amounts of armaments and munitions as well as raw materials – steel, copper, aluminum, lumber – and foodstuffs, including millions of bushels of wheat and barrels of flour. During the first two years of the war alone, Canada shipped to Britain, besides wheat and flour, more than one and one-half billion pounds of food – pork, apples, cheese, evaporated milk, eggs, canned tomatoes, honey and beans.

*Canadian food companies quickly used wartime images in the '40s.*

Courtesy of Specialty Brands and The Country Guide/Farm Business Communications

On pages 94 – 95:   Come for coffee: Sandwiches, Cheese Dreams, Pickled Beets, Queen Elizabeth Cake, Victory Cake and Icebox Cookies.

*The war effort extended to the kitchen as this booklet encouraged cheap and cheerful cooking.*

Courtesy of Best Foods Canada Inc.

*Tea, coffee and sugar were the first foods rationed; meat and butter followed.*

Montreal Gazette Collection/National Archives of Canada/#PA-108300

## HEADLINES

**1940** First self-propelled combines from Massey Harris.

**1940** Unemployment Insurance introduced.

**1941** Canada's Population: 11,506,700.

**1941** Record wheat harvest: half-billion bushels.

**1941** Wartime Prices and Trade Board announces wage and price freeze.

**1942** Food rationing introduced.

**1942** Alaska Highway opens.

**1944** Veterans' Land Act helps settle returning servicemen.

**1944** D-Day: Invasion of Normandy.

**1945** Germany surrenders May 8 (VE Day).

**1945** Japan surrenders August 15 (VJ Day).

**1945** Canada signs U.N. founding charter.

**1945** "Baby Bonus" cheques mailed under Family Allowance Bill.

**1947** Polish refugees arrive: first of displaced persons from Europe.

**1947** Formation of GATT with promise of new markets for agricultural products.

**1947** Oil strike at Leduc in Alberta.

**1947** Canadian Association of Consumers established.

**1949** Sale of margarine in Canada becomes legal.

**1949** Newfoundland joins Confederation as Canada's 10th province.

By the end of the decade, Canada had been transformed from a depression-poor, largely rural country to an agricultural giant and one of the major industrial and trading nations of the world. By war's end, more than a million Canadians had served in the Armed Forces, and over a million civilians had worked in war industries at home.

A large proportion of those workers were women. While nearly 50,000 women, many of them defying tradition and families, joined the military as nursing sisters, CWACs (Canadian Women's Army Corps), WDs (Women's Division of the Air Force), and Wrens (Women's Royal Naval Service), more than 250,000 others donned Rosie the Riveter overalls and joined factory assembly lines making planes and guns and bombs.

Many more took over the traditionally male jobs left vacant – driving buses, working on the railroad and in lumber mills, running the family farm. To keep up food production, large numbers of young people were recruited to "land armies" to help with the harvest in fields and orchards. One Torontonian, Marguerite McKinnon, recalled (in a letter to George Gamester's "nostalgia" column in the Star in 1990) her teenage summers with a group of fellow volunteers, "Early every morning we'd be picked up by a Labatt's van at King and Bay and dropped off at Leaver's farm in Oakville to dig potatoes and cut the tops off carrots all day. En route we'd sing the *Land Army Song* to the tune of *Cheers, Cheers for Old Notre Dame*:

'We are the girls of the Land Army Corps, / We are out to help win the war…. / We pick potatoes, we hoe the corn, / Hitler will wish he'd never been born, / So send somebody out for me, / We're the girls of the Land Armeee.'"

There were also vast brigades of volunteers collecting clothing for the Red Cross, organizing

*Grocery stores like Woodward's in Vancouver encouraged use of Canada's new food rules.*

National Film Board Collection 1971-271/National Archives of Canada/#PA-803923

*Victory gardens were planted in backyards and empty city lots.*

Courtesy of Metropolitan Life Insurance Company, Ottawa

## LOOKING BACK

*Food writer and cookbook author Kay Spicer reminisces about growing up in small-town Saskatchewan:*

When I think of food in the '40s, I see my mom, busy with all the activity involved in its preparation. I loved watching and copying. Learning to cook was part of growing up; with our mothers we peeled, sliced, stirred, mixed, cleaned up. By the time I was six, I was cooking – real food for all of us to eat.

My mother learned to cook from her Ukrainian mother (my "Baba") and older sisters. Mom baked wonderfully light white bread while Baba made heartier wholegrain loaves, and in the tradition of the old country "put down" barrels of sauerkraut, sour cabbage for cabbage rolls, crocks of pickles and salted meats.

In Radisson everyone bought their groceries at the Red and White; other towns had an OK Economy, Safeway or Co-op, and all had butcher shops. My sister and I were often sent to buy 10 cents worth of liver or 25 cents worth of ground beef.

The kitchen table was the hub of the home – the place for doing home-work, cutting fabric, playing cards, paying bills, and for listening to the noon news while we ate "dinner." The evening meal was usually a light supper and most families also had a snack before bedtime.

In the afternoons, there were regular Ladies Aid, Homemakers, Lodge or Bridge Club teas where everyone showed off their finest cakes, squares and the little lemon tarts we all loved.

Whatever the meal or the occasion, I remember that home-cooked food was always good – wholesome, full of warmth and comforting.

fund-raising bazaars, holding dances for the boys on leave and packing ditty bags and food parcels for those overseas.

In the autumn of 1941, the government set up the Wartime Prices and Trade Board, which froze prices, wages and rents, and eliminated unnecessary frills on consumer goods. Shortages of wool fabric outlawed such items as double-breasted jackets; women's fashion switched to shorter skirts and smaller hats. New cars were non-existent and gasoline scarce. Kitchen appliances had to be repaired, not replaced. But after a decade of depression, Canadians were used to scrimping and gamely made the best of it.

Advertisements for consumer products reflected and reinforced a patient patriotism: "Perhaps they're bombing Berlin tonight!...with the metal that might have gone into my new Findlay range."..."Don't blame your dealer if he's out of Crisco. We are doing our best to keep him supplied; keep asking for it."..."But Lady, we haven't got any Shirriff's Desserts today! It's not the grocery boy's fault. Production of sweetened foods is limited in wartime, so Shirriff's have to distribute the reduced supply as fairly as possible."

Food rationing was introduced in 1942, and home cooks juggled menus and recipes to stretch their allotment of sugar, butter, coffee, tea and meat as well as many other ingredients in short supply. Hard-to-get items included everything from refrigerators to silk stockings. Improvisation was often ingenious: women baked "eggless, butterless, sugarless" cakes and painted "stockings" on their legs, complete with seams down the back.

Homemakers were constantly reminded of the importance of their role in the war effort. One ad trumpeted: "Wear this uniform proudly.... It's just a kitchen apron, yet you who wear it perform a service without which this war cannot be won. Mending, painting, making things do. Planning good meals with rationed foods. Keeping everyone on the job.

*Thousands of English war brides arriving with their children soon learned Canadian food ways.*

Canadian Army Photo, courtesy of Public Archives of Nova Scotia/#G1066-2

*From Below The Bridge (1979) by Helen Porter, who was born and raised on the South Side of St. John's, Newfoundland.*

There's really nothing quite like eating, is there? Succulent chops just nicely browned with onions, rabbit stew with a pastry over it, flipper pie, partridge-berry jam on thick white homemade bread, salt meat and cabbage with creamy hot pease pudding . . . . I once read that eating is the last joy left to us when all the others have faded or been removed. "There's nothing like a good feed," I've heard Mom say hundreds of times, and Aunt Viley, and Nanny, and many, many other people on the South Side . . . .

Some of my food memories are a lot more ordinary . . . . Molasses water for our trips up over the hill, an ice-cream soda at the Mayfair Restaurant on a hot summer day, a bottle of Ironbeer thrown over a scoop of ice cream at Power's on New Gower Street and a bag of homemade candy from the same store on the way home from church. Jelly and custard and potted meat sandwiches at birthday parties, tea tossed in the kettle on our summer outings on the rocks in Manuels River, chocolate mice and banner caramels from Knight's Shop, turnip tops and beet greens in the summer. And, of course, the dandelion.

Food still makes me feel good. . . . a plate of good hot food in front of me and the Southside Hills within my view . . . . Perhaps, even though I still don't like dandelion, I'm as authentic a southsider as even Aunt Viley could ever wish for me to be.

Holding home together, no matter what." Another promoting Canada corn starch and Karo syrup referred to homemakers as "Canada's 'Housoldiers'."

Moms who went out to work in the war plants quickly learned to simplify their cooking and shift to easier, faster meals. And women who stayed home often had extra mouths to feed (boys on leave or stationed nearby, visitors en route to new postings, evacuees from Britain). "Oven meals" (main course, side dishes and dessert all in the oven at the same time) were encouraged for saving both time and fuel.

The influx of wartime industries and mobile populations into major cities, especially embarkation centres like Halifax, caused severe housing shortages. Cramped quarters, shared facilities and tiny kitchens were the norm. Boarding houses handled a deluge of transients – and good home cooking, usually found by sheer good luck, was never more appreciated.

Kids learned to cook for themselves and to pack lunch-boxes. And although everyone complained about shortages of candy, chocolate bars, soft drinks and ice cream, school children enthusiastically joined Boy Scouts and Girl Guides in salvage drives, collecting soft drink bottles and foil from cigarette packages. Homemakers dutifully saved flattened tin cans, empty toothpaste tubes, bacon fat and rubber rings off sealer jars.

Production of homegrown food was enthusiastically promoted, and Victory gardens appeared on every vacant lot and corner. A city office-worker remembers that "newspapers ran diagrams on how to lay out the garden, Kiwanis gave prizes, people used to take baskets of vegetables to work and put them on a desk and people would take their pick." Everyone was encouraged to preserve and pickle as much produce as possible, and extra ration coupons were allowed for sugar for jam-making.

*The National Film Board produced a film on wartime nutrition.*

National Film Board Collection 1971-271/National Archives of Canada/#PA-116120

*Magazine ads offered tested recipes from major food companies.*

Courtesy of Maple Leaf Foods

## NUTRITION

- Second World War made good nutrition patriotic duty. Adequate diet seen as means of making men healthy for war service, keeping up industrial production and preventing time lost through illness.

- Division of Nutrition created by Dominion Department of Pensions and National Health; provinces also set up nutrition committees. Nutrition surveys showed deficiencies in calcium, iron, thiamin, vitamins A and C. Nutrition and health education introduced in schools.

- 1942: Canada's first dietary guidelines published as *Canada's Official Food Rules*, listing seven essentials: milk; fruits; vegetables; cereals and bread; meat, fish, etc.; eggs; fish-liver oils.

- 1942: "Vitamin B" flour and bread (labelled "Canada Approved") introduced. The flour was partially milled to retain percentage of nutrients found in whole grain flour. "Enriching" or "fortifying" flour (adding nutrients back in after milling) not allowed.

- The coffee break probably originated in mid-'40s when dietary studies noted a mid-morning break prevented work slow-downs before lunch.

- Apple juice fortified with vitamin C.

- Vitamin D added to evaporated milk to prevent rickets in children.

- 1948: Vitamin B12 discovered.

- In early '40s, goitre still serious problem. Iodized salt not in wide use except by military. In 1949, adding iodine to table salt became mandatory, and goitre all but disappeared.

The "Food for Britain" campaign, which started in 1942, prompted community groups all across Canada to organize projects. One of the biggest in fruit-growing areas such as the Fraser Valley was making jam for Britain. One worker remembers: "All the Red Cross chapters would work with the Women's Institutes and we'd collect all the berries and fruit in the valley that was donated and it would come in wagons, sacks and boxes – mountains of fruit and berries of every kind. I remember our quota in 1945 was 60 tons of jam. Now that's a lot of jam!"

Magazine articles, cooking columns in newspapers and radio broadcasts provided endless advice for wartime cooks. Marie Holmes, who wrote for *Chatelaine* in the '40s, had a "Cooking Chat" column in the *Toronto Star* in the '30s, and her cookbook, *Food from Market to Table*, was ready to go to press when war broke out in 1939. She quickly added a chapter on wartime cookery and coping with shortages.

*Canadian Home Journal* in 1943 updated "Mrs. Canada's Market Basket" after new nutrition guidelines came from the federal government. *Country Guide* offered "150 Ways to Save Sugar" and *National Home Monthly's* recipes for Christmas baking suggested, "As a patriotic gesture we feel icings on cakes should be 'out' this year."

The *Vancouver Daily Province* in September 1943 gave tips for packing overseas parcels. The weight limit was 11 pounds for men in the services, five pounds for civilians. Christmas cakes were recommended because they were the correct weight and size, travelled well and improved with aging en route.

The *Halifax Herald* published a wartime cookbook supplement in April 1945, including recipes for sugar savers such as Sugarless Rhubarb Pie (made with rhubarb, dates and corn syrup) and Butter Stretcher (with milk and gelatin added).

Swift's Weekly Food Hints (a wartime newspaper cooking column by Martha Logan) included cheerful encouragement with recipes:

*Salvage collecting was as much a part of the war effort as serving coffee and doughnuts or knitting socks.*

Metropolitan Toronto Library/Ref #939 S2/12

*Basic recipes were converted to quantity for wartime cooks (many never before in a kitchen) feeding our servicemen and factory workers.*

## DO YOU REMEMBER?

- The end of food rationing in 1947.
- Barbara Ann Scott's world figure skating win.
- P.E.I. last province to end prohibition.
- Big bands and jitterbugging.
- Radio's "Wayne & Shuster" and "Share the Wealth."
- The first time you watched TV.
- A prime rib roast for a dollar.
- Zoot suits and slick chicks.
- Ganong's ribbon candy and chicken bones.
- "Don't say bread, say McGavin's."
- Blue Bonnet margarine's "yellow-quick" bag.
- The *Toronto Star* for 3 cents.
- War Savings Stamps and Certificates.
- Spanish Rice and "Creole" everything.
- The New Look.
- Moir's chocolates in cedar boxes.
- The Garden Brigade in Nova Scotia.
- Coke Floats.
- Making syrup from sugar beets.
- Winston Churchill's "Some chicken, some neck."
- Love, the Flavour Man.
- Tube steaks.

"Sometimes it is a problem to know what to serve after the Red Cross or church war-group meeting, especially as you can't use too much sugar or butter these rationed days. Be the talk of the neighbourhood with these biscuits that are savoury or sweet" and "Serve the service men something piping hot before they shove off for camp....They'll be in fine fettle for parade next day if you top their evening with delicious frankfurters or hamburgers in barbecue or tomato sauce."

Despite the many changes and disruptions that wartime brought to Canadian families, meal patterns in most homes remained much the same as always – three-squares-a-day, and still favoring a plain meat-and-veg Britishness. At the same time, however, many families whose origins were elsewhere served their traditional dishes either regularly or on special occasions.

Certainly compared to conditions in Europe during the war, food shortages in Canada were more an inconvenience than a real hardship: the butter ration never fell below six ounces per person per week or meat below one and one-half pounds. In 1941, the *Free Press Prairie Farmer* reported B.C. strawberries rolling in by the carload every day and gave recipes for strawberry whip, trifle, jam and ice cream. And the *Vancouver Sun* in 1942 still took superb seafood for granted: "By serving a shellfish meal at least once a week we can ease up tremendously on the demand for meat, and a 15-cent crab will serve three people generously." Still, everyone knew the war was finally over when boxes of mandarin oranges from Japan arrived once more at Christmas.

The end of the war brought Canadians the momentous changes that go with a return to peacetime and normal life. An even greater adjustment was ahead for the 40,000 war brides, mostly from Britain, who arrived in Canada with 20,000 children. One in five Canadian soldiers

*Honest-to-goodness home cooking was shared with servicemen and their families from far and wide.*
Saskatchewan Archives Board, Saskatoon/Ref #S-B6434

*Grocery delivery boys like this one in 1943 collected ration coupons at the door.*
Courtesy of Canadian Home Journal © Maclean Hunter Ltd.

and airmen who went over a bachelor came home married. Many brides and children had to live with in-laws at first.

Canadian military headquarters in London established the Canadian Wives Bureau to dispense information about Canada. In Canada, Red Cross and other homemakers' services taught war brides how to cope with supermarkets, Canadian cooking measurements and unfamiliar foods.

In 1949, Newfoundland joined Confederation as Canada's tenth province. Despite the protests of many Newfoundlanders, incorporation was accepted as a way to a better economic future. In the meantime, however, longtime isolation and shortage of agricultural land kept food supplies restricted. Especially in the outports and rural areas, where people lived mainly on what foods they could hunt, fish, or grow, Newfoundland's unique, traditional cooking stayed the same as it had been for countless generations.

The postwar years brought to Canadians most of the goods and services first previewed in 1939 and interrupted by the war: faster cars, better highways, cheap gasoline, frequent air service and television. Cities spread into suburbia with building lots provided by the Veteran's Land Act. An influx of new immigration from Europe along with soldiers' memories of friendly pubs and cafés abroad stimulated a new casualness and changing attitudes to food.

Shopping was easy with well-stocked supermarket shelves and market stalls. Eating out was a new pleasure, too, even in department stores, where the food service staff maintained high standards in food and presentation not only in their restaurants, such as Eaton's Georgian Room and Simpson's Arcadian Court, but at the lunch counters, too.

By the late '40s, magazines were offering surprisingly sophisticated food ideas. An up-scale cooking column in *Saturday Night* magazine admonished, "Post-war cooking is casual but shouldn't be careless." Magazines also featured themes that we associate with later years, such as quick recipes using canned soup, cheesecake birthday cakes and Canadian specialty foods from each province. In 1949 Canada Packers sponsored a $100-a-recipe contest.

Kitchens changed, too. New methods and new equipment made food easier to prepare; pressure cookers were must-haves. Wartime had sped up development of new food techology, and the research that produced powdered milk and dried eggs now turned to the development of new convenience foods such as cake mixes and instant coffee. Women were back in the kitchen, with new family priorities as the postwar baby boom began.

*Wartime weddings such as this nursing sister's in Ottawa, May 1945, still meant fruitcake and fancy baking.*

Department of National Defense/National Archives of Canada/#PA-128247

*The abundance of postwar shopping was a welcome change.*

Provincial Archives of Alberta, Garneau Studio Collection, #256

*The new electric kitchen included a top-loading dishwasher. This B.C. Electric example is late '40s.*

Vancouver Public Library/Photo #26792

# Cookbook Sampler

## THE FORTIES

For more cookbooks of the decade, see Bibliography p. 234.

# SEVEN-LAYER DINNER

*Sausages instead of ground beef were often placed on top. In the '90s, it makes sense to partially cook the sausages in the microwave first and drain off the excess fat.*

| | | |
|---|---|---|
| 1 | can (12 oz/341 mL) kernel corn | 1 |
| 1 | can (14 oz/398 mL) tomato sauce | 1 |
| 1 tsp | salt | 5 mL |
| | Pepper | |
| 1 | large potato, thinly sliced | 1 |
| 1 | medium onion, chopped | 1 |
| 1/2 cup | parboiled rice | 125 mL |
| 1 cup | frozen peas | 250 mL |
| 3/4 lb | lean ground beef, crumbled | 375 g |
| 3 | strips bacon, halved and partially cooked | 3 |
| 1/3 cup | shredded Cheddar cheese | 75 mL |

Drain corn, reserving liquid in measure; pour in enough water to make 1 cup (250 mL). Stir into tomato sauce along with salt, and pepper to taste.

In greased 6-cup (1.5 L) casserole, layer potato, onion, then rice; pour half the tomato sauce mixture over top. Layer with corn, peas and beef; top with remaining sauce. Cover and bake in 350°F (180°C) oven for 1-1/2 hours. Top with bacon and cheese; bake, uncovered, 15 minutes. Makes 6 servings.

## VARIATIONS:

Use 1 cup (250 mL) grated carrot instead of corn.
Use 1 lb (500 g) link (breakfast) sausages, partially cooked, in place of beef; omit bacon.

One of the first casserole meals, this was the answer to a busy cook's prayers – just put everything into one dish, bake and serve. Called **Shipwreck** in some books, variations included rice, macaroni or broken spaghetti and were often made with a can of tomato soup.

# SALMON LOAF

*Often this loaf was served with a cream sauce mixed with parsley or chopped egg, or a simple Tartar Sauce made by mixing mayonnaise with chopped sweet pickle or pickle relish.*

| | | |
|---|---|---|
| 2 | cans (7.5 oz/213 g each) salmon | 2 |
| 3/4 cup | (approx) milk | 175 mL |
| 1 cup | dry bread or cracker crumbs | 250 mL |
| 2 | eggs, lightly beaten | 2 |
| 1 cup | finely chopped celery | 250 mL |
| 1 | small onion, chopped | 1 |
| 1 tbsp | chopped fresh parsley | 15 mL |
| | Salt and pepper | |

Drain salmon, reserving liquid in measure; add enough milk to make 3/4 cup (175 mL). In bowl, mix salmon, bread crumbs, eggs, celery, onion, milk mixture, parsley, and salt and pepper to taste. Pack into greased 8- x 4-inch (1.5 L) loaf pan. Bake in 350°F (180°C) oven for 45 minutes. Let stand in pan 10 minutes. Makes 6 servings.

## VARIATION:

**Tuna Loaf:** Substitute canned tuna for salmon.

Canned salmon was a staple in homes all over Canada and was as versatile an ingredient as any cook would want. In the '40s, cookbooks offered recipes for Creamed Salmon and Peas on Toast, Salmon Loaf, Salmon Roll, Scalloped Salmon, Salmon Pie, Salmon Cakes and assorted dishes simply called Salmon Supper Dish.

# SWISS STEAK

*Adapted from* Cooking Under Pressure: A Modern Guide to Pressure Cookery, *by Edith Adams (the* Vancouver Sun, *1947), this recipe, which freezes well, works in a pressure cooker, on stove top, or in the oven. A June '47 ad in the* Toronto Star *had Presto Cookers for $15.95 at Simpson's.*

| 2 lb | round steak | 1 kg |
|------|-------------|------|
| 3 tbsp | all-purpose flour | 50 mL |
| 1 tsp | salt | 5 mL |
| | Pepper | |
| 2 tbsp | vegetable oil | 25 mL |
| 1 | clove garlic, minced | 1 |
| 2 | onions, sliced | 2 |
| 1/2 cup | sliced celery | 125 mL |
| 1 | sweet green or red pepper, chopped | 1 |
| 2 cups | canned tomatoes (or one 19 oz/ 540 mL can) | 500 mL |

Trim visible fat from meat. Combine flour, salt, and pepper to taste; sprinkle half over one side of meat and pound in with mallet or edge of plate. Repeat on other side. Cut into serving-size portions.

Pressure Cooker Method: In pressure cooker, heat oil over medium-high heat; brown meat on both sides. Add garlic, onions, celery and sweet pepper; stir for 1 minute. Add tomatoes. Cook at 15 pounds pressure for 25 minutes.

Stove Top Method: In large skillet over medium-high heat, brown meat, garlic and onions in oil. Drain tomatoes and add juice to pan; reduce heat, cover and simmer for 1 hour. Add celery, sweet pepper, and tomatoes (breaking up with spoon); simmer, covered, for 30 minutes or until meat is tender.

Oven Method: Follow stove top method, but add undrained tomatoes, breaking up with spoon. Bake, covered, in 325°F (160°C) oven for 1 hour. Add celery and sweet pepper; bake 30 minutes.

Makes 6 to 8 servings.

Postwar brides, housewives and those determined to cook in a hurry bought pressure cookers. At first, basic recipes were very plain. Gradually, adventurous cooks learned to adjust and create tastier foods. They also discovered that pressure cooking was a great way to tenderize tough cuts of venison, moose and beef. Pressure canners were a necessity for those who still canned vegetables, meat or fish in the '40s. Today in the '90s, pressure cookers are once again being promoted for fast and easy (time- and energy-saving) cooking.

# CABBAGE ROLLS

*Often the remaining cabbage not used for the rolls is chopped and placed in the bottom of the baking dish or layered with the rolls before the tomatoes are poured over top. Serve with sour cream, if desired.*

| | | |
|------|----------------------------------|--------|
| 1 | head cabbage, separated | 1 |
| 1/2 cup | long-grain rice | 125 mL |
| 2 tbsp | vegetable oil | 25 mL |
| 1 | small onion, chopped | 1 |
| 1 | carrot, grated | 1 |
| 1/2 lb | ground beef | 250 g |
| 1 tsp | salt | 5 mL |
| | Pepper | |
| 2 cups | canned tomatoes or tomato juice | 500 mL |
| 2 tbsp | lemon juice | 25 mL |
| 2 tbsp | packed brown sugar | 25 mL |

Steam cabbage leaves until partially wilted. Reserve about 15 for rolls; chop remaining leaves coarsely and line baking pan. Partially cook rice in boiling water; drain.

In skillet, heat oil; cook onion and carrot until softened. Add beef and cook, breaking up meat, just until no longer pink; drain off fat. Stir in rice, salt, and pepper to taste.

Place a little meat mixture on each leaf; roll up and arrange seam-side down over chopped cabbage. Mix tomatoes, lemon juice and sugar; pour over rolls. Cover and bake in 325°F (160°C) oven for 1-1/2 hours. Makes 6 servings.

Cabbage rolls (*holubsti*) vary from region to region and home to home in Canada, just as they do in Ukraine and Poland. Fillings may include meat, rice, kasha (buckwheat) or carrots, depending on the taste of the cook and the trend of the day.

German, Hungarian and Ukrainian versions often used sour cabbage or sauerkraut, or softened the cabbage leaves in vinegar and boiling water. In the North West Territories, **Caribou Cabbage Rolls** were the order of the day. As time went on, tomato soup versions became commonplace.

# CHEESE DREAMS

*Monda Rosenberg, Chatelaine's food editor, updates this sandwich for the '90s with goat cheese, strips of prosciutto and a sprinkling of thyme.*

| | | |
|--------|----------------------------|--------|
| 1 cup | shredded Cheddar cheese | 250 mL |
| 3 tbsp | mayonnaise | 50 mL |
| | Butter | |
| 8 | slices bread | 8 |
| 8 | slices bacon, partially cooked | 8 |

Mix cheese and salad dressing. Butter bread; spread with cheese mixture. Criss-cross bacon on top. Bake on greased baking sheet in 375°F (190°C) oven until bubbly and brown. Makes 8 servings.

Two kinds of Cheese Dreams appear in 1940s' cookbooks. A sweet version, like cheese shortbread with a tart jelly layer in the centre, was popular for tea time.

The other version was a savory – simply slices of bread (usually white store-bought) spread with a cheese mixture, topped with bacon strips and broiled. Or cheese was sandwiched between two slices of bread, lightly buttered on the outside and toasted in the oven. When electric frypans came along, this sandwich became the ever-popular grilled cheese.

# PARTY SANDWICH LOAF

*First introduced in the '20s as an elegant make-ahead recipe, this was popular at the endless stream of postwar showers and bridal luncheons. Vary fillings to suit your taste; choose chicken salad, thinly shaved ham with mustard, or tuna filling for a change. Garnish the loaf with parsley sprigs, radish slices, chives and watercress.*

| 1 | loaf unsliced sandwich bread | 1 |
|---|---|---|
|  | Butter or mayonnaise |  |
| *Filling:* | | |
| 1 lb | cream cheese, softened | 500 g |
| 1/4 cup | (approx) light or 18% cream | 50 mL |
|  | Chopped parsley, radishes, chives or watercress |  |

Remove crusts and slice loaf lengthwise into four 1/2-inch (2 cm) thick slices. Spread with butter, then filling. Stack slices; wrap and chill for 4 hours or overnight.

Blend cheese with cream until spreadable. Frost sides, ends and top of loaf. Using piping bag, decorate with any remaining cheese. Makes 12 servings.

**Salmon Filling:** Combine 1 can (7.5 oz/213 g) drained red salmon, 2 chopped green onions, 2 tbsp (25 mL) finely chopped celery and 2 tbsp (25 mL) mayonnaise.

**Egg Salad Filling:** Combine 3 chopped hard-cooked eggs, 2 tbsp (25 mL) mayonnaise, 1 tbsp (15 mL) minced onion or chives and 1 tbsp (15 mL) chopped pimiento.

**Ham Filling:** Combine 1 cup (250 mL) minced ham, 2 tbsp (25 mL) each mayonnaise and chopped sweet pickle and 1 tsp (5 mL) prepared or Dijon mustard.

The same fillings were used to make fancy sandwiches:

**Pinwheels:** Remove crusts from sandwich loaf; cut lengthwise into 1/3-inch (8 mm) thick slices. Flatten each slice slightly with rolling pin. Spread each slice with butter, then filling. Place a row of olives, gherkins, cooked asparagus or banana along long side and roll up lightly from that side. Wrap well; refrigerate. Slice at serving time into 1/2-inch (1 cm) thick rounds.

**Ribbons:** Use 2 slices brown and 1 slice white bread, crusts removed. Butter one side of brown slices and both sides of white slice. Spread buttered side of one brown slice with filling; top with white slice. Spread with filling; cover with second brown slice, buttered-side down. Wrap tightly; refrigerate. Cut at serving time into 1/2-inch (1 cm) slices; cut each into thirds.

# WHITE WEDDING SALAD

*Called **Bride's Salad**, 24-Hour Salad or **White Wedding Salad**, this was a must for bridal showers or luncheons. A nice make-ahead, it is best chilled 24 hours to mellow flavors.*

| | | |
|---|---|---|
| 1 | can (19 oz/540 mL) pineapple chunks, drained | 1 |
| 2 cups | seedless green grapes, halved | 500 mL |
| 1 | large banana, sliced | 1 |
| 2 cups | miniature marshmallows | 500 mL |
| 1 cup | toasted sliced almonds | 250 mL |
| 2 | eggs | 2 |
| 2 tbsp | packed brown sugar | 25 mL |
| 1/2 cup | light cream | 125 mL |
| 1/2 tsp | grated lemon rind | 2 mL |
| 1/4 cup | lemon juice | 50 mL |
| 1 cup | whipping cream | 250 mL |
| | Lettuce | |
| | Mint or watercress | |

In bowl, combine pineapple, grapes, banana, marshmallows and almonds; refrigerate. In double boiler, combine eggs, sugar, light cream and lemon rind; gradually blend in lemon juice. Cook over boiling water, stirring, until thickened; chill.

Whip cream; fold into lemon mixture. Pour over fruit; stir gently. Refrigerate for 24 hours. Serve in lettuce cups; garnish with mint. Makes 8 servings.

**Frozen Pineapple Salad** was a variation on the same theme. Frozen or refrigerated in loaf shape or individual moulds, this was served on lettuce leaves as a ladies' luncheon special. Considered dainty fare, the moulds were featured in Kraft television commercials (or maybe that's where the idea came from).

Cream together 4 oz (125 g) cream cheese and 1/2 cup (125 mL) cooked salad dressing or mayonnaise. Stir in 1 can (14 oz/ 398 mL) crushed pineapple, drained, 1/4 cup (50 mL) chopped maraschino cherries, 1 cup (250 mL) snipped marshmallows and 1/2 cup (125 mL) flaked coconut. Whip 1 cup (250 mL) whipping cream with 1 tbsp (15 mL) icing sugar; fold into fruit mixture. Spoon into 8- x 4-inch (1.5 L) loaf pan; freeze until firm. Remove to refrigerator 30 minutes before slicing. Makes 8 servings.

# PICKLED BEETS

*Pickled beets need about three weeks to develop their flavor.*

| | | |
|---|---|---|
| 1-1/2 cups | granulated sugar | 375 mL |
| 1 cup | vinegar (preferably cider) | 250 mL |
| 1 cup | water (or drained cooking liquid) | 250 mL |
| 1/2 tsp | whole cloves | 2 mL |
| 1/2 tsp | whole allspice | 2 mL |
| 1 | cinnamon stick | 1 |
| 3 lb | small fresh beets, cooked and peeled | 1.5 kg |

In large saucepan, combine sugar, vinegar and water. Add cloves, allspice and cinnamon tied in cheesecloth; bring to boil. Add beets and simmer 10 minutes. Discard spices. Pack beets into canning jars; add liquid to come within 1/2 inch (1 cm) of tops. Seal and process 10 minutes in boiling water bath. Makes 4 cups (1 L).

Victory gardens meant preserving, and pickling was popular. Onions, beans, carrots, cucumbers (**Icicle Pickles, Bread and Butter Pickles**), watermelon rind, crabapples – you name it, Canadians pickled it. There were 7-day, 9-day and 11-day pickles, even "9-day pickles to make in 3 days." Dills (often kosher) were fresh-packed in brine in crocks or sealed in jars and often aged for two months before opening.

The most perfect small beets (Aylmer canned them as "rosebuds") were pickled whole. Others were sliced or diced. Beets were also served as a vegetable in a sweet and tangy sauce and called **Harvard Beets**.

In the '40s, a boiling water bath probably meant hauling out Grandma's big old copper boiler, now museum and antique dealers' prizes.

# CHILI SAUCE

*Granulated sugar may be used in place of brown sugar. Hotter versions included some dried chili peppers.*

| | | |
|---|---|---|
| 12 cups | chopped seeded peeled tomatoes | 3 L |
| 4 cups | chopped onions | 1 L |
| 3 | sweet red or green peppers, chopped | 3 |
| 2 cups | chopped celery | 500 mL |
| 1 cup | cider vinegar | 250 mL |
| 2 tbsp | coarse pickling salt | 25 mL |
| 1/2 tsp | each cloves, ginger, cinnamon, celery seed, nutmeg and pepper | 2 mL |
| 1-1/2 cups | packed brown sugar | 375 mL |

In large kettle, combine tomatoes, onions, sweet peppers, celery, vinegar, salt, cloves, ginger, cinnamon, celery seed, nutmeg and pepper; bring to boil. Reduce heat and simmer, uncovered, for 1-1/2 hours or until thickened, stirring often. Add sugar; simmer for 30 minutes, stirring often. Immediately pour into hot canning jars. Seal and process in boiling water bath for 15 minutes. Makes about 16 cups (4 L).

### VARIATION:

**Fruit Chili Sauce:** In large heavy saucepan combine 4 cups (1 L) chopped tomatoes, 1 cup (250 mL) each chopped peeled peaches, pears and apples, 1 cup (250 mL) each chopped onion and sweet red pepper, 1-1/2 cups (375 mL) each cider vinegar and brown sugar, 1 tbsp (15 mL) coarse pickling salt, 2 tbsp (25 mL) pickling spice (tied in cheesecloth bag) and 1 cinnamon stick.

Bring to boil; reduce heat and simmer, uncovered, stirring frequently, for about 1 hour or until thickened. Remove spices. Immediately pour into hot canning jars. Seal and process in boiling water bath for 15 minutes. Makes about 6 cups (1.5 L).

Most old cookbooks, especially fundraisers and church books, contain at least one recipe for Chili Sauce. Often the recipe includes peaches, pears or apples. Particularly appealing are the simple ones that have long lists of ingredients and then simply say, "Cook until thick; seal."

Chili sauces varied from thick to watery, chunky to finely chopped. The variety of relishes was unlimited: corn, cranberry, cucumber, pepper and hot dog (mustardy) were in cookbooks all over the country. Sauerkraut filled the house with a sour odor, but it was worth it. **Chow Chow** was a mixture of vegetables, including tomatoes and cabbage.

**Piccallili** was usually made with green tomatoes. Since recipes were often passed on by word of mouth, inadvertent changes often crept in. Maybe that's why one book had a recipe for Pickled Lillie.

# PEACH CONSERVE

*Be sure that each jar of this conserve gets two or three maraschino cherries. During the '80s, a popular drink was a Fuzzy Navel made with peach schnappes. For **Fuzzy Navel Conserve**, top each jar with 1 tbsp (15 mL) peach schnappes before sealing.*

| | | |
|---|---|---|
| 3 | oranges | 3 |
| 1 | lemon | 1 |
| 12 | peaches, chopped | 12 |
| 7 cups | (approx) granulated sugar | 1.75 L |
| 1/2 cup | blanched almonds (whole or slivered) | 125 mL |
| 1/2 cup | drained maraschino cherries | 125 mL |

Squeeze juice from oranges and lemon into bowl. Using food grinder or processor, finely grind oranges and lemon (pulp and rind); add to bowl along with peaches.

Measure fruit and add equal amount of sugar. Cook over medium heat, stirring, until boiling. Reduce heat and cook, stirring often, for 1 hour or until thickened and peaches are translucent. Add almonds and cherries; cook 5 minutes. Remove from heat; skim off foam. Pour into hot sterilized Mason-type jars; seal with two-piece lids. Makes about 8 cups (2 L).

Just as their mothers and grandmothers did, homemakers still made lots of jams and jellies. There were jams from berries – strawberry, raspberry, blackberry; jams and conserves from tree fruit – cherry, peach, pear; jellies from grapes and red and black currants; conserves from rhubarb and pineapple; marmalades from oranges, lemons and even carrots.

Sugar was rationed, but extra rations were allowed for those who grew more or preserved more. At the same time, the Red Cross and the Women's Institutes were again charged with producing vast quantities of "Jam for Britain."

# CORNBREAD

*Cornbread, called **Johnnycake** in many regions, was staple fare for decades. It was often served with meat dishes, chili or for breakfast.*

| | | |
|---|---|---|
| 1 cup | yellow cornmeal | 250 mL |
| 1 cup | all-purpose flour | 250 mL |
| 1/4 cup | granulated sugar | 50 mL |
| 1 tbsp | baking powder | 15 mL |
| 1/2 tsp | salt | 2 mL |
| 2 | eggs | 2 |
| 1 cup | milk | 250 mL |
| 1/4 cup | butter, melted | 50 mL |

In bowl, combine cornmeal, flour, sugar, baking powder and salt. Beat eggs until frothy; beat in milk and butter. Add to dry ingredients; mix well.

Pour into greased 8-inch (2 L) square cake pan. Bake in 350°F (180°C) oven for 30 to 35 minutes or until cake tester comes out clean. Let cool slightly in pan. Cut into squares and serve warm.

In *Muskie Jones's Northwoods Cookery*, reference is made to Paper Bread. "If'n you like cornmeal … this here recipe for Paper Bread makes mighty good eatin! Take 3 or 4 handfuls of cornmeal and a little salt. Add enough water to make a gruel and cook it until it's like porridge. Then, heat a big flat rock (or large frypan) on your fire until a drop of water flies off. Take some dough in your hand and wipe it quickly across the rock. It cooks right off so you peel it off when it crinkles at the edges...."

**Sausage Cornbread** had precooked sausages baked in the cornbread and was usually served with maple syrup. Cornmeal also appeared on many Canadian tables as **Cornmeal Mush** (cooked cornmeal spread in a pan until set, cut into squares and fried – very much like Italian polenta). **Tamale Pie**, a popular supper dish, was a spicy meat mixture topped with cornbread. In the '80s, cornbread was dressed up with jalapeño peppers, shredded Cheddar or Monterey Jack cheese and often a can of corn.

# BASIC SWEET DOUGH FOR ROLLS

*This dough can be baked in plain or fancy shapes.*

| | | |
|---|---|---|
| 1 tsp | granulated sugar | 5 mL |
| 1/2 cup | warm water | 125 mL |
| 1 | pkg active dry yeast | 1 |
| 1/2 cup | milk | 125 mL |
| 3 tbsp | granulated sugar | 50 mL |
| 3 tbsp | butter or shortening | 50 mL |
| 1 tsp | salt | 5 mL |
| 1 | egg, beaten | 1 |
| 4 cups | (approx) all-purpose flour | 1 L |

Dissolve 1 tsp (5 mL) sugar in warm water; sprinkle in yeast and let stand for 10 minutes or until frothy. Meanwhile, in saucepan, heat milk, sugar, butter and salt until lukewarm, stirring to dissolve sugar and melt butter.

In large bowl, combine milk mixture, dissolved yeast and egg. Beat in about one-third of the flour until smooth. Gradually add enough remaining flour to make soft, slightly sticky dough. Knead on lightly floured surface for 5 minutes or until smooth and springy.

Place dough in greased bowl, turning to grease all over. Cover and let rise until doubled, about 1-1/2 hours. Punch down and form into two smooth balls; let rest 10 minutes. Shape as desired (see below). Cover and let rise until doubled. Bake in 375°F (190°C) oven for 15 to 20 minutes or until golden brown. Makes 2 to 3 dozen rolls.

**Pan Buns:** Form each ball of dough into a long roll and cut each into 16 pieces. Shape pieces into balls; place in greased 8-inch (1.2 L) round or square pan.

**Parkerhouse Rolls:** Roll out each ball of dough 1/4 inch (5 mm) thick. Cut rounds with biscuit cutter; brush with melted butter. Crease centre and fold over. Place on greased baking sheet.

**Cloverleaf Rolls:** Roll small pieces of dough into 1-inch (2.5 cm) balls. Place three in each greased muffin cup; brush with melted butter.

**Bowknots:** Roll pieces of dough into ropes about 6 inches (15 cm) long and 1/2 inch (1 cm) thick. Tie each into loose knot. Place on greased baking sheet.

**Crescents or Butterhorns:** Roll each ball of dough into circle about 1/4 inch (5 mm) thick. Brush with melted butter. Cut into 12 wedges. Starting at wide end of each wedge, roll up tightly, sealing point with fingers; curve into crescents. Place on greased baking sheet.

**Fantans:** Roll out each ball of dough into 12- x 10-inch (30 x 25 cm) rectangle. Cut lengthwise into 5 strips; brush with melted butter. Pile strips on top of one other; cut into 12 pieces. Place in greased muffin cups, cut side up, separating slices at top slightly.

## VARIATIONS

**Rich Sweet Dough:** Increase sugar and butter to 1/3 cup (75 mL) each and use 2 eggs.

**Refrigerator Dough:** After kneading, place dough in greased bowl, turning to grease all over. Cover tightly with plastic wrap. Store in refrigerator up to 2 days. If not doubled in bulk, let rise at room temperature before punching down and shaping

In the '40s, small, light rolls were very popular for teas and luncheons. Parkerhouse rolls had been made for decades, and cloverleafs also appear in some old cookbooks; other fancy shapings gained favor.

By the late '40s, fast-rising granulated dry yeast was an alternative to yeast cakes. Also new were "straight-dough" methods which simplified bread making; most earlier recipes used the "sponge" method, which started with a yeast mixture that had to stand several hours or overnight.

The post-war years also brought new recipes for refrigerator yeast dough, promoted by flour companies as a convenient new way of making bread and rolls. This dough could be stored in the refrigerator up to a week, using portions for fresh rolls when desired. Most recipes for refrigerator dough were the same as for regular sweet dough but used water instead of milk and called for little or no kneading.

**Hot Cross Buns:** Make Rich Sweet Dough, adding 2 tsp (10 mL) cinnamon and 1/2 tsp (2 mL) each nutmeg and allspice to the flour, and kneading in 1/2 cup (125 mL) each raisins, currants and chopped candied peel.

After first rising, shape dough into 18 small balls. Place on greased baking sheet; let rise double. Bake for 15 to 20 minutes in 375°F (190°C) oven; brush with glaze (mixture of 2 tbsp/25 mL each sugar and water); return to oven for 5 minutes. Brush again with glaze. When cool, pipe icing cross on top of each.

# BRAN MUFFINS

*In the '40s, fibre was called bulk or roughage. All-Bran cereal and prunes were the best-known sources. Along with muffins, recipes for gingerbread, waffles, refrigerator rolls, cookies and pancakes made with All-Bran appeared.*

| | | |
|---|---|---|
| 1/2 cup | boiling water | 125 mL |
| 1-1/2 cups | All-Bran or 100% Bran cereal | 375 mL |
| 1 | egg, lightly beaten | 1 |
| 1/4 cup | molasses | 50 mL |
| 1/4 cup | vegetable oil | 50 mL |
| 1 cup | buttermilk | 250 mL |
| 1/2 cup | all-purpose flour | 125 mL |
| 1/2 cup | whole wheat flour | 125 mL |
| 1/3 cup | granulated sugar | 75 mL |
| 1 tsp | baking soda | 5 mL |
| 1 tsp | baking powder | 5 mL |
| 1/4 tsp | salt | 1 mL |
| 1/2 cup | raisins, chopped dates or currants | 125 mL |

Pour boiling water over cereal; let cool. Mix together egg, molasses, oil and buttermilk.

In large bowl, combine all-purpose and whole wheat flours, sugar, baking soda, baking powder and salt; add cereal mixture along with buttermilk mixture and raisins. Fill muffin cups two-thirds full. Bake in 400°F (200°C) oven for 20 minutes or until firm to the touch. Makes 12.

**VARIATIONS:**

**Blueberry Muffins:** Fold in 1/2 cup (125 mL) fresh or frozen (unthawed) blueberries.
**Nut Muffins:** Fold in 2/3 cup (150 mL) chopped nuts.
**Date Muffins:** Substitute 1/2 cup (125 mL) chopped pitted dates for the raisins.
**Refrigerator Bran Muffins:** Double or triple this recipe; refrigerate batter, covered, up to 2 weeks. Bake as needed.

# LEMON CAKE PIE

*This has a light lemon filling very similar to Lemon Sponge Pudding.*

| | | |
|---|---|---|
| 1/2 cup | granulated sugar | 125 mL |
| 2 tbsp | butter, melted | 25 mL |
| 2 tbsp | all-purpose flour | 25 mL |
| 1/4 tsp | salt | 1 mL |
| 2 | eggs, separated | 2 |
| 2/3 cup | milk | 150 mL |
| 1 tsp | grated lemon rind | 5 mL |
| 1/4 cup | lemon juice | 50 mL |
| 1 | (unbaked) 8-inch (20 cm) pie shell | 1 |

In bowl, combine sugar, butter, flour, salt, egg yolks, milk, lemon rind and juice. Beat eggs whites until stiff; fold into lemon mixture. Pour into pie shell. Bake in 350°F (180°C) oven for 30 minutes or until golden and firm to the touch. Cool.

**Lemon Sponge Pudding** was a favorite dessert in the '40s that came out of the oven with a layer of light cake on top of lemon pudding: In bowl, combine 3/4 cup (175 mL) granulated sugar, 3 tbsp (45 mL) melted butter, 3 tbsp (45 mL) all-purpose flour, 1/4 tsp (1 mL) salt, 3 egg yolks, 1 cup (250 mL) milk, 1 tsp (5 mL) grated lemon rind and 1/3 cup (75 mL) lemon juice. Beat 3 egg whites until stiff; fold into batter. Bake in 8-cup (2 L) casserole set in pan of hot water in 350°F (180°C) oven until set and lightly browned, 30 to 40 minutes. Makes 6 servings.

# FRUITCAKE

*This medium-dark cake may be served plain, brushed with corn syrup that has been heated to thin it, or covered with almond paste and a thin layer of decorator frosting.*

*Seeded raisins, so popular in the '40s, are rarely used in the '90s. Newfoundlanders use their traditional salt pork in place of butter.*

| | | |
|---|---|---|
| 2 cups | Sultana raisins | 500 mL |
| 2 cups | golden raisins | 500 mL |
| 2 cups | currants | 500 mL |
| 1 cup | chopped pitted dates, prunes or dried apricots | 250 mL |
| 2 cups | walnuts or almonds (whole or chopped) | 500 mL |
| 2 cups | candied mixed peel | 500 mL |
| 1 cup | diced candied pineapple | 250 mL |
| 1 cup | candied cherries | 250 mL |
| 1/3 cup | brandy, rum or sherry (or fruit juice) | 75 mL |
| 1 cup | butter | 250 mL |
| 1 cup | granulated sugar | 250 mL |
| 6 | eggs | 6 |
| 1/4 cup | molasses | 50 mL |
| 1-3/4 cups | all-purpose flour | 425 mL |
| 1-1/2 tsp | baking powder | 7 mL |
| 1/2 tsp | salt | 2 mL |
| 2 tsp | cinnamon | 10 mL |
| 1/2 tsp | each allspice, nutmeg and cloves | 2 mL |
| 1/2 cup | grape or orange juice | 125 mL |

In bowl, combine Sultana and golden raisins, currants, dates, walnuts, peel, pineapple and cherries; toss with brandy. Cover and let stand overnight.

In large bowl, cream butter with sugar until light and fluffy. Add eggs, one at a time, beating well after each addition. Blend in molasses. Combine flour, baking powder, salt, cinnamon, allspice, nutmeg and cloves; remove 1/2 cup (125 mL) and toss with fruit mixture. Add remaining dry ingredients to creamed mixture alternately with grape juice, beating well. Stir in fruit only until well distributed.

Grease 8-inch (3 L) square fruitcake pan; line with heavy brown paper and waxed paper, then grease again. Spoon in batter; spread evenly, smoothing top. Bake in 275°F (140°C) oven for about 3 hours or until cake tester inserted in centre comes out clean. Cool for 5 minutes; turn out onto rack to cool completely. To store, wrap tightly in several layers sherry- or brandy-soaked cheesecloth; overwrap in foil. Store in cool place for several weeks, occasionally moistening cheesecloth.

Perfect for wedding cakes for all the wartime marriages, this fruitcake was a good "keeper" and travelled well in parcels to servicemen. Other favorite recipes made white or light fruitcakes. Some old cookbooks from the Maritimes gave two wedding-cake recipes: a white plain Bride's Cake and a dark fruitcake Bridegroom's Cake.

Butter and sugar were rationed, but good cooks saved them for the traditional treat of Christmas baking. Recipes for very dark fruitcakes often contained strawberry jam or grape jelly, molasses or coffee, even chocolate. If almonds for almond paste were scarce, they were replaced by mashing sweet or white potatoes with almond extract and lots of sugar. A layer of hard ornamental icing, Royal Icing, sealed flavor and moisture in the cake.

In the '60s and '70s, recipes for no-bake fruitcakes were developed in test kitchens of food companies to promote such products as graham wafer crumbs, condensed milk and marshmallows.

# Orange Chiffon Cake

*Chiffon cakes may be frosted, but a simple glaze is pleasant (see Vanilla Glaze or Citrus Glaze, p. 87).*

| 2-1/4 cups | sifted cake-and-pastry flour | 550 mL |
|---|---|---|
| 1 tbsp | baking powder | 15 mL |
| 1 tsp | salt | 5 mL |
| 1-1/2 cups | granulated sugar | 375 mL |
| 1/2 cup | vegetable oil | 125 mL |
| 6 | eggs, separated | 6 |
| 3/4 cup | orange juice | 175 mL |

In bowl, combine flour, baking powder, salt and 3/4 cup (175 mL) of the sugar; gradually beat in oil until smooth. Blend in egg yolks and orange juice; beat for 1 minute.

In large bowl, beat egg whites to soft peaks; gradually beat in remaining sugar to stiff shiny peaks. Fold in egg yolk mixture until no streaks remain. Do not overfold.

Pour into ungreased 10-inch (4 L) tube pan. Bake in 350°F (180°C) oven for 1 hour or until cake springs back when lightly touched. Invert and cool in pan. Loosen edges; remove to serving plate.

### VARIATIONS:

**Lemon Chiffon:** Use 2 tsp (10 mL) lemon juice plus water to make 3/4 cup (175 mL) instead of orange juice. Add grated rind of 1 lemon.
**Mocha Chiffon:** Use 3/4 cup (175 mL) strong coffee and 1 tsp (5 mL) vanilla instead of orange juice.
**Chocolate Chiffon:** Reduce flour to 2 cups (500 mL) and sift 2/3 cup (150 mL) cocoa with dry ingredients. Use 1 cup (250 mL) water instead of orange juice. Add 1 tsp (5 mL) vanilla.

Marjorie Thompson Flint, food columnist for *Saturday Night* magazine in the late '40s, remembers the great excitement when chiffon cakes hit the cooking scene from California. And *Chatelaine* called this the cake-making discovery of the century. Even in the '40s, a lot of our trends had their roots in California. Different from an angel cake, a chiffon cake is made with oil and includes egg yolks. It stays moist for days in a cake tin and freezes well.

# Victory Cake

*Sugar rationing meant less-sweet cakes or replacing granulated sugar with corn syrup or sweetened condensed milk. Butter rationing gave rise to shortening-based cakes.*

| 2-1/4 cups | sifted cake-and-pastry flour | 550 mL |
|---|---|---|
| 2 tsp | baking powder | 10 mL |
| 1/4 tsp | salt | 1 mL |
| 1/2 cup | shortening | 125 mL |
| 1 cup | light corn syrup | 250 mL |
| 1 tsp | vanilla | 5 mL |
| 2 | eggs | 2 |
| 1/2 cup | milk | 125 mL |

Sift together flour, baking powder and salt three times. In bowl, cream shortening until fluffy; gradually beat in corn syrup and vanilla. Add one-quarter of the dry ingredients; beat well. Add eggs, one at a time, beating well after each addition.

Blend in remaining dry ingredients alternately with milk, beginning and ending with dry; beat well. Pour into two greased 8-inch (1.2 L) round pans. Bake in 375°F (190°C) oven for 30 minutes or until cake tester comes out clean. Let cool 5 minutes; turn out onto racks and cool completely.

Favorite frosting recipes during wartime used corn syrup or melted jelly instead of sugar.

**Quick Fluffy Frosting:** Beat 1 egg white to soft peaks; gradually beat in 1/2 cup (125 mL) boiling corn syrup to stiff peaks. Blend in 1/2 tsp (2 mL) vanilla. Frost cake at once.

If you were lucky enough to be at the grocery store when a case of sweetened condensed milk arrived, you could make a batch of Overseas Fudge, a caramel pudding made by heating the can in boiling water (not recommended today) or this **Magic Quick Chocolate Frosting:** In double boiler over boiling water or heavy saucepan over medium-low heat, combine 2 oz (60 g) unsweetened chocolate, 1-1/3 cups (325 mL) sweetened condensed milk and 1 tbsp (15 mL) water; cook, stirring often, for 10 minutes until thickened. Let cool.

# QUEEN ELIZABETH CAKE

*This date and nut cake always included a broiled topping.* **Lazy Daisy** *was a plain white cake with the same topping.*

| 1 cup | boiling water | 250 mL |
|---|---|---|
| 1 cup | chopped dates | 250 mL |
| 1 tsp | baking soda | 5 mL |
| 1/2 cup | butter | 125 mL |
| 1 cup | granulated sugar | 250 mL |
| 1 | egg | 1 |
| 1 tsp | vanilla | 5 mL |
| 1-1/2 cups | all-purpose flour | 375 mL |
| 1 tsp | baking powder | 5 mL |
| 1/2 tsp | salt | 2 mL |

Pour water over dates and soda; let stand until lukewarm. In bowl, cream butter with sugar; beat in egg and vanilla. Mix together flour, baking powder and salt; add to creamed mixture alternately with date mixture. Spread in greased and floured 9-inch (2.5 L) square cake pan. Bake in 350°F (180°C) oven for 40 minutes or until tester comes out clean.

**Broiled Topping:** In small heavy saucepan, combine 1/4 cup (50 mL) butter, 1/2 cup (125 mL) packed brown sugar, 1/4 cup (50 mL) light cream and 3/4 cup (175 mL) shredded coconut (half nuts if desired). Bring to boil, stirring; boil gently for 1 minute. Spread over warm baked cake; broil until bubbly and lightly browned, watching carefully.

Queen Elizabeth cakes have appeared in cook books coast to coast for many years. Some claim that the recipe was a favorite of the Queen Mother and given to worthy groups as a fund-raiser during World War II. One from Quebec's Eastern Townships includes a footnote that says: "This is not to be passed on but must be sold for charitable purposes for 15 cents."

In a reply to our query about the name of this recipe, the Queen Mother's Lady-in-Waiting writes: "I fear I have to tell you that, although we have known about this recipe for many years, it did not originate from either Buckingham Palace or Clarence House....However, as Her Majesty has always made it a rule, due to the number of requests received, never to give 'favourite recipes', I fear I have to tell you that should you wish to include this recipe in any cookbook it should only be called 'a date and walnut cake' with no reference to The Queen Mother."

# ICEBOX COOKIES

*Later called* **Refrigerator Cookies** *or* **Slice-and-Bake Cookies**, *this dough was the basis for many different kinds of cookies. Having this dough on hand was a novelty in the '40s and meant fresh home baking at a moment's notice.*

| 1/2 cup | butter | 125 mL |
|---|---|---|
| 1/2 cup | packed brown sugar | 125 mL |
| 1/2 tsp | vanilla | 2 mL |
| 1 | egg | 1 |
| 1-1/2 cups | all-purpose flour | 375 mL |
| 1-1/2 tsp | baking powder | 7 mL |
| 1/4 tsp | salt | 1 mL |

In bowl, cream butter with sugar until light; add vanilla and egg, mixing well. Combine flour, baking powder and salt; stir into creamed mixture. Shape into 2-inch (5 cm) diameter roll; wrap and chill thoroughly. Cut into 1/4-inch (5 mm) slices; place slightly apart on greased baking sheet. Bake in 400°F (200°C) oven for 5 to 8 minutes or until almost firm. Remove to rack. Makes about 4 dozen.

### VARIATIONS:

Divide dough into three parts; to each, add one of the following: 1 oz (30 g) unsweetened chocolate, grated; 1/4 cup (50 mL) finely chopped candied cherries; 1/4 cup (50 mL) chopped nuts.

Creative cooks impressed guests with pinwheels or striped cookies simply by combining doughs of different colors, or even square cookies.

**Pinwheel Cookies:** Divide dough in half. Add 2 oz (30 g) melted unsweetened chocolate to one half. Roll each portion into equal rectangles; place one on top of the other and roll up like jelly-roll. Chill, slice and bake as for Icebox Cookies.

**Ribbon Cookies:** Divide dough into thirds. Add 1/4 cup (50 mL) chopped maraschino cherries to one part; 2 tbsp (25 mL) each cocoa and nuts to second; 2 tsp (10 mL) grated orange rind to third. Flatten and pack in layers in waxed paper-lined 9- x 5-inch (2 L) loaf pan. Chill overnight; turn out and slice. Bake as for Icebox Cookies.

*There is no virtue in doing things the hard way....It's fun getting acquainted with the newest mixes, the fabulous instants, the ready-to-go canned and frozen foods. Our jet-age cooking would have astounded Grandma who, when she wanted gelatine, had to boil a pot of calves' feet for hours. Now we simply reach for a package. A package plus imagination adds up to food anyone can be proud of.*

– Muriel Wilson
*Colonist Cookbook (Victoria)*

They were the Boom Years, the Fat Fifties, a decade of mass media, mass buying, mass traffic jams. British dominance gave way to an ethnic mosaic, teens became a force to be reckoned with, and television ruled the waves.

Full employment, family allowances, unemployment insurance, unions, credit cards – happy days were here again. To those who had lived through the austerity of the Depression and the war years, the '50s represented unimagined security and prosperity.

Young marrieds wanted a family, a savings account and a house with a yard. The result was a mass exodus to the new suburbs. Here the stay-at-home moms – perky, shirtwaisted, aproned – nestled down in rows and crescents of tidy bungalows with picture windows, fenced yards and neat lawns. Life was safe, friendly and conformist. The new houses not only looked alike but ran alike, with new gadgets in the kitchens, a new barbecue on the patio and often a second car in the driveway. Nearby were schools, churches and fancy new shopping centres.

Suburban subdivisions sprouted almost overnight, as did planned communities, such as Don Mills in Toronto, which were designed as towns within towns, where people could live, work, play, shop and attend school and church all within walking distance. In the North,

industry created brand-new boom towns like Kitimat, Uranium City and Elliot Lake.

At the same time, rural areas were installing updated plumbing and electricity and modernizing kitchens. School buses on newly paved roads delivered kids to consolidated schools. Family farms were embracing scientific methods; agricultural colleges and experimental farms provided up-to-date information from seeding time to harvest.

Most urban households could manage comfortably on one salary – the husband's – and many wives left the workforce to stay at home. Happiness was a family – and a "baby bonus" cheque. The '50s baby boom produced more births than in any previous decade; by 1955, the Canadian population had increased by 40 per cent since the war, and one-third were under the age of 14.

Bringing up baby in the suburbs seemed the ideal scenario to many. Even those who moved to

---

*Stay-at-home moms were great cookie bakers.*

Courtesy of Dairy Farmers of Canada and Dairy Bureau of Canada

**It's a Date...**
WITH MILK AND COOKIES

*By Marie Fraser*
**DAIRY FOODS SERVICE BUREAU**
*A Division of Dairy Farmers of Canada*
*409 Huron Street, Toronto 5, Ontario*

**On pages 116 – 117:   Rec room buffet: Chips & Dip, Tuna Noodle Casserole, Golden Glow Salad, Lettuce with Thousand Island Dressing and Ambrosia-Filled Angel Cake.**

*"Media moms" were pert and stylish, and the object of countless recipe promotions.*

Toronto Star

the city from the farm, while missing the cheeriness of the old woodstove, enjoyed the streamlined sleekness of the new kitchens. Household science courses designed work-flow patterns in a "work triangle" (sink, stove, fridge) to save steps in the kitchen. Spic-and-span efficiency was the goal, with built-in cupboards, arborite countertops, vinyl tile floors, double sinks with garburetors, big fridges and freezers, stoves with pushbuttons and hoods with fans, the first wall ovens and dishwashers. Everyone had to have a new electric frying pan, kettle, waffle iron, blender and countertop mixer. Wrought-iron room dividers sprouted philodendrons and knickknacks; café curtains and wooden spice racks were added for a cosy touch.

Cooking in these kitchens still included the familiar old favorites from grandma's day, especially home baking, and at Christmas everyone automatically turned out the traditional fruitcakes, plum

puddings and a dozen kinds of cookies. But a new and stronger influence came from the myriad of new "convenience foods" appearing on store shelves and in magazine and TV ads. The "modern" housewife felt she had to try everything new and time-saving. Food companies jumped on the bandwagon with an avalanche of packaged mixes, dehydrated dinners, and canned and frozen foods (starting with frozen orange juice and progressing to a hundred varieties of TV dinner).

Many perceived needs were in fact created by lavish advertising. New product promotions convinced homemakers that the ultimate in culinary chic was producing four-layer cakes covered with fluffy frosting mix, glazing Klik or Prem with pineapple and calling it "Hawaiian," topping sweet potatoes with marshmallows and adding canned soup to every casserole. All kinds of recipes called "never-fail" beckoned irresistibly from food ads.

*The latest stoves were streamlined and built-in, with see-through oven windows and automatic timers.*

Courtesy of Chatelaine © Maclean Hunter Ltd

*Weekly grocery shopping in well-stocked supermarkets became a family affair.*

Malak/National Archives of Canada/#PA-145867

## LOOKING BACK

*From* The Morningside Papers *(1985) by Peter Gzowski.*

The time was the 1950s when, as you may remember, much of Canada was going through a culinary revolution, turning from overdone beef and boiled vegetables to at least an experimentation with lighter meats and seafood, crisper greens.

We lived . . . in a quarter of Toronto that was inexorably turning Italian . . . . We were learning to shop in the new places, sampling eggplant and zucchini, white veal, black olives, virgin oils, sculpted pastas.

And one day we saw snails. It was a Saturday. The snails were in a basket on a sidewalk stand. We bought two dollars' worth. . . . There were only two things different from the snails we had already courageously sampled in our restaurant adventures – escargots. For one thing, ours were smaller . . . for another, they were alive . . . .

Undaunted, we consulted our small shelf of cookbooks. In a paperback on French cooking, we found what we were looking for. The remainder of that Saturday and much of Sunday morning, we worked with painstaking care. . . .

Early Sunday afternoon one of Canada's most distinguished magazine writers arrived. . . . He smelled the snails. "What's that?" he said. We told him. "I've never had snails," he said. We offered him one, showed him how to spear it, still broiling hot, with a pin. He swallowed it, smiled, licked his lips, speared another. . . . He ate them all. All the snails. All the garlic, butter, parsley, wine. . . .

Later, I think, that same writer wrote one of the original series of memorable meals in *Maclean's*. He never mentioned our snails.

Probably the greatest influence on what we cooked, where we ate and when we ate it was television. Flickering only in black-and-white at first, this electronic marvel nonetheless revolutionized family life. Dining rooms almost disappeared; rec rooms, dens, living rooms – wherever the TV stood, that's where many families ate, TV tables at the ready. Alternatively, whole families moved to one side of the dining room table.

Mesmerized by U.S. television (if we lived within receiving distance) or by CBC productions such as "Wayne and Shuster," "Our Pet Juliette," "Front Page Challenge" or Wally Koster and Joyce Hahn on "The Hit Parade," we remained glued to the set even during food commercials. Thousands who drooled over Kraft's creations with Miracle Whip, Cheez Whiz and caramels remember the dulcet tones of announcer Bruce Marsh describing the lastest taste treat. It was a pleasant respite from cold Canadian winters.

Entertaining at home become much more casual. Outdoor barbecuing established Dad as steak-cooker and Mom as salad-maker and grill-scrubber. The family station wagon served up tailgate picnics and transported camping and cottage gear, as new expressways and longer paid vacations made travelling popular. In the winter, buffet parties and potluck suppers (often eaten in front of the TV during hockey playoffs or Grey Cup football games) replaced sit-down dinners. Informal cocktail parties served up chips-and-dips, cheese balls and meatballs on toothpicks.

Eating out went casual too, with drive-in service for burgers, pizza and soft ice cream. Pancake houses with voluminous menus, silver-dollar-sized portions for kids and "Swedish" pancakes with fruit syrups attracted whole families at all times of the day.

Meanwhile, still going strong were familiar restaurant chains like White Spot in Vancouver (since the late '20s), Salisbury House in

*Home-cooking moved outdoors as hamburgers, hot dogs and steaks were barbecued over charcoal.*

Courtesy of Best Foods Canada Inc. and Reynolds Aluminum Company of Canada

## LOOKING BACK

*Writer-broadcaster Helen Gougeon looks back at the role of food in women's lives.*

I remember our teenage parties at home. We rolled up thin slices of bread spread with canned mushroom soup and toasted them in the oven. We thought that was cooking. At 25, I moved to Montreal to be an editor at *Weekend* magazine where I was to write for women – in those days, that meant food, fashion and beauty.

In the '50s, canned soup was often the secret ingredient of a cherished recipe. I collected recipes for jellied concoctions and "candle salads" (a banana set like a candle in a slice of pineapple) on my cross-country trips to meet readers. My thickest file was labeled "Cookies and Squares." But I reveled in my "glamorous" job, picked up techniques from professional chefs, took cooking classes in France.

Later, living in suburbia with a husband and three children, food still dominated my life. I prided myself on not buying commercial bread and there were always bake sales or church suppers in need of a blueberry torte.

By the late '60s I was again writing a column and teaching groups of homemakers. We also talked about our lives and engaged in consciousness-raising. Some of us prepared a brief to the Royal Commission on the Status of Women and shook up some husbands.

But as long as I can remember, food was inextricably entwined with the prevailing attitudes about marriage and the home. Even when I began to pick up my career I didn't cut corners. I was trying to be the ideal woman of the TV sitcoms. Each night we would eat a three-course meal at the dining room table, which gave us time to talk. I've never regretted that tradition even though it was hard being superwoman.

Winnipeg (famous for their hamburger "nips" since 1931) and Fran's in Toronto (since 1940). Lunch counters in Woolworth's, Kresge's, and Eaton's and Simpson's basements were packed every noon hour.

Also, every small-town main street and city neighborhood had a favorite café or restaurant ("diner" was more an American term) where everyone hung out. It was a haven for teens after school, movies, dances and on Saturday afternoons, and a regular stop for taxi drivers, shopkeepers on coffee breaks and whole families on Sundays. Most had booths or tables as well as a lunch counter; some were truck stops with cute names like the Dew Drop Inn or Edna's Place. They all had soda fountains and jukeboxes but otherwise were an extension of the home kitchen, serving up blue-plate specials (meat loaf with gravy, roast turkey, chicken à la king), hot beef sandwiches (always on

white bread with gravy, mashed potatoes and canned peas) and homemade desserts (apple pie, chocolate cake, rice pudding) along with short-order classics (soups, burgers, grilled cheese and club house sandwiches) and a long list of soda fountain treats

Many of these restaurants were owner-operated, with the whole family working in the kitchen and living upstairs, often the first enterprise of immigrants The chefs may have been Greek in the East or Chinese on the Prairies, but their menus were all the same, except for one or two special dishes from the home country. Any other deviation from the standard fare was regional, such as fish cakes or chowder in the Maritimes, cabbage rolls or perogies in Winnipeg.

Affluence and babysitters afforded more opportunity to eat out, but special-occasion restaurant choices, even in big cities, were often limited to formal

*"Mrs. A." dispensed recipe ideas and household hints on radio and in print.*

From THE KATE AITKEN COOKBOOK by Kate Aitken. Copyright © 1950 by Kate Aitken. Published by Wm. Collins & Co. Ltd.

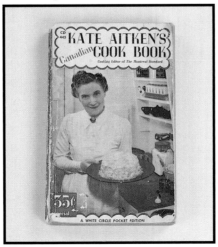

*Baking competitions remained popular at district fairs across Canada.*

Courtesy of The Yorkton Exhibition, Yorkton, Saskatchewan

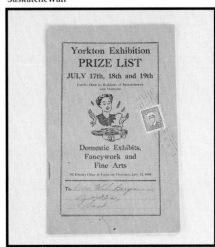

## NUTRITION

- 1950: Canada developed own Dietary Standard outlining daily nutrient requirements for calories, protein, calcium, thiamine, riboflavin, niacin and vitamin A. Before this, Canada had adopted American recommended allowances.

- 1952: Enrichment of flour allowed as direct result of Newfoundland joining Dominion. The new province, which had been using enriched flour for some time, made its continued use a condition of joining Confederation.

- 1952: Debate began about fluoridation of water to promote dental health.

- 1953: Food and Drugs Act of 1920 amended; act remains essentially same today.

- Focus of nutritionists to improve health in vulnerable populations: expectant mothers, infants, preschoolers, mothers, schoolchildren and convalescents.

- In early '50s, nutrition education encouraged in schools; for example, rat-feeding experiments popular to compare health effects of diet of white bread, cake and candy with one based on *Canada's Food Rules*.

- By 1953, vitamin A added to margarine, vitamin D to milk.

- Obesity new health problem. Dietitians warned against fad diets such as "seven-day diet" and "milk and banana diet."

- Emerging trends:
  - Idea of balance in diet.
  - Weight control (prevention) rather than weight reduction.
  - Sugar blamed for bad teeth.
  - Recognition that heart disease related to diet.
  - Concern about increasing use of food additives.

hotel dining rooms (serving English-style roast beef just like at home), steak houses (an American import) or Chinatown. But changes in archaic provincial liquor laws in the '50s brought a big increase in dining out (and improvement in food quality). Except in Montreal, which always had a lively night life, drinking had been restricted to private clubs, beer parlours or under-the-table brown bagging in supper clubs all across Canada. Vancouverites remember the advent of cocktail bars and licensed restaurants in 1952 as a pivotal event. The adventurous now ordered wine (though never on Sunday) with dinner at the Sylvia Hotel or the Georgia's Cavalier Grill. Some people even started serving a little wine (remember rosé?) with meals at home.

Canadians also began to discover the charms of spaghetti-and-Chianti dinners in romantic little cafés with red-checkered tablecloths. A new interest in "foreign" food was one of the major trends revolutionizing our tastes in the '50s. For one thing, jet travel was creating a demand for the flavors of other cultures, as tourists returning from the café tables of France or Italy started searching out the same dishes in restaurants here. Better transportation systems also brought to our supermarkets more out-of-season and exotic products (such as fresh pineapples, avocados and artichokes) from faraway places.

At the same time, a massive new wave of immigration was making a significant change in the country's demographics. More than 1.5 million newcomers – mostly from Hungary, southern Italy, Poland, Ukraine, Germany and Holland – came to Canada during the decade, and for the first time the proportion of Canadians of British origin declined to less than 50 per cent of the population.

Multicultural food styles would eventually find their way into all Canadian kitchens but at first were most apparent in city neighborhoods. Toronto's Italian community numbered nearly 150,000 by the

*New products and new appliances attracted women to local cooking demonstrations. This one, sponsored in 1954 by Robin Hood Flour and Inglis gas ranges, was held in a church hall in Toronto.*

Consumers Gas Archives

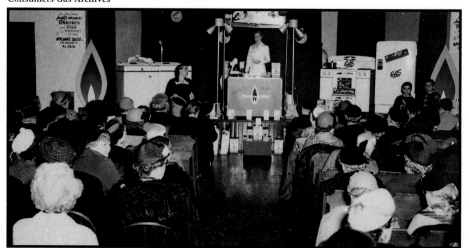

end of the decade, and the west end blossomed with outdoor cafés, cappuccino bars, cheese shops and baskets of bright red tomatoes on the sidewalk.

Longer-established ethnic groups began to acknowledge their own distinct contributions to the culinary history of Canada. The first cookbooks that truly reflected regional traditions were a revelation to the food media and quickly became best-sellers. *Dutch Oven*, a cookbook of traditional recipes compiled by the Ladies Auxiliary of the Lunenburg, Nova Scotia, Hospital Society in 1953, marked the 200th anniversary of the landing of the first German settlers.

*From Saskatchewan Homemakers' Kitchens*, put together by the Homemakers' Clubs in 1955 to honor the province's Golden Jubilee, had an account of "The Rural Home" from 1912 to the '50s. *Traditional Ukrainian Cookery* (1957) by Savella Stechishin was the first complete collection of authentic Ukrainian-Canadian recipes. The British Columbia

Women's Institutes' *Centennial of B.C. Cookbook* (1958) was filled with the history and food styles of every region, from sourdough days in Barkerville to Doukhobor cooking in the Kootenays.

Women from the Atlantic to the Pacific were busy fund-raising with cookbooks, teas, bake sales, canasta or euchre parties and bridge luncheons; many people felt sorry for women who "had to work" at jobs outside the home. Women's groups were expected to cater church suppers and weddings, and their daughters were expected to help. "We learned by osmosis," says Ontario home economist Evelyn Hullah, remembering how girls just seemed to pick up the skills of cooking, serving and cleaning up.

But for most Canadian teenagers in the '50s, life was much easier than it had been for their parents. Raised in an era of greater affluence, staying in school instead of going to work, they became the first generation in history to form a separate "teen" subculture between child-

*Instant puddings and other mixes marked the beginning of the convenience food era.*

Courtesy of Kraft General Foods Canada Inc.

*Test kitchens provided recipes galore for home baking.*

Courtesy of Dairy Farmers of Canada and Dairy Bureau of Canada

hood and adulthood. Pony-tailed girls in calf-length full skirts went steady with guys in strides or drapes, leather jackets, brush cuts or ducktail haircuts. They jived at sock hops in school gyms and platter parties in rec rooms, bought Hit Parade 45s and new LPs, turned on to rock'n'roll and Elvis. A few rebelled à la James Dean and Natalie Wood, but most conformed to established social codes and gender roles just as their parents were doing.

For young women graduating from high school in the '50s, career choices were slowly expanding. Some entered engineering, but more became stewardesses or secretaries (often to support a husband through college); most headed into the traditional fields of nursing, teaching and home economics.

"Home Ec" graduates, however, found themselves entering a new era of job opportunities beyond the expected dietetics and teaching. With so much focus on new products, food and appli-

ance companies were expanding their test kitchens and home service departments. Many home economists became well-known by their pseudonyms on packages and recipe books: "Betty Crocker" at General Mills, "Martha Logan" at Swift Canadian, "Brenda York" at Canada Packers, "Anna Lee Scott" at Maple Leaf Milling, "Rita Martin" at Robin Hood. Provincial utility companies personalized their messages with names like "Betty Bright" at Consumer's Gas and "Penny Power" at SaskPower. Food producers' associations also began hiring home economists for promotion: Jean Fewster became "Marie Fraser" for the Dairy Foods Service Bureau; Dorothy Batchellor-McKinnon did national promotion for the Poultry Products Institute.

Many food companies sent their home economists across the country conducting cooking classes in town halls and church basements. Provincial depart-

ments of agriculture employed large numbers of extension workers who travelled the countryside giving food and nutrition courses for 4H clubs and Women's Institutes. The WI was still going strong across Canada, with new branches starting in the Northwest Territories and the Yukon in 1956.

Cooking schools attracted large crowds in the cities, too. At the Canadian National Exhibition in Toronto, the Kitchen Theatre presented a steady diet of demonstrations, and the Food Building offered enough free samples to make a meal. At large exhibitions and smaller fairs coast to coast, traditional baking competitions still attracted large numbers of entries. At the Maritime Winter Fair in 1950, the newly established Women's Work division upstaged the livestock show by exhibiting a model farm kitchen and utility room.

Rural women's lives were changing, too; gone were the huge meals for threshing crews

*Baking contests sponsored by major food and appliance companies attracted thousands of entries.*

Courtesy of Maple Leaf Foods

*Bread baking remained popular as quicker methods streamlined the process.*

Courtesy of Robin Hood Multifoods Inc.

as self-propelled combines became common. Dinnertime began to switch from noon to evening as it had for commuters in city suburbs. Cooking became a little lighter and less traditional. In 1951, Emmie Oddie's popular column, "I'd Like to Know," in the *Western Producer* still included old favorites like Christmas cakes and peppermint candy (made with mashed potato) but readers were also requesting recipes for Fig Bars ("like we buy in the store") and homemade Chow Mein.

Rural kitchens reflected the same influences affecting city cooks, such as the new interest in "foreign food." "It was considered very avant-garde to make spaghetti with your own homemade Italian sauce," says Toronto home economist Margaret Howard. "It was our first brush with ethnic cuisine. But we also loved tuna casserole made with mushroom soup and crushed potato chips on top; we even served it to company. Then we filled angel food cake, made from

a mix, with lemon pie filling and whipped topping mix. It was such a switch from the '40s food we had grown up on – roasts, heavy meat dishes, overcooked salmon steaks."

We were still overcooking fish in the early '50s, but by 1958 the federal Department of Fisheries' "Canadian Rule for Fish" (baking in a hot oven 10 minutes per inch of thickness) was being adopted by culinary experts all over the continent.

People were also discovering calories and dieting began to be fashionable, though certainly not to the extremes that came later. Salads of all kinds had become much more popular, but no one hesitated over an extra spoonful of creamy dressing.

The 1959 issues of *Chatelaine* brought a popular lineup of food articles: "101 Recipes from Brand-name Products"; "A Summer Party" (Watermelon Basket, Rotisserie Wieners, Can-opener Casserole); "Food Fit For a Queen" (in honor of the opening of the St. Lawrence Seaway);

and "Fun Fare for the Rumpus Room" (Deckered Sandwiches, Hi-Fi Punch and Howdy Doodies).

The carefree attitudes of the '50s extended to university campuses, where students enrolled without much competition, had a wide choice of job offers after graduation, and in between partied at frat houses and football weekends.

But by the end of the decade, the capers were wearing a bit thin. Attention shifted to new scientific technology and a more serious world of space satellites, nuclear missiles and an increasingly chilly Cold War. Civil defense programs across Canada taught schoolchildren about fallout shelters. In 1958, the Department of Health and Welfare even issued a booklet, "Your Evacuation Pack," about stocking emergency food supplies.

All this led to a reassessment of the status quo and the first glimmers of protest. The happy-days '50s were about to become the rebellious '60s.

---

*The average Canadian ate little fish except on Fridays and during Lent.*

Courtesy of Fisheries and Oceans Canada

*A can of soup was often the key ingredient in '50s recipes.*

Courtesy of Campbell Soup Company Ltd.

*Kraft creations were among the first TV commercials to entrance Canadian viewers.*

Courtesy of Kraft General Foods Canada Inc.

# Cookbook Sampler

## THE FIFTIES

For more cookbooks of the decade, see Bibliography pp. 234-235.

# THREE-WAY CHEESE SPREAD

*This basic cheese mixture yields three shapes and flavors to serve with crackers.*

| | | |
|---|---|---|
| 4 cups | shredded old Cheddar cheese | 1 L |
| 3/4 lb | cream cheese | 375 g |
| 2 tbsp | milk | 25 mL |
| 2 tsp | horseradish | 10 mL |
| 1 tsp | Worcestershire sauce | 5 mL |
| 1 tbsp | caraway seeds | 15 mL |
| 1/4 cup | chopped dried prunes | 50 mL |
| 2 tbsp | chopped nuts | 25 mL |
| 2 tbsp | sweet pickle relish | 25 mL |
| 1/2 cup | chopped fresh parsley | 125 mL |

Blend together Cheddar, cream cheese and milk; divide into three portions. To one portion, add horseradish and Worcestershire sauce. Shape into 1-inch (2.5 cm) diameter roll; roll in caraway seeds.

To second portion, add prunes and nuts. Shape into 1-inch (2.5 cm) square log. To third portion, add relish. Shape into 1-inch (2.5 cm) triangular-shaped log; coat with parsley.

Wrap and refrigerate logs until 30 minutes before serving. Makes 3 logs.

The '50s was the era of Lipton's Onion Soup dip, Nuts and Bolts and fancy appetizers for casual home parties. Cream cheese was indispensable. Tiny balls of it were rolled in finely chopped nuts or parsley, or it was wrapped around nuts or olives. Celery was filled with cream cheese or crab salad, slices of bologna were sandwiched with cream cheese and cut into wedges to serve on toothpicks. Tomato roses (tomatoes with cream cheese petals) effectively centred the appetizer tray.

**Cheese Balls** were mixtures of two or three kinds of cheese (for Christmas parties, almond-studded and shaped into a pine cone) served with assorted crackers, thin rye bread or melba toast. *Chatelaine's* "401 Tested Recipes" (1956) suggests stuffed dried fruit, nut balls and "Cheese Dunk 1 and 2."

Many recipes recommended cutting a pineapple in half and studding each half with cheese balls on toothpicks.

# SWEET AND SOUR PORK

*Serve over hot fluffy rice and pass extra soy sauce. Toasted almonds or cashews add a special touch.*

| | | |
|---|---|---|
| 1 lb | cubed lean boneless pork | 500 g |
| 2 tbsp | vegetable oil | 25 mL |
| 1 | clove garlic, chopped | 1 |
| 1 | small onion, chopped | 1 |
| 2/3 cup | sliced celery | 150 mL |
| 1 | sweet green pepper, cut in strips | 1 |
| 1 | can (14 oz/398 mL) pineapple chunks | 1 |
| 2 tbsp | cornstarch | 25 mL |
| 1/3 cup | granulated or packed brown sugar | 75 mL |
| 1/3 cup | vinegar | 75 mL |
| 2 tbsp | soy sauce | 25 mL |

Lightly brown pork in oil. Add garlic, onion, celery and green pepper; stir-fry until tender-crisp, about 3 minutes. Remove and keep warm.

Drain pineapple, reserving liquid in measure; add enough water to make 2/3 cup (150 mL). Blend in cornstarch, sugar and vinegar; pour into pan. Cook, stirring, until smooth and thickened; stir in soy sauce. Add pork mixture and pineapple; simmer 5 to 10 minutes or until heated through. Makes 4 servings.

Pretending to be very good at cooking international fare, we made things like **Polynesian Chicken** with coconut, or **Hawaiian Shrimp** with pineapple. Canadians were eating North American versions of Chinese food in restaurants from coast to coast. A sweet and sour dish, whether pork or chicken, was one of the first ventures into Oriental cooking at home. Chicken strips or cubes, or meatballs, in a similar sauce were also popular.

# Spaghetti Sauce with Meat

*For a meatless version simply omit beef. For a mushroom sauce, cook sliced mushrooms along with the onion.*

| | | |
|---|---|---|
| 2 tbsp | vegetable oil | 25 mL |
| 1 cup | chopped onion | 250 mL |
| 2 | cloves garlic, minced | 2 |
| 1 lb | ground beef | 500 g |
| 1 | can (28 oz/796 mL) plum tomatoes (undrained) | 1 |
| 1 | can (7-1/2 oz/213 mL) tomato sauce | 1 |
| 1 | can (5-1/2 oz/156 mL) tomato paste | 1 |
| 1-1/2 cups | water | 375 mL |
| 1 tsp | each salt, dried oregano and basil | 5 mL |
| 1/2 tsp | each pepper and dried thyme | 2 mL |
| 1 | bay leaf | 1 |
| 2 tbsp | grated Parmesan | 25 mL |

In large heavy saucepan, heat oil over medium heat; cook onion and garlic just until soft. Add meat and cook, stirring to break up, until no longer pink.

Add tomatoes, crushing to break up, tomato sauce, tomato paste, water, salt, oregano, basil, pepper, thyme and bay leaf; bring to boil, stirring. Reduce heat and simmer, uncovered and stirring occasionally, for 1 hour or until thickened. Remove bay leaf. Stir in Parmesan, adding more to taste. Makes about 5 cups (1.25 L).

## VARIATION:

**Spaghetti and Meatballs:** Omit beef in sauce. For meatballs, combine 1 lb (500 g) ground beef (or half beef, half pork), 1/2 cup (125 mL) fine fresh bread crumbs, 1 egg, 1 small onion and 1 clove garlic, minced, and 1/4 tsp (1 mL) each salt and pepper. Shape into small balls; brown in oil in skillet. Cook meatballs in sauce for 30 minutes.

Through the late '50s and the '60s, a big pot of spaghetti sauce was a reliable standby in many kitchens, especially for those on tight budgets. A lot of young singles and college couples (many with the wife supporting a husband through school, or at home with a baby or two) perfected their favorite sauces and exchanged recipes over red-checkered tablecloths and candles stuck in Chianti wine bottles.

Most sauces were based on canned tomatoes, and many called for a spoonful of sugar or honey to cut acidity. Others used a combination of tomatoes, tomato paste and tomato sauce for a balanced taste, because plum tomatoes were not readily available then and regular tomatoes took a long time to cook down.

# Oven-Barbecued Ribs

*In place of spareribs, chicken pieces can be used.*

| | | |
|---|---|---|
| 2 lb | spareribs | 1 kg |
| 1 | onion, chopped | 1 |
| 1/2 cup | ketchup | 125 mL |
| 1/2 cup | tomato juice | 125 mL |
| 1/4 cup | vinegar | 50 mL |
| 2 tbsp | brown sugar | 25 mL |
| 1 tsp | salt | 5 mL |
| 2 tsp | Worcestershire sauce | 10 mL |
| 1/2 tsp | each dry mustard and chili powder | 2 mL |
| 1/4 tsp | hot pepper sauce | 1 mL |

Cut spareribs into two-rib portions. Bake in single layer in baking dish in 350°F (180°C) oven, covered, for 30 minutes. Drain off excess fat.

Combine onion, ketchup, tomato juice, vinegar, sugar, salt, Worcestershire sauce, mustard, chili powder and hot pepper sauce; pour over ribs. Cover and bake for 30 minutes. Turn ribs and baste; bake, uncovered, for 30 minutes. Makes about 4 servings.

Toward the end of the '50s, outdoor barbecuing was a constant summer feature in suburban backyards. In winter, "oven-barbecuing" took its place, using the flavors of barbecue sauces.

To barbecue these spareribs outdoors: After baking or simmering them in water for 30 minutes, grill over medium-hot coals (or medium setting on a gas barbecue), brushing with sauce, for 10 to 20 minutes or until coated but not charred.

# CHILI CON CARNE

*Chili was a regular dish served at home as well as at the speedy lunch counters or cafés of the '50s. Chili Con Carne was usually served with toast. The same mixture (without the beans) served over hamburger buns became **Sloppy Joes**. With the addition of rice, similar mixtures were used for **Stuffed Green Peppers** and for meatballs cooked in tomato sauce, called **Porcupines**.*

| | | |
|---|---|---|
| 1 tbsp | vegetable oil | 15 mL |
| 1 | large onion, chopped | 1 |
| 1 | clove garlic, minced | 1 |
| 1 | small sweet green pepper, chopped | 1 |
| 1 lb | lean ground beef | 500 g |
| 2 | cans (each 14 oz/ 398 mL) kidney beans (undrained) | 2 |
| 1 | can (28 oz/796 mL) tomatoes | 1 |
| 1 | can (7-1/2 oz/213 mL) tomato sauce | 1 |
| 1 tbsp | (approx) chili powder | 15 mL |
| 1 tsp | salt | 5 mL |

In large saucepan, heat oil over medium-high heat; sauté onion, garlic and green pepper for 5 minutes or until softened. Remove and set aside. Add beef to pan and cook, breaking up meat, just until no longer pink; drain off fat.

Add kidney beans, tomatoes, tomato sauce, chili powder, salt and reserved vegetables; bring to boil. Reduce heat and simmer, covered, for 1 hour or until thickened. Season with more chili powder to taste. Makes about 8 servings.

**Stuffed Green Peppers:** Cook chili mixture, omitting green pepper, until meat is browned, draining off fat. Add 1 cup (250 mL) cooked rice and one-half of a 14 oz (398 mL) can tomato sauce. Season with salt and pepper to taste, mixing well.

Cut stem end from 6 green peppers; remove seeds and membranes. Cook peppers in boiling water for 5 minutes; drain. Stand peppers in ungreased baking dish. Lightly stuff peppers with meat mixture. Pour remaining tomato sauce over peppers. Cover; bake in 350°F (180°C) oven for 45 minutes. Uncover and bake 10 minutes longer. Makes 6 servings.

# Meat Loaf

*Rolled oats give a coarse texture; slightly dry bread crumbs make a denser meat loaf. Use all beef or half ground beef and half ground pork. Some stores sell meat loaf mixtures.*

| 1-1/2 lb | ground beef | 750 g |
|---|---|---|
| 3/4 cup | rolled oats | 175 mL |
| 1/2 cup | milk | 125 mL |
| 3/4 cup | chopped onion | 175 mL |
| 1 tsp | salt | 5 mL |
| 1/2 tsp | pepper | 2 mL |
| 1/2 tsp | dried savory (optional) | 2 mL |
| 1 | egg, lightly beaten | 1 |

Mix together beef, rolled oats, milk, onion, salt, pepper, savory (if using)

and egg. Pack into 8- x 4- inch (1.5 L) loaf pan. Bake in 350°F (180°C) oven for 1 hour or until juices run clear. Drain off fat. Makes 4 to 6 servings.

### VARIATIONS:

**Glazed:** Bake for 45 minutes. Spread mixture of 1/3 cup (75 mL) ketchup and 2 tbsp (25 mL) brown sugar over top. Bake for 15 minutes.
**Italian:** Add 1/3 cup (75 mL) chopped sweet green pepper, 1 clove garlic, minced, and 1/2 tsp (2 mL) each dried oregano and basil. Use tomato sauce in place of milk. When baked, top with mozzarella cheese slices and let stand until melted.
**Tex-Mex:** Add 1/4 cup (50 mL) chopped sweet pepper, 1 to 2 tbsp (15 to 25 mL) chopped jalapeño peppers and 2 tbsp (25 mL) chopped fresh cilantro.

Meat Loaf has been around as long as there has been ground beef. Comfort food for many over the years, new and old versions are still popular. There are people who associate meat loaf with army, boarding school or Depression-era cooking, when there was little else and meat loaf could be so easily extended to feed many mouths. To this day, they don't know that meat loaf can be delicious.

# Roast Wild Duck / Wild Fruit Jelly

*Tart jellies or fruit sauces were popular accompaniments to meats, especially wild birds and game.*

### ROAST WILD DUCK:
Thoroughly wash prepared bird; pat dry. Stuff with a seasoned bread stuffing if desired, or simply stuff with quartered onions; skewer shut. Cover breast with bacon strips. Roast, breast side up, on rack in shallow roasting pan in 350°F (180°C) oven for 1 hour and 15 minutes or until juices run clear.

### WILD FRUIT JELLY:
Cover fruit with water and simmer until fruit is softened. Transfer to dampened cheesecloth-lined colander. Let drip overnight. Measure extracted juice.

For pin cherries, chokecherries and blackberries, add 1 cup (250 mL) gran-

ulated sugar for each 1 cup (250 mL) juice. For cranberries, crabapples or grapes, add 2/3 cup (150 mL) sugar for each 1 cup (250 mL) juice.

In heavy stainless steel or enamel saucepan, combine juice and sugar. Bring to boil, stirring until sugar dissolves; boil vigorously until jelly setting point of 218° to 220°F (103° to 104°C), or until jelly sheets (cold metal spoon dipped in boiling jelly and held above the pot has 2 side-by-side drops that come together). Remove from heat and skim off foam. Pour into sterilized jars and seal.

Note: Manufacturers of commercial preserving jars and pectin offer recipe booklets designed to help you successfully preserve berries and other fruit. You'll also find standard tests for pectin in fruit to determine if fruit will jell.

Prairie autumn meant hunting season, and wild birds such as duck and prairie chicken abounded. Newfoundlanders and northerners relished partridge, turrs and wild geese. Ontarians savored wild grouse and pheasant.

To serve with these flavorful birds, each region had special jellies. Pin cherries, saskatoon berries or chokecherries were favorites on the Prairies; partridgeberries (redberries), and bakeapples in Newfoundland and Labrador were often submerged in water to store all winter, along with sealers (jars) of jams and jellies. Highbush and low-bush cranberries and wild blueberries grew in many regions. Wild grapes made a tangy jelly, but as they disappeared in time, Concord grapes took their place.

# Seafood Coquilles

*Chicken stock may be used in place of white wine. If scallop shells are unavailable, bake in a shallow buttered casserole for 20 to 30 minutes until bubbly.*

| | | |
|---|---|---|
| 1 lb | scallops | 500 g |
| 1/2 cup | dry white wine | 125 mL |
| 1/2 cup | water | 125 mL |
| 1/4 cup | finely chopped onion | 50 mL |
| 1 cup | sliced mushrooms | 250 mL |
| 1/4 cup | butter | 50 mL |
| 1/4 cup | all-purpose flour | 50 mL |
| 1 cup | light cream | 250 mL |
| | Salt and pepper | |
| 1 cup | soft bread crumbs | 250 mL |
| 1/4 cup | grated Parmesan cheese | 50 mL |
| 2 tbsp | butter, melted | 25 mL |

Cut scallops in halves, or quarters if large; simmer in saucepan with wine and water for 2 minutes or until barely opaque. Drain and reserve liquid.

In heavy saucepan, cook onion and mushrooms in butter just until softened. Stir in flour; cook until bubbly. Stir in cream and reserved liquid; cook until thickened. Add salt and pepper to taste. Add scallops; spoon into scallop shells on baking sheet.

Combine crumbs, Parmesan and butter; sprinkle on top. Bake in 400°F (200°C) oven for 10 to 15 minutes until lightly browned. Makes 4 to 6 servings.

Fish and seafood were always important in the diet of Canadians on both coasts, where fresh fish was always available. In other regions, frozen fish was the closest a lot of people came to good fish. Canada's Department of Fisheries promoted the use of fish with all kinds of booklets, full of recipes created in their test kitchens. New recipes from one of their booklets for the '50s included **Crispy Baked Fillets** (with Corn Flake crumbs), Fillets Florentine and Seafood Soufflé. Nevertheless, for many Canadians, fish was still reserved for Friday and Lent.

**Scallop Bubbly Bake** from the same recipe booklet was similar to coquilles, but the scallops were not cooked first, simply thawed if frozen. One cup (250 mL) chopped celery was cooked with the onion and mushrooms, and milk replaced the cream. Placed in a buttered casserole, it was baked in a 375°F (190°C) oven 20 minutes.

# Tuna Noodle Casserole

*The quintessential '50s dish, this was called Perfect Tuna Casserole, Tuna Fantasy or Hong Kong Casserole. A recipe for **Salmon Almond Casserole Deluxe** was a salmon version of this tuna casserole.*

| | | |
|---|---|---|
| 1 | can (7.5 oz/213 g) tuna, drained | 1 |
| 1 | can (10 oz/284 mL) mushroom soup | 1 |
| 1/4 cup | milk | 50 mL |
| 1 cup | sliced celery | 250 mL |
| 1/4 cup | chopped green onion | 50 mL |
| 1 cup | chow mein noodles | 250 mL |
| 1/2 cup | chopped toasted almonds or crushed potato chips | 125 mL |

Mix together tuna, soup, milk, celery, onion and noodles. Spoon into greased 6-cup (1.5 L) casserole. Top with almonds. Bake in 350°F (180°C) oven for 45 minutes or until toasted on top and heated through. Makes 4 servings.

### VARIATIONS:

**Crunchy Mock Chicken:** Use chicken soup instead of mushroom.
**Salmon Noodle Casserole:** Use celery soup instead of mushroom, and salmon instead of tuna.
**Lobster Mushroom:** Use canned lobster instead of tuna.

Everyone over the age of 30 has eaten this casserole of canned tuna, mushroom soup, noodles and nuts or potato chips at some time or other. A similar recipe-contest winner was named **Pick-up-sticks Casserole** after the popular game of that decade.

Casseroles with even a hint of Oriental flavor were often labelled Chinese, Oriental, Hong Kong and Far East. As long as soy sauce, chow mein noodles, canned bamboo shoots or water chestnuts were ingredients, the recipe qualified.

Slightly more elegant, but still using the miracle of cans, was **Seafood Mull:** onions, garlic and celery sautéed with bacon, then mixed with tomatoes and a can each of shrimp, crabmeat and lobster. Just before serving, butter and sherry were added. All was served over rice or noodles.

# SALMON MOUSSE

*This mousse, often made in a fish-shaped mould, is similar to one in a '50s booklet put together by the Calgary Wesley United Church Women's Association. Typical of dozens of group fund-raisers, the loose-leaf booklet is hand-typed with an oilcloth cover. Serve slices of this mousse on greens.*

| | | |
|---|---|---|
| 1 | envelope unflavored gelatin | 1 |
| 2 tbsp | cold water | 25 mL |
| 1-1/2 tsp | all-purpose flour | 7 mL |
| 1/2 tsp | salt | 2 mL |
| Pinch | cayenne pepper | Pinch |
| 2 | egg yolks | 2 |
| 3/4 cup | milk | 175 mL |
| 1/4 cup | vinegar | 50 mL |
| 4 tsp | butter, melted | 20 mL |
| 1-1/2 cups | flaked cooked salmon (2 cans 7.5 oz/213 g each) | 375 mL |
| 1/2 cup | whipping cream, whipped | 125 mL |

Sprinkle gelatin into cold water; let stand to soften. In top of double boiler over boiling water, combine flour, salt, cayenne, egg yolks and milk; cook, stirring, until thickened. Add vinegar; cook until thickened again. Add butter. Add gelatin, stirring until dissolved. Stir in salmon; let cool until slightly thickened. Fold in whipped cream. Turn into 4-cup (1 L) mould; chill thoroughly. Makes 8 servings.

---

### VARIATIONS:

**Chicken Mousse:** Substitute 1-1/2 cups (375 mL) cubed cooked chicken for salmon.

**Ham Mousse:** Substitute 1-1/2 cups (375 mL) finely diced ham for salmon.

In the '50s, everything was jellied – chicken, ham, tuna, vegetables or fruit – and the simplest way was with a package of lemon jelly powder. A little lemon juice or vinegar masked the sweetness, tomato juice turned it into tomato aspic, and it was simple and fast.

Adding chopped vegetables and fruit led to endless variations.

**Sunshine** (or **Golden Glow**) **Salad** was orange jelly with grated carrots and crushed pineapple. Another popular one was **Emerald Ribbon Salad**, a lime two-tone salad flavored with mayonnaise or cream cheese, which was clear on the bottom (sometimes containing fruit or vegetables) and creamy on top.

# THOUSAND ISLAND BLENDER DRESSING

*Blenders were to the '50s what food processors were to the '80s. To be able to whip up an unusual dressing, even just to top the familiar wedge of iceberg lettuce, was a step forward. Other pourable dressings, like French, Italian and Russian, were served in restaurants and duplicated at home.*

| | | |
|---|---|---|
| 1 cup | mayonnaise | 250 mL |
| 1/4 cup | chili sauce | 50 mL |
| 1 | small sweet green pepper, cut in chunks | 1 |
| 1 | clove garlic | 1 |
| 8 | stuffed olives | 8 |
| 2 | hard-cooked eggs, quartered | 2 |
| 2 | sprigs fresh parsley | 2 |
| 2 tbsp | chopped dill pickles | 25 mL |
| 2 tsp | chopped fresh chives | 10 mL |
| 1 tsp | Worcestershire sauce | 5 mL |
| | Milk or cream | |

In blender, combine mayonnaise, chili sauce, green pepper, garlic, olives, eggs, parsley, pickles, chives and Worcestershire sauce; whirl at high speed until coarsely chopped. Thin with a little milk, if necessary. Makes about 2 cups (500 mL).

**Blender Mayonnaise:** In blender, combine 1 egg or 2 egg yolks, 1 tsp (5 mL) Dijon mustard, 1/2 tsp (2 mL) salt and 1 tbsp (15 mL) vinegar or lemon juice. Measure 1 cup (250 mL) vegetable oil; add 2 tbsp (25 mL) of this oil to blender; blend for 30 seconds. With blender still running, slowly drizzle remaining oil into mixture until all the oil is used and mixture is thick. Taste and adjust seasoning. Makes 1 cup (250 mL).

# EVERLASTING COLESLAW

*A make-ahead salad, this was popular for large parties, to carry to potluck suppers or just to keep on hand in summer or winter.*

| | | |
|---|---|---|
| 8 cups | shredded cabbage | 2 L |
| 1/2 cup | chopped celery | 125 mL |
| 1/2 cup | chopped Spanish onion | 125 mL |
| 1 | small green or red pepper, slivered (optional) | 1 |
| 2 | carrots, grated | 2 |
| 1/2 | white vinegar | 125 mL |
| 1/4 cup | vegetable oil | 50 mL |
| 1/3 cup | granulated sugar | 75 mL |
| 1 tsp | celery seeds | 5 mL |
| 1 tsp | salt | 5 mL |
| 1/2 tsp | dry mustard | 2 mL |
| 1/4 tsp | pepper | 1 mL |

Toss together cabbage, celery, onion, green or red pepper and carrots. In small saucepan combine vinegar, oil, sugar, celery seeds, salt, mustard and pepper. Bring to boil, stirring until sugar dissolves. Pour over cabbage mixture; stir to mix well. Cover and chill. Keeps up to 1 week in refrigerator. Makes about 12 servings.

**Cabbage Salad:** Toss shredded cabbage (green, Savoy or red, or a mixture of red and green) with enough salad dressing or mayonnaise to coat; season to taste with salt and pepper. Add one or two of the following: diced unpeeled red or green apple, coarsely grated carrot, raisins, chopped walnuts, chopped sweet green or red pepper, chopped Bermuda-type onions, or caraway seeds, if desired.

# SWEDISH TEA RING

*Impressive but easy to make, this fancy bread always produced "ohs" and "ahs" from audiences at baking demonstrations. Use the basic recipe for Rich Sweet Dough; half of the dough (one ball) makes one Swedish Tea Ring.*

| | | |
|---|---|---|
| 1 | ball Rich Sweet Dough (recipe, p. 111) | 1 |
| 2 tbsp | butter, melted | 25 mL |
| 1/2 cup | brown sugar | 125 mL |
| 1 tsp | cinnamon | 5 mL |
| 1/2 cup | raisins | 125 mL |
| | **Melted butter** | |
| | **White icing (optional)** | |

Roll dough to 12- x 9-inch (30 x 23 cm) rectangle. Brush with butter. Mix together brown sugar, cinnamon and raisins; sprinkle over dough. Roll up from long side; seal edge. Place seam-side down on greased baking sheet. Form into ring and seal ends together. Cut ring into 1-inch (2.5 cm) slices, almost through to centre. Twist each slice slightly onto its side. Brush lightly with melted butter. Cover and let rise until doubled, about 45 minutes.

Bake in 375°F (190°C) oven for 25 to 30 minutes or until golden brown. If desired, drizzle with icing when cool.

---

### VARIATIONS:

**Cinnamon or Chelsea Buns:** Warm from the oven, these were and are perennial favorites. Pull-apart buns were most popular, but sometimes large muffin tins were used to make individual buns. Prepare roll of dough as for Swedish Tea Ring. Instead of shaping into ring, cut roll into 9 slices. In 9-inch (2.5 L) square cake pan, mix together 1/4 cup (50 mL) melted butter and 1/2 cup (125 mL) brown sugar. (For Chelsea Buns, sprinkle with pecan halves and maraschino cherry halves.) Place slices of dough on top. Cover and let rise until doubled, about

45 minutes. Bake in 375°F (190°C) oven for 25 to 30 minutes or until golden brown. Invert and remove pan.

**Hungarian Coffee Cake:** Also called Bubble Bread, this novel shape was a new hit. Using one ball of Rich Sweet Dough, form into long cylinder and cut into 16 pieces. Shape pieces into small balls. Melt 1/2 cup (125 mL) butter and use some of it to grease 9-inch (3 L) tube pan. Dip balls of dough into melted butter, then into mixture of 1/2 cup (125 mL) granulated sugar and 1 tsp (5 mL) cinnamon. Arrange layer of balls, barely touching, in pan; sprinkle lightly with raisins, chopped nuts and halved maraschino cherries. Repeat layers. Cover and let rise until doubled, about 45 minutes. Bake in 375°F (190°C) oven for about 35 minutes or until golden brown. Loosen edges, invert and remove pan. To serve, break apart with two forks.

The '50s produced a flurry of new recipes for sweet yeast breads in fancy shapings. Braids, twists, rings and filled Danish pastries were all the rage at coffee klatches, teas and bake sales, along with the ever-popular cinnamon buns and fruit breads.

By the early '60s, pre-sifted flour appeared and flour companies produced booklets with recipes adjusted to no-sift baking and even fancier shapings – glamorous coffeecakes in round or oblong shapes with pineapple, date, apple or cinnamon swirl fillings; butterscotch pecan and cherry streusel rolls; frosted orange twists; braided wreaths decorated with icing and candied fruit.

For Christmas and Easter, traditional ethnic specialties were popularized – stollen, kulich, kolache, panettone and Lucia buns.

# Stained Glass Dessert

*Called Crown Jewel Dessert, Cracked Glass, Broken Glass Torte, Kaleidoscope Jelly or Colorful Christmas Dessert, this is still one of* Chatelaine *magazine's most-requested recipes. It appears in cookbooks from Labrador to Vancouver Island, and is impressive to serve. Since everything old is new again, General Foods featured this recipe in a 1990s advertisement.*

| 1 | each pkg (3 oz each) orange, cherry, lime and lemon jelly powder | 1 |
| --- | --- | --- |
| 1/2 cup | pineapple juice | 125 mL |
| 1-1/2 cups | graham wafer crumbs | 375 mL |
| 1/3 cup | butter or margarine, melted | 75 mL |

| 2 cups | whipping cream | 500 mL |
| --- | --- | --- |

Prepare orange, cherry and lime jelly powders separately, dissolving each in 1 cup (250 mL) boiling water, then adding 1/2 cup (125 mL) cold water. Pour each into separate 8-inch (2 L) square pan. Chill until firm, about 4 hours. Cut into 1/2-inch (1 cm) cubes.

In large bowl, dissolve lemon jelly powder in 1 cup (250 mL) boiling water; stir in pineapple juice. Chill until slightly thickened. Meanwhile, combine crumbs and butter; press onto bottom of 9-inch (2.5 L) springform pan.

Whip cream; fold into slightly thickened lemon jelly. Fold in jelly cubes; spoon into crust. Chill until firm, preferably overnight. Makes 12 servings.

Some refrigerated desserts were called icebox cakes, even though iceboxes were a thing of the past. There was **Jail Cake** or **Chocolate Wafer Roll** (chocolate cookies sandwiched with sweetened whipped cream, chilled then sliced diagonally for an unusual pattern). **Pineapple Icebox Dessert** was a light concoction with a graham wafer base, a buttery layer, then whipped cream and pineapple on top.

# Ambrosia-Filled Angel Cake

*Angel food cake mixes made easy and sensational refrigerator desserts, becoming the choice of hostesses from coast to coast.*

| 1 | 10-inch (25 cm) baked angel food cake | 1 |
| --- | --- | --- |
| 2 cups | whipping cream | 500 mL |
| 1 cup | chopped marshmallows | 250 mL |
| 1 | can (14 oz/398 mL) crushed pineapple, drained | 1 |
| 1/4 cup | chopped maraschino cherries | 50 mL |
| 1 tbsp | granulated sugar | 15 mL |
| 1 tsp | vanilla | 5 mL |

Cut 1-inch (2.5 cm) slice off top of cake; set aside. Hollow out cake, leaving 1-inch (2.5 cm) thick walls. Whip 1 cup (250 mL) of the cream; fold in marshmallows, pineapple and cherries. Spoon into cake tunnel, filling to top. Replace top slice. Refrigerate for 1 hour.

Whip remaining cream; add sugar and vanilla. Frost cake. Refrigerate for 1 hour, or overnight if desired. Makes 12 servings.

There were dozens of variations of filled angel food cakes. **Lemon Angel Refrigerator Cake** was tunneled and filled with lemon pie filling folded into whipped cream, then frosted with whipped cream and artistically garnished with swirls of pie filling. **Cherry-Filled Angel Cake** teamed whipped cream with black cherries and Jello. **Angel Food Deluxe** used chocolate-flavored whipped cream as a frosting with a generous covering of toasted almonds. A simplified version folded whipped cream with torn chunks of angel food cake and pineapple, which had to set in a rectangular pan before slicing into squares.

In Winnipeg, there was **Shmoo Torte**, a sponge cake that was split and filled with whipped cream and drizzled with a rich brown-sugar sauce.

# WACKY CAKE

*This easy mix-in-the-pan, moist, dark chocolate cake was a favorite for anyone in a hurry. It was also called Crazy Cake, Lazy Cake and Blue Monday Cake, and a similar cake was called Chocolate Weary Willie Cake in earlier years. For an easy frosting, top warm cake with chocolate chips or peppermint patties and spread when softened. Or frost cooled cake with chocolate icing.*

| | | |
|---|---|---|
| 1-1/2 cups | all-purpose flour | 375 mL |
| 1 cup | granulated sugar | 250 mL |
| 3 tbsp | unsweetened cocoa powder | 50 mL |
| 1 tsp | baking powder | 5 mL |
| 1 tsp | baking soda | 5 mL |
| 1/2 tsp | salt | 2 mL |
| 1/3 cup | vegetable oil or butter, melted | 75 mL |
| 1 tbsp | vinegar | 15 mL |
| 1 tsp | vanilla | 5 mL |
| 1 cup | warm water | 250 mL |

In ungreased 8-inch (2 L) square cake pan, combine flour, sugar, cocoa, baking powder, baking soda and salt; shake to level off. Make 3 holes in mixture; pour oil into one, vinegar into second and vanilla into third. Pour warm water over all; mix thoroughly with fork. Bake in 350°F (180°C) oven for 30 minutes or until tester inserted into centre comes out clean.

Fifties cake baking fell into one of three categories: fast and easy with a mix, classics like Mother made, or "different" – using wild methods and non-traditional ingredients. This was the era of **Tomato Soup Cake**, a spice cake made with a can of tomato soup, and **Miracle Chocolate Cake** made with salad dressing. **Red Velvet** was a chocolate cake containing a whole bottle of red food coloring. There was Jelly Powder Cake and Sauerkraut Chocolate Cake. Wacky Cake was silly, simple and fast, and produced a snacking cake similar to cake mixes so-named in the '70s. Kate Aitken suggested this as the first cake young girls learn to make. Even in the '90s, a recipe for Mix-Easy Chocolate Cake is on the Baker's chocolate package.

# CHOCOLATE ONE-BOWL CAKE

*Favorite frostings for this cake were Chocolate Fudge, 7 Minute Frosting or White Mountain Frosting, or **Quick Fluffy Frosting** (double the recipe p. 114).*

| | | |
|---|---|---|
| 2 cups | sifted cake-and-pastry flour | 500 mL |
| 1-1/3 cups | granulated sugar | 325 mL |
| 1 tsp | baking soda | 5 mL |
| 1/2 tsp | salt | 2 mL |
| 1/2 cup | shortening | 125 mL |
| 1 cup | buttermilk | 250 mL |
| 3 oz | unsweetened chocolate, melted | 90 g |
| 2 | eggs | 2 |
| 1 tsp | vanilla | 5 mL |

In bowl, stir together flour, sugar, baking soda and salt; add shortening, 2/3 cup (150 mL) buttermilk and chocolate. Beat at medium speed for 2 minutes.

Add remaining buttermilk, eggs and vanilla; beat 2 minutes. Pour into two greased and floured 8-inch (1.2 L) layer cake pans. Bake in 350°F (180°C) oven for 35 minutes or until cake tester comes out clean.

As cake mixes became popular, new recipes appeared for easier cake making. The traditional creaming method was upstaged by the one-bowl method using emulsified shortening. Home kitchens were equipped with countertop electric mixers, making the beating of cakes easy. Cake mixes flooded the market, with ads showing sky-high whipped frostings mounded on four-layer cakes.

# FRYPAN COOKIES

*There was no end to the number of "no-bake" cookie recipes created in the '50s. This one, sometimes called Saucepan Cookies, could now be made in an electric fry pan. Porcupines and Haystacks (Stooks in the West) were similar but usually rolled in toasted coconut.*

| 2 | eggs, beaten | 2 |
|---|---|---|
| 3/4 cup | granulated sugar | 175 mL |
| 1/2 cup | chopped dates | 125 mL |
| 1 cup | Rice Krispies | 250 mL |
| 1 cup | crushed Corn Flakes | 250 mL |
| 1 tsp | vanilla | 5 mL |
| | Flaked or desiccated coconut | |

Mix together eggs, sugar and dates; cook in heavy frypan over medium-low heat 8 minutes or until thickened, stirring constantly. Mix in Rice Krispies, Corn Flakes and vanilla. With wet hands, roll into small balls or logs; roll in coconut. Or press into 8-inch (2 L) square pan and sprinkle with coconut. Cool until set. Makes about 2 dozen.

Rice Krispie Squares were likely the first unbaked cookies. Jiffy Chocolate Balls and Brandy Walnut Balls were mixtures of melted chocolate and graham cracker or vanilla wafer crumbs. Marshmallow mixtures made Chocolate Chews, Chocolate Marshmallow Roll and all sorts of log-shaped concoctions to slice.

Chocolate Spiders or Frogs were made with chocolate and butterscotch chips and dry chow mein noodles.

Peanut butter was another ingredient for unbaked ball-shaped cookies or drop cookies like Peanut Butter Clusters (or Peanut Logs).

Cookie squares with the flavors of popular candy bars appeared in many cookbooks with names such as Sweet Maries, Oh Henrys, Eatmores and Turtles.

# CHOCOLATE CHIP COOKIES

*Life was simple once chocolate chips hit the market, imported Chipits from the United States first, then Canadian-made Baker's in the '50s. The Toll House Cookie recipe that appeared on chocolate chip packages was adapted from an older recipe that originally used chopped chocolate.*

| 1/2 cup | shortening (part butter, if desired) | 125 mL |
|---|---|---|
| 1/2 cup | packed brown sugar | 125 mL |
| 1/4 cup | granulated sugar | 50 mL |
| 1 | egg | 1 |
| 1 tsp | vanilla | 5 mL |
| 1 cup | all-purpose flour | 250 mL |
| 1/2 tsp | baking powder | 2 mL |
| 1/2 tsp | salt | 2 mL |
| 1 cup | chocolate chips | 250 mL |
| 1/2 cup | chopped nuts | 125 mL |

In bowl, cream shortening with brown and granulated sugars; beat in egg and vanilla. Stir together flour, baking powder and salt; gradually mix into batter. Stir in chocolate chips and nuts. Drop by teaspoonfuls (5 mL) onto ungreased cookie sheets. Bake in 375°F (190°C) oven for 10 to 12 minutes or until golden. Makes about 3 dozen.

Other favorites for the cookie jar included: Jumbles (drop cookies with additions like cereals, coconut, nuts, dates, raisins and gumdrops), Jam Jams (sandwich cookies filled with jam), Peanut Butter (with the familiar fork markings), and Date or Raisin Turnovers.

For Christmas, Fruit Drops and Sugar Cookie Cutouts (rolled, decorated and often iced) were perennial musts. At the same time we became aware of old-country favorites besides Scottish Shortbread: German Pfeferneusse, Lebkuchen, and Berliner Kranser (wreath shaped), Ukrainian Pyrizhky, Swedish Sandbakelser (sand tarts), Spritz in many shapes, and Springerle (cookie stamp). Jewish favorites for Hannukah included Hamentashen, Mandelbrot and Rugalahs. By the '70s we turned out Stained Glass Cookies (using colored Lifesavers), Brandy Snaps and Florentines.

# NANAIMO BARS

*During the '50s, a Dairy Foods Service Bureau recipe called Dominoes suggested piping a little of the middle layer into dots on top to give a domino pattern when cut.*

**Bottom Layer:**

| 1/2 cup | butter | 125 mL |
|---------|--------|--------|
| 1/4 cup | granulated sugar | 50 mL |
| 1/3 cup | unsweetened cocoa powder | 75 mL |
| 1 | egg, beaten | 1 |
| 1-3/4 cups | graham wafer crumbs | 425 mL |
| 1/2 cup | finely chopped nuts | 125 mL |
| 1 cup | shredded coconut | 250 mL |

**Middle Layer:**

| 1/2 cup | butter | 125 mL |
|---------|--------|--------|
| 3 tbsp | light cream | 50 mL |
| 2 tbsp | custard powder | 25 mL |
| 2 cups | icing sugar | 500 mL |

**Top Layer:**

| 4 oz | semisweet chocolate | 125 g |
|------|---------------------|-------|
| 2 tbsp | butter | 25 mL |

Nanaimo Bars, Dream Bars, Chocolate Chip Cookies

Bottom Layer: In double boiler, melt butter, sugar and cocoa; add egg and cook until thickened. Add crumbs, nuts and coconut. Press into ungreased 9-inch (2.5 L) square pan; chill.

Middle Layer: Beat together butter, cream, custard powder and sugar; spread over base. Chill.

Top Layer: Melt chocolate with butter; cool slightly. Pour over second layer; chill. Cut into bars.

Recipes for this no-bake treasure appear in countless cookbooks as Chocolate Fridge Cake, New York Slice, Miracle Bars, Ribbon Squares and many other names. But the origin of Nanaimo Bars is still a hot topic of debate.

The *Women's Auxiliary to the Nanaimo Hospital Cook Book* (1952) included three similar recipes (two called Chocolate Squares and one Chocolate Slice). The recipe appeared under the name Nanaimo Bars in the *Vancouver Sun* in the early '50s and in the B.C. Women's Institutes' *Centennial of B.C. Cookbook* in 1958. The test kitchens of food companies developed various versions with their own products.

Since the '50s, endless variations include Minted, Grand Marnier, Cherry, Pina Colada, Mocha and Peanut Butter Nanaimo Bars.

# DREAM BARS

*Called Dream Cake (or squares), Walnut Slice (or bars), Mystery Cake (or bars), some recipes added chopped candied cherries with the nuts and coconut.*

### Base:

| | | |
|---|---|---|
| 1/2 cup | butter | 125 mL |
| 1/4 cup | granulated sugar (or 1/3 cup/75 mL packed brown) | 50 mL |
| 1 cup | all-purpose flour | 250 mL |

### Topping:

| | | |
|---|---|---|
| 2 | eggs | 2 |
| 1 cup | packed brown sugar | 250 mL |
| 1 tbsp | all-purpose flour | 15 mL |
| 1/2 tsp | baking powder | 2 mL |
| 1/4 tsp | salt | 1 mL |
| 1 tsp | vanilla | 5 mL |
| 1/2 cup | chopped walnuts | 125 mL |
| 1/2 cup | shredded coconut | 125 mL |

### Icing:

| | | |
|---|---|---|
| 1-1/2 cups | icing sugar | 375 mL |
| 3 tbsp | butter | 50 mL |
| 1/2 tsp | vanilla | 2 mL |
| 1 tbsp | (approx) milk | 15 mL |

Base: Cream butter with sugar; blend in flour until crumbly. Press onto bottom of 8-inch (2 L) square cake pan. Bake in 350°F (180°C) oven for 10 to 15 minutes or until lightly browned.

Topping: In bowl, beat eggs; beat in sugar, flour, baking powder, salt and vanilla. Stir in nuts and coconut. Spread over base. Return to oven for 25 to 30 minutes or until dark golden and nearly set in centre. Let cool.

Icing: Beat together icing sugar, butter, vanilla and milk until spreading consistency, adding more milk if needed. Spread over cooled cake. Cut into bars.

## VARIATIONS:

Use same base as for Dream Bars.

**Lemon Squares:**
Topping: Combine 2 beaten eggs, 1 cup (250 mL) granulated sugar, 2 tbsp (25 mL) all-purpose flour, 1/2 tsp (2 mL) baking powder, 1/4 tsp (1 mL) salt, 3 tbsp (50 mL) lemon juice and grated rind of 1 lemon. Bake 25 to 30 minutes; cool. Sift icing sugar over top.

**Butter Tart Squares:**
Topping: Combine 2 beaten eggs, 1 cup (250 mL) packed brown sugar, 2 tbsp (25 mL) each melted butter and all-purpose flour, 1/2 tsp (2 mL) baking powder, 1 tsp (5 mL) vanilla and 1 cup (250 mL) raisins. Bake 30 to 35 minutes.

**Raspberry Coconut Squares:**
Topping: Spread 1/2 cup (125 mL) raspberry jam over base. Combine 1 beaten egg, 3/4 cup (175 mL) granulated sugar, 1 tbsp (15 mL) melted butter, 1 tsp (5 mL) vanilla and 2 cups (500 mL) unsweetened shredded coconut. Bake 30 to 35 minutes.

**Apricot Nut Bars:**
Topping: Cover 1 cup (250 mL) dried apricots with water; cook 10 minutes, drain and chop. Combine 2 beaten eggs, 1 cup (250 mL) packed brown sugar, 1/4 cup (50 mL) all-purpose flour, 1/2 tsp (2 mL) baking powder, 1/4 tsp (1 mL) salt, 1 tsp (5 mL) vanilla, 1/2 cup (125 mL) chopped nuts and the apricots. Bake 30 to 35 minutes.

Squares and bars came in all shapes and sizes and were the mainstay of suburban kitchens. Bazaars, teas, bridge luncheons, coffee parties, all required home baking. Recipes were traded (or guarded, depending on the owner). Preferred favorites were easy to cut and safe to transport.

**Marshmallow Squares:** Prepare base using 3/4 cup (175 mL) butter, 1/3 cup (75 mL) brown sugar and 1-1/2 cups (375 mL) flour. Press into 13-x 9-inch (3.5 L) pan. Bake 20 to 25 minutes or until golden. Cool.

Soften 2 envelopes gelatin in 1/2 cup (125 mL) cold water. In saucepan mix 2 cups (500 mL) sugar with 1/2 cup (125 mL) hot water; boil for 2 minutes. Dissolve gelatin in hot syrup. Pour into large bowl; beat with electric mixer until very stiff. Add 1 tsp (5 mL) almond flavoring and a few drops red coloring to make mixture pale pink. Stir in 1/2 cup (125 mL) each chopped maraschino cherries and chopped toasted almonds. Pour over shortbread layer. Let cool until set. Cut into about 60 bars.

# The SIXTIES

1960 — 1969

*It would be foolish to suggest that food isn't infinitely more varied and in many cases infinitely more tasty today for those who will take the trouble to enjoy it....Pizza, chow mein and pastrami may not be terribly exotic or even terribly authentic but they're a step in the right direction. Espresso coffee may have saved the nation, gastronomically speaking.*

> – Pierre Berton
> *The Centennial Food Guide*

The '60s were a whole new bag. The generation gap widened, the divorce rate rose, men landed on the moon. Canadians went to church less and travelled more. It was the decade of jumbo jets and miniskirts, color television and green garbage bags, Flower Power and protest marches and Pop-Tarts. We devoured freeze-dried coffee and Metrecal, Shake 'N Bake and instant mashed, but also discovered crêpes Suzette and chicken Cordon Bleu.

The '60s turned the world upside down. A decade that started out as an extension of the house-party '50s (adding the twist, beehive hairdos and the first of the baby-boom teenagers) became a decade of dizzying social and political change, of re-evaluation that ended with all the rules changed and a new liberalism in the air.

Baby boomers protested against most things their parents valued. Thousands joined marches for peace, equality, freedom. The women's liberation movement took root with a royal commission on the status of women. The pill, the Beatles, hootenannies in coffee houses, rock concerts in the park, meditation, encounter groups, long hair, granny glasses, peace symbols on neck chains, a new Canadian flag and a year-long wingding for our 100th birthday – all were part and product of the liberating '60s.

We also took a new look at what we were eating. Our '50s love affair with packaged convenience foods was challenged by culinary options of every philosophical stripe from macrobiotic brown-rice diets to classic French cuisine.

Julia Child's cooking show on American educational TV made her name a household word here. James Beard, Dione Lucas and Michael Field visited Canada to give a series of stylish food demonstrations titled "The Art of Cooking," presented by the women's committee of the Art Gallery of Toronto. Recipes for *suprème de volaille bourguignon* and *soufflé au grand marnier* started to make the rounds at modish dinner parties. Many Canadian cooks tried French onion soup, duck with orange sauce, French omelettes and crêpes for the first time.

Television still brought us lavish commerials for packaged food products, most of them time-savers: Dream Whip, canned puddings, boil-in-the-bag corned beef, gourmet soups like tomato bisque, Red Kettle dry soup

---

*"Gents going gourmet" was a popular theme for cooking schools, such as this one at Consumer's Gas in Toronto in 1967.*

Courtesy of Jane Martin

On pages 140 – 141: The fondue party: Beef Fondue with Tangy Tomato, Mustard and Horseradish Sauces, Caesar Salad and French stick.

*After learning to enjoy chianti and rosé, Canadians ventured into cooking with wines.*

Courtesy of The Canadian Wine Institute

*Many a fondue pot received as a '60s wedding gift found its way into the garage sales of the '80s and '90s.*

## HEADLINES

1960 Native women win the vote.

1961 Canada's population: 18,238,200.

1961 CTV national network begins.

1962 Trans-Canada Highway completed from St. John's to Victoria.

1962 Canada adopts new maple leaf flag.

1963 U.S. President John F. Kennedy assassinated.

1964 100th anniversary of Charlottetown meeting of Fathers of Confederation.

1964 Northern Dancer wins Kentucky Derby.

1966 Ottawa housewives spark nationwide supermarket boycott over prices.

1967 Canada celebrates centennial year.

1967 Expo '67 resounding success in Montreal.

1967 Navy, army and air force unite as Canadian Armed Forces.

1968 Canadian planes airlift food to starving Biafrans.

1968 Trudeau becomes new PM in landslide victory.

1969 Department of Health and Welfare bans cyclamate sweeteners.

1969 Canada bans use of DDT.

1969 U.S. astronaut Neil Armstrong becomes first man on moon.

mixes and all kinds of baking mixes.

Food writers jumped on the bandwagon with endless columns devoted to cooking with mixes or "creative tips" such as adding a little cooking sherry to the soup. Some branched off into recipes for "make-your-own" mixes (usually similar to packaged biscuit mix) with variations for muffins, quickbreads, cakes and cookies. But many home cooks continued to turn out the traditional baking they still considered their duty, especially for bake sales at churches and schools.

Homemakers wanting new food ideas or basic advice had a wealth of sources to choose from. Federal and provincial departments of health, agriculture and fisheries provided up-to-date information on nutrition, food shopping, cooking and preserving. All the large food and appliance companies, hydro and gas utilities, supermarket chains, producers' associations and marketing boards operated consumer

information centres and home service departments. Most of these had home economists and test kitchen staffs to answer consumer queries, providing a wide range of recipes, cookbooks, cooking demonstrations and courses; they also wrote package instructions, press releases, advertising and promotional copy, did food styling for photography and worked on new-product development.

Innovation was paramount in the new-product race, and, not surprisingly, results were varied. One instant-setting jelly powder, made from a form of seaweed, jelled solid while hot and never got past the test-market stage. Canned Arctic char was an expensive experiment that soon faded. But nondairy creamers, Saran Wrap, Baker's milk chocolate chips, Swift's Butterball turkeys, McCain's frozen french fries, Minute Rice and freezer jams made with Certo were '60s successes that are still with us today.

*Built-in appliances and arborite counter tops modernized kitchens during the '60s.*

Courtesy of Hanover Kitchens (Canada) Inc. 1952 - 1992...40 Years of Earning Your Trust...Everyday!

*Recipe booklets offered "101 new ways to save time and add variety to meals."*

Courtesy of Maple Leaf Foods

## LOOKING BACK

*From* Food That Really Schmecks
*(1968) by Edna Staebler.*

One of the joys of my life is to
visit my Old Order Mennonite
friends, the Martins, in their
sprawling fieldstone farmhouse
near the Conestoga River in
Waterloo County. Their large
old-fashioned kitchen, warmed
by a big black cookstove,
always has a homely fragrance
of wonderful things to eat...rivel
soup, roasting meat, baking
cinnamon buns or spicy
botzelbaum pie.

Bevvy, the plump little lady of
the house, is always busy
schnitzing (cutting up apples for
drying), canning or cooking...
"Of course you'll stay for supper," she says as she hangs up
my coat on a nail....

The food Bevvy cooks has
such mouth-watering savour
that no one can resist it. Like all
Mennonite cooking it is plain
but divinely flavoured...sour
cream salads...schnitz und
knepp...shoo-fly pie....

From a drawer in the cup-
board Bevvy brings me her most
treasured possession: a little
handwritten black notebook in
which she has copied recipes,
swapped and inherited...Aunt
Magdaline's Hurry Cake,
Grossmommy Martin's
Kuddlefleck....

"This is Cousin Katie's recipe
for fetschpatze [small fritters
called 'fat sparrows']; we eat
them hot and dunked in maple
syrup," Bevvy says as the deep-
fried golden balls are passed
around the table. And we all eat
so many that David says, "It
wonders me that we'll have
room after this for the pie. But
we will."

Salome glances at me and
laughs, "You look like you
have afraid you'll bust your
buttons."...David's eyes have a
teasing twinkle, "If she eats
with us for a week she'd be
wonderful fat."

Newspaper food editors produced large weekly food sections for
their legions of loyal readers. Marjorie Elwood at the *Star Weekly* and
Helen Gougeon and Margo Oliver at *Weekend* were familiar names in
magazine supplements to Saturday newspapers coast to coast. Other by-
lines that were popular for many years included those of Mary Moore
(in Hamilton, London and many other dailies), Helen Gagen at the
*Toronto Telegram*, Norah Cherry at the *Winnipeg Free Press* and Dorothy
Allen-Gray at the *Globe and Mail* and in Calgary. At the *Vancouver Sun,* the
Edith Adams department ( a name used for the *Sun*'s homemakers' service since 1912)  produced large food sections. (The first of their many
cookbooks had appeared in 1928, and their first in-house test kitchens,
Edith Adams Cottage, opened in 1947.)

Many regional television stations produced food shows whose popular hosts made cooking an entertainment. One of the longest careers
was that of Vancouver's Mona Brun, who started out in 1963 at BCTV
(on a show called "Woodward's Culinary Capers") and continued for 25
years doing TV food shows and consumer promotion. Mona's famous
sense of humour got her through many a sticky situation. "I remember
going to Edmonton to do a show about bread," she recalls, "which
meant that I had to start the dough in North Vancouver and take it on
the plane. I stashed the bowl of dough under the seat, where of course it
started rising and wafting the smell of yeast through the cabin, and I
had to punch it down with my feet all the way to Edmonton."

Transportation of food by airplane was more crucial in the Far
North, where supplies of grocery staples from the south stocked the
shelves of general stores like the Hudson's Bay Company.

In Newfoundland, electricity and refrigeration had reached the last
outlying regions. As a result, though still great fish-eaters, islanders
began to consume a lot more fresh meat and poultry. But at the same
time, like other Canadians coast to coast, they began to flock to takeout

*Typical of church groups catering to weddings and dinners, these St. Andrew's
Presbyterian Church women prepared pre-Stratford Festival dinners in 1963.*

In the '50s and early '60s, "live-to-air" TV commercial production could make life pretty traumatic for the food stylist. I remember watching the luscious caramel coating slide off five apples just seconds before airtime.

The majority of TV commercials promoting food products used the "hands" demonstration. This tabletop technique was a simple, direct way of presenting products and ways to use them. All kinds of new food products were being developed, and they were the stars – no gleeful actors needed.

The challenge for the stylist was to produce a foolproof clone of the home recipe. The food had to withstand hot lights, time delays and rough handling. Much fuss has been made about the fakery in food comercials during this period – shaving soap for whipped cream, mashed potatoes for ice cream and so on. Most food companies rejected these ideas, so with common sense and a little creativity, we developed alternate solutions such as stabilizing whipped cream with gelatin.

The advent of videotape in 1962 reduced the many live-to-air hazards, such as the sudden disappearance of a camera-ready food (the cast of a Wayne and Shuster show denuded a tray of hors-d'oeuvres meant for a cocktail party commercial). Now commercials were produced separately from shows and inserted later.

For the more than 10 years before color TV, varying shades of grey were the normal "colors" for food commercials. The big challenge was to achieve contrast in ingredients that registered the same tone. So it was a sheer delight to view a red tomato and green lettuce when color cameras arrived in 1966.

chicken chains; these became even more popular than fish-and-chip shops (which served malt vinegar on theirs, like the Brits) or deep-fried sweet-and-sours from Chinese takeouts.

Changing patterns of immigration continued to influence Canadian life. The '60s brought larger numbers of people from the West Indies, Hong Kong and southeast Asia. A steady stream of Vietnam war-resisters arrived from the United States. Our cities were becoming more and more cosmopolitan and lifestyles more varied.

As the number of restaurants and markets supplying ethnic dishes and ingredients expanded, so did our tastes. In Vancouver, Robson Street sprouted so many German bakeries, restaurants, delis and sausage shops it became known as Robsonstrasse. In Yellowknife, an Italian miner brought his wife over from Europe and opened a restaurant serving Sicilian-style home cooking.

Home cooks began to take "ethnic cooking" more seriously and to attempt more honest versions. Neighborhood gourmet clubs became popular, with members sincerely trying to research and prepare authentic recipes from other lands. But more often "international" still meant going "Hawaiian" or "Polynesian" (any recipe including pineapple and coconut), "Italian" (tomatoes, garlic, green peppers) or "Oriental" (soy sauce). On backyard barbecues, thick steaks were still the ultimate, and cheese-stuffed, bacon-wrapped wieners were considered a nifty dish.

For many people in large urban areas, sprawling suburbia was no longer the utopia it had once appeared. Some of the disenchanted left the city to set up idealistic communes or to find a cheaper, more peaceful lifestyle. The back-to-the-land movement gave rise to organically grown foods, "natural" ingredients and health food stores, and fostered a new distrust of food additives.

*Interest in our ethnic roots produced many books about regional food.*

From Sauerkraut and Enterprise by Edna Staebler. Used by permission of the Canadian Publishers, McClelland & Stewart, Toronto.

*The popularity of Italian restaurants led to the home-cooked pasta craze.*

Courtesy of Borden-Catelli Consumer Products

## NUTRITION

- Back-to-nature movement strong, organic and health foods flourished, vegetarian and macrobiotic diets fashionable.

- 1961: *Canada's Food Rules* revised and renamed *Canada's Food Guide*. Five food groups featured: milk, fruit, vegetables, cereals and breads, meat and fish. Recommended potatoes be eaten daily, eggs and cheese at least three times a week, butter or margarine daily.

- Very strong interest in obesity control. Fad diets popular.

- Food fads and nutrition misinformation growing concern.

- Evidence that fat and calories played role in development of heart disease.

- Breakfast-skipping cited as problem.

- Suspected nutrition deficiencies: vitamin A, vitamin D, iron.

- 1969: Studies showed about 22 per cent of food dollar spent away from home; nutritionists concerned about quality of fast food.

Others headed in the opposite direction – downtown. Urban renewal was giving lacklustre city centres new life, such as Ottawa's railway-station-turned-conference-centre, Halifax's Historic Properties and Regina's Wascana Park. Montreal was first with skyscrapers (Place Ville Marie) in 1962, followed by the Toronto-Dominion Centre in Toronto. High-rise apartment towers sprouted everywhere. Restoration of historic districts like Old Montreal, Gastown in Vancouver and Cabbagetown in Toronto created fashionable new addresses for residences and studios.

Renovating old houses became trendy, and updating the kitchens with the latest appliances was a high priority. An interest in "gourmet cooking" was part of the new lifestyle. In a 1991 column titled "You'll Eat Up the Sixties" *(Toronto Sun)*, Lucy Waverman recalled: "Inviting friends for dinner and spending all day in the kitchen cooking the *Gourmet* magazine centrefold was a Saturday occupation. A typical menu might be vichyssoise, beef Wellington and crêpes Suzette."

Fancy coffees also came into vogue. Along with international favorites like Irish or Spanish coffee, Canadian variations such as "Royal Canadian" (with rye whisky) and "Quebec Special" (with maple liqueur and whipped cream) appeared.

As the big cities grew bigger and more cosmopolitan, offering glamor, excitement and a richer cultural life to many, they also acquired big-city problems. Overcrowding in public housing, endless expressway expansion and industrial pollution gave rise to the "People Power" movements of the '60s. Tenants' associations grew and flourished. Groups such as Pollution Probe tackled environmental problems.

Education faced severe challenges as the baby boom generation had schools bursting at the seams and spilling out into portable classrooms. Enrolment at universities tripled over the decade. One faculty that attracted greatly increased numbers of students was home economics, as

*Stylish kitchens, like the fashions of the '60s, were sleek and uncluttered.*

Courtesy of Nestlé Canada Inc.

- Listening to hi-fi.
- The Twist.
- Diefendollars.
- The first polyester knits, perma-press, pantyhose.
- Coffee houses, Gordon Lightfoot, Ian and Sylvia.
- Electric hot dog cookers.
- Trying to light charcoal on the barbecue.
- The ubiquitous coffee carafe.
- Making your first uncooked freezer jam.
- Teased hair and beehives.
- White lipstick.
- Teflon.
- The first Corning ware casseroles with a cornflower pattern.
- The end of Friday fish day when Vatican II lifted the ban on eating meat on Fridays.
- Marshall McLuhan's *Understanding Media*.
- Canada's first McDonald's opening in Richmond, B.C.
- William Dixon of Brampton, Ontario winning the world ploughing match in France.
- The first green garbage bags.
- The last run of the Newfie Bullet.

Its programs broadened in response to runaway consumerism. The University of Guelph changed the name of its home economics faculty to Family and Consumer Studies. At the new community colleges, extensive courses for chefs reflected the booming hospitality and tourism industries.

In 1965, Canada's new flag with its red maple leaf was flying over schools, public buildings and shopping centres. Vast new malls, such as Yorkdale in Toronto, opened with dozens of stores under one roof. In smaller centres, large supermarkets replaced many smaller grocers and butcher shops. All catered to the shopper with a car. Weekly shopping for family groceries became the norm.

Many Canadians were on a spending spree. Credit buying bought dishwashers, microwaves, refrigerator-freezers, electric can openers, coffee grinders and electric knives. New homes acquired slim-lined Scandinavian furniture, usually teak. Kitchen shops devoted exclusively to stylish cooking gear appeared: Helen Gougeon's Belle Cuisine in Montreal was one of the first. In Toronto's Yorkville, Pearl Gineen opened her shop, The Compleat Kitchen, out of necessity; while teaching young marrieds how to cook, she had discovered that "most Canadians didn't have a decent pot or pan in their kitchens."

Canadians enjoyed more leisure time as prosperity brought a shorter work week and better working conditions. Membership in unions surged; most people worked a 40-hour week, with paid holidays; hospital insurance and old-age pensions were universal. Greater affluence plus the advent of plastic money put many Canadians on the move, and foreign travel and winter holidaying surged. The "snowbirds" from eastern Canada began annual migrations to Florida. Prairie farmers, tired of saving for a rainy day, became the country's most travelled people.

*In 1961 a sour cream coffee cake won top prize in a* Star Weekly *recipe contest.*

Toronto Star

*Madame Benoit on CBC's "Take Thirty" shared food and fun with Paul Soles, Ed Reed and Adrienne Clarkson.*

Courtesy of Bernard Benoit

# A CENTURY OF CANADIAN HOME COOKING

In 1967, Canada turned 100 and threw itself a yearlong, countrywide birthday party. Nearly every community sponsored special Centennial projects and events, from new parks and libraries to an All-You-Can-Eat Oyster Festival in Tyne Valley, P.E.I. and a Giant Potlach in Burnaby, B.C. Thousands of Canadians joined the 50 million visitors to Expo '67 in Montreal. The big show inspired in many Canadians a new and unabashed national pride, as well as giving them a first taste of a variety of international foods at the great pavillions.

Cookbooks were ideal Centennial projects, being historical markers as well as fund-raisers. The best-selling *Laura Secord Canadian Cook Book,* compiled by the Canadian Home Economics Association, was one of the first professional cookbooks to present a collection of Canadian recipes with regional references. Others such as *Food That Really Schmecks* by Edna Staebler (from Waterloo County, Ontario) attracted national as well as local attention. On the west coast, Liz and Jack Bryan were cooking up *Western Living* magazine, which began publication in 1969, establishing a unique regional perspective that included local food styles and products.

As Expo and the Centennial year closed, and with the strains of Bobby Gimby's "Ca-na-da" still ringing in their ears, Canadians found themselves looking ahead with a new optimism. We seemed to realize suddenly that the land we lived in was something to brag about. The euphoria of celebration, the new sense of social freedom and opportunity, followed in 1968 by a heady wave of Trudeaumania, launched Canada confidently into the '70s.

*Expo '67 brought the world to Montreal.*

Courtesy of John McNeill

The Laura Secord Cookbook *was one of the first to create an interest in regional Canadian recipes.*

Courtesy of Laura Secord Inc. (Book is out of print and not available from Laura Secord Inc.)

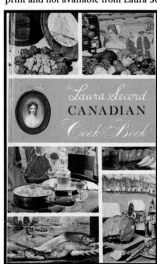

*Pride in Canadian foods and cooking appeared in many centennial brochures.*

Reproduced with the permission of the Minister of Supply and ServicesCanada, 1992.

# Cookbook Sampler

## THE SIXTIES

For more cookbooks of the decade, see Bibliography p. 235.

# CHICKEN LIVER PÂTÉ

*During the '60s, modifications to the ordinary pâté soon abounded, as various seasonings, ham or bacon and even apple were added.*

| | | |
|---|---|---|
| 1 lb | chicken livers | 500 g |
| 1/4 cup | butter | 50 mL |
| 3/4 cup | chopped onion | 175 mL |
| 2 | cloves garlic, minced | 2 |
| 1/4 cup | chicken stock | 50 mL |
| 2 tbsp | brandy | 25 mL |
| 3/4 cup | diced ham | 175 mL |
| 1/2 tsp | salt | 2 mL |
| 1/4 tsp | each pepper and allspice | 1 mL |
| 1/2 cup | whipping cream | 125 mL |

Cut livers in half; sauté in butter just until no longer pink. Add onion and garlic; cook, stirring, until softened. Stir in stock, brandy, ham, salt, pepper and allspice. Transfer to food processor or blender; add cream and purée until smooth. Transfer to small crock. Cover and refrigerate. Makes about 2-1/2 cups (625 mL).

The early '60s brought a deluge of snack and nibbler recipes for the rec-room crowd, for cocktail parties and predinner appetizers. At dinner parties, first courses (trying to duplicate "gourmet" restaurant fare) were shrimp cocktails, the shrimp perched around horseradish-flavored chili-sauce dips.

The first pâtés, usually smooth blender spreads made with sautéed chicken livers, were served with crackers or melba toast at parties. Winston's, an elegant Toronto restaurant where diners were reported to have their own keys to get in, was famous for a brandied version. The first baked pâtés and terrines appeared later in the decade as first courses at the table.

# PIZZA

*You can use other toppings, such as sliced mushrooms, chopped green pepper, crumbled browned beef, bacon and anchovies. The '80s introduced "designer pizzas," topped with things like artichokes, smoked salmon, goat cheese and sun-dried tomatoes.*

| | | |
|---|---|---|
| 1 tsp | granulated sugar | 5 mL |
| 1 | pkg active dry yeast | 1 |
| 1 cup | lukewarm water | 250 mL |
| 1/4 cup | vegetable oil | 50 mL |
| 2-1/2 cups | (approx) all-purpose flour | 625 mL |
| 1 tsp | salt | 5 mL |
| *Topping:* | | |
| 2/3 cup | tomato sauce | 150 mL |
| 1/2 tsp | each dried basil and oregano | 2 mL |
| 2 | green onions, sliced | 2 |
| 1/4 lb | pepperoni, sliced | 125 g |
| 3 cups | shredded mozzarella cheese | 750 mL |
| 2 tbsp | grated Parmesan cheese | 25 mL |

In large bowl, dissolve sugar and yeast in warm water; let stand 10 minutes or until bubbly. Stir in oil. Stir together flour and salt; stir half into yeast mixture, beating well. Add enough remaining flour until dough can be formed into sticky ball.

On lightly floured surface, knead dough until smooth and elastic, about 5 minutes. Cut in half; cover and let rest for 10 minutes. Roll out each half to 12-inch (30 cm) circle and place on lightly greased pizza pan, stretching carefully to fit pans. Let rest for 10 minutes.

Topping: Spread tomato sauce over dough. Sprinkle with basil, oregano, onions and pepperoni; top with mozzarella and Parmesan. Bake in 450°F (230°C) oven for 15 to 18 minutes or until crust is brown and cheese is bubbly. Makes two 12-inch (30 cm) pizzas.

In the '60s, cooking competitions at some provincial fairs included new categories. Under the label Foreign Pastries were such things as strudels and pizzas. In 1961, at the Saskatoon Exhibition, perennial winner Mrs. A.H. Trevoy impressed the judges with her winning pizza.

Although popular as take-out food, pizzas made from scratch at home seemed tedious. Frozen pizzas flooded the market and quick shortcuts invaded the kitchen. Rather than yeast dough for crusts, there were biscuit doughs (homemade, canned refrigerated doughs or biscuit mixes), hamburger buns, English muffins and eventually pita breads. Choice of toppings ranged from simply cheese on tomato sauce to a variety of familiar ingredients like bacon, ham and even pineapple.

**Food processor pizza dough:** Dissolve yeast in sugar and water as usual; place dry ingredients in processor and, with processor running, add liquids through feed tube. If dough is sticky, add more flour a little at a time until dough comes away from sides of bowl. Process 30 seconds to knead.

# BACON 'N' CHEESE DOGS

*Favorites with kids and adults alike, "dressed-up" hot dogs were popular in the '60s. Wieners were also served as cocktail fare. Cut into thirds and speared on cocktail picks, they were served with a tangy ketchup-based sauce or a mustard and grape jelly mixture.*

| 1 lb | wieners | 500 g |
|------|---------|-------|
| | Prepared mustard | |
| 6 to 8 | cheese slices | 6 to 8 |
| 8 to 10 | slices side bacon | 8 to 10 |

Split wieners lengthwise, cutting only 3/4 way through. Spread cut edges lightly with mustard. Cut cheese slices in strips; insert into wieners.

Partially cook bacon until almost cooked but not crisp; drain on paper towels. Wrap each cheese-stuffed wiener with a slice of bacon, securing with toothpicks. Place, cheese side up, on baking sheet. Bake in 350°F (180°C) oven for 15 minutes or until cheese is melted and bacon crisp. (Alternatively, broil until bacon is crisp.) Serve in toasted hot dog buns, if desired.

### VARIATION:

Saute 2 medium onions, thinly sliced, in 1 tbsp (15 mL) butter until golden brown. Spoon into slit wieners before adding cheese and wrapping with bacon.

To make **Tuna Rolls:** Combine 1 can (7.5 oz/213 g) flaked tuna, drained, with 1 cup (250 mL) shredded Cheddar cheese, 1 tbsp (15 mL) chopped sweet pickle and 2 tbsp (25 mL) each onion and prepared mustard. Stuff mixture into 6 split hot dog buns. Wrap each in foil; bake in 350°F (180°C) oven for 20 minutes. Makes 6 servings.

These rolls were sometimes called **Tuna Boats** or **TV Specials.** Kids loved this filling in hot dog buns, but it was nice for filling dainty Parkerhouse rolls for afternoon tea.

Long loaves of crusty bread were also filled with similar mixtures or Dagwood-style layers of fillings; these were called **Heroes, Poor Boys** or **Subs** and were served cut in thick chunks. For the weekly card game, this was the answer.

# Barbecued Shish Kebabs

*In the '60s, we learned that tomato barbecue sauces weren't the only choice, and we started cooking and basting with beer and wine. This sauce makes a good marinade for less tender cuts of beef.*

| | | |
|---|---|---|
| 1-1/2 lb | beef sirloin | 750 g |
| 12 | parboiled small onions | 12 |
| 1 | large sweet green pepper, cut in chunks | 1 |
| *Sauce:* | | |
| 2/3 cup | chili sauce | 150 mL |
| 1/2 cup | beer | 125 mL |
| 1/3 cup | packed brown sugar | 75 mL |
| 2 tbsp | vinegar | 25 mL |
| 2 tbsp | honey | 25 mL |
| 1 tbsp | lemon juice | 15 mL |
| 1 tbsp | Worcestershire sauce | 15 mL |

Sauce: In small saucepan, combine chili sauce, beer, sugar, vinegar, honey, lemon juice and Worcestershire sauce; stir over medium heat until sugar dissolves.

Cut beef into 1-1/2-inch (4 cm) cubes. Alternately thread beef, onions and green pepper onto skewers; brush with sauce. Grill over medium-hot coals or at medium setting, turning once and basting with sauce, to desired doneness. Serve with remaining sauce. Makes 6 servings.

Backyard barbecuing too often meant overcooked hamburgers or charred steaks.

Eventually, the popularity of steaks gave way to chicken and kebabs of beef, lamb or pork. In the Yukon, moose or caribou kebabs were teamed with wild mushrooms. In time, adventurous folk experimented with fish, vegetable or even fruit kebabs.

Greek restaurants serving **Souvlaki** (marinated chunks of lamb) were becoming fashionable. Always on the barbecue menu was **Garlic Bread**: a loaf cut in thick slices almost through to the bottom, then spread with a garlicky butter (which was first made with garlic powder, then later fresh garlic) and wrapped in foil. This was set on the grill when the foil-wrapped potatoes and the kebabs were nearly done.

# Chicken Cacciatore

*Meaty plum tomatoes, readily available today, are best in this recipe. Served over spaghetti in the '60s, Chicken Cacciatore would be tasty today served with a pasta such as fusilli, or over egg noodles or rice, and topped with freshly grated Parmesan.*

| | | |
|---|---|---|
| 2-1/2 lb | chicken pieces | 1.5 kg |
| | All-purpose flour | |
| 1/4 cup | olive or vegetable oil | 50 mL |
| 1 | onion, chopped | 1 |
| 2 | cloves garlic, minced | 2 |
| 1 | sweet green pepper, sliced | 1 |
| 1/2 cup | sliced celery | 125 mL |
| 1/2 lb | mushrooms, sliced | 250 g |
| 1 | can (28 oz/796 mL) tomatoes | 1 |
| 1 tbsp | tomato paste | 15 mL |
| 1/2 cup | white wine or chicken stock | 125 mL |
| 1/4 tsp | each dried basil and oregano | 1 mL |
| 1 | bay leaf | 1 |
| | Salt and pepper | |

Dust chicken with flour; brown in oil in large skillet. Remove chicken; set aside. Add onion, garlic, green pepper, celery and mushrooms; cook, stirring occasionally, for 5 minutes or until onion is softened.

Add tomatoes (crushed), tomato paste, wine, basil, oregano, bay leaf, and salt and pepper to taste; return chicken to skillet. Cover partially and simmer for about 30 minutes or until juices run clear when chicken is pierced. (Remove lid to thicken sauce if necessary.) Remove bay leaf. Makes 4 servings.

Italian-style main dishes became very popular in the '60s. North Americans loved the flavors and weren't concerned about whether the recipes were authentically Italian or not. Many versions appeared in recipe booklets from producers of tomato sauce, tomatoes and pasta.

Chicken cooked with tomatoes, peppers, garlic, herbs and sometimes mushrooms was often labelled Italiano, Napoli or Marengo. Cacciatore (or *chasseur* in French) means hunter's-style, and the dish originally used wild game, mushrooms and white wine. In today's adaptations, different kinds of peppers and even sliced zucchini may be added.

# TURKEY OR CHICKEN DIVAN

*In later versions of this recipe, cubed ham or sliced hard-cooked eggs replaced the turkey.*

| | | |
|---|---|---|
| 1 | bunch fresh broccoli | 1 |
| 1/4 cup | butter | 50 mL |
| 1/4 cup | all-purpose flour | 50 mL |
| 2 cups | chicken stock | 500 mL |
| 2 tbsp | sherry | 25 mL |
| 1/2 tsp | lemon juice | 2 mL |
| Pinch | nutmeg | Pinch |
| 1/2 cup | whipping cream | 125 mL |
| 1/2 cup | grated Parmesan cheese | 125 mL |
| | Salt and pepper | |
| 3/4 lb | turkey or chicken breast, cooked and sliced (6 to 12 slices) | 375 g |

Cut broccoli into spears. Cook in boiling salted water just until tender; drain and keep hot.

Meanwhile, in heavy saucepan, melt butter; stir in flour and cook until bubbly. Stir in stock and bring to boil; cook 2 minutes, stirring. Remove from heat; stir in sherry, lemon juice and nutmeg. Whip cream; fold into sauce along with half the Parmesan. Season with salt and pepper to taste.

Arrange broccoli in 10-cup (2.5 L) shallow baking dish or gratin dish; pour half the sauce over top. Arrange turkey on top; pour on remaining sauce. Sprinkle with remaining Parmesan. Broil at least 6 inches (15 cm) below heat until bubbling and golden. Makes 5 or 6 servings.

For **Quick Divan:** Combine 1 can (10 oz/284 mL) cream of chicken soup, 1/4 cup (50 mL) each mayonnaise and chicken stock, 1 tbsp (15 mL) dry sherry (if desired), 1/2 tsp (2 mL) each lemon juice and Worcestershire sauce, and 1/2 cup (125 mL) shredded Cheddar cheese. Layer with 2 cups (500 mL) broccoli and 2 cups (500 mL) cubed cooked turkey or chicken. Top with 1/2 cup (125 mL) dry bread crumbs mixed with 1/2 cup (125 mL) shredded Cheddar cheese. Bake in 350°F (180°C) oven for 30 minutes or until bubbling and lightly browned. Makes about 4 servings.

# BEEF STROGANOFF

*Stroganoff, served on egg noodles or rice and topped with chopped parsley, was rich and tasty. Variations for cheaper entertaining or family fare were **Hamburger Stroganoff** and **Tuna Stroganoff**.*

| | | |
|---|---|---|
| 3 tbsp | all-purpose flour | 50 mL |
| 1/2 tsp | salt | 2 mL |
| 1 lb | sirloin, cut in thin strips | 500 g |
| 1/4 cup | butter | 50 mL |
| 1 cup | thinly sliced mushrooms | 250 mL |
| 1/2 cup | chopped onion | 125 mL |
| 1 | clove garlic, minced | 1 |
| 1 tbsp | tomato paste | 15 mL |
| 1 cup | beef stock | 250 mL |
| 1 cup | sour cream | 250 mL |
| 2 tbsp | sherry | 25 mL |

Combine half the flour with salt; dredge meat in mixture. In skillet, brown meat lightly in half the butter. Add mushrooms, onion and garlic; cook 3 to 4 minutes or until softened. Remove meat and mushroom mixture to warm plate.

Add remaining butter to pan; blend in remaining flour. Add tomato paste. Gradually add stock; cook, stirring, until thickened. Return meat mixture to pan; stir in sour cream and sherry. Heat through. Makes 4 servings.

Stroganoff was a venture into "gourmet" home cooking. Serving it over rice or noodles made a nice change from the standard meat-and-vegetable main course. **Veal** (or **Chicken** or **Turkey**) **Tetrazzini** was made with spaghetti in a rich cream sauce. **Chicken Paprika** (a vaguely Hungarian chicken stew) was served with rice. Liberal toppings of toasted almonds and splashes of wine or sherry made any dish "gourmet."

# LASAGNE

*The '60s saw the beginning of the pasta phenomenon, with lasagne quickly becoming everyone's favorite.*

| | | |
|---|---|---|
| 9 | lasagne noodles (about 8 oz/250 g) | 9 |
| 1 lb | ricotta or cottage cheese | 500 g |
| 1 | egg | 1 |
| 3/4 cup | grated Parmesan cheese | 175 mL |
| 4 cups | Spaghetti Sauce with Meat (see p. 128) | 1 L |
| 3/4 lb | mozzarella cheese, thinly sliced | 375 g |

In large pot of boiling salted water, cook noodles until tender but firm; drain and rinse under cold water. Mix together ricotta, egg and 1/4 cup (50 mL) Parmesan.

Spread about 1 cup (250 mL) meat sauce in 12-cup (3 L) lasagne dish. Top with 3 noodles in single layer, then one-third ricotta mixture. Top with one-third mozzarella and one-third remaining meat sauce. Repeat layers twice. Sprinkle with remaining Parmesan. Bake in 350°F (180°C) oven for 30 minutes or until bubbling. Let stand 15 minutes before cutting into large squares. Makes about 8 servings.

## VARIATIONS:

**Rich Lasagne:** Use 2 cups (500 mL) besciamella (white) sauce in place of ricotta.

**Seafood:** Use Meatless Spaghetti Sauce (p. 128); add 2 cups (500 mL) mixed cooked seafood and fish (shrimp, scallops, salmon, etc.).

**Vegetarian:** Use Meatless Spaghetti Sauce (p. 128).

**Spinach:** Add 2 cups (500 mL) well-drained chopped cooked spinach to ricotta mixture.

The universal popularity of lasagne made it a standby for casual entertaining. Easy, make-ahead buffet menus (casserole, bread, salad and dessert) became first choice for late-evening suppers at house parties, après-ski or curling, and Grey Cup gatherings around the TV.

Other pasta casseroles (mostly combinations of noodles with ground beef and tomatoes or cream-sauced seafood) were almost as popular as lasagne. Later, as Canadians expanded their pasta horizons, recipes for stuffed cannelloni or manicotti made the rounds.

Spaghetti toppings also evolved past red tomato sauces. White Clam Sauce was an early favorite, followed by Spaghetti Carbonara (with egg and bacon) and Spaghetti à la Caruso (chicken livers). Most people discovered fettucine and linguine first in restaurants, but as grocers' shelves began to stock a large variety of intriguing pasta shapes, home cooks experimented with all kinds of noodles as well as shells, bow ties, rotini, fusilli, penne and rigatoni.

# BEEF FONDUE WITH SAUCES

*Fondue pots were all the rage for wedding gifts in the '60s, when fondue parties became a favorite choice for informal entertaining. Beef was followed by many variations: batter-coated seafood or vegetables (similar to Tempura), or chicken cooked in broth instead of oil (like the Oriental Hot Pot).*

| 3 cups | peanut oil or vegetable oil | 750 mL |
|--------|------------------------------|--------|
| 1-1/2 lb | lean tender beef, cut in 1-inch (2.5 cm) cubes | 750 g |
| | **Dipping Sauces (recipes follow)** | |

Heat oil to 375°F (190°C); transfer to fondue pot set over heat. Serve beef cubes to be skewered and cooked in oil. Serve with dipping sauces. Makes 4 servings.

**Tangy Tomato Sauce:** Combine 1 cup (250 mL) chili sauce, 1 tbsp (15 mL) each brown sugar, horseradish and Worcestershire sauce and 1 clove garlic, minced. Makes about 1 cup (250 mL).

**Mustard or Curry Sauce:** Combine 2/3 cup (150 mL) sour cream, 1/3 cup (75 mL) mayonnaise and 1 tbsp (15 mL) Dijon mustard or 1 tsp (5 mL) curry powder. Makes 1 cup (250 mL).

**Horseradish Sauce:** Combine 1 cup (250 mL) sour cream and 1/3 cup (75 mL) horseradish. Makes about 1-1/3 cups (325 mL).

Cheese fondue became an après-ski favorite, likely "discovered" by Canadians skiing in Switzerland. Other versions followed, such as Beer and Cheddar, and other kinds of cheeses. Sweet fondues of fresh fruit or pound cake dipped in chocolate or even butterscotch, usually liqueured, made novel desserts.

**Cheese Fondue:** Heat 1-1/2 cups (375 mL) dry white wine with 1 tbsp (15 mL) lemon juice and 1 clove garlic, smashed, over medium heat until bubbles form around edge. Remove garlic. Toss 4 cups (1 L) shredded Swiss cheese with 1 tbsp (15 mL) cornstarch. Add to wine, a handful at a time, stirring until melted and starting to bubble. Transfer to fondue pot. Makes 4 servings.

**Chocolate Fondue:** Melt 6 oz (175 g) semisweet chocolate with 1/3 cup (75 mL) whipping cream over hot water until smooth. Mix in 2 tbsp (25 mL) brandy or rum. Transfer to fondue pot. Makes 4 servings.

# TURNIP AND APPLE BAKE

*Over the years, Canadians sautéed, mashed, scalloped, baked, souffléd or layered turnip with apple, as in this recipe.*

| 1 | large turnip (rutabaga), 2-1/2 lb (1.25 kg) | 1 |
|---|-----|---|
| 1 tbsp | butter | 15 mL |
| | Salt and pepper | |
| 2 cups | thinly sliced apples | 500 mL |
| 2 tbsp | packed brown sugar | 25 mL |
| 1/4 tsp | each cinnamon and nutmeg | 1 mL |
| *Topping:* | | |
| 1/2 cup | dry bread crumbs | 125 mL |
| 2 tbsp | packed brown sugar | 25 mL |
| 2 tbsp | butter, melted | 25 mL |

Peel and cut turnip into chunks; cook in boiling salted water until tender. Mash with butter; season with salt and pepper to taste. Layer half in greased 8-cup (2 L) casserole. Toss apples with sugar, cinnamon and nutmeg; arrange evenly on top. Cover with remaining turnip.

Topping: Combine bread crumbs, sugar and butter; sprinkle on top. Bake in 350°F (180°C) oven for 50 to 60 minutes or until apples are fork-tender. Makes 6 servings.

Since the turn of the century, turnips and rutabagas have been mainstays of the Canadian diet. Good storage vegetables, they're available all year round. For years, the big round yellow root was called a turnip or a Swede, but it is now rightfully known as a rutabaga, while the smaller, whiter vegetable is called turnip.

# SPINACH SALAD

*One of the first salads beyond the iceberg-lettuce-with-bottled-dressing standard, spinach salad gained wide popularity at home after it appeared in restaurants.*

| | | |
|---|---|---|
| 1 | pkg (10 oz/284 g) fresh spinach | 1 |
| 1 | small red onion, sliced in rings | 1 |
| 1 cup | sliced mushrooms | 250 mL |
| 6 | slices bacon, cooked and crumbled | 6 |
| 2 | hard-cooked eggs, chopped | 2 |
| *Dressing:* | | |
| 3 tbsp | vinegar | 50 mL |
| 2 tbsp | granulated sugar or honey | 25 mL |
| 1/2 tsp | salt | 2 mL |
| 1/4 tsp | pepper | 1 mL |
| 1/4 tsp | dry mustard | 1 mL |
| Dash | Worcestershire sauce | Dash |
| 1/2 cup | vegetable oil | 125 mL |

Trim spinach and tear into bite-size pieces; place in salad bowl. Top with onion, mushrooms, bacon and eggs.

Dressing: Whisk together vinegar, sugar, salt, pepper, mustard and Worcestershire sauce; whisk in oil. Pour over salad and toss well. Makes 6 servings.

The earliest versions of spinach salad nearly always included bacon bits, chopped eggs and sliced mushrooms. A bit later, additional ingredients such as bean sprouts, water chestnuts, sesame seeds, pecans or toasted almonds, orange sections, cherry tomatoes, grated cheese and croutons created endless variations. The dressing was usually a sweet vinaigrette.

# THREE-BEAN SALAD

*A great make-ahead for potluck suppers and barbecues, this salad inspired many variations with different seasonings and vinegars. Some recipes expanded to four- or five-bean combinations, adding lima beans, white kidney beans or chick-peas.*

| | | |
|---|---|---|
| 1 | can (14 oz/398 mL) each cut green beans, yellow beans and red kidney beans | 1 |
| 3/4 cup | chopped celery | 175 mL |
| 1/2 cup | chopped onion | 125 mL |
| 1/2 cup | chopped sweet green pepper | 125 mL |
| 1/2 cup | white or cider vinegar | 125 mL |
| 1/2 cup | vegetable oil | 125 mL |
| 1/3 cup | granulated sugar | 75 mL |
| 1 tsp | salt | 5 mL |
| 1/2 tsp | pepper | 2 mL |
| 1 tsp | dried herbs | 5 mL |

Drain green, yellow and kidney beans; rinse with cold water. In bowl, combine beans, celery, onion and green pepper. Whisk together vinegar, oil, sugar, salt, pepper and herbs; pour over bean mixture and mix well. Cover and chill at least 8 hours. Drain before serving. Makes 8 servings.

**Schnippled Bean Salad:** This sour-cream bean salad is a Mennonite specialty. "Schnippel" means to cut beans on a slant into long thin slices (similar to frenched beans).

Trim and "schnippel" 1 lb (500 g) fresh green or yellow beans; cook in boiling salted water until barely tender. Drain and rinse under cold water. Thinly slice 1 small onion and sprinkle with salt; let stand 15 minutes, stirring 2 or 3 times.

In large bowl, mix together 2 tsp (10 mL) granulated sugar, 2 tsp (10 mL) cider vinegar, 1/2 tsp (2 mL) salt and 1/4 tsp (1 mL) pepper; blend in 3/4 cup (175 mL) sour cream. Squeeze juice from onion; add onion to dressing. Add beans and toss well. Cover and chill. Makes 6 servings.

# DILL CASSEROLE BREAD

*This is excellent served warm from the oven or toasted on the barbecue.*

| | | |
|---|---|---|
| 1 tsp | granulated sugar | 5 mL |
| 1/2 cup | lukewarm water | 125 mL |
| 1 | pkg active dry yeast | 1 |
| 1 cup | creamed cottage cheese, heated to lukewarm | 250 mL |
| 2 tbsp | grated Parmesan cheese | 25 mL |
| 2 tbsp | granulated sugar | 25 mL |
| 1 tsp | salt | 5 mL |
| 1/2 tsp | baking soda | 2 mL |
| 2 tsp | dill seed | 10 mL |
| 1 | small onion, finely chopped | 1 |
| 1 | egg | 1 |
| 2-1/2 cups | all-purpose flour | 625 mL |
| | Softened butter | |
| | Coarse salt | |

Dissolve sugar in warm water; stir in yeast. Let stand 10 minutes or until frothy. In large bowl, combine cottage cheese, Parmesan, 2 tbsp (25 mL) sugar, salt, baking soda, dill seed, onion and egg; add yeast and mix well. Add 1 cup (250 mL) flour; beat for 2 minutes. Gradually beat in remaining flour. Cover and let rise in warm place until doubled, about 1 hour.

Stir down dough; turn into greased 6-cup (1.5 L) casserole or soufflé dish. Cover and let rise again until doubled, about 45 minutes.

Bake in 350°F (180°C) oven for 40 to 50 minutes or until loaf sounds hollow when tapped on bottom. Remove from dish to rack. Brush top with butter; sprinkle with salt. Makes 1 loaf.

No-knead or casserole breads were a big hit in the '60s. Made with a fast-and-easy yeast dough, they could be plain or savory. Later versions added cottage cheese, herbs like oregano, dill, parsley and chives, and sometimes minced garlic. Soon ricotta was used in place of cottage cheese.

Olive Diefenbaker, wife of Canada's prime minister in the early '60s, had a recipe for **Featherbeds**, simple buns that didn't require kneading. A Nova Scotia recipe called **Goofy Rolls** was also no-knead and used both yeast and baking powder.

# SOUR CREAM COFFEECAKE

*Coffeecake in the '60s usually meant this one. Delicious when freshly baked, it also freezes and reheats well.*

| | | |
|---|---|---|
| 3/4 cup | butter | 175 mL |
| 1 cup | granulated sugar | 250 mL |
| 2 | eggs | 2 |
| 1 tsp | vanilla | 5 mL |
| 2 cups | all-purpose flour | 500 mL |
| 1 tsp | baking powder | 5 mL |
| 1 tsp | baking soda | 5 mL |
| 1/2 tsp | salt | 2 mL |
| 1 cup | sour cream | 250 mL |
| *Topping:* | | |
| 1/2 cup | packed brown sugar | 125 mL |
| 1/4 cup | finely chopped nuts | 50 mL |
| 1 tsp | cinnamon | 5 mL |

Topping: Combine sugar, nuts and cinnamon; set aside.

In bowl, cream butter with sugar; beat in eggs and vanilla. Mix together flour, baking powder, soda and salt; add to creamed mixture alternately with sour cream. Spread half in greased and floured 9- or 10-inch (3 or 4 L) tube pan or 10-inch (3 L) springform pan; sprinkle with half the topping. Repeat. Bake in 350°F (180°C) oven for 40 to 45 minutes or until tester comes out clean.

**VARIATIONS:**

**Oblong:** Spread batter in 13- x 9-inch (3.5 L) pan; sprinkle with topping. Bake for 30 minutes.

**Rhubarb Streusel:** Stir 2 cups (500 mL) finely chopped fresh rhubarb into batter. Spread in 13- x 9-inch (3.5 L) pan; sprinkle with topping. Bake 40 minutes.

**Berry Streusel:** Spread batter in 13- x 9-inch (3.5 L) pan; spoon 2 cups (500 mL) berries over top. Sprinkle with topping. Bake 40 to 45 minutes.

**Poppy Seed:** Combine 1 cup (250 mL) poppy seeds with the sour cream; let stand 1 hour before mixing into batter. Bake 40 to 45 minutes.

# PUDDING POUND CAKE

*One of the most popular recipes of the decade, this still surfaces in the '90s. By mixing and matching cake and pudding mixes, countless variations were possible. When bundt pans became popular in the '70s, this was one of the first recipes used.*

*Since today's cake mixes are richer-textured than those of the '60s, we have reduced the amount of oil in this old recipe.*

| | | |
|---|---|---|
| 1 | pkg (two-layer) cake mix | 1 |
| 1 | pkg (4 servings) instant pudding mix | 1 |
| 1 cup | water | 250 mL |
| 1/4 cup | vegetable oil | 50 mL |
| 4 | eggs | 4 |

In bowl, beat cake mix, pudding mix, water, oil and eggs for 2 to 5 minutes (longer beating produces finer texture).

Pour into greased and floured pan(s) and bake in 350°F (180°C) oven as follows: two 9- x 5-inch (2 L) pans for 45 minutes; one 10-inch (4 L) tube or bundt pan for 45 to 50 minutes; one 13- x 9-inch (3.5 L) pan for 40 to 45 minutes or until tester comes out clean. Let cool slightly; remove from pan.

**VARIATIONS:**

**Orange:** Add 1 tbsp (15 mL) grated orange rind. Use orange juice in place of water.

**Poppy Seed:** Substitute 1/3 cup (75 mL) poppy seeds soaked in 1 cup (75 mL) water for 1 hour for the water.

**Spice Swirl:** Combine 1/4 cup (50 mL) packed brown sugar, 3/4 tsp (4 mL) cinnamon and 1/4 tsp (1 mL) nutmeg; layer with batter in 3 layers in tube pan.

**Lemon Glaze:** Mix 1 cup (250 mL) icing sugar with 2 tbsp (25 mL) lemon juice. Poke holes in warm cake; pour glaze over.

Eventually, mixes other than pudding and cake were baked into desserts in great profusion.

**Dream Cake:** Combine a two-layer cake mix, an envelope of Dream Whip, 4 eggs and 1 cup (250 mL) cold tap water or orange or pineapple juice. Mix and bake as for Pudding Pound Cake.

**Dump Cake** was made with crushed pineapple, canned pie filling, nuts and cake mix topped with slices of butter, then baked.

**Friendship Cake** made the rounds again in the '80s. It began with a brandied "starter" of canned fruit, cake mix, eggs and oil, usually given to you by a friend. Then, using more cake mix, nuts, eggs and oil, you made enough starter and cake to give loaves to other friends.

**Sex-in-a-Pan** (or **Heaven-in-a-Pan** in a United Church cookbook from the '80s) was a rich and calorie-laden layered concoction of vanilla and chocolate instant puddings, whipped topping and melted chocolate.

# FUDGE BROWNIES

*Girl Guides and Brownies often made brownies to sell at bake sales. But the cookies they have sold across Canada for years are the familiar sandwich cookies imprinted with the Guides' trefoil. Originally, they sold raisin cookies in Prince Edward Island and sugar cookies in Manitoba.*

| 2 oz | unsweetened chocolate, melted | 60 g |
|------|-------------------------------|------|
| 1/2 cup | butter, melted | 125 mL |
| 1 cup | granulated sugar | 250 mL |
| 2 | eggs | 2 |
| 1 tsp | vanilla | 5 mL |
| 1/2 cup | all-purpose flour | 125 mL |
| 1/2 cup | chopped walnuts | 125 mL |

In bowl, combine chocolate, butter, sugar, eggs and vanilla; beat well. Gently stir in flour only until no streaks remain. Add nuts. Spread in greased 8-inch (2 L) square pan. Bake in 350°F (180°C) oven for 20 to 25 minutes until barely firm to the touch.

## VARIATIONS:

**Cake Brownies:** Increase flour to 2/3 cup (150 mL).
**Cocoa Brownies:** Omit chocolate. Add 6 tbsp (100 mL) unsweetened cocoa powder and 1 tbsp (15 mL) butter.
**Double Chocolate:** Add 1/2 cup (125 mL) white chocolate chips to batter.
**Coconut Brownies:** Substitute flaked coconut for nuts.
**Mocha Brownies:** Add 1 tbsp (15 mL) instant coffee granules to flour.
**Rocky Road:** Add 1 cup (250 mL) miniature marshmallows to batter.

Over the years, there have been many brownie variations, including **Blonde Brownies**, a rich brown-sugar bar with chocolate chips folded in, or added as soon as the squares come out of the oven, to be spread like icing when melted. Mint wafers are used as icing, as well.
**Mint-Frosted Brownies:** Beat together 1 cup (250 mL) sifted icing sugar, 2 tbsp (25 mL) butter, 1 tbsp (15 mL) milk and 1 or 2 drops peppermint extract. Spread over brownies. Drizzle with 1 oz (30 g) semisweet chocolate, melted.

# BAKED ALASKA

*Choose your favorite flavor of ice cream for this fairly easy dessert.*

| 4 cups | ice cream | 1 L |
|--------|-----------|-----|
| 1 | 9-inch (23 cm) round sponge cake, or Fudge Brownies baked in 9-inch (23 cm) round pan | 1 |
| 4 | egg whites | 4 |
| 1/2 tsp | cream of tartar | 2 mL |
| 1/2 cup | granulated sugar | 125 mL |

Pack ice cream into plastic-wrap-lined bowl slightly smaller in diameter than cake round; freeze. Remove and centre on cake; cover and freeze.

At serving time, beat egg whites with cream of tartar until frothy; gradually beat in sugar until stiff peaks form. Transfer cake and ice cream to wooden board. Cover with meringue. Bake in 500°F (250°C) oven for 2 to 3 minutes or until lightly browned. Serve at once. Makes 6 to 8 servings.

Spectacular flaming desserts such as **Bananas Flambé** were all the rage in the '60s.
**Cherries Jubilee:** Drain 14 oz (398 mL) can Bing cherries into chafing dish; mix in 2 tsp (10 mL) cornstarch and cook until clear. Add 2 tbsp (25 mL) red currant jelly; heat until melted. Stir in cherries. Add 1/4 cup (50 mL) cherry brandy. Ignite and spoon immediately over rich vanilla ice cream.
**Crêpes Suzette:** Make 12 to 15 dessert crêpes (see Crabmeat Crêpes, p. 200). Blend together 1/4 cup (50 mL) butter, 1/4 cup (50 mL) granulated sugar and 1 tbsp (15 mL) grated orange rind; spread on crêpes and fold each into quarters.

In chafing dish, combine 3/4 cup (175 mL) orange juice, 2 tbsp (25 mL) butter, 1/2 cup (125 mL) granulated sugar and 1/2 cup (125 mL) Grand Marnier or Cognac; bring just to boil; add folded crêpes. Flambé. Makes 4 to 6 servings.

# CHERRY CHEESECAKE

*By far the most popular cheesecake made and served at home in the '60s was a simple one with a can of cherry pie filling spooned on top.*

| | | |
|---|---|---|
| 1 cup | graham wafer crumbs | 250 mL |
| 3 tbsp | granulated sugar | 50 mL |
| 3 tbsp | butter, melted | 50 mL |
| *Filling:* | | |
| 1-1/2 lb | cream cheese (at room temperature) | 750 g |
| 1 cup | granulated sugar | 250 mL |
| 3 tbsp | all-purpose flour | 50 mL |
| 1 tbsp | grated lemon rind | 15 mL |
| 2 tbsp | lemon juice | 25 mL |
| 1/2 tsp | vanilla | 2 mL |
| 4 | eggs | 4 |
| 1 | can (19 oz/540 mL) cherry pie filling, drained | 1 |

Combine crumbs, sugar and butter; press onto bottom of 9-inch (2.5 L) springform pan. Bake in 325°F (160°C) oven 10 minutes. Let cool.

Filling: In bowl, blend cheese, sugar, flour, lemon rind and juice and vanilla; beat in eggs, one at a time, beating well after each addition. Pour over crust. Bake in 450°F (230°C) oven for 10 minutes; bake in 250°F (120°C) oven 30 minutes. Immediately run sharp knife around outside edge of cake to loosen; let cool in pan. Spoon cherry pie filling over top. Makes 8 servings.

## VARIATION:

**Blueberry Cheesecake:** Prepare cheesecake but omit cherry topping. In saucepan, combine 1/2 cup (125 mL) granulated sugar, 4 tsp (20 mL) cornstarch, 1/3 cup (75 mL) water and 3 tbsp (50 mL) lemon juice. Cook, stirring, until boiling and thickened. Let cool slightly; add 2 cups (500 mL) blueberries. Spoon over cake and chill.

Hadassah groups all over Canada use cookbooks as fund-raisers, and with great success. Each contains wonderful recipes for cheesecake. Winnipeg foodies have insisted for years that cheesecake be made with cream cheese from the People's Cooperative Dairy. Topped with sour cream, it gets full marks.

There are countless recipes for Chocolate, Marble, Pumpkin, Eggnog and Maple Syrup Cheesecake. Think of a flavor, and we make it in a cheesecake. Bonnie Stern, director of a cooking school in Toronto, is famous for her Amaretto "Love" Cheesecake. Recipes vary in density (richness), using 1/2 lb to 2 lb (125 g to 1 kg) cream cheese, and regional fruit such as cranberry and blueberry are favorite toppings. Not to be confused with classic baked cheesecakes, there are refrigerated versions often made with cottage cheese and sometimes with gelatin, which are light and delicious but not the same.

# STRAWBERRY PARFAIT PIE

*If desired, the top of the pie can also be covered with whole strawberries and just before serving, brushed with melted red currant jelly to glaze.*

| 1 | pkg (4 servings) strawberry jelly powder | 1 |
|---|---|---|
| 1-1/4 cups | boiling water | 300 mL |
| 2 cups | vanilla ice cream | 500 mL |
| 1-1/2 cups | sliced strawberries | 375 mL |

| 1 | baked 8- or 9-inch (20 or 23 cm) pastry shell or crumb crust | 1 |
|---|---|---|

*Garnish (optional):*

| | Whipped cream |
|---|---|
| | Strawberries |

In bowl, dissolve jelly powder in boiling water. Add ice cream by spoonfuls, stirring until melted. Chill, stirring occasionally, until slightly thickened. Fold in strawberries. Pour into pie shell. Chill until firm. Garnish with whipped cream and strawberries.

Parfait pies first appeared in the '50s, probably as promotions by jelly powder manufacturers. They were instantly popular because they were so easy to make. By the '60s, flavor variations included peach, pineapple, orange and raspberry, but strawberry is the all-time favorite.

# MAGIC LEMON PIE

*This is so named because the filling thickens without cooking. Old cookbooks have recipes for making your own sweetened condensed milk with skim milk powder, sugar, margarine and boiling water.*

| 1-1/4 cups | sweetened condensed milk | 300 mL |
|---|---|---|
| 1/2 cup | lemon juice | 125 mL |
| 1 tsp | grated lemon rind | 5 mL |
| 2 | eggs, separated | 2 |
| 1 | 8-inch (20 cm) baked pie shell or crumb crust | 1 |
| 1/4 tsp | cream of tartar | 1 mL |
| 1/4 cup | granulated sugar | 50 mL |

In bowl, mix sweetened condensed milk with lemon juice and rind. Blend in egg yolks; pour into pie shell.

Beat egg whites with cream of tartar until soft peaks form; gradually beat in sugar until stiff peaks form. Pile on filling, sealing to crust. Bake in 350°F (180°C) oven for 10 minutes or until lightly browned.

### VARIATION:

**Key Lime Pie:** Beat 3 egg yolks with 1 can (300 mL) sweetened condensed milk and 1/2 cup (125 mL) lime juice; fold in 3 egg whites, stiffly beaten. Pour into 9-inch (23 cm) crumb crust (see Flapper Pie, p. 66). Bake in 350°F (180°C) oven for 25 minutes.

The baking of the '60s was sweet, and condensed milk, usually referred to simply as Eagle Brand, was one of the reasons. Here are favorites that used condensed milk:

**Rocky Road Squares** had marshmallows and nuts.

**Hello Dollys** were layers of butterscotch and chocolate chips, coconut and nuts drizzled with condensed milk and baked.

**Neapolitan Squares** had a graham wafer base, coconut and condensed milk, which was baked and iced.

**Lemon Slice**, unbaked, had a base of whole graham wafers covered with the Magic Lemon Pie filling, then iced.

**Strawberries** were desiccated coconut and sweetened condensed milk, shaped and rolled in red jelly powder.

# BLUEBERRY PIE

*Use either wild or cultivated blueberries for this pie. For frozen berries, use 5 tbsp (75 mL) cornstarch instead of flour.*

| | | |
|---|---|---|
| 4 cups | fresh blueberries | 1 L |
| 2/3 cups | granulated sugar | 150 mL |
| 3 tbsp | all-purpose flour | 50 mL |
| 1 tbsp | lemon juice | 15 mL |
| 1 tbsp | butter | 15 mL |
| | Pastry for 9-inch (23 cm) double-crust pie | |

Combine berries, sugar, flour and lemon juice. Pour into pastry-lined pie plate. Dot with butter. Cover with top crust; seal and flute edges. Cut a few slashes in top crust. Bake in 425°F (220°C) oven for 15 minutes; reduce heat to 350°F (180°C) and bake for 35 to 45 minutes longer or until golden brown.

---

### VARIATION:

**Saskatoon Pie:** In saucepan, simmer 4 cups (1 L) saskatoon berries in 1/4 cup (50 mL) water for 10 minutes. Add 2 tbsp (25 mL) lemon juice. Stir in 3/4 cup (175 mL) granulated sugar mixed with 3 tbsp (50 mL) flour. Fill and bake as for Blueberry Pie.

Fresh berry pies have been made in every decade, the choice of fruit dictated by season and region. As home freezers became more common, commercial and home-frozen berries were used all year round.

The most popular wild berries for pies include blueberries, saskatoons (serviceberries), raspberries and partridgeberries. Cultivated blueberries are the low-bush variety in Quebec and Nova Scotia, high-bush in southern British Columbia. B.C. also grows blackberries and loganberries (a hybrid of blackberry and raspberry). In Saskatchewan, cultivated saskatoons became popular pick-your-owns in the '80s.

# CHERRY PIE

*Bright red sour Montmorency cherries (rather than the sweet Bings) are the choice for pies.*

| | | |
|---|---|---|
| 2 to 4 tbsp | cornstarch | 25 to 50 mL |
| 1 cup | granulated sugar | 250 mL |
| Pinch | salt | Pinch |
| 4 cups | pitted sour cherries (fresh or frozen, slightly thawed) | 1 L |
| 1/4 tsp | almond extract | 1 mL |
| 1 tbsp | butter | 15 mL |
| | Pastry for 9-inch (23 cm) double-crust pie | |

In saucepan, mix cornstarch (2 tbsp/25 mL for fresh cherries, 4 tbsp/50 mL for frozen) with sugar and salt. Stir in cherries. Heat over low heat until juicy. Bring slowly to boil, stirring; cook until liquid is thickened and clear. Add almond extract and butter. Cool to room temperature.

Spoon into pastry-lined pie plate. Cover with lattice or plain top crust; seal and flute edges. Bake in 425°F (220°C) oven for 15 minutes; reduce heat to 350°F (180°C) and bake for 35 to 40 minutes longer or until golden brown.

Cherry pie contests were very popular in the '60s. Inevitably the most attractive pies had lattice-top crusts, as they did in magazine ads and TV commercials from flour, shortening and lard manufacturers.

Cherry season is short in Canada, with only British Columbia and Ontario producing significant commercial amounts. Frozen pitted sour cherries, becoming more widely available commercially, are convenient to use year-round.

# CLASSIC APPLE PIE

*Over the years, apple pie has always been Canada's favorite pie. Whether it's the traditional two-crusted, a crumb-topped variation, or even baked in a brown paper bag (which was all the rage for a while), it's a dessert that's hard to beat, especially warm from the oven and served with ice cream, whipped cream or a slice of good Cheddar. In this recipe, adjust the ingredients according to the apples used (increase or decrease sugar if apples are very tart or very sweet; adjust flour if apples are very juicy or dry).*

| | | |
|---|---|---|
| 5 cups | peeled, sliced apples | 1.25 L |
| 3/4 cup | granulated sugar | 175 mL |
| 1 tbsp | flour | 15 mL |
| 1/2 tsp | cinnamon | 2 mL |
| 1 tbsp | lemon juice | 15 mL |
| 1 tbsp | butter | 15 mL |
| | Pastry for 9-inch (23 cm) double-crust pie | |
| | Glaze: cream or egg wash; sugar | |

Mix together apples, sugar, flour, cinnamon and lemon juice. Turn into pastry-lined pie plate. Dot with butter. Cover with top crust; seal and flute edges. Cut a few slashes in top crust. Brush lightly with cream or egg wash (egg beaten lightly with a teaspoon of water). Sprinkle with sugar.

Bake in 425°F (220°C) oven for 15 minutes; reduce heat to 350°F (180°C) and bake for 35 to 40 minutes longer or until pastry is golden brown and apples are tender.

**Streusel Topping:** Use in place of top crust, if desired. Combine 1/2 cup (125 mL) flour, 1/4 cup (50 mL) brown sugar and 1/4 tsp (1 mL) cinnamon; cut in 1/4 cup (50 mL) butter until crumbly. Sprinkle over filling before baking.

**Apple-Cranberry Pie:** Combine 4 cups (1 L) sliced apples, 1-1/2 cups (375 mL) cranberries, 1/2 cup (125 mL) raisins (optional), 1 cup (250 mL) sugar and 1 tbsp (15 mL) flour. Fill and bake as for Apple Pie.

**Schnitz Apple Pie:** Cut 4 to 5 peeled apples in fairly thick slices; arrange in pastry-lined pie plate. Combine 1 cup (250 mL) sour cream, 3/4 cup (175 mL) sugar, 3 tbsp (50 mL) flour and a pinch of salt; pour over apples. Sprinkle with mixture of 3 tbsp (50 mL) sugar and 1 tsp (5 mL) cinnamon. Bake in 425°F (220°C) oven for 15 minutes; reduce heat to 350°F (180°C) and bake about 30 minutes longer or until apples are tender and filling is set.

# RHUBARB CUSTARD PIE

*Creamy fruit custard pies have been favorites for many generations. Popular variations include peach, cherry, raspberry and gooseberry. This pie is best with a lattice top crust, although a plain crust (or no crust at all) is also common.*

| | | |
|---|---|---|
| 4 cups | fresh rhubarb, cut in 1/2 inch (1 cm) pieces | 1 L |
| 1-1/4 cups | granulated sugar | 300 mL |
| 1/4 cup | all-purpose flour | 50 mL |
| 2 | eggs, lightly beaten | 2 |
| 2 tbsp | melted butter | 25 mL |
| | Pastry for 9-inch (23 cm) double-crust pie | |

Mix together sugar, flour, eggs and melted butter. Combine with rhubarb. Turn into pastry-lined pie plate. Cover with top crust; seal and flute edges. Bake in 425°F (220°C) oven for 10 minutes; reduce heat to 350°F (180°C) and bake for about 35 minutes longer or until pastry is golden brown, rhubarb soft and filling set.

**Custard Pie:** An old-fashioned pie with a plain baked custard filling has been a treat since grandma's day. During the '60s, the possibility of a soggy undercrust was solved with **Slip-Slide Custard Pie**, made by baking the filling separately in a pie plate (set in a larger pan of hot water, as for individual baked custards) and then sliding it while lukewarm into a baked pastry shell.

For traditional custard pie, beat 4 eggs lightly and beat in 2/3 cup granulated sugar, 1/4 tsp (1 mL) each salt and nutmeg. Stir in 1-1/2 cups (325 mL) milk, 1 cup (250 mL) light cream and 1 tsp (5 mL) vanilla. Pour into pastry-lined pie plate. Bake in 425°F (220°C) oven for 15 minutes; reduce heat to 350°F (180°C) for about 30 minutes longer or until filling is set at edges but still slightly soft in centre. Serve slightly warm or cold.

The
SEVENTIES
1970 - 1979

*A friend said to me, "You're writing a book about a gourmet's Canada? That will be a short book." Nevertheless, I am convinced that the gourmet's desires can be fulfilled from Cape Onion, Newfoundland, to Peachland, British Columbia....We have a lot of good food in our country but we do not take care of it or eat it all or know enough about it....Gluttony tinged with nationalism would definitely help."*

*– Sondra Gotlieb*
*The Gourmet's Canada*

The '70s rolled in on a wave of new ideas, liberalism and optimism about the future. The '60s had swept away many of the old rules, and freed up the national psyche. We could be anything we wanted to be.

But "doing your own thing" means first of all checking out the choices, and the '70s were a decade of exploration. We tried anything and everything new. And just as clothing fashions offered everything from mini to midi, from designer denims to unisex business suits, cooking styles came in a multitude of choices.

New influences came from everywhere – nouvelle cuisine from France, "natural" foods from the back-to-the-land movement, health consciousness from the fitness boom, international tastes from travels abroad and multiculturalism at home, "gourmet" cooking (pseudo and otherwise) from cookbooks and television chefs.

As we entered the '70s, steak and pizza were still gastronomical heights for many Canadians. But a growing segment of the population had already tuned in to Julia Child and her friends, collected the right cookbooks (James Beard, Craig Claiborne and the *New York Times Cookbook*), experimented with French cooking and bought all the proper equipment (copper mixing bowls, whisks and Le Creuset sauté pans).

Cooking schools began to attract large numbers of home cooks eager to learn about new food fashions, ingredients, techniques and equipment. In 1971 Etta Sawyer established the Academy of Culinary Arts in Toronto; Bonnie Stern opened her Toronto school in 1973 and was one of the first to use the Cuisinart food processor. Other new schools of the '70s helped pave the way to a culinary mania that peaked in the early '80s.

The home economists of food companies and other home service departments that were so active in the '60s were still going strong with cooking shows and demonstrations. Local school boards also made major contributions to the cooking-school scene

---

*Dinner clubs like this one in Etobicoke, Ontario enjoyed both Canadian and international cooking styles.*

*A Brownie offers brownies to celebrate the diamond jubilee of the Girl Guides of Canada.*

Homemaker's *magazine featured a series on Canada's multicultural flavors.*

**On pages 164 – 165: A casual brunch with foreign flavors: Gazpacho, Quiche Lorraine, Spinach Salad and Grasshopper Pie Squares.**

**ETHNIC FOOD**
CANADIAN STYLE
Tangible evidence of Canada's rich cultural heritage

A special pull-out booklet

with popular courses offering everything from "International Vegetarian" to "Flambéing for Fun."

Along with the new wave of "gourmet" and international cooking came a revival of interest in our own culinary heritage. After the very few authentic regional cookbooks produced in previous decades, the '70s finally brought a succession of gems.

Madame Benoit's *The Canadiana Cookbook* (1970) was a collection of traditional recipes from every province. Marie Nightingale's *Out of Old Nova Scotia Kitchens* (1971) was the first comprehensive look at the province's diverse culinary heritage, including both history and recipes.

Sondra Gotlieb's *The Gourmet's Canada* created a buzz on the food scene in 1972. She was the first author to juxtapose the words "gourmet" and "Canada" and prove they were not a contradiction in terms. Aiming to make Canadians more aware of our gastronomic resources, she took us on a coast-

to-coast tour to sample wild rice, partridgeberries, Oka cheese, buckwheat honey, Manitoba caviar, rainbow trout, perogies, knishes, colcannon, cipaille and dozens of other delicious foods that many Canadians had never tasted or even heard of. She took us beyond supermarkets to cheese shops, bakeries, delis and farmers' markets, beyond meat-and-potatoes to a multi-ethnic Canadian feast. In 1976, she wrote *Cross-Canada Cooking*, visiting Canadian kitchens of various ethnic and regional heritage from Newfoundland Irish to Winnipeg Jewish to British Columbia Japanese.

Elizabeth Baird's *Classic Canadian Cooking* (1974) focused on Upper Canadian culinary traditions that evolved in the 1800s. While raising our awareness of this important heritage, Elizabeth praised the seasonal nature of the old time cooking: "There was a respect in it for the Canadian land and the fruits of it...a rhythm to it as rich and fluid as the seasonal cycle...."

*Fall festivals celebrated foods from around the world, such as delectable baked goods from Latvia.*
Courtesy of Frank Grant, GW Photography, Toronto

*In Italian neighborhoods, the annual production of tomato sauce was a familiar tradition.*
Courtesy of Ottmar Bierwagen, Toronto

*In* Classic Canadian Cooking *(1974) Elizabeth Baird described the first official Canadian Thanksgiving of a century before.  Later, in* Canadian Living, *she wrote about her own family's enduring traditions:*

Every Thanksgiving, my family gathers for noon dinner in the heart of Perth county in southern Ontario. Taking the gravel concession roads, we drive through the tiny North Thames village of Fullarton. . . and we pass the farm [our] Aberdeen ancestors cleared in the 1840s. . . .

At the community hall in Russeldale, three generations unload the wicker baskets. . . . Cousin Verlyn and Aunt Marjorie are already in the kitchen, cooking the rutabaga, mashing potatoes, mixing cranberry punch and making coffee. . . . Aunt Helen sets out her pumpkin pies . . . glistening amber-brown, with a swirl of cream baked in the centre.

The buffet table is a kaleidoscope of colors with cranberry-orange sauce, green and red cabbage salad, golden jellied salads and bright fall vegetables around a cheesy dip.  Uncle Clayton and my father . . . are each carving a turkey and proclaiming, as they do every year, that this year's birds smell and taste the best ever.

Outside, the autumn sunshine is still strong enough to warm the corn stubble in the fields and burnish the orange cheeks of the last pumpkins.

Bright blue silos full of chopped corn silage tower over 19th-century barns and farmhouses. The granaries are packed, lofts stacked with straw bales.  Fruit cellars and freezers are full; jars of preserves line the shelves. "Just the ploughing left to do," Uncle Ray says proudly. We relax, knowing that another cycle has come to a fruitful and prosperous end.  We give thanks and dig in.

Other notable regional cookbooks published in the '70s included *Nova Scotia Down-Home Cooking* by Janice Gill, *The Old Ontario Cookbook* and *Every Day A Feast* by Muriel Breckenridge, *The Northern Cook Book* by Eleanor Ellis, and *Fat-Back & Molasses* (Newfoundland and Labrador recipes compiled by Ivan Jesperson). In Quebec, many excellent collections of regional recipes were produced by women's organizations in every part of the province, from the Women's Institute in Hemmingford to the Cercle de Fermières in St-Gabriel.

The mid-'70s also brought the first of a stream of self-published cookbooks, mostly from Alberta, that were to become phenomenally successful in the years that followed. *The Best of Bridge,* put out in 1975 by the eight members of a Calgary bridge club, quickly passed the novelty stage to roar to million-dollar sales and several sequels.

In 1979, Books For Cooks (now The Cookbook Store), billed as the first cookbooks-only store in Canada (and in all North America, according to most sources), opened at Yonge and Yorkville in Toronto. Food writer Jim White in the *Toronto Star* listed the seven best-selling cookbooks in the Metro area (the top three were *Joy of Cooking, Better Homes and Gardens New Cook Book* and *The Canadian Cook Book*) and joined other forecasters in correctly predicting a major cookbook boom coming in the '80s.

In December 1975, the first issue of *Canadian Living* appeared in supermarkets, quickly gaining national distribution and a large and loyal following of home cooks. By 1978, the magazine expanded to 12 issues a year and produced the first of its popular magazine-format cookbooks focusing on seasonal recipes for family and entertaining.

*Homemaker's* magazine (which was launched in 1966) raised consciousness about women's issues, including their role in domestic life in the '70s, and also drew attention to the Canadian food scene with several series of articles, such as Carroll Allen's award-winning "This Bountiful Land," an in-depth look at our farming and fishing families. *Harrowsmith* magazine gained a wide readership among country

*With strong ties to the land and sea, fishing, farming and market gardening families – producers of our daily food – are very special Canadians.*

© BROCK MAY/OUTSIDE EXPOSURE

© BROCK MAY/OUTSIDE EXPOSURE

Courtesy of Mike Gluss, Ganges, BC

## LOOKING BACK

*From the series "This Bountiful Land" by Carroll Allen in Homemaker's (1978), this story foreshadowed the cod stock crises of the 1990s.*

The clapboard houses, in crisp new-crayon shades of blue, yellow, tan and white, huddle together at road's edge on the lip of the sea, united against the wind. The 1,100 inhabitants of Burin [Newfoundland] live daily with views that camera-toting tourists journey thousands of miles to see. But this is no tourist town – it's a working, fishing community.

When I interrupted Teddy Paul in midafternoon, he was on his wharf with his son Donald, hosing out the boat. They had been up since 3 a.m., chugged 16 miles out to sea, hauled 34 nets full of fish, pulled into the wharf at 9 a.m., and had several hours of fish- and net-cleaning still to do.

They fish for cod and flounder from May until November. Some years that's enough to support Teddy and Dorothy and their nine children. "But more years, it's not," Teddy says matter-of-factly. He doesn't urge his children to become fishermen unless they want to, but after 35 years, he doesn't want to do anything else.

Neither does Eugene Mayo, trawler mate for the past six years – though his wife Shirley wishes he were home more. When he started fishing 18 years ago [1960] a 24-hour tour in good weather would bring in a full load; now [1978] trawlers are coming in half-full after nine days at sea.

Whether he's an inshore fisherman battling an errant whale, or an offshore fisherman chopping ice off the spars in the middle of the night, the life is a rugged one. "Maybe I think flour costs too much," Teddy Paul observes, "but that's because I don't know what a farmer goes through to raise the wheat. Anybody who thinks fish costs too much just doesn't understand what we have to do to land it."

dwellers, armchair farmers and environmentalists, with good natural food as part of its appeal.

Seasonal homegrown produce was also getting a lot more attention with the rapid growth of farmers' markets in the '70s. The Kitchener market built a new complex in 1974 and continued to attract regular customers from miles around, although many of the Old Order Mennonites moved out to set up their stalls at the Waterloo and Elmira markets. Toronto's old St. Lawrence market expanded to a second building. The Saskatchewan farmers' market program opened six new markets. In 1979, Vancouver's Granville Island Public Market opened in a bright and airy new building with boats at the doorstep and stalls selling everything from salmon sushi to Okanagan peaches and Fraser Valley flowers.

Multiculturalism became official policy in Canada in 1973, but its culinary effects were already spicing up the food pages of newspapers and magazines. Moussaka, zabaglione, tempura and falafel were new adventures for many readers, who ate it all up and asked for more. As the decade progressed, articles on ethnic cuisine gradually presented more authentic versions of familiar dishes as well as introducing exotic new international recipes.

Food fairs and folk festivals brought dancing in the streets as well as samples of food from a dozen lands in one evening. Winnipeg's Folklorama festival began in 1970, joining Toronto's Caravan and Edmonton's Heritage Days in celebration of Scottish haggis, Greek souvlaki, Indian curries, Caribbean patties and Hungarian plum dumplings.

Technological developments kept pace alongside our romance with the past. Microwave ovens made their appearance on the Canadian market, and, never fazed by the new, Madame

*Multiculturalism brought new flavors, such as those from the Caribbean, to city markets like Toronto's Kensington.*

CHRISTOPHER CAMPBELL, Toronto

*Canadians became aware of the pleasures of traditional ethnic feasts, such as this Greek lamb barbecue in the park.*

Courtesy of Frank Grant, GW Photography, Toronto

## NUTRITION

- The '70s were the diet decade. Weight control was the big nutrition issue, resulting in phenomenal sales of diet books, proliferation of fad diets and emergence of diet clinics.

- 1970–72: National nutrition survey conducted by Nutrition Canada teams travelling country.

- 1974: Among findings of Nutrition Canada survey: half of adult Canadians overweight, lack of physical activity major contributing factor; high serum cholesterol levels, low folic acid, iron, vitamin D and calcium levels common.

- 1974: Health and Welfare department's document *A New Perspective on the Health of Canadians* (Lalonde report) officially recognized impact of diet on cardiovascular disease, paving way for wave of cholesterol consciousness. Report also credited with birth of "lifestyles era," in which responsibility for health was placed on individual.

- Formulated foods – instant breakfasts and meal replacements – appeared on market.

- 1977: Revised *Canada's Food Guide* reflected some 30 changes from 1961 version. Number of food groups changed from five to four (fruit and vegetables combined as one group).

Benoit led the way in turning Canadians on to them. Benoit travelled widely as spokesperson for Panasonic as well as beginning an encyclopedia series on microwave cooking.

In the '70s, Canada went metric, presenting a new hurdle for cooks. For the measuring of recipe ingredients, Canada (along with Australia and, tentatively, the United States) decided to keep its customary volume method for both liquid and dry ingredients rather than adopt European weighing methods. In Continental kitchens, dry ingredients are usually weighed on a metric scale (in grams) and liquids measured by metric volume (litres). British recipes generally call for imperial measures, with solids in ounces and pounds, and liquids in fluid ounces and pints. In Canada, metric recipes do not require kitchen scales; all measures are in volume (millilitres) as are the old imperial cups and spoons. The only weights in a Canadian metric recipe are for ingredients purchased by weight such as meats and produce.

Corning Canada's home service department, headed by Wendy Sanford, was instrumental in teaching consumers about metric (as they were with microwaving). Corning's Pyrex measures began to show both metric and imperial markings. The Canadian Home Economics Association also worked diligently to convert home cooks to metric as painlessly as possible, even producing a cookbook, *The Collage of Canadian Cooking,* with traditional regional recipes given in the new measures. Schools began teaching metric only, government-developed recipes began to switch, and magazines published conversion charts. But in the face of delays and some resistance, many food publications adopted a dual-measure style in writing recipes, giving both metric and imperial measures.

Meanwhile, other influences were effecting changes in Canadian kitchens. The natural-food movement had us eyeing package ingredient lists suspiciously. More focus on nutrition and concerns about food

Chatelaine *magazine eased readers into metric cooking with this chart.*

Courtesy of Chatelaine © Maclean Hunter Ltd.

Traditional breads remained an *important part of the Ukrainian heritage as well as a highlight of the annual festival in Dauphin, Man.*

Courtesy of Greg Eligh, Toronto

## DO YOU REMEMBER?

- Blender breakfasts.
- Your first pocket calculator, tape cassette, digital watch.
- '70s buzzwords: lifestyle, bottom line, hopefully and bor-ring.
- Participaction starting in 1971.
- The Drinking Man's Diet.
- Cellulite.
- The Hall–Dennis Report on education.
- Roasting bags and cooking film.
- The Julia Child spoof on "Saturday Night Live."
- Scares: PCBs, PVCs, mercury, asbestos, spray cans (fluorocarbons).
- "It's mainly because of the meat."
- The first UPCs and scanners.
- Square egg makers.
- Tupperware parties.
- Cuisine minceur.
- Dial-a-Dietitian.
- Self-basting turkeys.
- Subscribing to cable TV.
- Christie's antique cookie jar collection.
- Paul Henderson's winning goal in Canada-Russia series.
- The first female Mountie.
- The first Great Canadian Aunt Jemima pancake race in Peterborough (1978).
- Walter Stewart's *Hard to Swallow*.
- Jean Hoare's The Flying N restaurant near Claresholm, Alberta.

additives, chemical fertilizers and pesticides led to more organically grown foods and meat substitutes. A lot of test-kitchen hours were devoted to developing recipes using soybean protein derivatives, with varying success. Granola, bean sprouts, yogurt and tofu grew in popularity. Fresh fruit and vegetable consumption began to increase. Sugar, salt and white flour became the bad guys.

Health-consciousness showed up in new recipes. The winning entry in the 1979 Ontario Milk Marketing Board recipe contest was called Garden Pizza, which had a brown-rice crust. Blender breakfasts, especially those made with homemade yogurt, were considered stylishly wholesome. "Natural" ingredients appeared in all kinds of prepared food from breakfast cereals to frozen cheesecake.

A decade of diets began. At the same time, recipes for croquembouche, profiteroles and other "decadent" creations enjoyed great popularity, and Canadians still baked rhubarb pie every spring and demanded strawberry shortcake in June.

Television food shows reflected the same diversity. CTV's Ruth Fremes attracted a large daily audience with "What's Cooking," dispensing advice on good health in cooking. On CBC, Joan Watson co-hosted "Marketplace," raising consumer awareness about food safety, packaging and advertising. Meanwhile, the "Galloping Gourmet," Graham Kerr, charmed audiences into trying decadent recipes given to butter and cream, exotic herbs and spices and lacings of wine. Bruno Gerussi's CBC show "Celebrity Cooks" turned cooking into show-biz. (Margaret Trudeau cooked tempura and Toller Cranston made cheesecake.)

Innovative restaurateurs were also beginning to lead us in new directions. One of the earliest to

*Health-conscious eating and a decade of diets began a new awareness of nutrition.*

Courtesy of The Dairy Bureau of Canada, KRAFT GENERAL FOODS CANADA INC. and The Ontario Milk Marketing Board

*Television personality Ruth Fremes offered sound cooking advice daily on CTV's "What's Cooking."*

Courtesy of Frank Grant, GW Photography, Toronto

break through was Umberto Menghi, who saw that Vancouver was ready to graduate from spaghetti-and-meatballs to the upscale flavors of northern Italy. His restaurants offered an irresistible combination of classy cuisine and casual ambience, and Vancouverites ate it up. In Toronto, Fenton's and the Courtyard Café became meccas for fashionable foodies, and in Montreal, Les Halles stood out among a host of other trend-setting spots.

Restaurant styles varied as much as the cities themselves, but they all helped to create a new food consciousness and respect for high-quality cooking. Some still used the techniques of classic European cuisine, but some were picking up on the rule-breaking "nouvelle cuisine" of France. When the new French style crossed the Atlantic in the early '70s, it quickly evolved into many North American interpretations, but the principles were the same: fresh, seasonal, high-quality ingredients; beautifully balanced colors, flavors and textures; a simplicity that came from quick cooking and lighter sauces; stylish presentations that looked like still-life art on large plates.

At the same time, diners encountered some very silly abuses committed in the name of nouvelle cuisine. Some young chefs, short on experience and long on bravado, produced incompatible combinations like fish with blueberry sauce and pink peppercorns. And complaints about miniscule portions were legion. Cynthia Wine wrote in *Homemaker's,* "On a pristine white plate lay two little quail, their tiny feet helplessly in the air. Beside them rested two quarters of a pomegranate…. the plate was further garnished with two teensy-cute quail eggs and two leaves of a plant foreign to me…."

But, still, it was fun – something to talk about over salmon papillote with beurre blanc at the next dinner party. What was happening was that food was becoming fashion. Many of the Canadians enjoying all this new stuff were the same ones who were emulating Julia Child at the beginning of the decade, gathering a wad of cooking-school diplomas after that, collecting 10 years of *Gourmet* and a kitchen full of chic gear.

The late '70s blossomed into a whole new wave of culinary trendiness that would not end until a decade later.

---

*Classic French techniques were a hot topic in cooking schools such as Beverley Burge's in Toronto.*

Canada Wide/Bill Sanford

*Weekend magazine took readers through the basics in the '70s.*

Courtesy of Margo Oliver

**Margo Oliver's Weekend Cooking School**

Twenty lessons about basic cooking and baking techniques complete with recipes

*A stylish basketful of classy gourmet delights was a "must" gift for foodies.*

Courtesy of Fred Bird, Toronto

# Cookbook Sampler

## THE SEVENTIES

For more cookbooks of the decade, see Bibliography pp. 235-237.

# GAZPACHO

*At the start of the '70s, this was usually made in a blender, although purists did the chopping by hand.*

| | | |
|---|---|---|
| 2 | tomatoes, peeled, seeded and chopped | 2 |
| 1/2 cup | chopped cucumber | 125 mL |
| 1/2 cup | chopped onion | 125 mL |
| 1/2 cup | chopped sweet green pepper | 125 mL |
| 1 | clove garlic, minced | 1 |
| 2 tbsp | red wine vinegar | 25 mL |
| 1 tbsp | olive oil | 15 mL |
| 1/2 tsp | Worcestershire sauce | 2 mL |
| 1/4 tsp | hot pepper sauce | 1 mL |
| 3 cups | tomato juice | 750 mL |
| | Salt and pepper | |

*Garnish:*

| | | |
|---|---|---|
| | Lemon slices, celery spears | |

In blender or food processor, process tomatoes, cucumber, onion, green pepper, garlic, vinegar, oil, Worcestershire sauce and hot pepper sauce. Pour tomato juice into large pitcher; add vegetable mixture and stir well. Season with salt and pepper to taste. Garnish with lemon and celery. Makes 6 servings.

Starters or first courses were very trendy in the '70s, and cold soups were new. Vichyssoise was one of the first classics served.

As imports like avocados arrived in Canadian supermarkets, and winter vacations to Florida and Mexico made Guacamole a favorite, we added it to our repertoires, along with seafood salads heaped into avocado halves.

In summer, tomatoes, cucumber, garlic and all sorts of seasonings were quickly transformed into ice-cold soup, Gazpacho. In following decades, this soup was turned into a layered overnight salad, it was jellied, and it was frozen as a sorbet. However, it still remains a great summer refresher, especially for those perpetually dieting.

# LAYERED SPINACH AND CARROT TERRINE

*Serve slices of this terrine drizzled with mayonnaise thinned with milk and seasoned with a little mustard.*

| | | |
|---|---|---|
| 3 cups | soft bread crumbs | 750 mL |
| 1/2 cup | chicken stock | 125 mL |
| 1 | small onion, chopped | 1 |
| 2 tbsp | butter | 25 mL |
| 2 | egg whites | 2 |
| 6 cups | packed fresh spinach, cooked and squeezed dry | 1.5 L |
| 2 tbsp | chopped fresh dill | 25 mL |
| | Salt and pepper | |
| Pinch | nutmeg | Pinch |
| 1 tsp | Dijon mustard | 5 mL |
| 1/2 cup | whipping cream | 125 mL |
| 2 cups | sliced carrots, cooked and mashed | 500 mL |

Cook bread crumbs and stock, stirring, until heated through and in thick paste; let cool. Cook onion in butter until softened but not browned.

In food processor, blend bread mixture, onion, egg whites, spinach, dill, salt and pepper to taste, nutmeg and mustard until smooth. With machine running, gradually add cream; process until thickened.

Spread half the mixture in buttered 8- x 4-inch (1.5 L) loaf pan. Spread mashed carrots over top; top with remaining spinach mixture. Cover with buttered waxed paper; fit foil over pan and secure tightly.

Set pan in larger pan; add hot water to depth of 1 inch (2.5 cm). Bake in 375°F (190°C) oven for 45 minutes or until firm to touch and edges come away from pan. Let cool; chill overnight. Unmould. Makes 8 servings.

Light, pretty and healthy starter courses replaced heavier ones, such as meat or liver pâtés. Food processors made them easy to prepare and popular. Cooks who had grown used to moulded, layered jellied salads thought these were neat.

**VARIATIONS:**

**Asparagus Terrine:** Instead of spinach, use 1 lb (500 g) asparagus, cooked and cut into 2-inch (5 cm) lengths.
**Broccoli Terrine:** Instead of spinach, use 1 bunch broccoli, cooked and cut into chunks.

# LENTIL, BEAN AND RICE SOUP

*This flavorful soup is as hearty as a stew, and with some good crusty bread, it makes a satisfying lunch or supper dish. For a lighter soup, dilute it with stock, tomato juice or water. For a meaty version, brown 1/2 lb (250 g) ground beef or crumbled sausage meat and drain off the fat before adding remaining ingredients; use beef stock (diluted beef broth is fine).*

| 2 tbsp | vegetable oil | 25 mL |
|---|---|---|
| 1 | large onion, chopped | 1 |
| 2 | cloves garlic, minced | 2 |
| 1 cup | lentils | 250 mL |
| 8 cups | stock (vegetable, chicken or beef) | 2 L |
| 1/2 cup | brown or white rice | 125 mL |
| 2 | carrots, chopped | 2 |
| 2 | stalks celery, chopped | 2 |
| 1/2 cup | chopped sweet green pepper | 125 mL |
| 1 | can (19 oz/540 mL) tomatoes (undrained) | 1 |
| 1 | can (14 oz/398 mL) kidney beans | 1 |
| 1 | bay leaf | 1 |
| 1/2 tsp | dried basil | 2 mL |
| 1/4 tsp | dried thyme or oregano | 1 mL |
| | Salt and pepper | |

In large heavy pot, melt butter; cook onion and garlic until softened but not browned. Add lentils and stock. Bring to boil; reduce heat, cover and simmer 20 minutes. Add rice, carrots, celery, green pepper, tomatoes, kidney beans, bay leaf, basil, thyme, and salt and pepper to taste. Cover and simmer about 40 minutes or until lentils, rice and vegetables are tender. Remove bay leaf. Makes about 8 servings.

Following the back-to-the-earth, no-meat, brown rice, granola, macrobiotic '60s, the '70s brought a new wave of health-conscious eating, much of it vegetarian. Beans and legumes came into vogue as vegetarians became aware of the need to assure complete protein in daily meals. Francis Moore Lappé's *Diet for a Small Planet* showed them how to do it. In the '80s, Alice Jenner wrote *The Amazing Legume* to promote Saskatchewan's crops of peas, beans and lentils.

Recipes such as Mexican Beans and Rice and Lentil and Barley Stew became popular. Purists devised such things as Bulgur Burgers and other meatless mixtures. Tofu, in spite of its great ability to take on flavors and textures, was not something people used every day. For flavor, middle-of-the-roaders opted for combinations of beans, legumes and rice, often with a little meat added.

# YOGURT SHAKES

*Recipes for fast blender breakfasts appeared in food columns in answer to the powdered diet-shake mixes on supermarket shelves. Post-milkshake, they were invariably healthful, with egg, fruit, wheat germ, granola or other additions to make a meal-in-a-glass. Use strawberries, raspberries, blueberries, mango cubes, banana chunks, cantaloupe chunks, peach slices or apricot halves in this recipe.*

| | | |
|---|---|---|
| 1/2 cup | milk | 125 mL |
| 1/2 cup | plain yogurt | 125 mL |
| 1 | egg | 1 |
| 1 cup | fruit | 250 mL |
| 1/4 cup | frozen orange juice concentrate | 50 mL |

In blender, process milk, yogurt, egg, fruit and orange juice concentrate until smooth and frothy. Makes 2 servings.

During the '70s, Canadians discovered yogurt. Making your own was trendy, and electric yogurt makers for the home kitchen were all the rage. As dairies began marketing a wider range of flavors, it became quicker and easier to buy it than to "do it yourself," except to control the amount of fat, sugar or fruit added.

# MICROWAVED FISH WITH VEGETABLES

*Halibut, ocean perch and whitefish all work well in this recipe.*

| | | |
|---|---|---|
| 2 tsp | butter | 10 mL |
| 2 cups | sliced mushrooms | 500 mL |
| 1 | medium onion, chopped | 1 |
| 1/3 cup | chopped sweet green pepper | 75 mL |
| 1 | medium tomato, peeled and diced | 1 |
| 1 lb | fish fillets, thawed if frozen | 500 g |
| 2 tsp | soy sauce | 10 mL |
| 2 tsp | sherry | 10 mL |
| 1 tsp | lemon juice or rice wine vinegar | 5 mL |
| | Salt and pepper | |

In microwaveable pie plate or shallow round casserole, microwave butter at High for 20 seconds or until melted. Add mushrooms, onion, green pepper and tomato; microwave, covered, at High for 3 to 4 minutes or until barely tender, stirring once. Drain off liquid.

Arrange fillets with thickest parts to outside of dish, overlapping thinner parts. Combine soy sauce, sherry and lemon juice; pour over fish. Cover and microwave at High for 4 to 5 minutes until fish is opaque and vegetables tender, rotating dish once. Season with salt and pepper to taste. Let stand 5 minutes. Makes 4 servings.

Although microwave cooking had been demonstrated by home economists as early as 1959, the first things Canadians did with microwaves was heat rolls, reheat coffee and defrost frozen food for dinner. During the '70s, the number of households with microwave ovens was highest in Alberta, followed by Saskatchewan.

Fish was one of the first foods we cooked in the microwave oven, since the popular 1 lb (500 g) frozen blocks of fish could be defrosted and cooked in a hurry.

# PORK MEDALLIONS WITH GARLIC SHALLOT SAUCE

*Garnish these medallions with julienned carrots and celery, glazed unpeeled apple slices and wisps of chives.*

| | | |
|---|---|---|
| 2 tbsp | butter | 25 mL |
| 1 | clove garlic, smashed | 1 |
| 8 | pork medallions (about 1 lb/500 g) | 8 |
| 2 tbsp | chopped shallots | 25 mL |
| 1 tsp | crushed peppercorns | 5 mL |
| 1/4 cup | white vermouth | 50 mL |
| 2 tsp | Dijon mustard | 10 mL |
| 1/3 cup | whipping cream | 75 mL |

In skillet, melt half the butter; cook garlic until golden but not browned. Remove garlic. Add pork and sauté until lightly browned and cooked through; remove and keep warm.

Add remaining butter to pan; cook shallots and pepper gently until softened. Deglaze pan with vermouth, cooking until reduced to half. Blend in mustard and cream; boil until barely thickened. Spoon onto serving plates; top with medallions. Makes 4 servings.

### GLAZED APPLE SLICES:

| | | |
|---|---|---|
| 1 tbsp | butter | 15 mL |
| 2 tbsp | brown sugar (or maple syrup) | 25 mL |
| 4 | small apples, thinly sliced or cut in wedges | 4 |

In small skillet melt butter over medium heat. Stir in brown sugar and cook, stirring, until sugar has melted. Add apple slices and cook, stirring, just until apples are tender but still retain their shape.

Nouvelle cuisine brought a new focus on stylish presentation. Beautifully arranged and with colors balanced, it was elegantly "in." Fine fresh Canadian ingredients such as lean pork and seasonal vegetables adapted perfectly to this style of cooking.

Sliced pork or pink beef tenderloins, fanned out on the plate, lamb noisettes, or dainty selections of seafood were served with barely cooked fresh asparagus, turned (carved) potatoes and carrots, skinny green beans and designer-arranged snow peas. Large plates with bold borders or stark white or black plates framed these artful assemblies.

# QUICHE LORRAINE

*Quiche has been labelled the quintessential dish of the '70s.*

| | | |
|---|---|---|
| 4 | slices bacon, chopped | 4 |
| | Pastry-lined 10-inch (25 cm) quiche dish | |
| 1/4 cup | finely chopped onion | 50 mL |
| 1 cup | shredded Swiss or Cheddar cheese | 250 mL |
| 4 | eggs | 4 |
| 1-1/2 cups | light cream | 375 mL |
| 1/4 tsp | salt | 1 mL |
| Pinch | pepper | Pinch |

Cook bacon until nearly crisp; sprinkle in pastry shell along with onion and cheese. Beat eggs lightly; beat in cream, salt and pepper. Pour into pastry shell. Bake in 425°F (220°C) oven for 15 minutes; reduce heat to 350°F (180°C) and bake for 15 to 20 minutes longer or until filling is set in centre.

(To be sure crust bakes thoroughly, bake quiche on rack near bottom of oven, or prebake crust 5 minutes in 425°F/220°C oven before filling.) Let stand 5 minutes before cutting into wedges. Makes about 6 servings.

### VARIATIONS:

**Salmon or Seafood Quiche:** Instead of bacon, use 1 cup (250 mL) cooked or canned salmon, crabmeat, chopped lobster or small shrimp (or mixture). If desired, use green onions and add a little chopped celery, parsley or dillweed.
**Spinach and/or Mushroom Quiche:** Instead of bacon, use 1 pkg (10 oz/284 g) fresh spinach, cooked and chopped, and/or 1/2 to 1 cup (125 to 250 mL) lightly sautéed sliced mushrooms.
**Asparagus and Crabmeat:** Add 1 bunch thin asparagus, cut in half and blanched, and 1 cup (250 mL) cooked crabmeat.
**Mini Quiches:** For appetizers, bake filling in small pre-baked tart shells in 350°F (180°C) oven 15 minutes or until set.

One of the first of many French dishes introduced during the decade, quiche was regarded as fashionably Continental and quickly became ubiquitous with white wine for lunch at fern bars and outdoor cafés. Gradually quiche moved into home kitchens (via countless recipes in magazines and newspaper food pages and promotions such as those of the Milk Marketing Board), survived the real-men-don't-eat-quiche stage, and remained exotic only until home cooks realized it was as easy as pie and added it to their permanent recipe files. New variations continue to be created, from smoked salmon to fiddlehead to apple.

In the '80s, quichelike **Impossible Pie** became well-known fare. The original dish was a custardlike mixture, with coconut and flour that baked to form a crust. Then biscuit mixes were used to save time.

# CHEESE STRATA

*Choose firm-textured bread for this one-dish meal. Egg bread with sesame seeds makes a nice variation.*

| | | |
|---|---|---|
| 8 | slices bread, buttered | 8 |
| 1-1/2 cups | shredded Cheddar cheese | 375 mL |
| 1 | small onion, finely chopped | 1 |
| 4 | eggs | 4 |
| 1-2/3 cups | milk | 400 mL |
| 1/2 tsp | Worcestershire sauce | 2 mL |
| | Salt and pepper | |

Slice bread into quarters; place half in buttered 9-inch (2.5 L) square baking dish. Sprinkle with half the cheese and half the onion; repeat. Beat together eggs, milk, Worcestershire sauce, and salt and pepper to taste; pour over bread. Cover and refrigerate overnight.

Bake, uncovered, in 350°F (180°C) oven for 50 to 60 minutes or until set in centre and well browned. Let stand 5 minutes; cut into squares. Makes 4 to 6 servings.

Optional Additions: Add slivered ham, sliced cooked sausage, crisp bacon bits, flaked cooked crabmeat, 1 tsp (5 mL) dry mustard, or chopped cooked broccoli or asparagus.

Stratas have been around since the turn of the century, but under different names, like **Oven Fondue** or just **Supper Dish**. Simply a custard mixture poured over slices or cubes of bread and cheese, it was cheap and filling. *The Best of Bridge* cookbook had a version called **Christmas Morning Wife Saver**. Over the years, stratas have included crab, spinach and pizza flavors. In the '90s, we microwave the whole thing – not crusty and golden brown, but fast.

# Hungarian Goulash

*Goulash can be made with veal, lamb, beef or pork. By 1984, Cynthia Wine's* Hot and Spicy Cooking *gave a recipe for Hot Red Goulash using "the hottest paprika you can find." Thicken this dish with flour at the end of cooking time, if desired.*

| 1 lb | lean stewing beef | 500 g |
|---|---|---|
| 3 tbsp | vegetable oil | 50 mL |
| 2 | onions, chopped | 2 |
| 1 tbsp | sweet Hungarian paprika | 15 mL |
| 2 tsp | caraway seeds | 10 mL |
| 2-1/2 cups | beef stock | 625 mL |
| 3 | potatoes, diced | 3 |
| 4 | carrots, sliced | 4 |
| 1 | parsnip, sliced | 1 |

Cut meat into small cubes. In large saucepan, brown meat in oil. Add onions; cook, stirring, for 2 to 3 minutes. Add paprika and caraway; cook, stirring, for 1 to 2 minutes. Add stock; cover and simmer for 1 hour. Add potatoes, carrots and parsnip; cook for 15 to 20 minutes or until tender. Makes 4 servings.

### EGG DUMPLINGS OR *NOKEDLI:*

| 1 | egg | 1 |
|---|---|---|
| Pinch | salt | Pinch |
| 1 cup | all-purpose flour | 250 mL |

Beat egg with salt. Blend in flour and enough cold water to make thick paste. Drop by teaspoonful onto simmering stew. Cover and cook 10 minutes.

Many favorite old-country dishes that were brought to Canada included noodles or dumplings. One Polish version was **Galuska**. Dough was held over a pot of simmering water and small pieces were cut off to fall into the water. As they rose to the surface, the galuska were done. Similarly, German egg dumplings, called **Spaetzle**, were pressed through a pastry bag or colander. Unleavened Matzo Balls and Liver Dumplings have been Jewish favorites for years.

Etta Sawyer taught students at her Academy of Culinary Arts in Toronto to serve Goulash with noodles or *nokedli*. Proud of her Hungarian heritage, Etta adapted these dumplings to top her homeland's **Goulash Soup** – almost a meal in itself.

# Chicken Cordon Bleu

*Instructions for boning were included in most recipes calling for boneless, skinless chicken breasts in the '70s.*

| 6 | boneless skinless chicken breasts | 6 |
|---|---|---|
| 6 | slices Swiss cheese | 6 |
| 1 tbsp | chopped chives | 15 mL |
| 6 | thin slices ham | 6 |
| 1/4 cup | all-purpose flour | 50 mL |
| | Salt and pepper | |
| 1 | egg | 1 |
| 2 tbsp | milk | 25 mL |
| 1 cup | dry bread crumbs | 250 mL |
| | Butter | |

Flatten chicken between sheets of waxed paper. Top each with cheese slice, chives and ham slice. Fold or roll up, securing with toothpicks if necessary.

On waxed paper, combine flour, and salt and pepper to taste. Beat egg with milk in pie plate. Spread crumbs on more waxed paper. Coat chicken with flour; dip into egg mixture. Roll lightly in bread crumbs to coat. (Dish can be prepared to this point and refrigerated for several hours.)

Sauté chicken in butter until golden, 2 to 3 minutes per side. Transfer to greased baking dish; bake, uncovered, in 350°F (180°C) oven for 8 to 10 minutes or until chicken is no longer pink inside. Makes 6 servings.

### VARIATION:

**Veal Cordon Bleu:** Use veal scaloppine in place of chicken.

International influences were still strong during the '70s, and recipes for Chicken Kiev, Coq au Vin, Beef Bourgignon and Beef Wellington were popular. Flambéing was impressive, and often a Steak Diane, as seen in restaurants, was attempted at home.

Sit-down dinner parties returned to popularity. Main dishes that could be assembled ahead allowed the hostess time to add finishing touches to the table, offer nibblers with predinner drinks and serve the main course at the last minute.

## GARLIC ROSEMARY BARBECUED LEG OF LAMB

*Barbecuing reached new heights in the '70s. Gas barbecues or covered charcoal-burning ball-shaped models were standard equipment for all suburban patios. Entire meals were cooked out of doors. Small boneless beef or pork roasts, whole chickens, legs of lamb or whole stuffed fish were surrounded with potatoes, which were wrapped in foil or oiled and set on the grill. Foil packets of fresh asparagus with butter and lemon, or buttered squash halves, or skewers of onions, mushrooms, green pepper chunks and cherry tomatoes were added during the cooking.*

| 6 lb | leg of lamb, bone-in | 2.5 kg |
|---|---|---|
| 6 | cloves garlic, slivered | 6 |
| | Fresh rosemary | |
| 1 | lemon, thinly sliced | 1 |
| | Pepper | |

Cut tiny slits in fatty side of lamb; insert garlic sliver in each. Sprinkle with rosemary; overlap lemon slices on top. Generously grind pepper over all.

Set lamb on greased grill over drip pan with medium-hot coals on either side. (Alternatively, set lamb over gas burners; turn burner off directly under meat, leaving other burner on.) Cover barbecue and grill for about 1-1/2 hours or until meat thermometer reaches 140°F (60°C) for rare or until desired doneness. Makes 8 servings.

New Zealand lamb, available and easy on the food budget, helped to promote the use of lamb in Canada, where supplies were seasonal. To cottagers in Ontario's Muskoka area, barbecued fresh Ontario lamb was a succulent summer treat. Port Carling butcher Morley Stephens still does a roaring business in fresh lamb from June to Thanksgiving. Before boneless butterflied legs of lamb became so popular in the '80s and '90s, a whole leg of lamb was a popular choice.

# LAYERED OVERNIGHT SALAD

*Variety is the key to this salad. Mix and match your favorite salad greens in place of the iceberg lettuce to suit your taste.*

| | | |
|---|---|---|
| 1 | small head iceberg lettuce | 1 |
| 1 cup | thinly sliced celery | 250 mL |
| 1 cup | chopped sweet green pepper | 250 mL |
| 2 cups | frozen green peas | 500 mL |
| 1 cup | thinly sliced green onion | 250 mL |
| 3 | hard-cooked eggs, sliced | 3 |
| 1 cup | mayonnaise | 250 mL |
| 1 tbsp | vinegar | 15 mL |
| 1 tsp | granulated sugar | 5 mL |
| 4 | slices bacon, cooked and crumbled | 4 |
| 1/2 cup | shredded Cheddar cheese | 125 mL |

In deep glass bowl, layer lettuce, celery, green pepper, peas, onion and eggs. Combine mayonnaise, vinegar and sugar; spread over top to edge of bowl. Refrigerate, covered, overnight. To serve, sprinkle with bacon and cheese. Makes 6 to 8 servings.

Layered salads, sealed with mayonnaise on top and refrigerated overnight, were one of the favorite make-aheads of this decade. Recipes appeared in community cookbooks from coast to coast.

# CAESAR SALAD

*After watching waiters toss this salad tableside in restaurants, everyone tried it at home. If desired, you can coddle the egg by simmering it for 1 minute.*

| | | |
|---|---|---|
| 2 | heads romaine lettuce, in bite-size pieces | 2 |
| 2 cups | croutons | 500 mL |
| | Grated Parmesan cheese | |
| *Dressing:* | | |
| 2 or 3 | cloves garlic, chopped | 2 or 3 |
| 3 | anchovy fillets | 3 |
| 1 | egg or 2 yolks | 1 |
| 2 tbsp | red wine vinegar | 25 mL |
| 1 tbsp | lemon juice | 15 mL |
| 1 tsp | Dijon mustard | 5 mL |
| 1/2 tsp | Worcestershire sauce | 2 mL |
| 1/4 tsp | pepper | 1 mL |
| 1/4 cup | grated Parmesan cheese | 50 mL |
| 3/4 cup | olive oil | 175 mL |
| | Salt | |

Dressing: In large salad bowl, mash garlic and anchovies into a paste; beat in egg until smooth. Beat in vinegar, lemon juice, mustard, Worcestershire, pepper and Parmesan; gradually whisk in oil. Season with salt to taste. Add romaine; toss well. Sprinkle with croutons, and Parmesan to taste. Makes about 8 servings.

**Easy Caesar Dressing:** As a fast alternative to classic Caesar salad, this blender method gives you a smooth, thick Caesar-flavored dressing that is good with romaine or spinach. In blender, process all dressing ingredients except oil a few seconds. With machine running, add oil gradually in steady stream. Makes about 1 cup (250 mL).

# BRANDIED FRUIT

*Small peaches, nectarines or apricot halves by themselves make a nice change from mixed fruit in this recipe.*

| | | |
|---|---|---|
| 2 cups | granulated sugar | 500 mL |
| 4 lb | peaches or nectarines, pears and apricots (about 8 each) | 2 kg |
| 1/2 cup | brandy | 125 mL |

In large heavy saucepan, bring sugar and 1-1/2 cups (375 mL) water to boil, stirring to dissolve sugar. Simmer, uncovered, for 10 minutes.

Peel and quarter peaches and pears; cut nectarines (if using) and apricots in half. Add to syrup; simmer for 5 minutes or until barely tender. With slotted spoon, transfer fruit to 4 hot sterilized 2-cup (500 mL) canning jars. Add 2 tbsp (25 mL) brandy to each.

Boil syrup for 10 minutes; pour over fruit, leaving 1/2-inch (1 cm) headspace. Seal and process in boiling water bath for 10 minutes. Cool, label and store for at least 3 weeks before using. Makes about 8 cups (2 L).

The '70s was the decade of boozy preserves. **Rumptoff** (rumpot) was in style, starting with fresh strawberries in June, sugar and rum or brandy, then adding layers of cherries, peaches, apricots and other seasonal fruits as they ripened. Eaten as is, or spooned over ice cream, it is still delicious.

Brandied fruit in fancy preserving jars made trendy hostess gifts. Pickled Cherries, Cranberry Ketchup and Raspberry Vinegar were also popular, but spirited fruit seemed new and naughty as well.

# CRANBERRY ORANGE TEA BREAD

*Cranberries are easiest to chop if fresh or frozen (not thawed).*

| | | |
|---|---|---|
| 2 cups | all-purpose flour | 500 mL |
| 1 cup | granulated sugar | 250 mL |
| 1 tsp | baking powder | 5 mL |
| 1/2 tsp | baking soda | 2 mL |
| 1/2 tsp | salt | 2 mL |
| 1 tsp | grated orange rind | 5 mL |
| 3/4 cup | orange juice | 175 mL |
| 1/4 cup | butter, melted | 50 mL |
| 1 | egg | 1 |
| 1 cup | cranberries, chopped | 250 mL |
| 1/2 cup | chopped nuts | 125 mL |

In bowl, combine flour, sugar, baking powder and soda, salt and orange rind. Blend together orange juice, butter and egg; add to bowl and beat well. Stir in cranberries and nuts.

Pour into greased 8- x 4-inch (1.5 L) loaf pan. Bake in 325°F (160°C) oven for 1 hour or until cake tester comes out clean. Remove from pan; cool on rack. Cuts best after 24 hours.

Fruit breads were still popular in the '70s. Along with the familiar favorites – banana nut, apricot almond, date nut – cranberry bread was a recent addition.

In British Columbia's lower mainland, boxes of harvested cranberries are lifted by helicopter from the bogs. Ontario's Muskoka cranberries are harvested by flooding the bogs, stirring the water with a machine called an egg beater, then corralling the floating berries with booms and pushing them to shore.

Maritimers had enjoyed local cranberries for decades, and *The Cranberry Connection,* first in a series of berry cookbooks by Beatrice Ross Buszek of Nova Scotia, showed the versatility of this native fruit. Add them to muffins and crisps, use them raw in relishes or salads, or cook them in the traditional festive-season sauce. Wild low-bush cranberries can be used if available locally.

# POPPY SEED TORTE

*This simple Ukrainian version can be varied by folding 1 cup (250 mL) chocolate chips into the batter before layering it with the cocoa mixture.*

| | | |
|---|---|---|
| 1/4 cup | poppy seeds | 50 mL |
| 1 cup | buttermilk | 250 mL |
| 1/2 cup | butter | 125 mL |
| 1/2 cup | shortening | 125 mL |
| 1-1/2 cups | granulated sugar | 375 mL |
| 4 | eggs, separated | 4 |
| 1 tsp | vanilla | 5 mL |
| 2-1/2 cups | all-purpose flour | 625 mL |
| 2 tsp | baking powder | 10 mL |
| 1 tsp | baking soda | 5 mL |
| *Filling:* | | |
| 1/3 cup | granulated sugar | 75 mL |
| 2 tsp | unsweetened cocoa powder | 10 mL |
| 1 tsp | cinnamon | 5 mL |

Soak poppy seeds in buttermilk for 1 hour. In bowl, cream butter and shortening with sugar until light and fluffy; add egg yolks one at a time, beating well after each addition. Add vanilla.

Stir together flour, baking powder and baking soda; add to creamed mixture alternately with buttermilk, beating well after each addition. Beat egg whites until stiff peaks form; fold into batter. Spread one-third in greased 10-inch (4 L) Bundt pan.

Filling: Combine sugar, cocoa and cinnamon; sprinkle half over batter. Spread with half of the remaining batter; sprinkle with remaining cocoa mixture. Spread remaining batter over top. With knife, cut through batter to give marbling effect. Bake in 350°F (180°C) oven for 1 hour or until cake tester comes out clean. Let stand for 10 minutes before removing from pan to cool.

European versions of cakes with poppy seeds appeared in many cookbooks. One Polish version, **Makowiec Torte,** starts by boiling poppy seeds, then draining and grinding them with honey. Besides adding a crunch to cakes and squares, poppy seed has for decades been a favorite filling in **Danish Pastries,** usually with cream cheese, as well as in rich spicey **Strudels.**

# GRASSHOPPER PIE SQUARES

*A few drops of green food coloring may be added to the filling. Garnish with grated chocolate or sprinkle with chocolate wafer crumbs.*

| | | |
|---|---|---|
| 1-1/2 cups | chocolate wafer crumbs | 375 mL |
| 1/4 cup | butter, melted | 50 mL |
| *Filling:* | | |
| 30 | large marshmallows (or 3 cups/750 mL miniature) | 30 |
| 1/2 cup | milk | 125 mL |
| 1/4 cup | green crème de menthe | 50 mL |
| 1/4 cup | white crème de cacao | 50 mL |
| 1 cup | whipping cream | 250 mL |

Combine chocolate crumbs and butter; press into 8-inch (2 L) square pan. Chill.

Filling: In saucepan, melt marshmallows with milk over low heat, stirring constantly. Chill until slightly thickened. Blend in liqueurs. Whip cream; fold into filling. Pour over base. Chill until firm. Makes 6 servings.

Fancy drinks and liqueurs were included in most home entertaining in the '70s, and clever hostesses served desserts laced with these flavors. **Black Bottom Pie** included Tia Maria, **Harvey Wallbanger Cake** had Galliano, and there was **Brandy Alexander Pie, Bacardi Rum Cake, Grasshopper Pie** and **Grasshopper Crêpes. Grasshopper Cake** had four chocolate cake layers filled and frosted with whipped cream that was flavored with crème de menthe and crème de cacao. Authentic **Black Forest Cake** was a chocolate genoise sprinkled with kirsch, filled with kirsch buttercream and topped with whipped cream, drained cherries and chocolate curls.

# CARROT CAKE

*Whole wheat flour may be used for half the flour, and 1 cup (250 mL) drained crushed pineapple can replace 1 cup (250 mL) grated carrots.*

| 2 cups | all-purpose flour | 500 mL |
|---|---|---|
| 2 tsp | baking powder | 10 mL |
| 1 tsp | baking soda | 5 mL |
| 1 tsp | salt | 5 mL |
| 2 tsp | cinnamon | 10 mL |
| 1 tsp | nutmeg | 5 mL |
| 1/2 tsp | cloves | 2 mL |
| 4 | eggs | 4 |
| 1 cup | packed brown sugar | 250 mL |
| 1/2 cup | granulated sugar | 125 mL |
| 1-1/4 cups | vegetable oil | 300 mL |
| 2-1/2 cups | grated raw carrots | 625 mL |
| 1 cup | raisins | 250 mL |
| 1/2 cup | chopped nuts | 125 mL |

Combine flour, baking powder, baking soda, salt, cinnamon, nutmeg and cloves. In bowl, beat together eggs, brown and granulated sugars and oil; stir in dry ingredients, mixing well. Stir in carrots, raisins and nuts.

Pour into greased and floured 10-inch (4 L) bundt or tube pan or 13- x 9-inch (3.5 L) baking pan. Bake in 350°F (180°C) oven for 40 to 45 minutes for oblong, 60 to 70 minutes for bundt, or until cake tester comes out clean. Cool.

## CREAM CHEESE FROSTING:

| 4 oz | cream cheese | 125 g |
|---|---|---|
| 1/4 cup | butter | 50 mL |
| 2 cups | sifted icing sugar | 500 mL |
| 1 tsp | vanilla | 5 mL |

Cream together cheese and butter; blend in sugar and vanilla until spreading consistency.

As healthy became fashionable but desserts were difficult to give up, this was a nice way to have your cake and eat it, too. Gradually those who disliked fruitcake chose this as an alternative for wedding cakes. Often served with a dusting of icing sugar, Carrot Cake's traditional icing is made with cream cheese.

A **Passover Carrot Cake** is made with cake meal and potato starch, since leavening is not permitted in Jewish fare during this religious time.

# DUTCH APPLE CAKE

*Any apple works well in this recipe, but in wintertime, Spy, Golden Delicious or McIntosh apples are good for cooking.*

| | | |
|---|---|---|
| 5 | medium apples | 5 |
| 1/3 cup | packed brown sugar | 75 mL |
| 1 tsp | cinnamon | 5 mL |
| 1/2 cup | butter | 125 mL |
| 1/2 cup | granulated sugar | 125 mL |
| 3 | eggs | 3 |
| 1 tsp | grated lemon rind | 5 mL |
| 1-1/4 cups | all-purpose flour | 300 mL |
| 1-1/2 tsp | baking powder | 7 mL |
| 1/4 cup | milk | 50 mL |

Peel, core and slice apples; sprinkle with sugar and cinnamon. Set aside.

In bowl, cream butter with sugar until light; add eggs, one at a time, beating well after each addition. Add lemon rind. Mix flour with baking powder; add to butter mixture alternately with milk to make thick batter.

Spread half of batter in greased 8-inch (2 L) square pan. Cover with half of apples; spread evenly with remaining batter. Top evenly with remaining apples. Bake in 325°F (160°C) oven for 1 hour or until tester comes out clean. Serve warm or cold.

> Dutch apple cakes have been made over the years with either a cakelike dough or a rich biscuit dough, layered with sliced apples or topped with them in rows, then sprinkled with sugar and cinnamon.

# CHOCOLATE MOUSSE

*This makes a creamy, soft mousse. For a denser mousse, omit either egg whites or whipped cream.*

| | | |
|---|---|---|
| 1 cup | semisweet chocolate chips (175 g pkg) | 250 mL |
| 1/3 cup | boiling hot coffee or water | 75 mL |
| 3 | eggs, separated | 3 |
| 2 tbsp | brandy or rum (optional) | 25 mL |
| 1/2 cup | whipping cream | 125 mL |
| 1/4 cup | granulated sugar | 50 mL |
| *Garnish (optional):* | | |
| | Whipped cream | |
| | Chocolate curls | |

In blender, combine chocolate chips and coffee; blend a few seconds until smooth. Add egg yolks, and brandy (if using); blend 30 seconds. Transfer to large bowl. Whip cream; fold into chocolate mixture.

Beat egg whites to soft peaks; gradually beat in sugar to stiff peaks. Fold into chocolate mixture. Spoon into parfait glasses or dessert cups. Chill thoroughly, at least 2 hours. If desired, top each with dollop of whipped cream and/or chocolate curl. Makes about 6 servings.

> One taste of this rich, creamy dessert at a restaurant or dinner party sent everyone scrambling for a good recipe. Classic chocolate mousse recipes, calling for chopped chocolate and careful cooking in a double boiler, were sometimes intimidating, but the popular blender method was fast and no-fail delicious.

# The EIGHTIES

## 1980 – 1989

# A CENTURY OF CANADIAN HOME COOKING

*We Thai'd one on, nixed nouvelle cuisine, O.D.'d on oat bran, said say-onara to sushi, and got kiwi'd out…the 1980s had its share of food fads. But as we raise a glass to another bygone decade, it's good to know that, in many ways, we came to our senses on the subject of food.*

– Marion Kane
*Toronto Star*

It was a decade of culinary contradictions, of fads and fashions and "what's-hot" lists that seemed to change overnight. Pink peppercorns and white chocolate were "in" one year, upstaged by golden caviar and purple broccoli the next. Our consuming passions went upscale and downscale, nouvelle to nostalgic, grazing to cocooning. We hopped from fat-and-sassy to lean-and-mean, junk food to spa cuisine, muffin mania to mussel power, sinful chocolate truffles to extra-virgin olive oil.

But the '80s were also the greatest culinary consciousness-raising decade of them all. Never before had we tasted so many new foods or cooked in so many new styles. Dining out and travelling broadened our culinary horizons, and exotic international ingredients became widely available in supermarkets. We tried out Tex Mex and Cajun, Northern Italian and Southeast Asian, bought pasta machines and paella pans, discovered *herbes de Provence* and Chinese five-spice powder.

And best of all, we discovered the pleasures of our own homegrown products. We learned to appreciate fruits and vegetables in season, fresh herbs and properly cooked seafood. Farmers' markets, specialty food shops, gourmet takeouts, wine bars, sidewalk cafés and cookbook stores blossomed all over the country.

In many ways, the '80s were a coming-of-age for Canadian cuisine. Our best chefs helped lead the way by capturing all the gold medals at the 1984 International Culinary Olympics in Frankfurt, putting Canada on the world-class culinary map with their prize-winning platters of lobster, mussels, caribou, fiddleheads, Alberta beef, Manitoba wild rice, Nova Scotia smoked salmon and Vancouver Island mountain squab.

Many Canadian restaurants followed suit, creating distinctively regional menus, using local ingredients in innovative new dishes or updated versions of traditional favorites. At Sooke Harbour House on Vancouver Island, Sinclair Philip had already established one of the most acclaimed interpretations of regional cuisine in the Pacific northwest. Every ingredient, from salad flowers and chanterelles to abalone and oysters, came from the inn's gardens, island farms, mountain forests and the sea. In Digby, Nova

---

*Elegant bazaars such as the Sugar Plum Fair sponsored by The National Ballet School were Christmas shoppers' delights.*
Courtesy of Frank Grant, GW Photography, Toronto

On pages 186 – 187: The artful presentation of food as fashion: Pasta Primavera with Seafood, salad of greens and flowers, and Tuiles with Sorbets and Raspberry Coulis.

*Home cooks were inspired by restaurants like La Goéliche on Île d'Orléans where traditional dishes were given a nouvelle touch.*
Courtesy of Frank Grant, GW Photography, Toronto

*The light and lean look came from combinations of exercise and at-home spa cooking.*
Courtesy of Fred Bird, Toronto

Scotia, chef Bernard Meyer at The Pines resort hotel did justice to the famous scallops and commissioned local gardeners to grow fine salad greens and vegetables. In Toronto, Mark Bussières updated Ontario country cooking (corn muffins with peppers, grilled rabbit with lemon and basil) on his all-Canadian menus at Metropolis.

But probably the greatest trendsetter of all, at least in the cities, was "yuppie culture." The baby boomers had become the decade's largest target market, and the yuppies (young urban professionals) in fact represented only a small proportion of that group. However, their upscale tastes produced a ripple effect that set the tone for most lifestyle advertising and editorializing in the '80s. And as an important part of the envisaged "good life," food became high fashion. A new breed of young chefs and food gurus became media stars. Trends and attitudes were swept along on a wave of journalistic hype (in fact, the media were sometimes accused of setting the trends themselves).

The '80s brought an annual parade of "What's In and What's Out" lists in food magazines and newspapers. It all started out innocently enough. At first the lists simply banished anything smacking of the "dark ages" (the '50s and '60s) – shrimp cocktail, sweet-and-sour anything, packaged cheese slices, Baby Duck. Soon many standbys of the '70s were added to the "outs" – French onion soup, escargots in garlic butter, anything flambéed or en croûte (but quiche was still okay, even for real men). Kiwi fruit, beurre blanc and other clichés of nouvelle cuisine were also pronounced passé. All these sins were to be replaced by fresh pasta (preferably home-made), chocolate truffles, croissants, vegetable terrines, raspberry vinegar, dried mushrooms and amaretto.

Within a few years, keeping abreast of current fads required great devotion. Out went

*Consuming passions flavored the '80s.*

Courtesy of KRAFT GENERAL FOODS CANADA INC. and Toronto Life magazine

## LOOKING BACK

*From* Across The Table *(1985) by Cynthia Wine.*

We have the world's most succulent beef and even the Russians envy our wheat. How did we manage to turn them into the hot beef sandwich?

What's worse is that visitors to Canada often get the impression that there's nothing better to chew on here. I gained eleven new pounds eating across Canada, and not one is owed to the hot beef sandwich. Those pounds are in place because of lobster chowder made with cream in Prince Edward Island . . . maple bread spread with salt pork in Quebec . . . cinnamon buns sticky with glazed sugar and sweet butter in Manitoba.

As I travelled across the country, within each area I found foods I'd never heard of. When they were especially good, I wondered why. At my first taste of cod in cheese in Newfoundland, triple-crust blueberry pie near the Bay of Chaleur or bannock baked light and flaky in Whitehorse, I wondered how I could have lived so many years next to these dishes without knowing what I was missing. We know more about the food of northern Italy.

The Canadian stomach, it seems, doesn't travel in Canada. . . . Our good food tends to stay put . . . and our eating regions are very distinct. . . .

We are finally discovering foods that are wonderful to eat in Canada. But we are keeping many more dishes a secret in their own regions. They are at their best in their own homes, surrounded by people who love them. . . . Find fish that has been cooked fresh and flaking in the East, or berry pies that squirt bright juice at first bite in the North. You can't eat better anywhere.

amaretto, in came frangelico or anything hazelnut. Also out was everything else that was in the year before. Stylish shopping baskets now overflowed with fresh herbs (especially basil), real Parmigiano-Reggiano, extra-virgin olive oil, balsamic vinegar and sundried tomatoes; ice cream machines churned out sorbets of passionfruit, pomegranate and figs; baby vegetables garnished every platter.

The food frenzy peaked around 1985 as leading-edge Canadian cooking came under the influence of the "new American cuisine" movement in the United States. Creative young chefs there had taken the country by storm with innovative cooking styles based on locally grown ingredients and ethnic influences. The trend was especially identified with California, where a raft of luminaries (such as Alice Waters at Chez Panisse and Wolfgang Puck at Spago) were turning restaurants into theatre and cooking into a new religion. Trademark foods included game and fish grilled over mesquite, blue cornmeal and designer pizzas.

Meanwhile, back in our home kitchens, what were we actually cooking? Certainly, many of the trendy fashions filtered down and we experimented with all kinds of new dishes. But our habits and attitudes were influenced more by our changing practical needs. By the mid-'80s, families were more fragmented, schedules were tighter. The majority of households now had two working adults, and the kids were just as busy; sitting down together for a meal became an increasingly rare occasion. At the same time, families were getting smaller; the numbers of singles, childless couples and single-parent families were rising rapidly. All these groups were united in their demand for fast and easy cooking. But otherwise they came up with a great variety of eating styles based on personal priorities and interpretations of the many choices available. Breakfast might be oatmeal-and-orange-juice or croissants-and-cappuccino; lunch could mean brown-bagging at a desk or grazing at a sushi bar. Dinner in many households meant teaching the kids to microwave

*A wave of new cookbooks hit the market as microwave ovens became popular.*

Courtesy of Joyce Webster, Margaret Eckford, and Ruby Juss

### LOOKING BACK

*Adapted from "A Taste of Five Cities" in* Canadian Living's *FOOD magazine (1988). Judy Schultz, food editor at the* Edmonton Journal, *reflects on the local food scene:*

To eat well in Edmonton today, you have only to ferret out two particular aspects of the city – the ethnic restaurant/food shops and the farmers' markets.

For me, it starts Saturday morning around 8:30 when I head for the City Market on 97th Street. A nice fresh chicken, a loaf of Hungarian onion bread, a sack of wild mushrooms, a jar of rosehip jam. I revel in the noise, the color, the musical babble of five or six languages I don't understand. And the small-town welcome. "Where were you last week for my rye bread?" "Here, try my new cookies." "Hey, how about those Oilers?" and so forth. . . .

If I feel like dim sum, I drop into any of a dozen restaurants in the area doling out har gow and noodles. . . . North of the railway underpass is more Chinatown – bakeries, restaurants, shops selling barbecued meats, live fish. . . .

Two blocks east is Little Italy where you can order your wine grapes, choose olives from five or six barrels, buy real Parmesan. The bakers, the butcher, the ice-cream makers are all here, and if you haven't cooled a hot August afternoon with a gelato from the Bar Italia and Billiards, you haven't lived.

I've left out too much – the hot sauce at my favorite Ethiopian restaurant, the delis and ethnic eateries on 118th Avenue or 124th Street, old Strathcona. . . . And what about the prime beef and pork, the cheesemakers, the golden caviar from Slave Lake, the buffalo burgers? Call me, we'll eat.

and stir-fry, and that pizza's okay when Mom and Dad are both working late. Entertaining could mean four courses by candlelight or a casual gathering around a pot of good chowder.

Adapting to this diverse market was a whole new ballgame for food marketers and researchers. During the '80s, Canadian consumers were analysed, labelled and targeted as never before. Distinct "market segments" were identified and given psychographic labels such as "chase-and-grabbits" (young, upwardly mobile, eating on the run), "achievers" (urban careerists, affluent, status cooks), "experientialists" (concerned about health and environment, experimental cooks) and "belongers" (comfortable traditionalists, conservative cooks).

An "average Canadian" was getting hard to define; "middle Canada" had become a very big place. Our food styles were as varied as our lifestyles and as diverse as the regions we lived in. But as the decade progressed, certain trends emerged.

Health and diet became a major obsession. Fad diets and calorie-counting were replaced by a quest for overall fitness (fuelled in part by the boomers' first intimations of mortality). In typical '80s style, nutrition was seized upon obsessively, with the focus on one fashionable issue at a time – cholesterol, calcium, fibre (especially oat bran). Popular nutrition columns in newspapers expanded greatly in number and length, attempting to sort out the fads and facts for readers. More help came from the Canadian Cancer Society and the Canadian Heart and Stroke Foundation who both produced new dietary guidelines that were incorporated into Anne Lindsay's best-selling cookbooks, *Smart Cooking* (1986) and *The Lighthearted Cookbook* (1988).

Fat phobia gave rise to countless new "lite" and low-fat prod-

*The Northwest Territories adapted Canada's Food Guide to its own native foods.*

"N.W.T. Food Guide." 1987. Medical Services Branch, NWT Region. Used with Permission of Department of Health, Government of the NWT, 1992

**N.W.T. FOOD GUIDE**

*Eat foods from each group every day for Health*

*Nutritional buzzwords for the '80s included fibre, calcium and heart-smart.*

Courtesy of Kellogg Canada Inc., The Dairy Bureau of Canada, and The Heart and Stroke Foundation of Canada

## NUTRITION

- Nutrition came into its own as fitness became fashionable.
- Reducing dietary fat key nutrition issue of decade. Canadians advised to reduce fat intake to 30 per cent or less of calories.
- 1982: *Canada's Food Guide* revised again, primarily to stress variety, energy balance (calorie intake and output), and moderation in consumption of fat, sugar and salt.
- In Yukon and Northwest Territories, food guide illustrated four food groups with native foods and encouraged their use.
- 1983: *Canada's Dietary Standard* updated as *Recommended Nutrient Intakes for Canadians*, including intake levels for calories and 17 other nutrients.
- Popular food and nutrition issues: cholesterol, oat bran, calcium, osteoporosis.
- Serious issue of decade: growing problem of eating disorders such as anorexia and bulimia.
- Fads of decade: hypoglycemia (low blood sugar); sugar as cause of hyperactivity in children.
- Nutrition and health programs entered workplace as larger corporations recognized that healthy employees more productive.
- Canadian Cancer Society and Heart and Stroke Foundation promoted new dietary guidelines.
- 1989: Food and Drug Regulations amended to allow nutrition labelling of foods and permit greater number of nutrition claims to be made.

ucts in supermarkets. We were seduced by anything labelled "no cholesterol" even when the product was not new and had never contained cholesterol in the first place. New takeout restaurants offered stylishly "healthful" salads and sandwiches for lunch. Even fast-food chains added fish and chicken to their burger menus. Salad bars blossomed, bran muffins replaced croissants, popcorn (especially microwavable and air popped) became the snack of the decade. Low-fat sour cream, yogurt and cheese moved into the dairy case. Consumer fear of cholesterol reduced red meat consumption for a while but was countered by promotions for the new lean beef and pork, both of which had become much leaner through improved breeding, feeding and grading systems in recent years. Lean turkey became available in a wide variety of cuts and products from boneless roasts and cutlets to sausage and sandwich meats. Fish became a fashionable dish in restaurants grilling exotic new varieties like orange roughy, swordfish and mahi-mahi.

All this emphasis on healthy eating co-existed crazily with a passion for decadent desserts. Many restaurant-goers chose virtuous salad plates so they could indulge in desserts such as double-chocolate pecan pie, triple-chocolate mousse cake or four-layered hazelnut torte with whipped cream.

In a decade of mood swings, old-fashioned favorites like chicken pot pie and blackberry crumble began to appear on the "what's-hot" lists, this time recycled as "comfort food," in a backlash to the chic skimpiness of nouvelle cuisine. But when fashionable foodies predicted a return to the simpler, more satisfying foods of the past and announced "Meat loaf is back," many Canadian home cooks simply rolled their eyes and replied, "I didn't know it had left." The old favorites were indeed still staples in most home kitchens and would continue to be. But just as we'd adapted them over previous generations, we continued to update them now, streamlining preparation to save time and cutting

*Producers' associations and marketing boards offered a wide variety of recipe books with '80s themes.*

Courtesy of The Beef Information Centre, Canada Pork Inc., Canadian Chicken Marketing Agency, Canadian Egg Marketing Agency, Canadian Turkey Marketing Agency, Dairy Bureau of Canada and Fisheries and Oceans Canada. "Get Cracking" is a trade-mark of the Canadian Egg Marketing Agency.

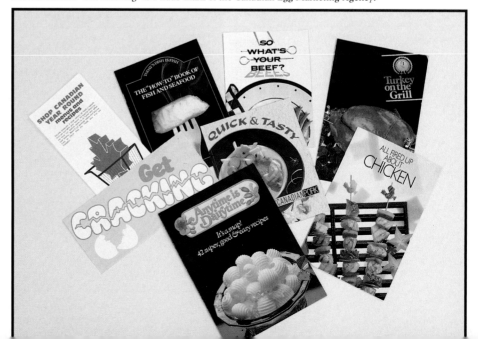

## DO YOU REMEMBER?

- Power breakfasts.
- Wellness cuisine.
- National Seafood Month in November; Canadian Meat Month in February.
- Beaver tails (deepfried pastries) at Winterlude in Ottawa.
- Passions of Food series on TV.
- Your first tastes of sushi, dim sum, Szechuan, Thai noodles.
- Hosers Bob and Doug McKenzie, eh?
- Micro breweries, wine coolers, Beaujolais Nouveau.
- Buffalo burgers on bannock buns at Expo '86.
- The Grocery Hall of Fame opening in Vancouver.
- Living lettuce (hydroponic).
- Bistro food and diner food.
- Simmering potpourri (apple pie, gingerbread, peach cobbler).
- Drinking "caribou" at the Quebec Winter Carnival.
- The first annual Culinary Masters and Taste & Tour Festival in P.E.I. (1989).
- Howard Dill's prize pumpkin in Nova Scotia.
- Opening of the West Edmonton Mall.
- Elephant garlic, baby eggplants.
- The "tainted tuna" scandal in 1985.
- Old fashioned church picnics at Leitch Collieries in Crow's Nest Pass.
- Cabbage Patch dolls.

back a bit on the butter, sugar and salt. We also created new recipes using familiar home-grown ingredients: pumpkin in mousses, fiddleheads in quiches, smoked salmon in savory cheese-cakes.

The personal recipe collections of most Canadian cooks had become an eclectic mix of old and new, some adapted from old-country traditions, but even more from recent decades when the latest recipes got passed around through women's clubs and other networks. During the '80s, many of these collections, from both individuals and groups, became part of a deluge of grassroots cookbooks (often self-published or printed regionally) that suddenly issued from every corner of the country. Typical of these were *I've Got to Have That Recipe!* from three women running a dessert business in Victoria; *Country Church Cooking*, from the Josephburg, Saskatchewan, Men's Choral Society; and Jean

Paré's phenomenally successful *Company's Coming* series from Alberta, beginning with *150 Delicious Squares* in 1981 and going on to *Pies*, her 18th, in 1992.

Comprehensive research on the country's culinary history, however, was still sporadic in most provinces, with the notable exception of Quebec. In 1985, *Cuisine du Québec* was published by the Institut de tourisme et de l'hôtellerie, the Montreal-based tourism and hotel school that trains the province's young chefs. The result of a five-year project, the book divided the province into 18 regions, each with its own food traditions – from the seafood pies of Gaspé and maple tartes of the Beauce to braised partridge in Gatineau and blue-berry pudding in Saguenay. Publicizing the distinct culinary stamp of each region not only helped preserve the old traditions but resulted in a whole new wave of contemporary re-

*Busy lifestyles left little time to bake, but updated traditions continued through get-togethers for cookie swaps and "stirring parties" (to make Christmas cakes or puddings).*
Courtesy of Fred Bird, Toronto

*Traditions were alive and well at this feast prepared by the Ladies' Auxilliary of the Lebanese Club of Charlottetown.*

Courtesy of Frank Grant, GW Photography, Toronto

gional specialties created and served in restaurants all over Quebec.

Awareness of homegrown products was strengthened in every province by the promotional efforts of provincial ministries of agriculture and fisheries. Newspaper, magazine, radio and television advertising, recipe booklets, demonstrations, cooking contests and seasonal guides to farmers' markets and pick-your-own farms all contributed to increased use of local ingredients.

Alongside the wealth of products long famous in each province (from B.C. salmon to P.E.I. lobster), a new generation of specialty foods began to appear in markets: fancy cheeses of all kinds, smoked trout, whitefish caviar, cultured mussels and farmed salmon, Oriental bok choy, Italian rapini, mâche, Belgian endive, wild mushrooms, flavored honeys, snow crab, game birds, quail, rabbit. British Columbia began to harvest kiwifruit, southwestern Ontario to

grow peanuts and Saskatchewan successfully to cultivate saskatoon berries.

Greenhouse and hydroponic production of cucumbers, tomatoes and lettuces grew to thriving industries especially in British Columbia and Ontario. New game farms in many regions produced pheasant, partridge, pintade (guinea fowl), buffalo, wild boar and venison. Some farms began specializing in "natural" products to supply the growing demand of many restaurants and retail stores for more organic, preservative-free produce and free-range or hormone-free poultry and meats. Bourgeoning cottage industries evolved from home kitchens, producing specialty mustards, honeys, herbed vinegars and oils, sweet preserves and gourmet sauces. Small wineries developed new vintages from local products (such as saskatoon, rhubarb and wild rose honey wines from Grand Paririe, Alberta).

During the '80s, *Canadian Living* magazine produced the

Great Canadian Cookbook series of articles featuring local products from each province and territory. Enthusiastic reader response prompted many other cross-Canada food series in the magazine: big-city farmers' markets (from Edmonton to Saint John); the food of our historic river valleys (including the Red, Ottawa and Annapolis); food festivals (from Penticton Peach to P.E.I. Potato); and country inns from Vancouver Island to Grand Manan.

With so much happening on the food scene, new Canadian magazines began to appear that were devoted wholly to gastronomy. The sophisticated but short-lived *Epicure* and the Montreal-based *Wine and Dine* were launched in 1980, followed in the next few years by several others such as *Sel et Poivre* from Quebec, *Recipes Only* (later incorporated into *Homemaker's*) and *à la carte* (which became *Travel à la carte*). *Canadian Living's FOOD* was launched in January '88 and later incorporated into *Select Homes and*

---

*The '80s brought a wave of new Canadian magazines devoted to food.*

*Canadian Living's food pages expanded into popular, seasonal specials.*

Courtesy of Canadian Living (Telemedia Publishing), Homemaker's magazine (Telemedia Procom Inc.), and Ian Campbell (Westside Studios, Toronto)

Courtesy of Canadian Living - Telemedia Publishing

*Food.* The first issue of *FOOD* wrapped up the diversity of the Canadian food scene in the late '80s with a "Cross Canada" column on what was cooking coast to coast (everything from soup at the Stock Market on Granville Island to wild boar in Winnipeg, Rodney's Oysters in Toronto and Julie Watson's barbecued fish in Charlottetown).

Cooking schools also changed gears during the '80s to cater to more diverse tastes and schedules. Home entertaining remained a popular cooking-class topic, as did chocolate and desserts. But there was more interest in new courses designed to help people set up a business (catering, baking). Daytime classes fell off, evenings being preferred by both men and women. Saturday classes for children filled up as parents did the weekend shopping.

By the end of the decade, the lists of ins and outs tapered off, the fads faded and a new buzz word emerged: real. "Getting real" was the new concept for selling everything from soft drinks to oatmeal. The hard practicalities of life were again taking over. The 30-something generation was beginning a belated baby boom of its own, and the combined demands of career and family moved "convenient" to the top of the grocery list.

Canadians were also starting to get more frugal. The tightening economy had many households adapting to reduced economic expectations. Growing families and working parents meant expensive day care or nannies. Also, an increasing number of grown children were returning to their parents' nest because they couldn't pay the rent elsewhere.

The last months of 1989 brought a major change in attitudes. As the drama of events in Eastern Europe transformed the world almost overnight, many Canadians found themselves also shifting their personal perspectives. They were tired of career-climbing and trend-consuming, tired of keeping up appearances, tired of acquiring. Priorities turned to more private satisfactions, home and family.

The yuppie cupboard was overflowing and it was time for a clean-out. The "I-want-it-all" attitude of the '80s shifted to "Who needs it?" After a decade of fads, we were ready for a return to the basics.

*All across Canada women farmers worked hard not only to keep family farms going but also for recognition of their contributions.*

Courtesy of Frank Grant, GW Photography, Toronto

*Canadian regional products began to take the spotlight through promotional pamphlets.*

Courtesy of B.C. Hothouse Growers, Manitoba Agriculture, Ontario Ministry of Agriculture (Foodland Ontario), Prince Edward Island Potato Board, Riverbend Plantation (Saskatoon), and Shoal Lake Wild Rice Ltd. (Keewatin, Ontario)

*Springridge Farm near Milton, Ontario, one of many pick-your-own farms, sells delectable home-baked tarts.*

Courtesy of Fred Bird, Toronto

# Cookbook Sampler

## THE EIGHTIES

For more cookbooks of the decade, see Bibliography pp. 237-240.

## RHUBARB AND SUMMER BERRY SOUP

*Serve this soup well chilled in frosted glass cups with a swirl or dollop of sour cream, softly whipped cream or yogurt on top. Alternatively, blend 1 cup (250 mL) light cream into soup; drizzle a swirl of fresh berry purée on each serving.*

| | | |
|---|---|---|
| 2 cups | sliced rhubarb | 500 mL |
| 1 cup | dry red wine | 250 mL |
| 1 cup | water | 250 mL |
| 1/2 cup | granulated sugar | 125 mL |
| 1 | small stick cinnamon | 1 |
| Pinch | nutmeg | Pinch |
| 2 cups | fresh strawberries | 500 mL |
| 1 | pkg (425 g) frozen raspberries | 1 |

Bring rhubarb, wine, water, sugar, cinnamon and nutmeg to boil, stirring until sugar is dissolved. Simmer 5 minutes or until rhubarb is very tender. Drain in sieve, reserving juice; let cool. Squeeze out any remaining juice. Chill.

Purée strawberries and raspberries (sieve to remove seeds, if desired). Add to reserved rhubarb juice. Chill. Makes about 6 servings.

Canada's wide variety of fruit became a natural for cold soups in the '80s. Chilled melon with yogurt, seasonal berries (strawberries, raspberries, blueberries, cranberries) or sour cherries were the basis of refreshing starter soups for summer meals. As well, chilled almond soup and variations of vichyssoise (with watercress or apple added) became other cold soup favorites. Gazpacho was made with zucchini instead of cucumber, carrot soup was flavored with orange and served chilled.

New hot soups combined flavors of the South Pacific: hot and sour, coriander and ginger, lemon shrimp and noodles.

Garnishing became an art form in the '80s and soups were strewn with chopped herbs, swirled with yogurt or sour cream, drizzled with purées (which were then pulled into cobweb or heart patterns) or dusted with spices. Two soups were often poured at the same time into serving bowls to form a divided pattern.

## BAKED GOAT CHEESE

*Warm Brie, en croûte (wrapped in pastry and baked) or coated with a crumb mixture and baked, was likely the trendsetter for this recipe. Serve in wedges on a pool of cranberry sauce, Cumberland sauce or red pepper jelly.*

| | | |
|---|---|---|
| 1 lb | fresh goat cheese (chèvre) | 500 g |
| 1/2 cup | extra-virgin olive oil | 125 mL |
| 1/2 tsp | coarse cracked pepper | 2 mL |
| 1 tbsp | chopped fresh basil | 15 mL |
| 1 cup | fresh bread crumbs | 250 mL |
| 1/3 cup | finely chopped toasted almonds | 75 mL |

Cut cheese into serving-size portions; marinate in oil, pepper and basil for at least 4 hours or overnight. Drain. Combine crumbs and almonds; coat cheese wedges. Place on ungreased baking sheet; refrigerate for 1 hour. Bake in 450°F (230°C) oven for 5 to 7 minutes or until cheese starts to soften but still holds shape. Makes 8 servings.

Chèvre, originally imported from France, is a piquant cheese made with goat's milk. In the '80s, to satisfy the demand for European tastes as well as Caribbean dishes, small Canadian cheese-makers, particularly in Quebec, Ontario and Nova Scotia, began raising more goats and marketing these soft cheeses. As a result, recipes appeared in magazines and newspaper food columns for chèvre everything, from deep-frying it to stuffing it under the skin of chicken breasts. But mostly chèvre was the basis of spreads and dips for appetizers.

# BRUSCHETTA

*A favorite snack of sunny, rustic Italy, Bruschetta was traditionally made by simply toasting crusty bread over an open fire, then rubbing it with garlic and drizzling with olive oil.*

| | | |
|---|---|---|
| 12 | plum or 4 large tomatoes | 12 |
| 2 | cloves garlic, minced | 2 |
| 2 tbsp | minced shallots or mild onion | 25 mL |
| 1/4 cup | chopped fresh basil | 50 mL |
| 1 tsp | chopped fresh oregano | 5 mL |
| 1/4 cup | extra-virgin olive oil | 50 mL |
| | Salt and pepper | |
| Dash | hot pepper sauce (optional) | Dash |

| | | |
|---|---|---|
| 12 | thick slices crusty Italian bread, about 4-inches (10 cm) diameter | 12 |
| 1 | large clove garlic, halved | 1 |
| | Freshly grated Parmesan cheese (optional) | |

Halve tomatoes and squeeze out seeds and juice; chop finely to give about 3 cups (750 mL). Combine with minced garlic, shallots, basil, oregano and 1 tbsp (15 mL) olive oil. Season generously with salt and pepper to taste and hot pepper sauce (if using). Let stand at room temperature for 1 to 2 hours; drain off liquid.

Grill or broil bread until golden on both sides. Brush one side with remaining olive oil and rub with garlic halves. Spoon tomato mixture on top. Sprinkle with Parmesan (if using). Broil for a few minutes if desired. Serve immediately. Makes about 6 servings.

An interesting array of international breads gained popularity in the '80s.
**Crostini:** Thin toasts are drizzled with oil and topped with a smooth, savory (often olive-based) spread.
**Focaccia:** A savory flatbread with a chewy texture is usually topped with garlic, onion, olive oil and coarse salt.
**Pita Bread:** Often called pocket bread, the dough puffs up as it bakes, then deflates, leaving a pocket when cool.
**Persian Flatbread:** Long, ridged breads about 1-inch (2.5 cm) thick and usually covered with sesame seeds.
**Armenian Flatbread:** Thin, crisp breads, almost like large crackers, are often topped with sesame or poppy seeds.
**Tortillas:** Thin breads, more like crêpes, these are the basis of many Mexican dishes. Corn tortillas can be filled and served soft as enchiladas, or fried until crisp, filled and served as tacos. Flour tortillas are usually rolled around fillings and served as burritos.

# CHICKEN WINGS WITH TWO DIPS

*Often marinated or coated with batter, wings were baked, microwaved or deep-fried. Serve these with dips.*

| | | |
|---|---|---|
| 3 lb | chicken wings | 1.5 kg |
| 1 tsp | paprika | 5 mL |
| 1 tsp | dry mustard | 5 mL |
| 1/2 tsp | salt | 2 mL |
| 1/4 tsp | pepper | 1 mL |
| 1/4 tsp | cayenne pepper | 1 mL |

Cut off wing tips; cut wings at joints if desired. In simmering water, cook for 15 minutes; drain and pat dry.

In bag, mix together paprika, mustard, salt, pepper and cayenne; add wings and toss to coat. Bake on greased baking sheet in 425°F (220°C) oven, or barbecue on greased grill, for 10 minutes. Turn wings; cook 15 minutes or until crisp and browned. Makes 6 servings.

**Blue Cheese Dip:** Blend 2/3 cup (150 mL) sour cream with 1/3 cup (75 mL) mayonnaise and 1 tbsp (15 mL) lemon juice. Add 2 oz (50 g) blue cheese, crumbled, 2 tbsp (25 mL) chopped chives and a dash of hot pepper sauce. Makes about 1-1/2 cups (375 mL).

**Hot and Spicy Dip:** In small saucepan combine 1/4 cup (50 mL) ketchup, 1/4 cup (50 mL) liquid honey, 1 tbsp (15 mL) vegetable oil, 1 tbsp (15 mL) lemon juice, 1/2 tsp (2 mL) hot pepper sauce and 1/4 tsp (1 mL) hot pepper flakes; heat just to boiling. Makes about 2/3 cup (150 mL).

Originally on menus as bar snacks or pub food, **Buffalo Wings,** spicy-hot and always served with a blue cheese dip, were the first of the chicken wings so enjoyed today. Along with wings, there were snacks like chicken fingers, ribs, or beef dip (sandwiches of roast beef shavings served with a tangy dip). The popularity of chicken gave rise to a wave of cookbooks and recipes using chicken wings and pieces.

# TACO PIE

*Serve this appetizer dip with tortilla chips.
A quicker version simply topped a layer of
whipped cream cheese with hot taco sauce,
grated cheese, chopped onions and shredded lettuce. The same ingredients appeared
in many other dishes, including salads
served in corn tortilla "bowls."*

| | | |
|---|---|---|
| 1 | can (14 oz/398 mL) refried beans | 1 |
| 1/4 cup | sour cream | 50 mL |
| 1/2 tsp | hot pepper flakes | 2 mL |
| 1/4 tsp | ground cumin | 1 mL |
| 1 | ripe avocado, peeled and mashed | 1 |
| 1 | small onion, chopped | 1 |
| 2 tbsp | mayonnaise | 25 mL |
| 1 tbsp | lemon juice | 15 mL |
| Dash | hot pepper sauce | Dash |
| 2/3 cup | sour cream | 150 mL |
| 2 cups | shredded Monterey Jack cheese | 500 mL |
| 4 | green onions, sliced | 4 |
| 1/2 cup | sliced black olives | 125 mL |
| 2 | tomatoes, chopped | 2 |

Blend together refried beans, 1/4 cup
(50 mL) sour cream, hot pepper flakes
and cumin; spread in 9-inch (23 cm)
pie plate or quiche dish. Mash together
avocado, onion, mayonnaise, lemon
juice and hot pepper sauce; spread over
bean layer. Spread sour cream over top,
sealing to edge. Garnish with concen-
tric circles of cheese, onions, olives and
tomatoes. Makes 8 to 10 servings.

For grazers, the '80s offered more variety than ever in cocktail fare and
starter courses: **Caviar Pie** (a pie plate
of cream cheese topped with three colors of caviar), **Taramasalata** (a Greek
spread made with fish roe), **Hot
Artichoke Dip** (puréed artichoke
hearts, mayonnaise and Parmesan
cheese) and spinach dip served in a
hollowed-out pumpernickel loaf.
Blocks of cream cheese were smothered with chutney, red pepper jelly,
or seafood sauce and shrimp.
**Hummus** (a chick-pea and sesame
dip), **Caponata** (eggplant spread or
dip), **Tapenade Dip** (tuna and
lemon), **Nachos** (corn chips with
melted cheese) and crisp potato skins
were favorites. Terrines and pâtés, like
veal with pistachios, or smoked
salmon or trout, were served with pita
crisps or crackers.

By the end of the decade, Spanish
tapas (small appetizers) were "in" and
many non-Spanish foods were included as tapas. Beans were once
again fashionable, and Mexican and
Southwestern fare was trendy.

# CRABMEAT CREPES

*This filling, enough for 12 to 15 crêpes, can be varied by substituting shrimp or mixed seafood, or broccoli or asparagus.*

|  | Crabmeat Filling (recipe follows) |  |
|---|---|---|
| 2 tbsp | butter, melted | 25 mL |
| 1/4 cup | shredded Swiss cheese | 50 mL |
| 2 tbsp | grated Parmesan cheese | 25 mL |
| *Crêpes:* |  |  |
| 4 | eggs | 4 |
| 1 cup | milk | 250 mL |
| 1/4 cup | water | 50 mL |
| 2 tbsp | butter, melted | 25 mL |
| 1 cup | all-purpose flour | 250 mL |
| 1/2 tsp | salt | 2 mL |

Crêpes: In blender or food processor, blend eggs, milk, water, butter, flour and salt for 1 minute until smooth. Cover and refrigerate for 1 hour.

Heat 7- to 8-inch (18 to 20 cm) crêpe pan over medium-high heat; brush with unsalted butter. Using 1/4 cup (50 mL) batter for each crêpe, pour batter into pan, tilting to cover bottom. Cook about 1 minute or until lightly browned; turn and cook other side.

Place spoonful of crabmeat filling in centre of each crêpe; roll up and arrange in one layer in baking dish. Drizzle with butter; sprinkle with Swiss and Parmesan cheeses. Bake in 400°F (200°C) oven for about 10 minutes or until heated through and lightly browned. Makes 4 to 6 servings.

### CRABMEAT FILLING:

| 3 tbsp | butter | 50 mL |
|---|---|---|
| 1/2 cup | sliced mushrooms | 125 mL |
| 2 tbsp | minced onion | 25 mL |
| 3 tbsp | all-purpose flour | 50 mL |
| 1 cup | light cream | 250 mL |
| 1/4 cup | dry white wine | 50 mL |
| 6 oz | cooked or canned crabmeat | 175 g |
| 2 tbsp | chopped chives or fresh parsley | 25 mL |
|  | Salt and pepper |  |

In small heavy saucepan or skillet, melt butter; cook mushrooms and onion until softened. Stir in flour; cook until bubbly. Stir in cream and wine; bring to boil and cook 2 minutes. Add crabmeat, chives, and salt and pepper to taste.

### VARIATIONS:

**Dessert Crêpes:** Add 1 tbsp (15 mL) granulated sugar to batter. Fill crêpes with fresh berries or sliced fruit; top with whipped cream. Hot fillings such as sliced apples cooked with brown sugar and cinnamon are good with a hot rum or lemon sauce.

**Blintzes:** Fill dessert crêpes with cottage cheese filling (1 lb/500 g pressed cottage cheese beaten smooth with 2 eggs, 1/4 cup/50 mL granulated sugar, 2 tsp/10 mL grated lemon rind and a dash of vanilla). Fold in sides, then roll up. Brown lightly in butter in skillet. Serve with sour cream.

The interest in French cooking that started in the '60s made crêpes a standard in recipe repertoires by the '70s and led to all kinds of stylish variations in the '80s. Everything from smoked salmon to spicy ratatouille inspired new fillings. Crêpe batters were varied with buckwheat and other flours, or even the addition of chopped spinach. **Beggar's Purses** were small crêpes gathered around a filling of caviar and sour cream and tied with green onions into a pouch.

In the early '80s, many new wrappers appeared: tortillas for Mexican recipes, egg rolls and rice paper for Oriental, pitas for Middle Eastern. Frozen puff pastry became widely available in supermarkets and made great sausage rolls and filled pastries.

Phyllo was a hot item, and the fragile, multi-layered pastry was a welcome shortcut for making apple strudel. By the late '80s, phyllo had become very popular for appetizers such as baked triangles of phyllo-wrapped cheese (first Cheddar, then feta and chèvre) and had replaced puff pastry in desserts. Formed into cups, twisted like party cracker or layered in baklava, phyllo was impressive.

# TERIYAKI SALMON

*This marinade works well with lean lamb chops or loins, pork tenderloin or boneless chicken breasts.*

| | | |
|---|---|---|
| 1 cup | tamari sauce or soy sauce | 250 mL |
| 1/4 cup | sherry or sake (rice wine) | 50 mL |
| 2 tbsp | granulated sugar | 25 mL |
| 2 | cloves garlic, minced | 2 |
| 2 tbsp | minced gingerroot | 25 mL |
| 2 lb | salmon fillets, 1-1/2 to 2 inches (4 to 5 cm) thick | 1 kg |

In shallow dish, combine tamari, sherry, sugar, garlic and ginger. Add salmon and marinate for at least 30 minutes or refrigerate overnight, turning occasionally.

Reserving marinade, barbecue or broil salmon 6 inches (15 cm) from heat, turning once, for 10 minutes per inch (2.5 cm) of thickness, basting with marinade, or until fish flakes easily when tested with fork. Serve hot or cold. Makes 6 to 8 servings.

This marinade, which reflects the popularity of Oriental flavors, especially in British Columbia, quickly became a favorite for backyard grilling across Canada.

During the '80s, the enjoyment of sushi reached a high. While few attempts were made to recreate these artfully designed morsels at home, a restaurant lunch of sushi was extremely popular, as was dim sum, an array of Chinese appetizers.

# PASTA PRIMAVERA

*For a light variation, just toss pasta with a little olive oil and crisp-cooked garden vegetables. Add lightly-cooked seafood if desired, and vary the vegetables to your taste.*

| | | |
|---|---|---|
| 2 tbsp | butter | 25 mL |
| 1 | small onion, chopped | 1 |
| 1 | clove garlic, minced | 1 |
| 1/2 lb | asparagus, sliced | 250 g |
| 1 | sweet red or green pepper, chopped | 1 |
| 2 cups | thinly sliced mushrooms | 500 mL |
| 1 | medium zucchini, sliced | 1 |
| 1 | carrot, thinly sliced | 1 |
| 1 cup | fresh or frozen peas | 250 mL |
| 2 tbsp | chicken stock | 25 mL |
| 1 cup | whipping cream | 250 mL |
| 2 tbsp | chopped fresh basil | 25 mL |
| | Salt and pepper | |
| 1/2 lb | fettuccine or linguine | 250 g |
| 1/2 cup | grated Parmesan cheese | 125 mL |

In wok or deep skillet, heat butter; cook onion and garlic until softened, about 2 minutes. Add asparagus, red pepper, mushrooms, zucchini, carrot and peas; stir-fry for 2 minutes.

Add stock; cover and steam for 2 to 3 minutes or until vegetables are tender-crisp. Remove with slotted spoon and keep warm. Increase heat to high; boil cream and basil until reduced slightly, about 3 minutes. Season with salt and pepper to taste.

Meanwhile, cook pasta in large pot of boiling water, until al dente (firm to the bite); drain.

Return vegetables to wok; toss to coat. Serve over pasta. Sprinkle each serving with cheese. Makes 4 servings.

Not only did we learn about good Italian cooking from neighbors with gardens of basil and huge pots of tomato sauce bubbling in backyards each fall, but Canadians travelled more and ate things like the authentic Fettuccine Alfredo in Rome. Our big-city cooking schools featured demonstrations by Italian food gurus Giuliano Bugialli and Marcella Hazen. And who can forget TV chef Pasquale, with his bright-red hat, cooking with love and singing his way through his Italian favorites.

New pasta dishes appeared on restaurant menus. Italian delis displayed an array of pasta salads and a multitude of pasta shapes flavored with intriguing sauces. Fresh pastas were made with spinach, red pepper or even squid ink for a change in color and flavor.

Soon the pasta craze hit the home cook. Hand-cut pastas and pasta machines were widely popular. No longer content to merely serve spaghetti with clam sauce, we tossed fettuccine with chives, asparagus and peppers; linguine with smoked salmon; or any pasta with pesto.

## BROCCOLI CHEESE FRITTATA

*Serve this frittata hot or cold. Vary the recipe by substituting chopped drained marinated artichokes, sautéed mushrooms and zucchini, or sliced nectarines or peaches for the broccoli. Canned or smoked salmon, or bacon or prosciutto can also be added.*

| | | |
|---|---|---|
| 1 cup | sliced leeks | 250 mL |
| 2 tbsp | butter | 25 mL |
| 1 | small sweet red or green pepper, chopped | 1 |
| 1/4 cup | chopped fresh parsley | 50 mL |
| 4 | eggs | 4 |
| 1/3 cup | fresh bread crumbs | 75 mL |
| 1/4 tsp | hot pepper sauce | 1 mL |
| | Salt and pepper | |
| 2 cups | blanched broccoli florets | 500 mL |
| 1 cup | shredded Cheddar cheese | 250 mL |

In skillet, cook leeks in butter until tender but not browned. Add red pepper and cook, stirring once or twice, for 3 minutes. Stir in parsley; remove from heat.

Whisk eggs until frothy. Stir in bread crumbs, hot pepper sauce, and salt and pepper to taste. Fold in broccoli, leek mixture and cheese. Pour into greased 8-inch (20 cm) quiche dish. Bake in 350°F (180°C) oven for 25 to 30 minutes or until golden and just set in centre. Makes 4 servings.

Frittatas (classic Italian omelettes) were introduced to many Canadians during the '80s, and all sorts of variations appeared in magazines. Some versions were simply crustless quiches. Frittatas also became popular as a way of increasing our broccoli consumption (which nutritionists were advising). Using zucchini instead of broccoli was a great way to use up the garden overflow.

# Microwave Artichokes with Hollandaise

*When microwaved, artichokes cook very quickly and retain a bright color, and sauces become virtually foolproof.*

| | | |
|---|---|---|
| 4 | artichokes | 4 |
| Half | lemon | Half |
| 1/4 cup | water | 50 mL |

Remove tough outer leaves of artichokes; cut off stem. With scissors, cut tips off each leaf. Rub cut edges with lemon. Arrange artichokes, upright, in microwaveable dish. Add water; microwave, covered, at High for 6 to 10 minutes, rotating dish twice, until artichokes are tender when pierced with tip of sharp knife. Let stand for 5 minutes. Makes 4 servings.

**HOLLANDAISE SAUCE:**

| | | |
|---|---|---|
| 1/2 cup | butter | 125 mL |
| 3 tbsp | lemon juice | 50 mL |
| Pinch | each dry mustard and cayenne pepper | Pinch |
| 3 | egg yolks, lightly beaten | 3 |

In 2-cup (500 mL) bowl, microwave butter at High for 45 to 60 seconds or until melted but not bubbling. Whisk in lemon juice, mustard and cayenne. Whisk in egg yolks. Microwave, uncovered, at Medium-Low (30% power) for 1 to 3 minutes or until thickened, whisking every 30 seconds. (If sauce curdles, whisk in 1 to 2 tbsp/15 mL to 25 mL cold water.) Makes about 1 cup (250 mL).

During the '80s, Canadians went from reheating coffee and defrosting in the microwave to trying all sorts of recipes, some good, some dreadful. Scores of cookbooks appeared, many self-published and most by westerners. By the mid-'80s, microwaving finally went epicurean and was endorsed by foodies, who then turned out interesting recipes that showed off microwaving at its best. As the microwave oven took its place as the best time-saving tool in the kitchen, we wondered how we ever cooked without it.

# Wild Rice and Barley Pilaf

*Pilafs like this one can also be used as poultry stuffing. You can substitute white long-grain or brown rice for barley in this pilaf. For a change of flavor, add currants, toasted slivered almonds, chopped hazelnuts, cashews or pistachios, dried apricots, green onions or grated orange rind.*

| | | |
|---|---|---|
| 1/2 cup | wild rice | 125 mL |
| | Salt and pepper | |
| 3/4 cup | pearl barley | 175 mL |
| 1/4 cup | butter | 50 mL |
| 2 cups | sliced mushrooms | 500 mL |
| 1 | small onion, chopped | 1 |
| 1 | stalk celery, chopped | 1 |
| 1-1/2 cups | chicken stock | 375 mL |
| 1/4 cup | chopped fresh parsley | 50 mL |

Rinse rice in sieve under cold running water. Bring 3 cups (750 mL) water to boil; add rice and 1/2 tsp (2 mL) salt. Cover and boil gently for 45 minutes or until tender but still chewy. Drain and rinse in sieve under cold water; set aside.

In large skillet, melt half the butter; sauté mushrooms lightly. Remove and set aside. Add remaining butter to skillet; cook barley, onion and celery, stirring, until vegetables are softened. Stir in stock; bring to boil. Reduce heat; cover and simmer for about 35 minutes or until liquid is absorbed and barley is tender but still chewy, adding more stock if necessary. Season with salt and pepper to taste. Add parsley, wild rice and mushrooms; mix gently. Makes 6 to 8 servings.

As complex carbohydrates and fibre became nutrition buzzwords, grains were in vogue. Pilaf rose in popularity. Middle-eastern recipes suited familiar Canadian grains: barley, kasha (toasted buckwheat groats, good for stuffings as well) and bulgur (steamed and dried cracked wheat kernels, available in three sizes, the largest for pilafs, the smallest for tabbouleh salad).

Rice appeared in more varieties. White, brown, Thai, pecan and basmati were used alone, mixed, or combined with other grains. Italian Arborio rice was a favorite for risotto. Wild rice, actually an aquatic grass rather than a grain, adds a wonderful nutty taste and texture.

# WARM SEAFOOD SALAD

*Warm salads make delightful first courses or light suppers. For the greens, combine romaine, spinach, Boston or leaf lettuce with some sturdy varieties that don't wilt as quickly, such as radicchio, curly endive, Belgian endive, arugula or watercress. Either raw or cooked shrimp may be used. Lightly cooked shrimp with tails left on are available at many fish counters and are convenient to use.*

| 8 cups | assorted torn salad greens | 2 L |
|--------|----------------------------|-----|
| 1/2 lb | scallops | 250 g |
| 1/2 cup | olive oil | 125 mL |
| 1/4 lb | shrimp (raw or cooked), peeled, tails on | 125 g |
| 2 | cloves garlic, minced | 2 |
| 2 tbsp | chopped shallots or mild onion | 25 mL |
| 1/4 cup | white wine vinegar | 50 mL |
| 1 tbsp | lemon juice | 15 mL |
| Pinch | dried dillweed or tarragon | Pinch |
| 1/4 cup | chopped fresh parsley | 50 mL |
| | Salt and pepper | |

Arrange salad greens on individual plates. Cut scallops in half if large. In skillet, heat 2 tbsp (25 mL) oil over medium-high heat; sauté scallops and shrimp (if raw) for 1 minute. Add garlic and shallots; cook 1 minute. Add remaining oil, vinegar, lemon juice, dillweed, parsley and shrimp (if cooked); cook about 1 minute or until scallops are opaque and shrimp are pink. Season with salt and pepper to taste. Pour hot dressing over greens; spoon seafood on top. Makes 4 servings.

## VARIATIONS:

**Warm Chicken or Turkey:** Use thinly sliced grilled chicken or turkey breast in place of seafood; rosemary instead of dillweed.

**Warm Lamb:** Use grilled strips of boneless lamb in place of seafood; red wine vinegar instead of white; rosemary instead of dillweed.

**Warm Chicken Liver:** Use lightly sautéed chicken livers in place of seafood; balsamic vinegar in place of white wine vinegar.

Salads began changing with the arrival of more specialty greens at the supermarket, and fresh herbs in gardens and at produce stores. Edible flowers became trendy. Greens like arugula, mâche (lamb's lettuce) and beautiful hydroponic lettuces formed the base of the salad plate. Radicchio, Belgian endive and assorted fresh herbs completed the arrangement. Vinaigrettes, made with extra-virgin olive oil alone or in combination with oils like walnut or sesame, and vinegars (homemade or from specialty stores) included fruit- or herb-flavored ones.

Topping off crisp salad greens with a hot dressing and sautéed seafood, grilled chicken or strips of steak created sizzling new taste and texture sensations – a very '80s interpretation of the wilted salads of Grandmother's time.

# FRESH TOMATO SALSA

*Salsa is simply the Spanish word for sauce, but it generally refers to fresh, uncooked sauces of chopped vegetables.*

| 2 | large ripe tomatoes or 6 plum tomatoes | 2 |
|---|----------------------------------------|---|
| 1/4 cup | chopped green onions | 50 mL |
| 1 | clove garlic, minced | 1 |
| 1 tsp | minced jalapeño pepper | 5 mL |
| 1 tbsp | wine vinegar or lime juice | 15 mL |
| 1 tbsp | olive oil | 15 mL |
| | Salt and pepper | |

Cut tomatoes in half and squeeze out seeds; chop finely and place in bowl. Add onions, garlic, jalapeño pepper, vinegar, oil, and salt and pepper to taste. Let stand 1 hour to blend flavors. Makes about 2 cups (500 mL).

Salsas are fast, fresh tasting, light and low-cal. Use tomato salsa for topping tacos, nachos, burgers, omelettes, fish or chicken. Make salsa very chunky if desired, or purée part of it in blender for smoother sauce. For salsa variations, add to taste: chopped fresh coriander (cilantro), parsley, fresh herbs, red or green sweet peppers, cucumbers, or fruit such as mango or peaches.

# PESTO

*Fresh basil flourishes in Canadian gardens, and basil pesto became almost as familiar as tomato sauce during the '80s. If you make this in large batches for freezing, omit the cheese and add it just before serving. Pesto can also be made with fresh parsley or coriander (cilantro).*

| 2 cups | packed fresh basil leaves | 500 mL |
|---|---|---|
| 2 | cloves garlic | 2 |
| 1/4 cup | pine nuts | 50 mL |
| 1/2 tsp | salt | 2 mL |
| 1/4 tsp | pepper | 1 mL |
| 1/2 cup | olive oil | 125 mL |
| 1/2 cup | grated Parmesan cheese | 125 mL |

In food processor or blender, combine basil, garlic, pine nuts, salt and pepper; process until chopped. With motor running, drizzle in oil, processing until smooth. Add cheese. Refrigerate for up to 3 days. Makes about 1 cup (250 mL).

> To use pesto for pasta sauce, dilute slightly with a little of the pasta cooking water, or mix pesto with cream. For salad dressings, add pesto to vinaigrettes, mayonnaise, sour cream or yogurt.

# STIR-FRY PORK AND VEGETABLES

*Make up the 3 cups (750 mL) vegetables by mixing and matching carrot, zucchini, broccoli, red or green pepper or green beans. Or choose Chinese vegetables like bok choy, fresh bean sprouts or snow peas. Serve over hot fluffy rice.*

| 2 tbsp | soy sauce | 25 mL |
|---|---|---|
| 2 tbsp | sherry | 25 mL |
| 1 tbsp | cornstarch | 15 mL |
| 3/4 lb | lean pork or boneless chicken breasts, cut in strips | 375 g |
| 2 tbsp | vegetable oil | 25 mL |
| 1 | clove garlic, chopped | 1 |
| 1 | onion, chopped | 1 |
| 1 tbsp | finely chopped gingerroot | 15 mL |
| 3 cups | sliced or slivered vegetables | 750 mL |
| 1/2 cup | chicken stock | 125 mL |

In bowl, combine soy sauce, sherry and cornstarch; add pork and marinate for up to 30 minutes. Remove with slotted spoon, reserving marinade. Heat 1 tbsp (15 mL) oil in wok or skillet; stir-fry pork until lightly browned and no longer pink. Remove and keep warm.

Add remaining oil to pan; stir-fry garlic, onion, gingerroot and vegetables, adding vegetables according to cooking time necessary (carrot or turnip first, green beans or broccoli next, cabbage or snow peas last, stir-frying each for 2 to 3 minutes before adding next).

Add chicken stock; cover and simmer for 3 to 4 minutes or until vegetables are tender-crisp. Blend in reserved marinade; add reserved pork. Cook, stirring until sauce is thickened and clear and meat is heated through. Makes 4 servings.

> Chinese cooking, stir-frys in particular, appealed to the desire for healthy eating, more vegetables and fast cooking in the '80s. Martin Yan, with his "Yan Can" series on Canadian television, made stir-frying look easy and lots of fun. Woks became stylish, and a basic stir-fry was simple to adapt to whatever vegetables were handy. Beef, pork or chicken were interchanged in recipes.

# OAT BRAN MUFFINS

*You can vary this recipe by substituting natural wheat bran for oat bran, or chopped dates or prunes for raisins. Any all-purpose flour (regular, unbleached or with bran) may be used.*

| | | |
|---|---|---|
| 1 cup | oat bran | 250 mL |
| 1-1/4 cups | buttermilk | 300 mL |
| 1 | egg | 1 |
| 1/3 cup | vegetable oil | 75 mL |
| 1/2 cup | packed brown sugar | 125 mL |
| 1/4 cup | honey or molasses | 50 mL |
| 1 tsp | vanilla | 5 mL |
| 1 cup | all-purpose flour | 250 mL |
| 1 tsp | baking powder | 5 mL |
| 1 tsp | baking soda | 5 mL |
| 1/2 tsp | salt | 2 mL |
| 1/2 tsp | cinnamon (optional) | 2 mL |
| 1 cup | raisins | 250 mL |

In bowl, combine bran and buttermilk; let stand 5 minutes. Beat together egg, oil, sugar, honey and vanilla; mix into bran mixture. Combine flour, baking powder, soda, salt, cinnamon (if using) and raisins; stir into bran mixture just until combined.

Spoon into greased or paper-lined muffin tins, filling three-quarters full. Bake in 375°F (190°C) oven for 20 minutes or until tops are firm to the touch. Makes about 12.

In the early '80s, mega muffins (with little regard for calories) became all the rage. Cookbooks of muffin recipes were published in great profusion. Flavors ranged from bacon-corn niblet to orange-date to zucchini to chocolate chip, but oat bran remained the most popular of all.

A batch of muffin cookbooks by Canadians hit the bookstore shelves in the '80s, including *Mad About Muffins* by Angela Clubb; *Muffins: A Cookbook* by Joan Bidmosti and Marilyn Wearring; *Muffin Mania* by Cathy Prange and Joan Pauli; *101 Marvelous Muffins* by Adele Marks; *Heather's Muffin Cookbook* by Heather Irwin; and *Just Muffins* by Gaye Hansen.

# ZUCCHINI BREAD

*This easy recipe makes two moist loaves that freeze well. Peel the zucchini only if it's large and tough, or if you prefer the bread not speckled with green.*

| | | |
|---|---|---|
| 3 | eggs | 3 |
| 1-1/2 cups | granulated sugar | 375 mL |
| 1 cup | vegetable oil | 250 mL |
| 2 tsp | vanilla | 10 mL |
| 2 cups | packed finely shredded zucchini | 500 mL |
| 3 cups | all-purpose flour | 750 mL |
| 1-1/2 tsp | baking powder | 7 mL |
| 1 tsp | baking soda | 5 mL |
| 1/2 tsp | salt | 2 mL |
| 1-1/2 tsp | cinnamon | 7 mL |
| 1 cup | raisins | 250 mL |
| 1/2 cup | chopped nuts | 125 mL |

In bowl, beat eggs; beat in sugar, oil and vanilla. Stir in zucchini. Stir together flour, baking powder, soda, salt and cinnamon; stir in raisins and nuts. Stir into zucchini mixture. Pour into two greased 8- x 4-inch (1.5 L) loaf pans. Bake in 350°F (180°C) oven for 50 to 60 minutes or until tester comes out clean. Makes 2 loaves.

> As soon as Canadians learned to love zucchini, they had to deal with the annual garden overflow. Recipes for zucchini in every possible guise – cakes, breads, muffins, stuffed, baked, breaded – filled the late-summer food pages of every newspaper.
>
> Variations of the following quick supper dish were popular. **Skillet Zucchini with Tomatoes and Basil:** In a little oil in skillet, cook a sliced or chopped onion until softened. Add 3 or 4 thinly sliced zucchini and a crushed garlic clove; cook and stir 2 minutes. Add 8 tomato wedges or cherry tomatoes; cook 2 minutes. Add chopped basil, salt and pepper to taste. Makes 3 or 4 servings.

# GLAZED FRESH FRUIT PIE OR TARTS

*Colorful glazed pies and tarts show off Canadian summer fruit at its best. One kind of fruit or a mixture may be used for this recipe. A tart red jelly is a good glaze for berries; apricot jam can be used for a lighter-colored glaze.*

| | 9-inch (23 cm) baked pie shell or 8 to 12 tart shells | |
|---|---|---|
| 3 cups | fresh fruit* | 750 mL |
| 8 oz | cream cheese | 250 g |
| 2 tbsp | orange juice or liqueur | 25 mL |
| 3/4 cup | red currant jelly | 175 mL |

Cream together cheese and orange juice until smooth. Spread in bottom of baked pie shell. Arrange fruit attractively on top. Melt jelly and cook slightly. Spoon over fruit. Chill pie until set.

*Small or sliced strawberries, raspberries, sliced peaches and kiwifruit are attractive together, but mix and match fruit according to season and taste.

**Food Processor Sweet Pastry:** Into food processor bowl measure 1-1/2 cups (375 mL) all-purpose flour, 1/4 cup (50 mL) icing sugar, 1 egg and 1/3 cup (75 mL) cold butter cut in pieces. Process for 10 seconds or until dough begins to form a mass on the blade. Gather into ball; refrigerate for 30 minutes.

Roll out on lightly floured surface; ease into flan or tart pans, pressing gently into sides of pan. Trim; prick bottom. Bake in 425°F (220°C) oven for 10 minutes or until golden. Cool.

> Recipes in the '80s for open-faced pies or tarts provided countless variations. The earliest recipes were for glazed strawberry pies and often called for making the glaze by crushing part of the fruit and cooking it with cornstarch. Later recipes used a quicker glaze of melted jelly. Regular pie plates were upstaged by shallower, straight-sided flan pans for the classic look of French pastry-shop tartes. Butter pastry became easy to make with a food processor, or store-bought spongecake flans were quickly and easily filled.
>
> For weekend cooks, Pavlovas or individual meringues filled with fruit and whipped cream were popular. And the craze to garnish everything with kiwifruit started in the '80s.

# CHOCOLATE TRUFFLE RUFFLE CAKE

*To add a touch more decadence, garnish with Chocolate Truffles.*

| | | |
|---|---|---|
| 4 oz | semisweet chocolate | 125 g |
| 2 tbsp | rum or strong coffee | 25 mL |
| 1/2 cup | unsalted butter | 125 mL |
| 2/3 cup | granulated sugar | 150 mL |
| 3 | eggs, separated | 3 |
| 1/3 cup | finely ground almonds | 75 mL |
| 3/4 cup | sifted cake-and-pastry flour | 175 mL |
| 1/2 tsp | salt | 2 mL |
| 2 tbsp | granulated sugar | 25 mL |
| **Glaze:** | | |
| 1 cup | semisweet chocolate chips | 250 mL |
| 1/2 cup | sour cream | 125 mL |
| **Garnish:** | | |
| | Chocolate ruffles, curls or shavings | |
| | Candied violets | |

Melt chocolate; stir in rum. Set aside. In bowl, cream butter with sugar; beat in egg yolks, one at a time, beating well. Blend in chocolate mixture. Add almonds and flour, mixing well.

Beat egg whites with salt until frothy; gradually beat in 2 tbsp (25 mL) sugar until soft peaks form. Fold into batter. Pour into buttered 8-inch (1.2 L) round cake pan. Bake in 350°F (180°C) oven for 25 to 30 minutes or until edge is cooked and centre is barely soft to the touch. Let cool in pan for 5 minutes; remove to rack and let cool completely.

Glaze: Melt chocolate chips; blend in sour cream. Refrigerate until spreadable. Spread over cake, smoothing top. Garnish with chocolate ruffles and candied violets.

**CHOCOLATE TRUFFLES:**

| | | |
|---|---|---|
| 6 oz | semisweet chocolate, coarsely chopped | 175 g |
| 6 tbsp | whipping cream | 100 mL |
| 2 tbsp | rum or orange-flavored liqueur | 25 mL |
| | Unsweetened cocoa powder, icing sugar, finely chopped nuts or melted semisweet chocolate | |

In bowl, slowly melt chocolate with cream over hot water or in microwave, stirring often. Remove from heat; beat well. Blend in rum. Chill until firm. Roll into small balls. Roll in cocoa, icing sugar or nuts, or dip into melted chocolate. Chill until serving. Makes about 30.

"Decadent" desserts (served in small portions) were a popular antidote for a surfeit of "healthy" eating. Many recipes produced cakes that were so rich in butter and chocolate that they dipped in the centre during baking. Ingredients like white chocolate, macadamia nuts, liqueurs, pistachios, ground almonds, dark chocolate (curls, shavings or ribbons) were always the very best quality. The chocolate was usually imported Swiss, French or Belgian. Dainty candied violets or fresh flowers were garnishes.

**Chocolate Mousse Cake** usually had layers of chocolate mousse and chocolate cake but was sometimes simply a rich mousse in a cake shape.

# Tuiles with Sorbets and Raspberry Coulis

*Make coulis by puréeing 1 pkg (425 g) thawed raspberries, straining if desired, and flavoring with framboise liqueur and sugar. Spoon onto individual plates. Drizzle or dab with crème fraîche, sour cream or softly whipped cream to form pattern. Centre tuile on coulis; fill with sherbet. Garnish with fruit, fresh mint, flowers, or a light dusting of icing sugar around the rim of the plate.*

| | | |
|---|---|---|
| 2 | egg whites | 2 |
| 1/2 cup | granulated sugar | 125 mL |
| 1/3 cup | all-purpose flour | 75 mL |
| 1/4 cup | butter, melted | 50 mL |
| 2 tsp | water | 10 mL |
| 1 tsp | vanilla | 5 mL |

Grease and flour 3 baking sheets or line with parchment paper.

In bowl, beat egg whites, sugar, flour, butter, water and vanilla just until blended. Using 3 tbsp (50 mL) for each tuile, drop onto baking sheets, spreading each into 6-inch (15 cm) circle. Bake, one sheet at a time, in upper half of 400°F (200°C) oven for 6 to 8 minutes or just until edges begin to brown.

Remove baking sheet from oven. Immediately remove tuiles, one at a time, and invert over lightly greased inverted tall glass, about 1-1/2-inches (4 cm) in diameter. Working quickly, shape warm tuile with fingers to create fluted cup. Repeat with second tuile. (If too firm to mould, reheat 15 to 30 seconds or until softened.) Let cool completely on glass. Repeat with remaining batter. Makes 6 tuiles.

Designer desserts, often known as "puddle-and-drizzle" cuisine, were fashionable in upscale restaurants and often imitated at home, especially by those taking cooking classes. The drizzles, such as melted chocolate, caramel or crème fraîche, topped the puddles, such as custard, sour cream or coulis (purées of lightly cooked or fresh fruit). Melted white chocolate or softly whipped cream dribbled over raspberry purée or chocolate sauce were favorites.

Tuiles (crisp sugar cookies curved after baking to form a cup shape), chocolate cups (formed in paper-lined muffin tins) or brandy snaps shaped into lacy cups were filled with tiny scoops of exotic sorbets or rich ice creams.

# Tiramisu

*The name means "pick-me-up," and this delectable coffee-and-chocolate-flavored Italian trifle certainly seemed to give dessert lovers a lift in the '80s. Tiramisu was on all the fashionable restaurant menus, and recipes quickly made the rounds for dinner parties at home.*

| | | |
|---|---|---|
| 1/2 cup | strong espresso coffee | 125 mL |
| 3/4 cup | coffee liqueur | 175 mL |
| 16 | (approx) ladyfinger biscuits | 16 |
| 1 lb | mascarpone cheese | 500 g |
| 1/4 cup | granulated sugar | 50 mL |
| 2 cups | whipping cream | 500 mL |
| 3 oz | semisweet chocolate, grated | 90 g |

Combine coffee and 1/4 cup (50 mL) liqueur. Dip ladyfingers in coffee mixture; set aside. In bowl, beat together mascarpone, sugar and remaining liqueur until smooth and light. Whip cream, reserving half for topping. Fold remainder into cheese mixture.

In serving bowl, arrange single layer of ladyfingers; spread with layer of cheese mixture. Sprinkle with layer of chocolate. Repeat layers, reserving a little chocolate for garnish. Top dessert with reserved whipped cream and chocolate. Cover and chill several hours. Makes about 12 servings.

There are many versions of tiramisu, both classic and current. Mascarpone cheese is the key ingredient and available in most Italian and specialty food shops, but a good quality soft cream cheese (or half cream cheese, half ricotta) makes a satisfactory substitute.

**Zabaglione** (sabayon in French) is another classic Italian dessert that became very popular here in the '80s. Variations flavored with everything from orange juice to champagne can be used as dessert sauces over fruit. Classic Zabaglione is easy to make: For 4 servings, beat 4 egg yolks with 1/4 cup (50 mL) granulated sugar until pale and creamy. Set bowl in saucepan of barely simmering water; add 1/2 cup (125 mL) dry Marsala wine, and whisk until tripled in volume and holds soft peaks. Pour into stemmed glasses and serve immediately.

# A CENTURY OF CANADIAN HOME COOKING

*It's Friday, and weekend plans are exchanged. When asked, I say, "I'm cocooning," and someone mutters about another one of my new words for the '90s. The word isn't new and neither is the concept. We simply lost sight of it during the '80s....Now, doing nothing is the best treat of the week....The most obvious cocoon is home, where you can lock the front door on Friday night with everyone you love inside, make popcorn, bring out a cosy afghan and watch movies.*

– Bonnie Baker Cowan
*Canadian Living*

Comfort, caring, common sense. Balance and moderation. Slow down, simplify, deschedule. The "new-attitude" buzzwords of the early '90s represented a giant pendulum swing away from the "shop-till-you-drop" codes of the fast-lane '80s.

A new credo emerged: conspicuous consumption was out; frugality and a return to traditional values were in. We were scaling down, staying in and preparing home-cooked meals again.

A taste of hard times certainly helped change our priorities. The '90s staggered in on an economic recession that forced major changes in many people's lives. "I'm worth it" became "I can't afford it." The recession that was supposed to be short-lived just wouldn't quit; economic woes were very severe in many regions, with thousands of people out of work.

But even for those who escaped the crunch, attitudes toward spending changed. The post-yuppie counterreaction to the excesses of the '80s made scaling down downright fashionable. Discount-store bargains acquired the previous cachet of designer-shop labels; boomers bragged about eating meat loaf instead of nouvelle cuisine. Consumers embraced recycling, denounced excess packaging and began worrying about the environment.

A new consciousness was emerging, with the focus on figuring out what really mattered. That wasn't easy. The political and social order of the whole planet was changing with mind-boggling speed, while closer to home we were struggling with our own future as a nation, facing a unity crisis and trying to redefine ourselves nationally and regionally. And on top of it all was the recession. No wonder we turned to cocooning.

Home and family provided a refuge from the uncertainties of the world outside. Eating together at home became important again. Combination kitchen/family rooms became action central; video rentals and VCR sales soared. Entertaining shifted to more casual neighborhood and co-op gatherings; an article in the *Winnipeg Sun* suggested a potluck party for the Grey Cup weekend, with finger foods such as Buenos Nachos and Super Sassy Wings.

Sit-down dinners hearkened back to Grandma's day, with

---

*"Everything old is new again."*

On pages 210 – 211: The new naturals: Market Garden Vegetables with Dipping Sauces, Grilled Salmon with Lime Cilantro Marinade and Salad of Black Beans, Grains and Rice.

*"Cocooning" includes cosy dinner parties and gatherings at home.*

Courtesy of Frank Grant, GW Photography, Toronto

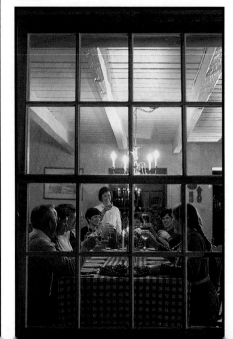

*Nostalgia and comfort foods are back.*

Courtesy of Ashley-Koffman Foods (Division of Hagemeyer Canada Inc.)

tables set with good china and crystal but serving basic meals such as roast chicken and fresh vegetables. The past was fondly recalled as a simpler and more satisfying time. Nostalgic cookbooks appeared, including Kay Spicer's *From Mom with Love* (which grew into a cooking show on TV Ontario), Anita Stewart's *From Our Mothers' Kitchens* and Rose Murray's '90s-style *Comfortable Kitchen Cookbook*.

In the *Toronto Sun*, Cynthia David reported that when Johnny came marching home again from the Gulf War, he'd want "mom food" – be it pot roast and chocolate cake, home-made pizza and lasagne, or cabbage rolls and perogies. A food article in *Chatelaine* updated the familiar casseroles, tuna melts and desserts of the '50s and '60s, giving them a '90s spin (faster, healthier, livelier flavored). Retro food created from packaged mixes and back-of-the-box recipes got a rerun as "kitsch cuisine" – the stuff that

horrifies food snobs but everyone else gobbles up, like meat loaf made with onion soup mix and hopscotch bars (peanut butter, butterscotch chips, chow mein noodles and marshmallows).

A '50s look reappeared in kitchen designs, too, with classic appliances such as Sunbeam Mixmasters and Osterizer blenders replacing high-tech multi-purpose kitchen machines. Bread machines brought back the old-time aromas of home baking without all the work.

Preserving made a comeback and new booklets from Bernardin (makers of preserving jar lids) and Certo featured recipes for herbed vinegars, red and green pepper jellies and wild berry jams. Home canners had shifted mainly to exotic treats, although many people still enjoyed making their traditional chili sauce and pickles, and every fall Canadians of Italian background still turned bushels of plum tomatoes into tomato sauce.

*Toronto's Cookbook Store held an old-fashioned Chili Sauce contest in 1991.*

Canada Wide/Warren Toda

*Cookbooks for a cause are an important theme of the "caring" '90s.*

Canada Wide/Veronica Milne

The recession prompted all kinds of articles on "hard-times cooking." In February 1991, the combination of recession, war in the Gulf and gloomy winter weather inspired one in the *Toronto Star* titled "Good Food for Bad Times," welcoming back cheap and comforting fare such as chicken pot pie, rice pudding, and wholewheat carrot apple honey cake.

Many newspapers featured tips and reminiscenses from people who had lived through the Depression of the '30s and the food-rationing of the '40s. People with '90s war jitters seemed to feel a sudden urge to make marmalade or get out the old Spam recipes. Other recipes that resurfaced were for "mock" foods such as raspberry jam made with green tomatoes and raspberry jelly powder; a '30s favorite, Mock Apple Pie, re-appeared on Ritz cracker boxes.

Recession was also the big bad word on the restaurant scene. Downscaling was one answer; many luxury restaurants switched to simpler fare and a more casual ambience, providing a welcome cocoon of sociability along with lower prices.

Meanwhile, food banks across the country were trying to cope with the largest numbers of needy people ever. By 1991 there were over 300 food banks in Canada. The first one had been formed in Edmonton in 1981 as a temporary measure, handing out 50 hampers a month; 10 years later the number had grown to 3000 hampers. In Toronto, the Daily Bread food bank was feeding 125,000 people a month by Thanksgiving 1991, up 44 per cent from the previous year; other charities such as Second Harvest collected surplus food from restaurants and caterers and distributed it to the poor; breakfast clubs for kids were formed in inner-city schools. In Montreal, a project called Cuisine Collective brought low-income mothers together for regular cooking bees that provided each family with four or five casseroles.

Cooking schools also went back to basics, offering a new curriculum: common sense, comfort and confidence. In a 1990 newspaper

*Cooking with kids is a popular activity, shown here by cooking school teacher Bonnie Stern and friend.*

The Toronto Star/Ken Faught

*The Millers at Riverside Lodge in Trinity Bay serve a Newfoundland special – partridgeberry pudding.*

Courtesy of George Kapelos, Toronto

## LOOKING BACK

Today's kids are adept at using microwave ovens but they aren't being taught basic culinary skills at home or school. A lot of 11- and 12-year-olds are cooking for their families, and I have been yelling about cuts being made in Family Studies by school boards across Canada.
– *Pam Collacott, author of* Pam's Kitchen, *cooks with kids on YTV's "Take Part" (June 1991)*

We had no choice but to change because of the tough times, but we don't consider our new lifestyle a sacrifice anymore. . . in becoming less consumption-oriented we ended up freeing ourselves from a treadmill – from yearning for things that don't really make you happy anyway. . . .We're spending a lot less than we ever did, but in many ways our quality of life is far better.
– *Janet McCallum,*The Frugal Times *newsletter (February 1992)*

Shepherd's pie topped with buttery mashed potatoes, creamy macaroni and cheese, lemon pie piled high with meringue . . . the simple foods from a gentler time are fast becoming the culinary hallmarks of the '90s. We've had our fill of oversauced dishes and nouvelle cuisine. Now, we're swooning over the dishes many of us ate as kids.
– *Monda Rosenberg,* Chatelaine *(March 1991)*

article, Bonnie Stern summed up the trends: "People are getting into cooking again; they want old-fashioned food but they want it fast and healthy. They're on tighter budgets, eating out less, entertaining at home more." Her new courses reflected those interests: Lite Cooking, Eat and Run, Microwave Gourmet, California Bistro, Fast and Stylish, Modern Basic Cooking.

"New basics" cookbooks became best-sellers. What was hot at bookstores had changed dramatically. Out went anything faddy or fancy. In came fitness, freshness, fibre, fat-free, fast, frugal and environmentally friendly.

The Green Revolution was under way. "Reduce, reuse, recycle" became the new three Rs. Grocery shoppers added ethical and environmental considerations to their lists. In newspapers, ecology-begins-at-home articles featured "green" recipes for everything from soup to household cleansers.

Part of the revolution was a concern about pollution and the safety of our food supply. Government departments of health and agriculture launched campaigns to promote food safety in the home as well as to educate consumers about Canada's stringent food inspection systems, since so much information coming from the United States didn't apply here.

Our interest in healthful eating was here to stay, but the '80s obsession with nutrition began to give way to a more balanced approach to health and fitness. The fixation on cholesterol, calcium and fibre lessened as consumers showed more confidence in food choices, selecting more vegetables, fruits, whole grains and legumes and smaller, leaner portions of fish, poultry and red meat. Many leading voices in the food media began to protest against the nutrition excesses of "food terrorists" who would reject all fat, sugar and salt; instead

*Sensible healthy eating continues but with moderation in mind.*

Courtesy of Canadian Egg Marketing Agency, Effem Foods Ltd. and KRAFT GENERAL FOODS CANADA INC.

*Pristine freshness is the key to today's quality-conscious consumer, as seen in this seafood display at Granville Island Market in Vancouver.*

Courtesy of Frank Grant, GW Photography, Toronto

## NUTRITION

- Keen interest in nutrition continues, with focus on social and environmental concerns.
- 1990: Health and Welfare Canada published *Canada's Guidelines for Healthy Eating*, outlining eating style to reduce risk of nutrition-related health problems.
- Food safety from perspective of environmental contaminants and food additives is major concern.
- 1992: New guide called *Canada's Food Guide to Healthy Eating* places greater emphasis on grains, fruits and vegetables, and lower fat choices in milk and meat categories.
- Fat reduction continues to be important, but increased emphasis now on shifting dietary intakes to include more carbohydrate-rich foods.
- Fresh and organically grown food continues to be stressed.
- Poverty–related hunger in Canada becomes major issue.

they preached moderation and enjoyment at the table. Most experts now recommended simply reducing the overall amount of fat in our diet while keeping food satisfying. "Recipe makeovers" offered healthier updates of favorites such as lasagne, french fries and carrot cake.

Convenience and speed remained top priorities in both food shopping and preparation. Microwave cooking became firmly entrenched; 75 per cent of homes had one oven, 10 per cent had two. Over half of all new convenience food products were for the microwave. Sales of one-serving suppers increased among singles and seniors; breakfast and lunch items were popular for the office microwave.

Pressure cookers, crock pots and automatic oven timers were dusted off as "new old-fashioned" tools of convenience. One-pot, slow-cooked meals (hearty soups, baked beans, pot roasts) made a comeback for taste, low cost and nutrition as well as convenience (especially for the growing number of people working at home who could take a brief break from the computer to stir a stew).

Food writers catered to an increasing demand for fast and easy recipes, or menus that combined home-cooked and purchased foods. Meat and produce departments offered more partially prepared choices: precut meats and vegetables for stir-frying, marinated steaks, salad mixtures, fresh pasta sauces. Supermarkets extended their shopping hours and expanded their nonfood departments (pharmacies, books, hardware) and services (bank machines, video rentals) to lure busy shoppers.

But our preoccupation with convenience didn't mean we were willing to sacrifice high quality, endless variety and interesting flavor – quite the contrary. In 1990 surveys, most grocery shoppers rated taste as even more important than cost. Freshly prepared dishes from gourmet takeouts were hot sellers even at high prices. Supermarket-style frozen entrees, especially diet products, improved to meet consumer demand

*Rush-hour cooking continues to be a prime concern of '90s cooks.*

The Toronto Star/Ken Faught

## DO YOU REMEMBER?

- Eating more ice cream and doughnuts (consumption went up during recession).
- Predictions that Russian cuisine would be "in" in the '90s.
- Shopping organic at the new Knives & Forks market in Toronto.
- The first Rain Forest cookies.
- 100th anniversary celebrations at the Algonquin Hotel, St. Andrew's by the Sea, New Brunswick (1990).
- The unveiling of the giant perogy sculpture in Glendon, Alberta.
- 1991 opening of Knob Hill Farms' Cambridge/Waterloo Food Terminal, billed as world's largest retail food outlet.
- Taste of the Nation fundraiser at top of CN Tower.
- Simplesse and Olestra (fake fats), Splenda (new super sweetener).
- Teenage Mutant Ninja Turtle dinners.
- Roberta Bondar, Canada's first woman astronaut.
- Muskox jerky, caribou burgers, smoked char at Aurorales in the Canadian pavilion at Expo '92 in Seville.
- And watch for:
  - Pizza perogies.
  - Wheat meat.
  - Seal sausages.
  - Muskox pepperoni.
  - Puffed wild rice.
  - Buzzwords: clanning, burrowing.

that "healthy" foods had to taste just as good as "regular" foods. More international flavors (often in crosscultural combinations of "East meets West") found their way to our tables. Even the "new traditionalists" found plain meat-and-potatoes a trifle boring; a recipe booklet from the Canadian Meat Council featured roast beef flavored with Dijon mustard, crushed peppercorns and oregano, and lamb chops with rosemary, ginger and soy sauce.

The *Vancouver Sun*'s 1990 listing of five-star recipes offered a typical sampling of the year's eclectic tastes: an aromatic beef stew with cilantro and curry; grilled peppers with feta, olives and balsamic dressing; ginger orange muffins; roast rack of lamb with Asian marinade. International flavors also predominated in their top microwave recipes: couscous paella, lasagne rolls and enchilada casserole.

As the '90s progress, we continue to add interesting new flavors to our menus while retaining our tried-and-true traditions. We are learning to blend the best of the old with the best of the new, and are interpreting that combination in many individual ways. Fads and fashions have been replaced by more honest cooking and a more philosophical approach to food in general.

As we relax our culinary attitudes along with our lifestyles, we are exploring new ways to enjoy the world of food. Cookbooks, for instance, have always made delicious reading for armchair cooks, and even more so today. Curled up in our cocoons, we can also dip into some of today's tasty literary fare, such as Margaret Visser's *Much Depends on Dinner* and *The Rituals of Dinner*.

Or we can plan next year's gastronomic vacation (no

*Familiarity with traditional northern foods increases through samplings like those for the Circumpolar Conference in '92, provided by Elizabeth Hansen of Inuvik and Helen Gruben of Tuktoyaktuk.*

Canada Wide/Ken Kerr

*Lovesick Lake Native Women's Association provides traditional foods for the annual Wildmeat Dinner at the Curve Lake First Nations Reserve near Peterborough, Ontario.*

The Toronto Star/Bob Olsen

problem if the recession restricts us to domestic destinations). Check out all the goodies published by the provincial ministries of tourism, such as the *Taste of Nova Scotia* dining guide (regional tours, best known delicacies and favorite recipes) or Quebec's unique *Tables Champêtres* (rural cuisine), listing regional farms where visitors can make reservations for special home-cooked dinners featuring fresh local ingredients.

Our interest in our regional culinary traditions continues to grow. More than ever in the '90s, we seem to need reminders of our roots. People are flocking to farmers' markets, not only for freshness and good prices but also for the earthy atmosphere and friendly service so different from the impersonality of supermarkets.

Country fairs are alive and well across the land, with city slickers coming in droves to buy eiderdown quilts and sample hot cinnamon buns and juicy raspberry pies. Day-tripping and leisurely weekend touring have become popular ways to explore our own regions, whether in the countryside or urban ethnic neighborhoods.

Canadians are also realizing that some of the best cooking in the country is tucked away in the home kitchens of our regional heartlands, and are seeking out country inns, vacation farms and bed-and-breakfasts serving local specialties. Travelling to different parts of the country is also a great way to sample many regional products that are often unavailable elsewhere in Canada, such as Arctic char and moose burgers in the North, Wheat Nuts (crunchy puffed wheat kernels) in Saskatchewan, Manitoba smoked goose and buckwheat honey, snow crab and Matane shrimp from the Gulf of St. Lawrence, dulse and fried clams in the Maritimes, and partridge-berries in Newfoundland.

Hundreds of food festivals coast to coast are attracting larger crowds every year. Many are held in honor of local products (from lobster in Shediac, New Brunswick, bakeapples in Labrador and grapes and wine in Niagara to corn and apples in Morden, Manitoba and barbecued lamb in B.C.'s Gulf Islands). Others celebrate local history (from Loyalist Days in Saint John to Klondike Days in Edmonton) or ethnic roots (from Irish in the Maritimes to Italian in Toronto, Icelandic in Manitoba and German Oktoberfests everywhere). Huge multicultural festivals are popular in every region, with 1992 bringing the biggest and best ever, in celebration of Canada's 125th birthday.

*Canadian summer markets like this one in Nova Scotia are more popular than ever before, attracting throngs of people each summer from coast to coast.*

Compliments of the Nova Scotia Department of Tourism & Culture and Taste of Nova Scotia

*Okanagan's wine country is a perfect setting for the pleasures of fine wines, regional cooking and good company.*

Photo: David Gray

*The earthy pleasures of baskets of crisp, fall apples and old-fashioned apple pies such as these regional beauties from Georgian Bay, Ontario are truly Canadian.*

Courtesy of Frank Grant, GW Photography, Toronto

## LOOKING AHEAD

The future isn't what it used to be. Maturing boomers will be the most powerful force, in both numbers and affluence, in the marketplace. Their demands for healthier and more interesting foods will revolutionize the food industry.
– *Len Kubas, Kubas Consultants, Toronto-based marketing specialist*

Trends hint at a more natural reconciliation of epicurean pursuits and health consciousness. There will be less worrying and more healthy pleasure.
– *Scott Mowbray, editor of* Eating Well *and former editor of* Vancouver *magazine*

Dining will be more casual and take less time, with great emphasis on fresh food and healthy eating. The variety of exotic ingredients will increase, but dishes will be uncomplicated, simple and satisfying.
– *Barbara Gordon, owner of the Avocado Club (formerly Beaujolais) in Toronto, and previously of La Cachette in Vancouver*

# What's In Store For The Remainder Of The Decade?

Most forecasters expect the back-to-basics trends of the early '90s to continue, with the effects of the recession keeping us cautious about spending. Even when the economy recovers, the shift from conspicuous consumption to common sense will likely remain; people will be spending money again, but on different things and for different reasons. As we head toward the 21st century, consumer demand for faster, fresher, healthier, safer foods will accelerate along with several other major trends:

**Individualism:** This new buzzword refers to the emergence of more independent consumers – more confident in their values and tastes, more demanding in the marketplace, more willing to take responsibility for their own health and environment. They will no longer spend blindly on status symbols or faddy items and will want products they can relate to individually. Their personal lives, homes and families are becoming more important.

**Changing demographics:** Canadian population growth is slowing but diversity is increasing – a changing ethnic mix, an aging population, smaller households, more singles in all age groups. The fastest-growing age group is over 50; it's also the most affluent but many of this generation grew up in hard times and are careful spenders.

By the mid-'90s, however, they'll be joined by the oldest of the boomers – the well-fed, well-travelled generation that grew up with every indulgence. These will be middle-agers with a different attitude; they believe in getting better not older. They will be less concerned with price than with nutrition, flavor and variety in foods. Even those who had to scale down during the recession will still demand quality. Their food choices will be fashionably '90s-style: low-fat, fresh and never boring.

The next generation, the "after-boomers," will be more environmentally conscious, avoiding packaged and processed foods in favor of fresh and natural. But their cooking will be mainly microwave and they'll be a big market for prepared food and other services.

**Market fragmentation:** Mass marketing is giving way to "niche marketing," with products and services catering to different needs. Retailers predict a major split into high- and low-end shopping, with the biggest growth in the bargain-hunting segment – discount warehouses, factory outlets, price clubs and mega-stores with bag-your-own groceries, long lineups, no service but great prices. At the same time, there's a growing upscale market that wants high quality products, pleasant surroundings and personal service and is willing to pay for it. But even this group wants value for their money.

**Service with a smile:** Convenience and speed are highest priorities for many consumers who want faster checkouts, ordering by phone or fax, more delivery services, lunch counters in supermarkets. Eventually, eating-in at home will become a service industry, with "food care" as much in demand as day care; restaurants and supermarkets will offer more high-quality

## LOOKING AHEAD

Fresher, healthier, simpler is where it's at for the '90s. Consumers are seeking simplicity but not a return to the past. They want a change of pace, a new twist to make familiar foods interesting again.
– *Cecile Girard-Hicks, director, Consumer Centre, Kraft General Foods*

The leading edge of the next decade is "the furnished kitchen." Kitchens will be designed more like furnished rooms rather than the high-tech look. They will be wallpapered like living rooms; the jam cupboard will replace the wall cabinets and the harvest table will replace the island.
– *Lynette Jennings, host of* Homeworks *on CBC-TV and editor of* Select Homes and Food

Food technology promises so-called designer foods – calorie-free, fat-free, sugar-free, gluttony without guilt. But will these future foods bring us better health? Or is there really no such thing as a free lunch?
– *Denise Beatty, registered professional dietitian and nutrition columnist*

food-to-go; more catering services will deliver dinner, including a bottle of wine, fresh flowers and even a video if you like.

**More microwave:** Every workplace will be equipped with microwave ovens; most homes will have two or three. Kids' microwave ovens will have big buttons, symbols, talking voices, message centres with memos from Mom or Dad. Mini-microwave ovens could become popular options in vans, station wagons and car dashboards. Commuters who feel like cooking after work will use computers or car phones to program kitchen appliances to defrost foods, preheat ovens, even bake bread.

**Smart stores:** Supermarkets of the future will provide computerized customer services such as personalized shopping lists and discounts based on past purchases, and video-equipped shopping carts that help locate grocery items, suggest menus and recipes, provide nutrition information and entertain customers at the checkout.

**Freshness and variety:** Shoppers will get even fussier, insisting on highest quality and endless variety. Fresh products will replace many processed or frozen items. There will be more choice of local and seasonal products, such as freshly squeezed juices, fresh herbs, free-range poultry and game. More recipes and serving ideas for unfamiliar foods will be offered at produce and meat counters.

**Ecology and environment:** Growing numbers of ecology-minded consumers will demand less packaging, more bulk foods, more environment-friendly products (organic, recyclable, nonpolluting, energy-saving).

**Health and food safety:** More health-oriented products, especially low-fat, will continue to appear. High-tech packaging will create shelf-stable foods without chemical preservatives or freezing. Consumer concern about food safety will lead to more "sourcing" on labels, indicating where and how the food was produced. Demand for more nutrition labelling will also continue to grow (along with demand for less packaging, producing an obvious conflict between more information and smaller labels).

**Bio-technology:** Advances in genetic engineering will produce hardier crops, higher yields and pest control without chemicals. More fabricated foods will provide low-cost, high-quality protein; soybeans and "surimi" (a processed fish product) can be shaped and flavored to simulate anything. New kinds of fake fats will satisfy taste without adding pounds or clogging arteries. "Nutraceuticals" (imbuing foods with pharmaceutical properties) could produce such wonders as orange juice with as much calcium as milk, chocolate pudding with as much fibre as oatmeal, popcorn with as much protein as meat.

## WHAT WILL WE BE EATING IN THE YEAR 2000?

Breakfast from a microwave in the car? Hot dogs with all the nutrition you need in a day? Onions that don't make you cry? French fries with no fat? Processed fish that tastes like charbroiled steak?

With all that high-tech food, what will happen to good old-fashioned home cooking? Not to worry, say most futurists. Apparently the science fiction predictions of earlier decades were wrong and we won't all be popping an instant meal-in-a-pill three times a day. Most experts assure us that not only will our future food be healthier and more varied than ever, but our traditional foods will endure, too. Future generations will always love great-granny's recipes for tourtière, cabbage rolls or curried shrimp and will still demand their favorite chocolate cake for their birthdays.

As Madame Benoit said when people were worrying about the earlier transition to microwave cooking: "It's the same as the evolution from woodstove to electric stoves; we love the new technology but we will always keep our favorite foods, especially for special occasions like Thanksgiving and family reunions; we will always need the rituals."

Scientist David Suzuki, in a 1991 newspaper column, went a bit further on the subject of ritual and roots in Canadian culture: "Unlike the rituals, traditions and festivals of the First Nations peoples, our secular and religious holidays are not rooted in the land. They should be. Today our sanitized, overpackaged supermarket products bear little resemblance to their original living state . . . . We need to celebrate our link with the earth and to honor the plants and animals."

Environmentalists and political scientists see "global" as the key concept for the future. Food will become a major political issue as debate increases concerning trade and tariff barriers, global environment, food safety and Third World hunger.

Meanwhile, our Canadian resource industries, including agriculture and fisheries, are being swept by change. Adapting to shifting global markets, new technology and changing consumer tastes as well as the vagaries of nature are enormous challenges. The agri-food business is facing a drastic redesign all the way from farm gate to marketplace. Canadian family farms have become an endangered species, battling debt, dismal crop prices and urban encroachment. The Atlantic fishery is in serious crisis from depletion of cod stocks. But Canadian farming and fishing families are a very stubborn

breed with special ties that bind them to the land and sea. Determined to survive, and without romanticizing the past, one farmer simply states, "Our roots are terrible deep here."

At a Canadian university conference on ethics and technology at the beginning of the '90s, the chairman, political scientist Henry Wiseman, summed up the issues: "It's not that we should restrain scientific inquiry or technological innovation. But the best of all possible worlds must surely be based on the human spirit . . . and a profound concern for all life and the Earth itself. There are choices to be made."

Canadians are in a unique position to carry those philosophies into the 21st century. We are still close enough to our rural roots, to natural wilderness and the rhythm of the seasons to pass along to our children a respect for the sources of their daily food. We are also a society of richly diverse culinary traditions, with a long history of sharing that began with our first pioneers and has continued down through all the decades. Today as in the past, our Canadian cooking doesn't need defining; it needs sharing. When we pull our chairs up to each other's tables, we understand a little better who we are. Sounds like a good start for a brand new century.

# Cookbook Sampler

## THE NINETIES

For more cookbooks of the decade, see Bibliography pp. 240-241.

● ● ● ● ● ● ● ● ● ● ● ● ● ●

# Market Garden Vegetables With Two Dipping Sauces

*Serve a platter of barely cooked baby vegetables; choose from tiny blue or Yukon Gold potatoes, sunchokes (Jerusalem artichokes), yellow or green baby zucchini, dwarf pattypan squash, baby eggplant, broccoflower florets.*

### Roasted Pepper Dip:

| | | |
|---|---|---|
| 1 | sweet red pepper, roasted* and puréed | 1 |
| 1-1/2 cups | drained plain yogurt | 375 mL |

Mix pepper purée and yogurt; refrigerate until chilled. Makes 1-1/2 cups (375 mL).

### Herb Dip:

| | | |
|---|---|---|
| 1/2 cup | mixed chopped fresh herbs (parsley, rosemary, thyme, dill, basil, chives) | 125 mL |
| 1-1/2 cups | drained plain yogurt | 375 mL |
| 1 tsp | honey (optional) | 5 mL |
| | Pepper | |

Mix herbs into yogurt. Add honey (if using), and pepper to taste. Refrigerate until chilled. Makes 1-1/2 cups (375 mL).

*To roast pepper: Broil, turning, until blackened; place in paper bag 10 minutes; peel.

The '90s find the grazers of the '80s looking for ways to eat still tasty, but now low-fat morsels. We use skim milk, low-fat yogurt and light versions of sour cream, mayonnaise, cream cheese and vinaigrettes.

For those who miss the creaminess of high-fat ingredients, one answer is drained yogurt. Thick and creamy like sour cream, it makes a suitable substitute, albeit a bit tart and tangy. If yogurt is left to drain even longer, a delicious fresh "cheese" results.

To drain yogurt: Line a sieve with several thicknesses of cheesecloth; add 4 cups (1 L) yogurt. Set sieve over container; cover with plastic wrap. Refrigerate for 1-1/2 hours. Makes 3 cups (750 mL).

● ● ● ● ● ● ● ● ● ● ● ● ● ● ● ● ● ● ● ● ● ● ● ● ● ● ● ● ● ●

# Salad of Black Beans, Grains and Rice

*Many of the Tex-Mex flavors of the American southwest – corn, beans, chilies, cilantro – have gained popularity in Canada.*

| | | |
|---|---|---|
| 2 cups | cooked barley | 500 mL |
| 1 cup | cooked long-grain rice (white, brown or basmati) | 250 mL |
| 1 cup | cooked or canned black beans (or pinto) | 250 mL |
| 1 cup | cooked or canned red kidney beans | 250 mL |
| 1 cup | corn niblets | 250 mL |
| 1 | sweet red pepper, diced (roasted if desired, see above) | 1 |
| 1/4 cup | chopped fresh cilantro or parsley | 50 mL |
| 1/2 cup | chopped green onions | 125 mL |
| | Lettuce leaves | |

### Dressing:

| | | |
|---|---|---|
| 1/4 cup | red wine vinegar | 50 mL |
| 1 | clove garlic, minced | 1 |
| 1 tsp | chili powder | 5 mL |
| 1/4 tsp | hot pepper flakes | 1 mL |
| 1/2 tsp | salt | 2 mL |
| 1/4 tsp | black pepper | 1 mL |
| 1/2 cup | olive oil | 125 mL |

In large bowl, combine barley, rice, black and red beans, corn, red pepper, cilantro and onions.

Dressing: Whisk together vinegar, garlic, chili powder, hot pepper flakes, salt, pepper and olive oil. Pour over salad; toss to mix. Serve in lettuce-lined bowl. Makes 6 servings.

The popularity of grains continued into the '90s. Brown and white rice, wild rice, barley, buckwheat, orso (a rice-shaped pasta) and polenta (cooked cornmeal) remain fashionable. Quinoa, a high-protein grain from South America, is often touted by North American food mavens, even though our average protein intake is high, and our own Canadian grains are splendid.

To Cook Barley: Simmer 1/2 cup (125 mL) pearl barley in 2 cups (500 mL) water for 40 minutes. Makes 2 cups (500 mL).

To Cook Black Beans: Quick-soak 1/2 cup (125 mL) sorted dry black beans by covering with 2 cups (500 mL) water and bringing to boil; boil 2 minutes. Cover and let stand 1 hour; drain. Add 1-1/2 cups (375 mL) water; simmer for 45 minutes or until tender. Makes 1 cup (250 mL).

# SOUTHEAST SATAYS WITH PEANUT DIPPING SAUCE

*Satays were one of the first tastes of Southeast Asia tried in home kitchens. Easily adapted to barbecuing, these morsels on bamboo skewers are served as cocktail fare or main-course suppers. Increase the hotness of the sauce by adding more chili pepper.*

| | | |
|---|---|---|
| 1 lb | boneless chicken or lean pork, beef or lamb tenderloin | 500 g |
| 2 tbsp | soy sauce | 25 mL |
| 2 tbsp | rice wine or sherry | 25 mL |
| 1 tbsp | lime juice | 15 mL |
| *Peanut Sauce:* | | |
| 1 | clove garlic, chopped | 1 |
| 2 tbsp | soy sauce | 25 mL |
| 1/3 cup | smooth peanut butter | 75 mL |
| 2 tsp | packed brown sugar | 10 mL |
| 2/3 cup | water | 150 mL |
| 1 tbsp | chopped gingerroot | 15 mL |
| 1 | fresh hot red chili pepper, seeded and chopped | 1 |

Cut chicken into 1/2-inch (1 cm) wide strips about 1/4 inch (5 mm) thick. Marinate in refrigerator in soy sauce, rice wine and lime juice for 2 to 8 hours, stirring occasionally.

Peanut Sauce: In saucepan, whisk together garlic, soy sauce, peanut butter, sugar, water, ginger and chili pepper; bring to boil. Reduce heat and simmer 5 minutes or until slightly thickened. Cool to room temperature.

Thread chicken onto soaked wooden skewers. Grill or broil, brushing with some sauce, 2 to 3 minutes per side. Serve with remaining sauce. Makes about 8 appetizers.

In the '90s, cross-cultural cooking has taken off. East-meets-west cuisine, combinations of Oriental, European and North American flavors and techniques, came to our West Coast via California. As southeast Asian restaurants opened across Canada and travel to the Pacific increased, we sorted out Vietnamese, Thai, Malaysian, Indonesian and Filipino flavors. Ingredients like fiery peppers and *sambal olek* (Indonesian chili paste), *nam pla* (fermented fish extract), coconut milk, lemongrass, coriander, cellophane noodles and rice paper wrappers appeared on specialty shelves. Spring rolls, noodle salads with Thai flavors, curries, peanut dipping sauces and hot and sour soups have become familiar foods.

# JERK CHICKEN

*Usually served with Rice-and-Peas, this recipe is suitable for backyard barbecues.*

| | | |
|---|---|---|
| 2 tsp | each allspice, dried thyme and granulated sugar | 10 mL |
| 1 tsp | each hot pepper flakes and black pepper | 5 mL |
| 1/2 tsp | each cinnamon and nutmeg | 2 mL |
| 2 | cloves garlic, crushed | 2 |
| 1/4 cup | vegetable oil | 50 mL |
| | Grated rind and juice of 1 lime | |
| 2 tbsp | vinegar | 25 mL |
| 1/4 cup | orange juice | 50 mL |
| | Fresh thyme sprigs | |
| 2 lb | chicken legs (thighs attached) | 1 kg |

In shallow dish, mix together allspice, thyme, sugar, hot pepper flakes, black pepper, cinnamon, nutmeg, garlic, oil, lime rind and juice, vinegar and orange juice. Add thyme sprigs and chicken legs. Refrigerate for 4 hours or overnight, turning occasionally.

Grill over medium-hot coals or at medium-high setting, basting often, until juices run clear when chicken is pierced. Makes 4 servings.

Caribbean flavors abound in Canada. Caribana, a spectacular festival celebrated in Toronto each summer, brings music from the steel bands and flavors of "island food" with it. Shops in urban centres sell rotis, patties and the curry spices already mixed, or the seasonings to make your own. Readily available in the late '80s, the lush fruits of the tropics – mangoes, papayas, plantain, breadfruit, red bananas and coconut – continue to sell well right across Canada.

# CANADIAN CASSOULET

*You can substitute bite-size pieces of roast duck for the chicken, and also use any mixture of sausages: farmer's, garlic, kielbasa, Italian, fresh or smoked.*

| | | |
|---|---|---|
| 1/4 cup | vegetable oil | 50 mL |
| 3/4 lb | boneless pork, cubed | 375 g |
| 1/2 lb | boneless lamb, cubed | 250 g |
| 1 lb | chicken thighs, skinned | 500 g |
| 3/4 lb | farmer's sausage | 375 g |
| 2 | onions, chopped | 2 |
| 3 | cloves garlic, minced | 3 |
| 2 cups | tomato sauce | 500 mL |
| 1 cup | chicken stock | 250 mL |
| 1/2 cup | dry white wine | 125 mL |
| 1 | bay leaf | 1 |
| Pinch | dried thyme | Pinch |
| | Salt and pepper | |
| 6 cups | cooked white navy or pea beans | 1.5 L |
| 2 cups | coarse bread crumbs | 500 mL |
| 1/4 cup | butter, melted | 50 mL |

In large skillet, heat oil. Brown pork and lamb; remove and set aside. Brown chicken well; remove and cut meat from bones in large pieces; set aside. Cut sausage into 1/2-inch (1 cm) slices; brown and set aside. Cook onions and garlic until softened. Add tomato sauce, stock, wine, bay leaf and thyme; simmer 5 minutes, adding salt and pepper to taste. Add browned meats; simmer, covered, about 30 minutes or until tender. Remove bay leaf; taste and adjust seasoning.

Combine beans with about half of the sauce from skillet (mixture should be very moist; if necessary, add some extra stock). In large casserole, spread one-third bean mixture. Top with half of meat mixture and sauce. Repeat layers, ending with beans. Combine crumbs with butter; sprinkle over casserole. Bake, uncovered, in 350°F (180°C) oven for about 45 minutes or until bubbling and golden. Makes about 6 servings.

A renewed interest in classic comfort food has resulted in a lot of soul-satisfying eating in the '90s. This streamlined version of the traditional French cassoulet is the kind of fare that is as satisfying in your "cocoon" as it is in a warm bistro on a cold rainy night.

Canadian cooks, both in restaurants and home kitchens, have developed almost as many variations of cassoulet as there are in the regions of France. Many kinds of meats and sausages are layered with the beans; roast or preserved duck or goose *confit* are used for traditional flavor.

# LEAN TURKEY LOAF WITH GINGERED CRANBERRY CHUTNEY

*This mixture can also be shaped into patties for burgers, or rolled into small meatballs. Change ingredients for Italian-style flavors: use basil, tomato paste, pine nuts, olive oil for butter; or Pacific flavors: use ginger, cilantro, teriyaki or soy sauce.*

| | | |
|---|---|---|
| 6 | green onions, chopped | 6 |
| 1 | clove garlic, minced | 1 |
| 1 cup | chopped fresh mushrooms | 250 mL |
| 1 tbsp | butter | 15 mL |
| 1-1/2 lb | ground turkey or chicken | 750 g |
| 1 cup | fresh bread crumbs (preferably whole wheat) | 250 mL |
| 1/2 cup | chopped fresh parsley | 125 mL |
| 1 tsp | salt | 5 mL |
| 1/4 tsp | each dried thyme and savory | 1 mL |
| | Pepper | |

Sauté or microwave onions, garlic and mushrooms in butter. Mix with turkey, bread crumbs, parsley, salt, thyme, savory, and pepper to taste. Pack into 9-x 5-inch (2 L) greased loaf pan, gently shaping into loaf. Bake in 350°F (180°C) oven for 1 hour or until browned and juices run clear. Serve with Gingered Cranberry Chutney. Makes 6 servings.

**GINGERED CRANBERRY CHUTNEY:**

| | | |
|---|---|---|
| 4 cups | cranberries | 1 L |
| 3/4 cup | granulated sugar | 175 mL |
| 1 tsp | grated orange rind | 5 mL |
| 1/2 cup | orange juice | 125 mL |
| 1/3 cup | chopped preserved ginger | 75 mL |

In saucepan, combine cranberries, sugar, orange rind and juice, and ginger. Cook, stirring, until boiling. Simmer for 20 minutes or until most berries pop. Chill. Makes about 3 cups (750 mL).

**Microwave Cranberry Sauce:** In a 4-cup (1 L) microwaveable bowl or measure, combine 2 cups (500 mL) cranberries, 1/2 cup (125 mL) granulated sugar, 1 tsp (5 mL) grated orange rind and 1/4 cup (50 mL) orange juice. Cover and microwave at High for 6 to 8 minutes, stirring every 2 minutes, or until most berries pop. Let stand, covered, 5 minutes; chill. Makes 1-1/2 cups (375 mL).

# GRILLED CHAR OR SALMON WITH LIME CILANTRO MARINADE

*This marinade is also great for lamb chops, turkey cutlets or pork tenderloin.*

| | | |
|---|---|---|
| 4 | Arctic char or salmon steaks or large fillets | 4 |
| *Marinade:* | | |
| 1/4 cup | vegetable oil | 50 mL |
| 2 tbsp | fresh lime juice | 25 mL |
| 12 | peppercorns, cracked | 12 |
| 1 | clove garlic, crushed | 1 |
| | Hot pepper flakes | |
| 2 tbsp | chopped cilantro | 25 mL |
| 1 | Scotch bonnet or jalapeño pepper, seeded and chopped (optional) | 1 |

Marinade: In shallow dish, combine oil, lime juice, peppercorns, garlic, hot pepper flakes to taste, cilantro, and chopped pepper (if using). Add fish and marinate in refrigerator, turning occasionally, for at least 30 minutes or up to 2 hours.

Grill fish over medium-hot coals or on medium-high setting, covered and turning once, for 10 minutes per inch (2.5 cm) of thickness or until fish flakes when barely touched with fork. Makes 4 servings.

Arctic char, so popular in the North, is a firm fish, perfect for the barbecue. Shark, swordfish, monkfish, orange roughy, mahi-mahi, catfish and tilefish are all imports that are gaining popularity as fish becomes the healthy low-fat alternative to meats. Of course, salmon, halibut, cod and freshly caught lake trout, whitefish and pickerel are still favorites. Use a grilling basket or place fish on heavy foil, pricked with holes.

Along with fish, outdoor grills now sport new foods as accompaniments. Grilled fennel (*finocchio*), thick slices of polenta or eggplant brushed with oil and sprinkled with fresh basil, skewers of baby vegetables, corn-on-the-cob done in the husks, and marinated chunks of fruit are '90s choices.

# SPAGHETTINI WITH TOMATOES AND OLIVES

*Light, fresh tomato sauces are very stylish today; some are not cooked at all before tossing with hot pasta.*

| | | |
|---|---|---|
| 2 tbsp | extra-virgin olive oil | 25 mL |
| 2 | cloves garlic, minced | 2 |
| Pinch | hot pepper flakes | Pinch |
| 2 | large ripe tomatoes, chopped | 2 |
| 2 tbsp | slivered sun-dried tomatoes | 25 mL |
| 1/4 cup | coarsely chopped Greek olives | 50 mL |
| | Salt and pepper | |
| 2 tbsp | chopped basil | 25 mL |
| 1/2 lb | spaghettini | 250 g |
| | Crumbled feta cheese or grated Parmesan (optional) | |

In skillet, heat oil over medium heat; cook garlic and hot pepper flakes a few seconds without browning. Add chopped tomatoes; cook 2 minutes or until slightly softened. Add sun-dried tomatoes and olives; cook 1 minute. Season with salt and pepper to taste. Add basil.

Meanwhile, cook pasta; drain and toss with sauce. If desired, serve sprinkled lightly with feta. Makes 2 or 3 servings.

Mediterranean flavors are hotter than ever for the '90s because they adapt easily to today's recipes. Olive oil, one of the most popular mono-unsaturated oils, comes in many flavor variations. In fact, foodies hold olive oil tastings just as they do wine or cheese tastings.

Italian flavors have become familiar and beloved, but we are expanding our tastes to include Greek, Middle Eastern, Spanish and Portuguese.

# ZAP AND TOP POTATOES

*Bake and stuff potatoes as directed in sidebar; omit butter if desired. Top with one of the following additions, or Fresh Tomato Salsa (p. 204).*

*Broccoli Topping:*

| | | |
|---|---|---|
| 2 cups | blanched broccoli florets | 500 mL |
| 1/3 cup | drained yogurt (see p. 223) | 75 mL |
| 2 tbsp | chopped roasted sweet red pepper | 25 mL |

Mix together broccoli, yogurt and red pepper.

*Salmon and Onion:*

| | | |
|---|---|---|
| 1 | can (7.5 oz/218 g) salmon, drained | 1 |
| 1/4 cup | chopped celery or green onion | 50 mL |
| 1 tsp | lemon juice | 5 mL |
| 2 tbsp | light sour cream | 25 mL |

Mix together salmon, celery, pepper to taste, lemon juice and sour cream.

*Garden Vegetable:*

| | | |
|---|---|---|
| 2 tbsp | chopped onion | 25 mL |
| 1/2 cup | sliced mushrooms | 125 mL |
| 1/2 cup | slivered peppers | 125 mL |
| 2 tsp | olive oil | 10 mL |
| 2 tsp | chopped basil | 10 mL |

Lightly stir-fry onion, mushrooms and pepper in oil until softened; add basil.

Stuffed baked potatoes of yesteryear, loaded with cheese and butter, have been banished along with the "couch potatoes" to the jogging track. Now healthy potatoes are in style. And '90s kids can zap their favorites in the microwave, then top them with any number of flavors.

**Simple Baked Stuffed Potatoes:** Prick 2 baking potatoes and set on paper towel; microwave at High for 5 to 8 minutes until almost tender, turning and rearranging once during baking. Let stand 5 minutes. (Alternatively, prick and bake 2 large baking potatoes in 400°F/200°C oven for 45 to 60 minutes.)

Open potatoes; remove pulp and mash with a little milk and butter. Return to shell; brown under broiler. Set out light sour cream or yogurt, red (salmon) or golden (whitefish) caviar and a small dish of chopped chives to sprinkle over top.

# FRUIT-AND-YOGURT SPA MUFFINS

*Lightly greased muffin tins work best for this recipe; extra fruit tends to stick to paper baking cups.*

| | | |
|---|---|---|
| 1/2 cup | plain yogurt | 125 mL |
| 2 tbsp | vegetable oil | 25 mL |
| 1 | egg | 1 |
| 2/3 cup | whole wheat flour | 150 mL |
| 2/3 cup | all-purpose flour | 150 mL |
| 1/3 cup | wheat or oat bran | 75 mL |
| 1/3 cup | packed brown sugar | 75 mL |
| 1 tsp | baking powder | 5 mL |
| 1/2 tsp | baking soda | 2 mL |
| 1/4 tsp | salt | 1 mL |
| 1/2 tsp | cardamom | 2 mL |
| 1 cup | grated apple or pear (unpeeled) | 250 mL |
| 1/2 cup | chopped dates | 125 mL |

*Topping (optional):*

| | | |
|---|---|---|
| 2 tsp | granulated sugar | 10 mL |
| 1/2 tsp | cinnamon | 2 mL |

Combine yogurt, oil and egg. In bowl, stir together whole wheat and all-purpose flours, bran, brown sugar, baking powder, baking soda, salt and cardamom. With fork, stir in yogurt mixture just until moistened; fold in apple and dates. Spoon into greased muffin cups, filling two-thirds full.

Topping: Mix sugar and cinnamon; sprinkle on muffins. Bake in 375°F (190°C) oven for 18 to 20 minutes or until tops are firm to the touch. Makes 12 muffins.

You can cocoon at home and still stay fit with spa-style food from your own kitchen. Healthier baking in the '90s means reduced fat, sugar and salt, and increased fibre. This means cutting down on butter, oil and nuts to get rid of fat, and often using honey in place of sugar (it's sweeter and you can use less), or extra fruit to replace sugar and zip up the flavor. Part of the flour should be whole grain. In place of dates use other dried fruits: raisins, apricots, cherries, prunes, etc.

# THREE-GRAIN CARAWAY SODA BREAD

*Whole-grain flours and bran give a nutrition boost to traditional white soda bread. The optional rye flour and caraway seeds add intriguing flavor.*

| | | |
|---|---|---|
| 2 cups | all-purpose flour | 500 mL |
| 2 cups | whole wheat or rye flour (or half of each) | 500 mL |
| 1/4 cup | oat or wheat bran | 50 mL |
| 1/4 cup | packed brown sugar | 50 mL |
| 1 tbsp | caraway seeds (optional) | 15 mL |
| 1 tbsp | baking powder | 15 mL |
| 1 tsp | baking soda | 5 mL |
| 1 tsp | salt | 5 mL |
| 1/4 cup | butter | 50 mL |
| 1 | egg, beaten | 1 |
| 1-3/4 cups | buttermilk | 425 mL |

In bowl, combine flours, bran, sugar, caraway seeds (if using), baking powder, soda and salt; cut in butter finely. Combine egg and buttermilk; add all at once to flour mixture, stirring with fork to make soft, slightly sticky dough. Turn out onto floured surface; knead gently 10 times.

Divide in half; shape into two round loaves. Place on greased baking sheet. Cut X-shaped slash in top of each loaf. Bake in 375°F (190°C) oven for about 45 minutes or until loaf sounds hollow when tapped on bottom. Makes 2 loaves.

## VARIATIONS:

**Cheese:** Add 1-1/2 cups (375 mL) shredded Cheddar cheese.
**Beer:** Use 1 cup (250 mL) beer for 1 cup (250 mL) buttermilk.

In the '90s, as grains and complex carbohydrates remain the buzzwords of good eating, sorting out flours is important, especially for novice bakers.

**All-purpose flour:** Enriched white wheat flour, usually hard wheat, is essential for bread-making and is also used for general baking. **All-purpose with bran** and **unbleached** flour can be used interchangeably with all-purpose white.

**Cake-and-pastry flour:** Soft wheat flour, is best for more tender, finer-textured baking like cakes and pastries.

**Whole wheat** or **graham:** Brownish, containing some or all of the bran along with the rest of the wheat kernel, is usually used in combination with all-purpose flour to avoid a heavy texture.

**Stone-gound:** A whole wheat flour ground by large flat stones in a few small Canadian mills.

**Self-rising flour:** All-purpose flour that has salt and leavening added.

**Rye flour:** Usually used with all-purpose flour for a dark, heavy bread.

**Specialty flours:** Sold in small quantities, these include barley, buckwheat, cracked wheat, triticale (cross between wheat and rye), soy, potato, rice.

# FREE-FORM APPLE PIE

*More casual than traditional apple pie, this was a big hit, both with novice cooks who found traditional two-crusted pie-making intimidating and with experienced cooks who didn't have time to fuss. Just roll out the pastry and wrap it around the filling – it doesn't even require a pie plate.*

|  | Pastry for double-crust pie |  |
|---|---|---|
| 4 cups | sliced peeled apples | 1 L |
| 2/3 cup | granulated sugar (part brown, if desired) | 150 mL |
| 1/4 cup | all-purpose flour | 50 mL |
| 1 tsp | cinnamon | 5 mL |
| 1/4 tsp | nutmeg | 1 mL |
| 2 tbsp | butter | 25 mL |

On floured surface, roll out pastry to about 15-inch (38 cm) circle; transfer to baking sheet. Toss together apples, sugar, flour, cinnamon and nutmeg. Mound in centre of dough, leaving about 3-inch (8 cm) border. Fold border up over apples, pinching where necessary, but leaving apples showing in centre. Dot with butter.

Bake in 425°F (220°C) oven for 15 minutes. Reduce heat to 375°F (190°C); bake 30 to 40 minutes longer or until apples are tender and pastry is lightly browned. Serve slightly warm, dusted with icing sugar if desired.

This free-form shape adapts well to all sorts of fresh Canadian fruit, especially peaches or plums. Adding a few berries (cranberries, blueberries, blackberries) gives extra color and flavor.

The '90s have given us a new name for a mixed-berry pie. Whatever is handy can be baked into a **"Bumbleberry" Pie.**

The more casual styles of '90s desserts reflect the new "comfortable" culinary attitudes of the decade. But they still satisfy the passion for desserts that developed in the '80s, when fashion-conscious foodies were all making **Cherry Clafouti** (a custardy cake dotted with fruit) and **Tarte Tatin** (a classic French upside-down apple pie).

# RECESSION OATMEAL CAKE

*Delicious with just a dusting of icing sugar, this cake can also be topped with the traditional Broiled Topping (recipe p. 115).*

| | | |
|---|---|---|
| 1-1/3 cups | boiling water | 325 mL |
| 1 cup | rolled oats | 250 mL |
| 1/2 cup | butter | 125 mL |
| 1 cup | packed brown sugar | 250 mL |
| 1/2 cup | granulated sugar | 125 mL |
| 2 | eggs | 2 |
| 3/4 cup | all-purpose flour | 175 mL |
| 3/4 cup | whole wheat flour | 175 mL |
| 1 tsp | baking soda | 5 mL |
| 1/2 tsp | baking powder | 2 mL |
| 1/2 tsp | salt | 2 mL |
| 1 tsp | cinnamon | 5 mL |

Pour boiling water over oats; let cool. In bowl, cream butter with brown and granulated sugars until creamy. Add eggs, one at a time, beating well after each addition.

Combine flours, baking soda, baking powder, salt and cinnamon; stir into creamed mixture along with oats. Beat until smooth. Spread in 9-inch (2.5 L) square cake pan. Bake in 350°F (180°C) oven for 45 to 50 minutes or until tester inserted in centre comes out clean.

Easy, comforting, tasty and cheap, Oatmeal Cake is just right for recession times. As well, its healthy redeeming qualities – whole grains, no icing – appeal to today's eating habits.

### VARIATIONS:

**Apple Oatmeal:** Heat 1-1/3 cups (325 mL) applesauce just to boiling. Use in place of boiling water.
**Date Nut:** Add 1/2 cup (125 mL) each chopped pitted dates and nuts.
**Fruited Oatmeal:** Add 1 cup (250 mL) raisins or 1 cup (250 mL) dried sour cherries.

# NUTS-AND-SEEDS FRUIT CRUMBLE

*In every decade there have been crisps, crumbles and Bettys. This '90s version is good, and good for you, too. Serve warm or cold with light sour cream or whipped cream.*

| | | |
|---|---|---|
| 3 | peaches, peeled and sliced | 3 |
| 2 | apricots (or apples), sliced | 2 |
| 3 | pears, peeled and sliced | 3 |
| 2 | plums, quartered | 2 |
| 1 tbsp | all-purpose flour | 15 mL |
| 1 tbsp | lemon juice | 15 mL |
| 2 tbsp | liquid honey | 25 mL |
| *Topping:* | | |
| 2 cups | rolled oats | 500 mL |
| 1/3 cup | packed brown sugar | 75 mL |
| 1/4 cup | butter | 50 mL |
| 1/2 cup | chopped or sliced hazelnuts | 125 mL |
| 1/4 cup | sesame seeds | 50 mL |

In 9-inch (2.5 L) square baking dish or casserole, mix peaches, apricots, pears and plums. Sprinkle with flour, lemon juice and honey; toss to coat.

Topping: Blend oats, sugar and butter together with fingertips until crumbly. Stir in nuts and seeds. Sprinkle over fruit. Bake in 350°F (180°C) oven for 45 to 60 minutes or until fruit is tender and top lightly toasted. Makes 6 servings.

What goes around comes around, and while current updates are healthier and livelier, they still have to be close enough to the real thing to conjure up memories. In many parts of the country, baked puddings never went out of style: **Blueberry Grunt** with a sweet dumpling topping; **Cherry Cobbler** with biscuit dough; **Apple Crisp** as delicious as ever but perhaps made with a different variety of apple. And in Labrador and Newfoundland, they're still layering a crumb mixture of rolled oats, brown sugar and butter with bakeapples (which look like yellow raspberries) to make a most delicious **Bakeapple Crumble**.

New twists to old favorites are appealing. Mixing and matching fruits, adding seeds and nuts to toppings, and cutting back on butter and sugar justify baking old familiar Granny-style desserts.

# Selected Cookbook Bibliography

Our selected bibliography lists most of the important and popular cookbooks published in Canada in each decade. In addition, from among the hundreds of other titles published across the country, we have included a sampling of local community, charity, church and fundraiser books; government publications; food company booklets; textbooks; and French-language cookbooks.

Many books have had numerous printings, editions and revised editions over the years; not all are listed.

Most cookbooks from the early decades (and many later ones as well) are out of print. Some can be located in public archives and reference libraries. Or you might be lucky and spot them in antique or secondhand book stores, flea markets, or even grandma's attic.

To find out which books are still in print, check the current listings in the publication *Canadian Books In Print* (at all libraries and most booksellers).

## Pre-1900

A large number of cookbooks were in circulation in the 19th century and many of them were used regularly in Canadian households. Most of these books came from Great Britain (such as *Mrs. Beeton's Book of Household Management*, London, 1861), France (such as *La Cuisinière bourgeoise*, Paris, 1825) or the United States (such as *Miss Beecher's Domestic Receipt Book*, New York, 1854). The first cookbook published in Canada was called *The Cook Not Mad or Rational Cooking*. Published in Kingston, Canada West (Ontario) in 1831, it was in fact an American book.

The first truly Canadian cookbooks are believed to be two that were published in 1840: the French-language *La cuisinière canadienne* (later called *La nouvelle cuisinière canadienne*) from Quebec; and the English-language *The Frugal Housewife's Manual* by "A.B." of Grimsby, Ontario.

Many others followed in the last half of the century.

Some old cookbooks, such as *The Cook Not Mad*, *The Canadian Home Cook Book* (1877) and *The Galt Cookbook* (1898), were published in modern reprint editions in the 1970s.

## The 1st Decade

Allen, Mrs. Sarah. *The Common Sense Recipe Book*. Montreal: John Lovell & Son, 9th edition, 1903.

*The Berlin Cook Book*. Compiled by the ladies of Berlin (Kitchener), Ontario. News Record Print Shop, 1900.

*Blue Ribbon Cook Book*. Winnipeg: Blue Ribbon Limited, 1905.

Clarke, Anne. *The Dominion Cook Book*. Toronto: George J. McLeod Limited. Revised edition, 1901. Originally called *Mrs. Clarke's Cookery Book* (1883); appeared in many later editions under various titles.

*Culinary Landmarks*. Sault Ste. Marie: St. Luke's Woman's Auxiliary, 1909.

Gregory, Annie R. *Canada's Favorite Cook Book*. Brantford: The Bradley-Garretson Co., Ltd. and The Linscott Publishing Co., 1902.

Hoodless, Mrs. J. and Watson, Miss M.U. *Public School Household Science*. Toronto: The Copp, Clark Company Limited, 1905.

*Hughes' Household Calendar Cookbook*. Charlottetown: Geo. E. Hughes' Apothecaries' Hall, 1909.

*Laurel Cook Book*. Compiled by The Laurel Mission Circle of St. John Presbyterian Church, Hamilton, Ontario, 1909.

Lovell, Sarah. *Meals of the Day, A Guide to the Young Housekeeper*. Montreal: John Lovell & Son, 1904.

McMicking, Mrs. Robert Burns. *The King's Daughters Cook Book*. Victoria, 1904. 75th Anniversary Edition: Vancouver, The Unusual House, Inc., 1979.

*The New Cook Book, A volume of Tried, Tested and Proven Recipes by The Ladies of Toronto and other cities and towns.* Edited by Grace E. Denison (Lady Gay of Saturday Night). Toronto: Rose Publishing Co., 1903. Revised edition, The Musson Book Co., 1905.

*The New Household Manual and Ladies' Companion*. Saint John: R.A.H. Morrow, 1901.

*Ogilvie's Book for a Cook*. Montreal: The Ogilvie Flour Mills Company Limited, 1905.

*Royal Victoria Hospital W.A. Cook Book*. Barrie, Ontario, 1901.

*The Wheat City Cook Book*. Compiled by The Ladies of the Methodist Church. Brandon, Manitoba: Record Printing House, 1901.

## The 2nd Decade

*British Columbia Fruit*. B.C. Fruit Growers Association, 1918.

*Canadian Farm Cook Book*. Toronto: Compiled by the Woman's Department, Canadian Farm, 1911.

*Cowan's "Dainty Recipes"*. Toronto: The Cowan Company, Limited, 1918.

*Fish and How to Cook It*. Ottawa: Department of Naval Service, 1914.

*Five Roses Cook Book*. Montreal and Winnipeg: Lake of the Woods Milling Company Limited, 1915.

*The Great West Cook Book*. Vancouver: B.C. Sugar Refining Company Ltd., c. 1915.

*The Handy Home Book*. Montreal: Family Herald and Weekly Star, c. 1910.

*La cuisine raisonnée*. Quebec: Institution Chanoine-Beaudet (École Ménagère, Saint-Pascal de Kamouraska), Congrégation de Notre-Dame, 1919. Since 1967 published by Éditions Fides, Montreal.

Laird, A.L. and Pattinson, N.L. *L.M.S. Book of Recipes* (Lillian Massey School). Toronto, 1917.

Macfarlane, Margaret. *Preservation of Fruits & Vegetables for Home Use*. Ottawa: Dominion Experimental Farms, 1919.

McKenzie Hill, Janet. *The Whys of Cooking*. Hamilton: The Procter & Gamble Company, 1916.

*Metropolitan Cook Book*. Metropolitan Life Insurance Company, 1918.

*Modern Household Cookery*. Vancouver Gas, 1914.

*Moffat Cook Book*. Weston, Ontario: The Moffat Stove Company Limited, 1915.

Neil, Marion Harris. *A Calendar of Dinners*. Hamilton: The Procter & Gamble Company, 1917.

*Ogilvie's Book for a Cook*. Montreal: Ogilvie Flour Mills Co. Limited, 1916.

*Peterborough Summer Fair.* Compiled by The Ladies of the Autumn Booth, 1912.

*Purity Flour Cook Book.* Toronto and Winnipeg: Western Canada Flour Mills Co. Limited, 1917.

*The Real Home-Keeper. A Perpetual Honeymoon for the Vancouver Bride.* Vancouver: The Real Home-Keeper Publishing Co., 1913.

*Red Cross Cook Book.* Hamilton: The Ambulance Corps of the Women's Recruiting League, 1917.

*Reliable Recipes.* Hamilton: Egg-o Baking Powder Co., 1919.

Rorer, Mrs. *Robin Hood Cook Book.* Moose Jaw and Calgary: Robin Hood Mills Ltd., 1915.

Schneider, Henry, Chef de Cuisine, St. James' Club. *Practical Cookery.* Montreal, 1910.

Telford, Erma Paddock. *Standard Paper Bag Cookery.* Toronto; Copp Clark, 1912.

*Two Hundred Tested Recipes.* Saskatoon: St. John's Anglican Church, 1910.

*War Time Cook Book.* Compiled by Duke of Wellington Chapter of the Imperial Order of Daughters of the Empire, Sherbrooke, Quebec, c. 1915.

Young, Miss B. *Domestic Science Recipes.* Ottawa Gas Company, 1910.

## The Twenties

*Beach Frozen Dainties and Other Recipes.* Ottawa: Beach Foundry Limited, c.1925.

*Cheese - and ways to serve it.* Montreal: Kraft Phenix Cheese Company, 1928.

*Clark's Prepared Foods.* Montreal, c.1925.

*Cookery Arts and Kitchen Management* (Anna Lee Scott). Toronto: Maple Leaf Milling Co. Ltd., 1928.

Currie, Margaret (Montreal Star). *Margaret Currie Her Book.* Toronto: The Hunter-Rose Co., Limited, 1924.

*Fleischmann's Recipes.* The Fleischmann Company, 1924.

*Fruit & Vegetables Canning, Drying, Storing.* Ottawa: Department of Agriculture, 1924.

*The Girl at Catelli's.* Montreal: The C.H. Catelli Co., Limited, c.1920.

*Handbook of Practical Cookery.* Toronto: Board of Education, 1923.

*The Home Cook Book.* 100th edition. Toronto: Hunter, Rose and Company, 1923. Originally published in 1877 as *The Canadian Home Cook Book.* Compiled by Ladies of Toronto and Chief Cities and Towns in Canada. Appeared in many editions until 1929.

*Jell-O: Canada's Most Famous Dessert At Home Everywhere.* Bridgeburg, Ontario: The Genesee Pure Food Company of Canada, Ltd., 1922.

*La bonne cuisine canadienne.* Quebec: Ministère de la Voirie, 1927.

*The Little Blue Books* Home Series. Ottawa: Department of Health, 1922.

Martin, Virginia. *Salad Secrets.* Montreal: Colman-Keen (Canada) Limited, 1928.

*McClary's Household Manual.* London: The McClary Manufacturing Co., 1922.

*The Metropolitan Cook Book.* Metropolitan Life Insurance Company, c.1925.

*The Modern Cook Book for New Brunswick.* St. John: J & A McMillan, 1920.

*Moffat's Cookery Book.* Weston: Moffats Limited, 1926.

*Naomi Cook Book.* Compiled by Naomi Chapter of Hadassah, Toronto, 1928. Published in four editions to 1960.

*National Sea Food Recipes By the Women of The Maritime Provinces.* Halifax: National Fish Co. Ltd., 1923.

*The New Edwardsburg Recipe Book.* Montreal: The Canada Starch Co. Limited, c.1925

*Old Homestead Recipes.* Toronto: Maple Leaf Milling Co. Ltd., 1920–21.

Pattinson, Nellie Lyle. *Canadian Cook Book.* Toronto: The Ryerson Press, 1923. Revised by Helen Wattie and Elinor Donaldson after 1953.

*Prairie Rose Cookbook.* United Farmers of Canada, c.1925.

*The Purity Flour Cook Book.* Toronto, Western Canada Flour Mills Co., Limited, 1923.

*Queen Anne Cook Book.* Kitchener: The Queen Anne Chapter I.O.D.E., 1925.

*Rawleigh's Good Health Guide, Almanac and Cookbook.* W.T. Rawleigh Company, 1922.

*Recipes Wholesome Nutritious Economical.* Hamilton: Gunn's Limited Easifirst Shortening, c. 1925.

*Specially Selected Recipes.* The Western Home Monthly, c. 1920.

Souer Edith Sainte-Marie (Sister St. Mary Edith), Directrice de l'École Ménagère (The Montreal Cooking School), Congrégation de Notre-Dame. *Les secrets de la bonne cuisine* (English edition: *The Secrets of Good Cooking*). Montreal: La Compagnie d'Imprimerie et de Lithographie Canadienne Limitée/The Canadian Printing & Lithographing Company, 1928.

*The Unity Lodge Cook Book.* Compiled and published by Unity Lodge 499, L.O.B.A., Tuxford, Saskatchewan, c. 1925.

*Vancouver Girls Club Souvenir Cookbook.* Vancouver, 1927.

*The Westinghouse Refrigerator Book.* Canadian Westinghouse Co. Ltd., c. 1925.

*When We Entertain* (Anna Lee Scott). Toronto: Maple Leaf Milling Co., 1925.

*The Wimodausis Club Cook Book.* Toronto: The Hunter-Rose Co. Ltd., 1922.

## The Thirties

*Apple Secrets.* Vernon, B.C.: Associated Growers of British Columbia Ltd., 1931.

*Baking Made Easy.* Robin Hood Flour Mills Limited, 1938.

Brown, Cynthia. *Cooking – With a Grain of Salt.* Toronto: The Macmillan Company of Canada Limited, 1938.

*Canada's Prize Recipes.* Montreal: The Canada Starch Co., Limited, 1930.

*Canadian Grown Apples.* Ottawa: Department of Agriculture, 1937.

*Choice Tested Recipes.* Collected by Relief Committee Young People's Society, Revelstoke (B.C.) United Church, 1933.

*Community Booster Cook Book.* Melfort, Saskatchewan: The Business Men of Melfort, 1934.

*A Cookbook of Tested Recipes.* Compiled by The American Women's Club, Winnipeg, 1936.

*Coronation Cook Book.* London, Ontario: WA of Victoria Hospital, 1937.

*Davis Dainty Dishes.* Davis Gelatine (Canada) Limited, 1939.

*Delectable Dishes.* Montreal: Women's Guild of St. George's Church, 1936.

*Eclipse Tempting Recipes.* Winnipeg: Western Pure Foods Ltd., 1931.

*A Family Tradition: The Magic Baking Powder Cookbook.* Toronto: Standard Brands Limited, c. 1935.

*A Guide to Good Cooking* (Five Roses Cookbook). Montreal or Winnipeg: Lake of the Woods Milling Co. Ltd., 1932.

*Heinz Book of Salads and Meat Recipes.* Toronto: H.J.Heinz Co., 1938.

*The Housewife's Year Book of Health and Homemaking.* London, Ontario: Kellogg Company of Canada Limited, 1937.

*Jubilee Cookbook.* St. Catharines, Ontario: St. Georges Church, 1936.

*The Maple Leaf Canadian Recipe Book.* Ottawa, Department of Trade and Commerce, c. 1935.

*Maple Leaf Cooking School.* (Directed by Anna Lee Scott). Toronto: Maple Leaf Milling Co. Ltd., 1932.

*Mrs. Flynn's Cookbook.* Compiled by Mrs. Katherine C. Lewis Flynn. Charlottetown: published by The Ladies of St. Elizabeth's Aid Society of St. Vincent's Orphanage, 1931. (Reprinted by the Prince Edward Island Heritage Foundation, 1981.)

*The New Art.* Canadian General Electric, c. 1935.

*A New Way of Living.* The Kellogg Company of Canada, Ltd., 1932.

*Olympic Cook Book.* I.O.D.E. Olympic Chapter, Kentville, N.S., 1930.

*The Purity Cook Book.* Toronto: Western Canada Flour Mills Co. Limited, 1932.

Read, Jessie. *Three Meals a Day.* Toronto: Musson, 1938. *Three Meals a Day Recipe Review.* Toronto: The Evening Telegram, c. 1935.

*Rotary Ann Recipe Book.* Toronto: Rotary International, 1933.

*Shawinigan Falls Cook Book.* Shawinigan Falls, Quebec: Church of St. John, 1936.

*Tasty Meals for Every Day.* Compiled by Margaret H. Rees. Toronto: Canada Packers Limited, 1933.

*Tried and Tested Recipes.* Compiled by The Crumlin (Ontario) Women's Institute, 1937.

*Vincent Galleries Book of Cookery.* Compiled by Florence Elizabeth Stewart and Gretchen Day Ross. Vancouver: The Clarke & Stuart Co. Ltd., 1936.

*Watkins Cook Book.* Montreal, Winnipeg, Vancouver: The J.R. Watkins Co., 1935.

*Westminster Cook Book.* Saskatoon: Idylwyld Circle, Westminster United Church, c. 1935.

## The Forties

Aitken, Kate. *Kate Aitken's Cookbook.* Montreal: The Standard, 1945.

*The Black Whale Cook Book.* Compiled by Mrs. Ethel Renouf, Percé, Gaspé County, Quebec, 1948.

*Blossom of Canada Home Tested Recipes.* Toronto: Lakeside Milling Co. Limited, 1945.

*Borden's Eagle Brand Magic Recipes.* The Borden Company, 1946.

*Bread Baking Made Easy.* (Rita Martin). Robin Hood Flour Mills Limited, c.1945.

*Campbells Flour Home Tested Recipes.* Toronto: Lakeside Milling Co. Limited, 1947.

*Canadian Cook Book For British Brides.* Ottawa: Women's Voluntary Services Division, Department of National War Services, 1945.

*Canadian Favourites: CCF Cookbook.* Ottawa: C.C.F. National Council, 1944.

*Carnation Cook Book.* (Mary Blake). Toronto: The Carnation Company, 1943.

*The Cook's Tour to the Realm of Cakes* (Anna Lee Scott). Toronto: Maple Leaf Milling Co. Ltd., c. 1945.

*Cook To Win.* Calgary: Good Cheer Club, 1943.

*Cooking The Co-Op Way.* Regina: Federated Co-operatives Limited, 1946.

*Cooking Under Pressure.* Edited by Edith Adams, Vancouver Sun, 1947.

Cornell, Anna May. *Electric Cookery by Westinghouse.* Canadian Westinghouse Company Limited, 1946.

*Dover Daily Dainties.* Dover Centre (Ontario) United Church, 1948.

*51 Ways to a Man's Heart.* (Anna Lee Scott). Toronto: Maple Leaf Milling Co. Ltd., c. 1940.

*Food and the Family Income.* Montreal: J.B. Lippincott Company, 1945.

Gibson, Josephine. *How To Eat Well Though Rationed.* Toronto: Vital Publications, 1943.

*Hadassah Sonya Kaplan Chapter Cookbook.* Kirkland Lake, Ontario, 1946.

Holmes, Marie. *Food From Market to Table.* Toronto: Macmillan, 1940.

*Legion Ladies Cook Book.* Cornerbrook, Newfoundland, 1941.

*Les Conserves.* Quebec: Ministère de l'Agriculture, 1948.

*Martha Logan's Baking Lessons: I Like Your Crust* (Swift's Jewel Shortening Booklet). Also *One Good Cook Tells Another* and *You Too,* c. 1945.

*Presto Cooker Recipe Book.* Wallaceburg, Ontario: National Pressure Cooker Company (Canada) Limited, 1948.

*Purity Cook Book.* Toronto: Purity Flour Mills Limited. Revised edition, 1945.

*Robin Hood Prize Winning Recipes.* (Selected by Rita Martin). Robin Hood Flour Mills Limited, 1947.

*Rogers' Golden Syrup Recipe Book.* Vancouver: The B.C. Sugar Refining Co. Ltd., c. 1940.

*Sugar Savers.* Ottawa: Department of Agriculture, 1947.

*The Vancouver Sun's 11th Annual Cook Book.* Edited by Edith Adams, 1948.

*War Time Recipes.* Monteal: Fort Anne Chapter IODE, c. 1940.

Zinck, Helen. *Green Shutters Cookbook.* Mader's Cove, N.S., 1947. (Halifax: Nimbus Publishing, 1990.)

## The Fifties

Aitken, Kate. *Kate Aitken's Canadian Cookbook.* Toronto, Collins, 1950; *The New Kate Aitken Cook Book,* 1953.

Almon, Marg. *Woman's World Cook Book.* New Glasgow, N.S.: CKEC, 1957.

*Bluenose Cookbook.* Compiled in the '30s by the Ladies Auxiliary, YMCA, Yarmouth, N.S., 1959. (Halifax: Nimbus Publishing, 1990.)

*British Columbia Women's Institutes Centennial Cook Book.* Vancouver: Evergreen Press, 1955.

*Canadian Fish Cook Book.* Ottawa: Department of Fisheries, 1959.

Collett, Elaine. *Moffat Cook Book.* Toronto: Moffats Limited, c. 1955.

*Cooking The Co-Op Way.* The Manitoba and Saskatchewan Women's Co-operative Guilds in conjunction with Federated Co-operatives Limited, 1959.

*Coronation Cook Book.* Compiled by The Ladies of St. Matthew's Women's Missionary Society, Kitchener, Ontario, 1953.

*Dutch Oven.* Compiled by The Ladies Auxiliary of The Lunenburg (N.S.) Hospital Society, 1953. (Halifax: Nimbus Publishing, 1990.)

*Famous Chef Recipes.* Toronto: The Woman's Globe and Mail, 1957.

*Farm Women's Union of Alberta Cook Book.* Edmonton, 1956.

*Favorite Recipes from the United Nations.* Robin Hood Flour Mills Limited, 1951.

*Favourite Recipes.* Compiled by The Woman's Association of Bridge Street United Church, Belleville, Ontario, 1959.

*From Ottawa Kitchens.* Compiled for The Canadian Save the Children Fund, 1954; *More From Ottawa Kitchens,* 1960.

*From Saskatchewan Homemakers' Kitchens.* Compiled by Saskatchewan Homemakers' Clubs, 1955.

*Fun Fare.* Toronto: Canada Packers Limited, c. 1955.

*Janet Peters' Personal Cook Book from the pages of Canadian Homes and Gardens.* Toronto: Maclean-Hunter, 1956.

*Labtec Cook Book.* Compiled by the Saskatoon Academy of Laboratory Technologists, 1956.

Lewis, Gwen. *Buckskin Cookery*. Quesnell, B.C., 1957.

*Meeting Over Tea*. Toronto: The Tea Bureau, c. 1955.

*Metropolitan Cook Book*. Metropolitan Life Insurance Company, 1957.

*New Brunswick Recipes*. Compiled by The New Brunswick Home Economics Association, 1958.

*The New Purity Cookbook*. Toronto: Purity Flour Mills, 1959.

*Rare Recipes*. Compiled by The Woman's Association of Timothy Eaton Memorial Church, Toronto, 1958.

Robertson, Elizabeth Chant. *Good Food Makes Good Sense*. Toronto: McClelland and Stewart, 1951.

Stechishin, Savella. *Traditional Ukrainian Cookery*. Winnipeg: Trident Press Limited, 1957.

*Tested Recipes with Jewel Shortening*. Toronto: Swift Canadian Co. Limited, 1950.

*The Treasury of Newfoundland Dishes*. Cream of the West Flour: Maple Leaf Milling Co., Nfld., 1959.

*We Can Cook Too*. Compiled by Montreal branch, Canadian Women's Press Club, 1956.

*What's Cooking*. Vancouver Kiwassa Club, 1956.

*When You Bake – with Yeast*. (Fleischmann's) Montreal: Standard Brands Limited, 1956.

Wilson, Ann. *The Ann Wilson Cookbook*. Vancouver: Western Homes & Living Magazine, 1958.

*Women's Auxiliary to the Nanaimo Hospital Cook Book*. 1952.

## The Sixties

Aitken, Kate. *Kate Aitken's Cook Book*. Toronto: Collins, 1964.

Allen-Gray, Dorothy. *Fare Exchange*. Kingswood House, 1963.

*The All New Purity Cook Book*. Toronto: Maple Leaf Mills Limited, 1967.

*The Art of Home Baking*. Toronto: Maple Leaf Mills Limited, 1964.

Balcom, Joan. *Ripe 'N Ready: Apple recipes from Nova Scotia's famous Annapolis Valley*. Truro, N.S.: Howard H. Lettau, 1966.

Benoit, Jehane. *Encyclopedia of Canadian Cuisine*. Messageries du Saint-Laurent, 1963 (French) and 1965 (English).

Berton, Pierre and Janet. *The Centennial Food Guide*. Toronto: The Canadian Centennial Publishing Co. Ltd., 1966.

*Blue Flame Food Magic*. United Gas Company, c. 1965.

Boorman, Sylvia. *Wild Plums in Brandy*. Toronto: McGraw-Hill Ryerson, 1962.

Burbidge, Helen. *History in the Baking*. Midland, Ontario: The Huronia Historic Sites and Tourist Association,1964.

*Centennial Cook Book: Canada's Favourites*. Compiled by The Federal Women's Committee of the New Democratic Party, 1967.

Collett, Elaine. *The Chatelaine Cookbook*. Toronto: Maclean-Hunter/ Doubleday Canada, 1965.

*Cookbook For Diabetics*. Compiled by the Canadian Diabetic Association. Toronto: Burns and MacEachern Ltd., 1963.

*Discovering Canadian Cuisine*. The Canadian Gas Association,1966.

Ellis, Eleanor A. *The Northern Cook Book*. Ottawa: Department of Indian Affairs and Northern Development, 1967. Revised edition 1979: Supply and Services Canada/Hurtig Publishers, Edmonton.

*Food Fun: The Step by Step Cook Book for boys and girls*. Edited by Glenora Pearce. Saskatoon: Federated Co-operatives Limited,1963.

Gagen, Helen. *Helen Gagen's Summer Foods*. Toronto: The Telegram, c. 1965.

Goplen, Henrietta. *Saskatchewan Sportsman's Gourmet Guide*. Saskatoon: Western Producer Books,1968.

*A Guide To Good Cooking with Five Roses Flour*. Lake of the Woods Milling Company, 20th edition, 1962.

*The Heritage Collection of Home Tested Recipes*. Compiled by Chatelaine Institute. Toronto: Maclean-Hunter, 1968.

Kaplun, Lillian. *For The Love of Baking*. Toronto, 1960; *For The Love of Cooking*, 1968.

*The Laura Secord Canadian Cook Book*. Compiled by The Canadian Home Economics Association. Toronto: McClelland & Stewart, 1966.

MacIlquham, Frances. *Canadian Game Cookery*. Toronto: McClelland & Stewart, 1966.

*The Modern Hostess*. Toronto: Salada Foods, c. 1965.

Oliver, Margo. *Margo Oliver's Weekend Magazine Cook Book*. Montreal: The Montreal Standard, 1967.

*Our Favourite Recipes*. Compiled by Ryerson Home Economics Alumni Association, Toronto, 1960.

Staebler, Edna. *Food that Really Schmecks*. Toronto: McGraw-Hill Ryerson, 1968.

*Star Weekly Cook Book*. Edited by Marjorie Elwood. Toronto: Star Reader Service, 1967.

*Taste Temptations*. Compiled by Glenora Pearce. Saskatoon: Federated Co-operatives Limited, 1966.

*Traditional Macedonian Recipes*. Toronto: Ladies' Auxiliary, Macedonian Patriotic Organization,1969.

*A Treasury Of Nova Scotia Heirloom Recipes*. Compiled by Florence M. Hilchey, Nova Scotia Department of Agriculture and Marketing, 1967.

Vineberg, Trina. *Family Heirlooms*. Montreal/Toronto: McClelland & Stewart, 1965.

Watley, Ellen. *Food. . .Glorious Food*. Toronto: Clarke, Irwin & Company Ltd., 1966.

Wilson, Muriel. *Muriel Wilson's Colonist Cook Book*. Victoria, B.C.: The Daily Colonist,1963.

*The Yukon Gold Rush Festival Cookbook*. Compiled by Order of the Eastern Star, Dawson, 1962.

## The Seventies

Abrahamson, Una. *The Canadian Guide to Home Entertaining*. Toronto: Macmillan of Canada, 1975.

Baird, Elizabeth. *Classic Canadian Cooking*. Toronto: James Lorimer & Company, 1974; *Apples, Peaches and Pears*, 1977.

Beaulieu, Mirelle. *The Cooking of Provincial Quebec*. Toronto: Gage Publishing, 1975. Published in French by Les Éditions La Presse, Montreal.

Beaulieu-Roy, Thérèse. *L'Ordinaire 2*. Mont-Joli, Quebec: Les Ateliers Plein Soleil Inc., 1979.

Bennett, Jo-Anne. *The Complete Gas Barbecue Cookbook*. Burnstown, Ontario: General Store Publishing House.

Benoit, Jehane. *My Secrets for Better Cooking*. Montreal: Reader's Digest Canada, 1970; *The Canadiana Cookbook*. Toronto: Pagurian Press, 1970; *The Best of Madame Benoit*. Pagurian, 1972; *Enjoying the Art of Canadian Cooking*. Pagurian, 1974; *The Microwave Cook Book*. Toronto: McGraw-Hill Ryerson, 1975; *Mme. Jehane Benoit's Complete Heritage of Canadian Cooking*. Pagurian, 1976; *Madame Benoit Cooks at Home*. McGraw-Hill Ryerson, 1978; *Madame Benoit's Lamb Cook Book*. McGraw-Hill Ryerson, 1979.

*The Best Of Bridge*. Calgary: Best of Bridge Publishing Limited, 1976. Followed in the '80s by *Enjoy!*, *Winners* and *Grand Slam* (*More Recipes from The Best of Bridge*).

*The Best of Canadian Cooking*. Recipes from Canada's famous cooks. Toronto: Pagurian Press, 1977.

Bexton, Cecile. *With a Pinch of Love.* Toronto: General Foods Kitchens, 1970; *The Finishing Touch,* 1972.

*Boomtown's First Edition of the Women's Auxiliary Cook Book.* Saskatoon: The Western Development Museum, 1973. Followed by Second, Heritage and Fourth Editions (to 1990).

Borella, Ann. *In Glass Naturally.* Toronto: Simon & Schuster of Canada,1974.

Breckenridge, Muriel. *The Old Ontario Cookbook.* Toronto: McGraw-Hill Ryerson, 1976; *Every Day A Feast,* 1978.

Buszek, Beatrice Ross. *The Blueberry Connection.* Granville Centre, Nova Scotia: Cranberrie Cottage, 1979. Followed by *The Cranberry Connection, The Apple Connection, The Strawberry Connection* and *The Sugar Bush Connection.*

*Canadian Mennonite Cookbook.* Altona, Manitoba: D.W. Friesen & Sons Ltd.,1973. Revised edition of *Altona Women's Institute Cookbook,*1965.

Cartwright, Susan and Edmonds, Alan. *Capital Cookery.* Toronto: Pagurian Press, 1970; *The Prime Ministers' Cook Book,* 1976.

*Centennial Symphony of Cooking.* Compiled by St. Catharines Symphony Women's Committee, 1976.

Chevrier, Monique, c.n.d. *La Cuisine de Monique Chevrier.* Montreal: Éditions Mirabel, 1973.

*A Collage of Canadian Cooking.* Compiled by the Canadian Home Economics Association. Toronto: Van Nostrand Reinhold,1979.

Collett, Elaine. *The Chatelaine Cookbook.* Toronto: Maclean-Hunter/ Doubleday Canada, 1973.

*Cooking The Metric Way.* Compiled by the British Columbia Home Economics Association, 1975.

*A Cook's Tour of the ROM.* Toronto: The Members' Committee of the Royal Ontario Museum, 1978.

*The Country Kitchen Old and New.* Compiled by Women's Institutes of Nova Scotia, 1972; *Crocks, Pots and Whatnots,* 1973.

*crème de la crème.* Brantford, Ontario: The Art Gallery of Brant, 1975.

Crow, Elmay. *Grandma's Country Cooking.* Victoria, B.C., 1971.

Daniels, Adelaide. *Weight Watching Cookery.* Toronto: Clarke, Irwin and Company Ltd., 1972.

Dodd, Bert. *The Senior Chef.* British Columbia Ministry of Health, 1979.

*Epicure's Toronto Food Book.* Toronto Life/Greey de Pencier Books, 1978.

*Family Cooking Today.* Edited by Marilyn Clark. Calgary Co-Op Association, 1979.

*Fat-Back & Molasses.* Compiled by Ivan F. Jesperson. St. John's, Newfoundland, 1974.

Ferrier, Shannon and Shuttleworth, Tamara. *Kids In The Kitchen.* Toronto: James Lorimer & Company, 1978; *More Kids in The Kitchen,* 1980.

Fielden, Joan and Larke, Stan. *From Garden to Table.* Toronto: McClelland & Stewart, 1976.

*Food à la canadienne.* Ottawa: Food Advisory Services, Canada Department of Agriculture, 1970.

Fremes, Ruth. *The Canadian Woman's Almanac.* Toronto: Methuen, 1978.

Garrett, Blanche Pownall. *Canadian Country Preserves & Wines.* Toronto: James Lewis & Samuel, 1974.

Gill, Janice Murray. *Nova Scotia Down-Home Cooking.* Toronto: McGraw-Hill Ryerson, 1978.

Gotlieb, Sondra. *The Gourmet's Canada.* Toronto: New Press,1972; *Cross Canada Cooking.* Saanichton, B.C.: Hancock House Publishers, 1976.

Gougeon, Helen. *Helen Gougeon's Original Canadian Cookbook.* Montreal: Tundra Books,1975. (Originally *Helen Gougeon's Good Food,* Macmillan of Canada, 1958.)

*The Hadassah Cookbook.* Compiled by Sarah Goldenberg Chapter, Saskatoon, 1974.

Hansen, Gaye. *Just Muffins, Just Casseroles, Just for Tea, Just Cookies.* Cranbrook (B.C.), 1978 to 1984.

*Hillcrest Finnish Club Cookbook.* Thunder Bay, Ontario, 1979.

*The Kinnereth Cookbook.* Compiled by Hadassah-WIZO, Toronto, 1979.

*Les Recettes des Fermières du Québec.* Chomeday, Laval, Quebec: Les Éditions Pénelopé, Inc., 1978.

Lisko, Mary. *The Happy Cooker.* Oshawa, Ontario, 1976.

McColl Lindsay, Ann. *The Cookshop Cookbook.* London, Ontario, 1977.

McDougall, Sheila. *Cookbook for College Kids.* Calgary: Centax, 1978.

*Memorable Meals in B.C.: A Centennial Cook Book.* Edited by Margaret S. Pearlman. Victoria: The B.C. Centennial '71 Committee, 1971.

Meyer, Anna. *The Freezing and Cooking Book.* Toronto: Meyer Visual Productions, 1974.

Moore, Mary. *The Mary Moore Cookbook.* Toronto: Published by The Mary Moore Cookbook. Printed by D.G. Seldon Printing Ltd., Hamilton,1978.

Murray, Rose. *The Christmas Cookbook.* Toronto: James Lorimer & Company, 1979.

*Muskie Jones's Northwoods Cookery.* Cobalt, Ontario: The Highway Book Shop edition, 1975.

*Newfoundland Confederation Celebration Commemorative Recipe Cook Book.* Maple Leaf Mills Limited, 1974.

Nightingale, Marie. *Out of Old Nova Scotia Kitchens.* Toronto: Pagurian Press Limited,1971. (Halifax: Nimbus Publishing, 1990.)

*Northern Kitchen.* Compiled by Women's Auxiliary, Chapel of the Good Shepherd, Fort Churchill, and the Ladies Aid, St. Paul's Anglican Mission, Churchill, Manitoba,1973.

Oliver, Margo. *Weekend Magazine Menu Cookbook.* Montreal Standard Publishing,1972; *Stew and Casserole Cookbook.* Montreal: Optimum Publishing, 1975; *Most Treasured Recipes.* Montreal: Optimum Publishing, 1977.

Petch, Carol. *Old Hemmingford Recipes.* Hemmingford, Quebec, 1977.

*Reader's Digest Creative Cooking.* Montreal: The Reader's Digest Association (Canada) Ltd., 1977.

*Recipes of Note.* Compiled by Toronto Mendelssohn Choir, 1979.

Roland Bouchard, Cécile. *Le Pinereau: L'art culinaire au Saguenay-Lac Saint Jean.* Montreal: Les Éditions Leméac, 1971.

Sirrine, Patricia, Leavitt, Norma and Kiester, Elaine. *Eat Your Heart Out.* Calgary: Centax, 1978.

Sookavieff, Ellen. *The Sunflower Recipe Collection: A Doukhobor Cookbook.* Grand Forks, B.C.: MIR Publication Society, 1979.

Staebler, Edna. *More Food That Really Schmecks.* Toronto: McClelland & Stewart, 1979.

Stern, Bonnie. *Food Processor Cuisine.* Toronto: Methuen, 1978.

Temes, Sandra. *Welcome To My Kitchen.* Toronto: The Sandra Temes Cooking School, 1979.

*This is British Columbia: Recipes through the Years.* Victoria: Beautiful British Columbia Magazine and B.C. Ministry of Agriculture, 1979.

*Tillsonburg Centennial Cook Book.* Compiled by Tillsonburg (Ontario) District Memorial Hospital Auxiliary, 1972.

*Time-honoured Recipes of the Canadian West.* Vancouver: Nabob Foods Limited, 1973.

*The Treasury of Newfoundland Dishes.* Maple Leaf Mills Limited, 1976.

*Vancouver Aquarium Seafood Recipes.* Compiled by Ainley Jackson. Vancouver: Gordon Soules Book Publishers, 1977.

*The VanDusen Cook Book: Flavours of the Gardens.* Vancouver Botanical Gardens Association, 1979.

*Vers une nouvelle cuisine québecoise.* Institut de tourisme et d'hôtellerie. Québec: Éditeur officiel du Québec, 1977/Éditions Élysée, 1979.

*Western Favourites.* Calgary: Canadian Western Natural Gas Company, 1979.

## The Eighties

Ackerman, Caroline. *Cooking With Kids.* Winnipeg: Turnstone Press, 1982.

Adams, Mae. *Raves 'n Craves.* Vancouver, 1985.

Aitken, Julia. *Baker's Secret Quick & Easy Baking.* Toronto: Grosvenor House, 1986.

*All-Occasion Cooking.* A fund-raising project of Epilepsy Canada, 1981.

*The Atlantic Cookbook.* By the contributors and readers of Atlantic Insight, edited by Patricia Holland. Halifax: Formac Publishing, 1987.

Baird, Elizabeth. *Summer Berries.* Toronto: James Lorimer & Company, 1980; *Elizabeth Baird's Favorites,* 1984.

*Baker's Chocolate Celebration Cookbook.* Toronto: General Foods Inc., 1983.

Bannerman, Norma and Halliday, Donna-Joy. *Cooking With Cents.* Calgary: Cooking With Cents Publishing Company, 1983.

Bannock, Bill. *The Real Bill Bannock Cookbook.* The Pas, Manitoba: New North Ventures, 1987.

Barber, James. *James Barber's Immodest but Honest Good Eating Cookbook.* Vancouver: Douglas & McIntyre, 1987.

Barss, Beulah M. (Bunny). *The Pioneer Cook: A Historical View of Canadian Prairie Food.* Calgary: Detselig Enterprises, 1980; *Come 'n Get It: Favorite Ranch Recipes.* Saskatoon: Western Producer Prairie Books,1983; *Oh, Canada!* Calgary: Deadwood Publishing/Centax,1987.

*A Basketful of Favorites.* By food writers of The Globe and Mail. Toronto: Macmillan of Canada, 1988.

*Be My Guest.* Compiled by The Regina Y.W.C.A. Cookbook Committee. Regina: Centax, 1983.

Benoit, Jehane. *Madame Benoit's World of Food.* Toronto: McGraw-Hill Ryerson, 1980; *Convection Oven Cook Book.*

McGraw-Hill Ryerson, 1981; *My Grandmother's Kitchen.* McGraw-Hill Ryerson, 1981; *The Encyclopedia of Microwave Cooking.* Saint Lambert, Quebec: Les Éditions Héritage, 1985.

*The Berton Family Cookbook.* Toronto: McClelland & Stewart, 1985.

*Best of the Fairs.* Canadian Association of Exhibitions/Robin Hood Multifoods, 1986.

*The Best of Thunder Bay Cookbook.* Compiled by the United Women's Groups of Thunder Bay, Ontario, 1980.

*The Big Carrot Vegetarian Cookbook.* Compiled by Anne Lukin. Toronto: Second Story, 1989.

Bizier, Richard. *Les grand dames de la cuisine au Québec.* Montreal: Les Éditions La Presse, 1984. Volume II, 1986.

Black-Crowley, Linda. *The Avalon Dairy Cookbook.* Vancouver: Black Publications, 1983.

Braun, Linda and Cox-Lloyd, Barbara. *Going Wild.* Saskatoon: Western Producer Prairie Books, 1987.

Brownridge, Eleanor. *I'm Hungry.* Toronto: Random House of Canada, 1987.

Bruyère, Serge. *À la table de Serge Bruyère.* Montreal: Les Éditions La Presse, 1984.

Budge, Ann. *Fit To Eat.* Edmonton: Hurtig, 1983.

Calder, Susan. *Welcome to Microwave Cooking.* Victoria, B.C.: Centax, 1983; *Welcome to Microwave Living,* 1988.

*Caledon Cooking.* Compiled by the Caledon (Ontario) Information Centre, 1984.

*Canada Cooks!* Series. Vancouver: Whitecap Books, Vancouver, 1980s.

Canadian Diabetes Association. *Choice Cooking.* Toronto: NC Press,1987.

*The Canadian Living Barbecue and Summer Foods Cookbook.* By Margaret Fraser and the food writers of Canadian Living magazine. Toronto: Random House of Canada, 1988.

*The Canadian Living Cookbook.* By Carol Ferguson and the food writers of Canadian Living magazine. Toronto: Random House of Canada, 1987.

*The Canadian Living Microwave Cookbook.* By Margaret Fraser and the food writers of Canadian Living magazine. Toronto: Random House of Canada, 1988.

*The Canadian Living Rush Hour Cookbook.* By Margaret Fraser and the food writers of Canadian Living magazine. Toronto: Random House of Canada, 1989.

*The CanLit Foodbook.* Compiled by Margaret Atwood. Toronto: Totem Books, 1987.

Carpino, Pasquale and Drynan, Judith. *La Cucina di Pasquale.* Toronto: Horizon Publishing, 1980.

Cassidy, Julie and Parker, Kathleen. *Recipes From Toronto's Historic Ward 5,* 1987.

Clement, Diane. *Chef on the Run.* Vancouver: Sunflower Publications, 1982; *More Chef on the Run,* 1984.

Clery, Val and Jensen, Jack. *From the Kitchens of the World: A Canadian Feast.* Toronto: Clarke Irwin, 1981; Clery, Val. *The Solo Chef.* Toronto: Prentice-Hall Canada, 1981.

Cohen, Julie. *Tennis & Truffles.* Toronto: The Inn and Tennis Club at Manitou, 1985.

Cohlmeyer, David. *The Vegetarian Chef.* Toronto: Oxford University Press, 1985.

Comfort, Judith. *Some Good!* Halifax: Nimbus Publishing, 1985; *Spuds! Dulse! Fiddleheads!* 1986; *Judith Comfort's Christmas Cookbook.* Toronto: Doubleday Canada, 1988.

*Cooking Collections, Canadian Feasts From Land and Sea.* Compiled by Federated Women's Institutes of Canada. Ottawa: Centax, 1988.

*Cooking with Campbell's Today.* Toronto: Campbell Soup Co. Ltd., 1980.

*The Cottage Cookbook.* Compiled by Georgian Bay cottagers. Pointe au Baril, Ontario: The Ojibway Club, 1983.

*Country Church Cooking.* Compiled by Josephburg Men's Choral Society, Fort Saskatchewan, Alberta: Centax, 1984.

*Cuisine du Québec.* Institut de tourisme et d'hôtellerie du Quebec. Montreal: Les Éditions La Presse, 1985.

Crawford, Lee. *Good Mornings: A Breakfast Cookbook.* Toronto: Doubleday Canada, 1987.

Dams, Caralan and VanderVelde, Susan. *It's Microwaved.* Calgary: Centax, 1985; Dams, Caralan. *Let's Microwave,* 1987.

*Daughters of the Midnight Sun Cookbook.* Yellowknife, N.W.T., 1983.

*David Wood Food Book* (David Wood Food Shop, Toronto). Vancouver: Whitecap Books, 1989.

*A Different Kettle of Fish.* Halifax: The Book Room Limited, 1981.

Doell, Barbara, Pollard, Pat and Winsby, Dianne. *I've Got To Have That Recipe!* Victoria: 1986; *I've Got To Have That Recipe, Too!,* 1989.

Douglas, Joyce. *No-More-Than-Four Ingredient Recipes: A Cookbook for Kitchen Klutzes*. Toronto: Doubleday Canada, 1988.

Downie, Mary Alice and Robertson, Barbara. *The Well-Filled Cupboard*. Toronto: Lester & Orpen Dennys, 1987.

Dubrulle, Pierre. *The Great Canadian Chef from France*. Vancouver: Centax, 1986.

Dunton, Hope. *From The Hearth: Recipes from the World of 18th-Century Louisbourg*. University College of Cape Breton Press, 1987.

Dwillies, Eileen. *The Western Living Cookbook*. Vancouver: Whitecap Books, 1987.

*Eastern Townships Cookbook*. West Brome, Quebec: The Barn Press, 1986.

Elliot, Marion and Spicer, Ruth. *Christmas Through The Years*. St. Stephen, New Brunswick, 1982.

Enright, Nancy. *Nancy Enright's Canadian Herb Cookbook*. Toronto: James Lorimer & Company, 1985.

Evans-Atkinson, Mary. *British Columbia Heritage Cookbook*. Vancouver: Whitecap Books, 1984.

*Fare for Friends*. Compiled by Friends of Interim Place, Mississauga. Toronto: Key Porter Books, 1983.

*Favorite Recipes from the U.B.C. Bakeshop*. Edited by Shirley Louie. Vancouver: University of British Columbia Food Services, 1986.

Ferrier, Shannon and Shuttleworth, Tamara. *The Kidsfood Cookbook*. Toronto: James Lorimer & Company, 1982.

Fielden, Joan. *The Great Canadian Sandwich Book*. Toronto: Milmac Communications Inc., 1982.

*The Five Roses Complete Guide to Good Cooking*. 26th edition. Ogilvie Mills Limited, 1989.

Fraser, Margaret and MacDonald, Helen Bishop. *The Total Fibre Book*. Toronto: Grosvenor House, 1987.

Fremes, Ruth. *What's Cooking*, Books 1-5. Toronto: Methuen, 1980–84 .Fremes, Ruth and Sabry, Zak. *NutriScore*. Toronto: Methuen, 1981.

*Fresh From The Market*. Truro, N.S.: The Farmers' Markets Association of Nova Scotia, c. 1985.

*Freshwater Fish Cookbook*. Compiled by Nancy Prothero. Port Stanley, Ontario: Nan-Sea Publications, 1982.

*From Prairie Kitchens*. Recipes from Saskatchewan Women's Institutes, compiled by Emmie Oddie. Saskatoon: Western Producer Prairie Books, 1980.

*From The Collections: U.B.C. Museum of Anthropology Cookbook*. Vancouver, 1986.

*From The Villa With Love*. Toronto: Villa Colombo Ladies Auxiliary, Toronto, 1980.

*Georgian Bay Gourmet Winter Entertaining*. Midland, Ontario: Georgian Bay Gourmets' Publishing Ltd.,1980; *Summer Entertaining*, 1983.

Galioto, Renée. *The Flavour of Quinte: Cooking in Hastings and Prince Edward Counties*. Richmond Hill, Ontario: Renée Galioto Productions, 1982.

*The Gathering: The Rural and Native Heritage Cookbook*. Burleigh Falls, Ontario: Lovesick Lake Native Women's Association, 1985.

Gill, Janice Murray. *Canadian Bread Book*. McGraw-Hill Ryerson, 1980.

Glick, Julie and McLeod, Fiona. *The Granville Island Market Cookbook*. Vancouver: Talonbooks, 1985.

Gilletz, Norene. *Micro Ways*. Montreal: J & N Publishing, 1988.

Goodwin, Terry. *A Chuckwagon Load of Recipes*. Calgary: Rural Roots Publications, 1983.

*The Great Hadassah-WIZO Cookbook*. Compiled by the Edmonton chapter. Edmonton: Hurtig Publishers,1982.

*A Guide to Handling and Preparing Freshwater Fish*. Winnipeg: David Iredale and Roberta York, Freshwater Institute, Fisheries and Oceans Canada, 1983.

Hall, Marg. *Marg Hall's Cookbook*. Yellowknife, N.W.T.: printed by N.W.T. Power Corporation, 1989.

Halliday, Donna-Joy. *Entertaining Without Reservations*. Calgary: Cooking With Cents Publishing Company, 1985.

*The Harrowsmith Cookbook*. By the editors and readers of Harrowsmith Magazine. Camden East, Ontario: Camden House Publishing. Volume One, 1981; Volume Two, 1983; Volume Three, 1987; *The Harrowsmith Pasta Cookbook*,1984; *The Harrowsmith Fish and Seafood Cookbook*,1985; *The Harrowsmith Illustrated Book of Herbs*, 1986.

Hasselfield, Lesley. *A Month of Sundays*. Norway House, Manitoba: 1982; *Sunday Brunches*, 1983.

Haworth, Jan. *The Canadian Fish Cookbook*. Vancouver: Douglas & McIntyre, 1984.

*Heritage Recipes from the Maritimes and Newfoundland*. By the readers and contributors of Atlantic Insight. Halifax: Formac Publishing, 1988.

Hoare, Jean. *Best Little Cookbook in the West*. Claresholm, Alberta: Deadwood Publishing (Calgary)/Centax, 1983; *Jean's Beans*. Western Producer Prairie Books (Saskatoon)/Centax, 1986.

Hofer, Sam. *The Hutterite Treasury of Recipes*. Saskatoon: Hofer Publishing, 1986; *Soups and Borschts*, 1988.

Holland, Barb and McQuilkin, Roxanne. *Microwave Cooking With Style*. Toronto: McGraw-Hill Ryerson,1988.

*The Homemaker's Magazine Cookbook*. By the food editors of Homemaker's. Toronto: McClelland & Stewart,1986.

*Home On The Range*. Compiled by the Sorensen family, edited by Nancy Millar. Calgary: Homestead Publishing,1982.

*A Honey of a Cookbook*. Compiled by the Alberta Beekeepers' Association. Centax,1982; Volume 2, 1986.

Hooley, Larissa and Robinson, Josephine. *Vancouver Entertains*. Vancouver: Whitecap Books, 1986.

*Hospitality*. Compiled by the Women's Auxiliary of the Hospital for Sick Children, Toronto, 1983.

Hullah, Evelyn. *On The Go*. Toronto: Cardinal Kitchens, 1988.

Hunter, Alice. *Alice Hunter's North Country Cookbook*. Yellowknife, N.W.T.: Outcrop Publishers, 1986.

*Island Cookery*. Compiled by Quadra Island Child Care Society. Heriot Bay, B.C.: Ptarmigan Press, 1981.

Jenner, Alice. *The Amazing Legume*. The Saskatchewan Pulse Crop Growers' Association, 1984.

Johnson, Louise. *The Esperanza Cook Book: From Historic Vancouver Island's Rugged West Coast*. Surrey, B.C.: Maple Lane Publishing, 1989.

Juss, Ruby Schile. *Juss Microwaving*. Medicine Hat, Alberta: Juss Microwaving Publishing Co., 1987.

Kane, Marion. *Best Recipes Under The Sun*. Toronto: Totem Books, 1987.

Kane, Marion and Schwartz, Rosie. *The Enlightened Eater*. Toronto: Methuen, 1987.

Kates, Joanne. *The Joanne Kates Cookbook*. Toronto: Oxford University Press, 1984.

Kennedy, Jamie. *The Jamie Kennedy Cookbook*. Toronto: Oxford University Press, 1985.

Kenyon, Janice. *The Victoria Dinner Party Cookbook*. Victoria, B.C.: Kachina Press, 1985; *Light Fantastic*, 1989.

Kynaston, Jo. *Cooking in the Gulf Islands*. Sidney, B.C.: Mermaid Publishing, 1983.

Lafrance, Marc and Desloges, Yvon. *A Taste of History/Goûter à l'histoire: The Origins of Quebec's Gastronomy*. Canadian Parks Service and Les Éditions de la Chenelière, 1989.

*Let's Break Bread Together*. Recipes from the United Churches of Canada, compiled and published by the United Church in Meadowood, Winnipeg, 1988.

Lindsay, Anne. *Smart Cooking*. Toronto: Macmillan of Canada, 1986; *The Lighthearted Cookbook*. Toronto: Key Porter Books, 1988.

Logsdail, Barbara. *The Seasonal Gourmet*. Saskatoon: The Star-Phoenix/Centax, 1984.

Macdonald, Kate. *The Anne of Green Gables Cookbook*. Toronto: Oxford University Press, 1985.

MacIlquham, Frances. *Complete Fish and Game Cookery of North America*. Winchester Press, 1983.

Mackie, Joan. *A Culinary Palette*. Toronto/Vancouver: Merritt Publishing Company, 1981.

Margaret, Len. *Fish & brewis, toutens & tales*. St. John's: Breakwater Books, 1980.

Martin, Verneil. *Among Friends*. Calgary: Centax, 1987. Volume II, 1989.

Mason, Ruth and Silver, Sarah. *A Canadian Country Diary & Recipe Book*. Willowdale, Ontario: Hounslow Press, 1982.

McCall, Jeanette. *Wedding Cakes Simplified*. Toronto, 1984.

McCrorie, Brad. *Soups For All Seasons*. Toronto: Doubleday Canada, 1987.

McGinnis, Arthur. *Galley Magic*. Gibsons, B.C.: Gibsons Marina, 1987.

McQuade, Barbara. *The Sun's Five-Star Recipes*. The Vancouver Sun, 1985.

Mendelson, Susan. *Mama Never Cooked Like This*. Vancouver: Talonbooks, 1980; *Let Me In The Kitchen*. Vancouver: Douglas & McIntyre, 1982; *Nuts About Chocolate*, Douglas & McIntyre, 1983.

Menghi, Umberto. *The Umberto Menghi Cookbook*. Vancouver: Talonbooks, 1982; *Umberto's Pasta Book*. Vancouver: Whitecap Books, 1985; *The Umberto Menghi Seafood Cookbook*. Toronto: David Robinson/Key Porter Books, 1987.

Meyer, Bernard. *Bernard Meyer's East Coast Cuisine*. Halifax: Formac Publishing, 1988.

Murray, Rose. *Rose Murray's Vegetable Cookbook*. Toronto: James Lorimer & Company, 1983; *Secrets Of The Sea*. Toronto: Grosvenor House, 1989.

Nesbitt, Anne. *Parkland Palate*. Centax,1984; *Easy & Exciting*. Winnipeg: Ark Publishing, 1986.

*New Brunswick Women's Institute Cookbook*. Fredericton: Goose Lane Editions, 1987.

Newlove, Gloria. *Pacific Harvest Cook Book*. Campbell River, B.C., 1986.

*Nova Scotia Pictorial Cookbook*. Photographs by Sherman Hines. Edited by Anna Hobbs. Halifax: Nimbus Publishing, 1986.

*Okanagan Harvest*. Vernon, B.C.: DVA Publishing, 1988.

Oliver, Margo. *Cooking for Today*. Toronto: Today Magazine Inc., 1982; *Cookbook for Seniors*. North Vancouver: Self-Counsel Press, 1989.

*Old and New Pass Lake Cookbook*. Pass Lake, Ontario: Salem Danish Evangelical Lutheran Church, 1984.

Olson, Carol. *Berries Beautiful*. Spy Hill, Saskatchewan: Centax, 1985.

Paré, Jean. *Company's Coming: 150 Delicious Squares*. Vermillion, Alberta: Company's Coming Publishing Limited, 1981. First of the Company's Coming series of 18 titles.

Pentland, John (University Endowment Lands Fire Department, Vancouver). *Firehall Favourites Cookbook*. Burnstown, Ontario: The General Store Publishing House, 1989.

*Pioneer Cooking in Ontario: Recipes from Ontario Historical Sites*. Toronto: NC Press Limited, 1988.

*The Polish Touch*. Compiled by Marie Curie Sklodowska Society, Toronto, 1982.

Powers, Jo Marie and Stewart, Anita. *The Farmers' Market Cookbook*. Toronto: Stoddart,1984.

*Prizewinning Country Kitchen Recipes*. Baking contest winners at fairs in Ontario. Port Perry, Ontario: The Ontarian Group, 1980 edition.

*Recipes From Sea to Sea*. Compiled by Louisbourg, Nova Scotia branch, Navy League of Canada, 1985.

*The Recipes Only Cookbook*. By Carroll Allen and the food writers of Recipes Only magazine. Toronto: McGraw-Hill Ryerson, 1989.

Restino, Susan (Cape Breton). *Fresh From The Country*. Toronto: Key Porter Books, 1987.

Rodmell, Jane and Bush, Kate. *The Getaway Chef*. Toronto: Key Porter Books, 1983.

Roldan, Tony and White, Jim. *The Best of Canada Cookbook*. Toronto: McClelland & Stewart, 1981.

Sable, Myra. *Elegant Entertaining Cookbook*. Toronto: Bantam Books, 1986.

Sadkowski, May and Whitehead, Judith. *The Little Gourmet Gas Barbecue Cookbook*. Burnstown, Ontario: The General Store Publishing House, 1987.

Scace, Susan. *Take Me With You. . .Please*. Toronto: Eagle's Publications/ Centax, 1984.

Scargall, Jeanne. *Canadian Homestead Cookbook*. Toronto: Methuen, 1980. Formerly published as *Pioneer Potpourri*, 1974.

Schultz, Judy. *Nibbles & Feasts*. Edmonton: Tree Frog Press, 1986; *The Best of Seasons*. Red Deer, Alberta: Red Deer College Press, 1989.

*Seafood Celebration*. Prince Rupert, B.C.: 75th Birthday Committee, 1984.

*75 Favorites*. Calgary: The Blue Flame Kitchen, Canadian Western Natural Gas, 1987.

Sharp, J.J. *Flavours of Newfoundland & Labrador*. St. John's: Breakwater Books, 1981; *Flavours of Nova Scotia*, 1986.

Smith, Cathy. *Food 101*. Toronto: McGraw-Hill Ryerson, 1982.

Smith, Eleanor Robertson. *Loyalist Foods in Today's Recipes*. Hantsport, N.S.: Lancelot Press Limited, 1983.

Soeur (Sister) Berthe. *Cooking With Yogurt*. Montreal: Delisle Foods/ McClelland & Stewart, 1983.

Soeur Angèle. *À table avec Soeur Angèle*. Montreal: Insitut de Tourisme/ Les Éditions de l'Homme, 1984.

Spicer, Kay. *Light & Easy Choices*. Toronto: Grosvenor House,1985; *Choice Desserts*, 1986.

Staebler, Edna. *Schmecks Appeal*. Toronto: McClelland & Stewart, 1987.

Stamm, Fredy. *The Millcroft Inn Cookbook*. Erin, Ontario: The Porcupine's Quill, Inc., 1987.

Stancer, Claire. *The Ultimate Salad Dressing Book*. Toronto: McGraw-Hill Ryerson, 1988.

Stern, Bonnie. *At My Table*. Toronto: Methuen, 1980; *The Cuisinart Cookbook*. Toronto: Totem Books, 1984; *The CKFM Bonnie Stern Cookbook*. Toronto: Random House of Canada, 1987; *Desserts*. Random House, 1988.

Stewart, Anita. *Country Inn Cookbook*. Toronto: Stoddart, 1987; 2nd edition, 1990; *The St. Lawrence Market Cookbook*. Stoddart, 1988; *The Lighthouse Cookbook*. Madeira Park, B.C.: Harbour Publishing, 1988.

*Taste Niagara*. St. Catharines, Ontario: The Preservation of Agricultural Lands Society, Inc.: 1983.

*A Taste of Muskoka*. Bracebridge, Ontario: Cottage Country Cooks, 1986.

Thomson, Eleanor. *A Loving Legacy*. Westport, Ontario: Butternut Press, 1987.

Topp, Eleanor. *Feasts for Families*. Nepean, Ontario: Geertsema Publications, 1984. Topp, Eleanor and Shields, Betty. *Meals Microwave Style*. Carp,

Ontario: Gai-Garet Design & Publishing Ltd., 1988.

*The Toronto Symphony Cookbook.* Compiled by the Toronto Symphony Women's Committee, Toronto, 1980.

*Traditional Recipes of Atlantic Canada* (series of 13). Ultramar Canada Inc., 1988.

Trueman, Mildred and Stuart. *Favourite Recipes From Old New Brunswick Kitchens.* Willowdale, Ontario: Hounslow Press, 1983; *New Brunswick Heritage Cookbook*, 1986.

*Twillingate Times.* Compiled by Twillingate (Nfld.) Women's Institute, 1981.

Walker, Emily. *A Cook's Tour of Nova Scotia.* Halifax: Nimbus Publishing, 1987.

Warner, Joie. *The Complete Book of Chicken Wings.* Toronto: Totem Books, 1985; *A Taste of Chinatown.* Toronto: Little, Brown and Company, 1989; *All The Best* series including *All The Best Pasta Sauces.* Toronto: Prentice-Hall Canada, 1987 and 1988.

Warwick, Paul. *The Best of The Spirit of Cooking.* Vancouver: Centax, 1985.

*Waterloo County Cook Book.* Collected by Marcella Wittig Calarco. Kitchener, Ontario: 1980.

Watson, Julie V. *Favourite Recipes from Old Prince Edward Island Kitchens.* Willowdale, Ontario: Hounslow Press, 1986; *Cultured Mussel Cookbook.* Halifax: Nimbus Publishing, 1986; *Barbecuing Atlantic Seafood.* Nimbus, 1988; *Largely Lobster.* Nimbus, 1989.

Waverman, Lucy. *The Cooking School Cookbook.* Toronto: HarperCollins, 1988; *Lucy Waverman's Seasonal Canadian Cookbook.* Toronto: HarperCollins, 1989.

Waxman, Sara. *The King's Wife's Cookbook.* Toronto: Nelson Canada, 1980; *Back Roads & Country Cooking.* Toronto: McClelland & Stewart, 1985.

Webster, Joyce and Eckford, Margaret. *Yes You Can! Microwave.* Vancouver, B.C.: Micro Chefs Publishers, 1987.

*Welcome To Our World.* Compiled by The Regina Open Door Society. Regina: Centax, 1985.

*Wheatland Bounty.* Compiled by the Laboratory Technologists of Saskatchewan. Centax, 1981.

Wilson, Kasey. *Granville Island Cookbook.* Vancouver: Douglas & McIntyre, 1984. *Gifts from the Kitchen*, 1987. *Spirit & Style The New Home Cooking*, 1989.

Wine, Cynthia. *Hot and Spicy Cooking.* Toronto: Penguin, 1984; *Across The Table.* Toronto: Prentice-Hall of Canada, 1985.

Winfield, Joan. *Microwave Miracles.* Glanworth, Ontario, 1983.

Wong, Sandra. *Liqueurs for Dessert.* Vancouver, 1988.

Wood, Marjorie. *A Pinch of the Past.* Winnipeg: Hyperion Press, 1987.

Wylie, Betty Jane. *Encore: The Leftovers Cookbook.* Toronto: McClelland & Stewart, 1982.

Yan, Martin. *The Joy of Wokking* and *The Yan Can Cookbook.* Toronto: Doubleday Canada, 1982.

Yan, Stephen. *Chinese Recipes* (6th Edition). Port Coquitlam, B.C.: Yan's Variety Company Limited, 1980.

## The Nineties

*Acadian Pictorial Cookbook.* Photographs by Wayne Barrett. Introduction by Barbara LeBlanc. Halifax: Nimbus Publishing, 1991.

*Aces: More Recipes From The Best of Bridge.* Calgary: The Best of Bridge Publishing Ltd., 1992.

Armstrong, Julian. *A Taste of Quebec.* Toronto: Macmillan of Canada, 1990.

Azevedo, Carla. *Uma Casa Portuguesa.* Toronto: Summerhill Press, 1990.

Bright, Emily. *Bright Ideas: Microwave and Micro-Convection Cooking.* Niagara-on-the-Lake: Emily Bright Publications/Centax, 1990.

*The Canadian Living Cooking Collection* (series of 8). Toronto: The Madison Book Group, 1991.

*The Canadian Living Light and Healthy Cookbook.* By Margaret Fraser and the food writers of Canadian Living magazine. Toronto: Random House, 1991.

*Canadian Living's Country Cooking.* By Elizabeth Baird and the food writers of Canadian Living magazine. Toronto: Random House, 1991.

*Canadian Living's Desserts.* By Elizabeth Baird and the food writers of Canadian Living magazine. Toronto: Random House, 1992.

*The Cannery Book: Salmon Stories & Seafood Recipes.* Vancouver: Dobson Communications, 1990.

Casey, Pat. *Fort Steele – The Gold Rush Days: A Taste of the Past.* Cranbrook, B.C.: Casey Enterprises, 1990.

Clement, Diane. *Fresh Chef On The Run.* Vancouver: Sunflower Publications, 1991.

Collacott, Pam. *Pam's Kitchen.* Toronto: Macmillan of Canada, 1990; *The Best of New Wave Cooking.* Carp, Ontario: Creative Bound Inc., 1992.

Cormier-Boudreau, Marielle and Gallant, Melvin. *A Taste of Acadie.* Fredericton, N.B.: Goose Lane Editions, 1991. Originally published as *La cuisine traditionnelle en Acadie*, Les Éditions d'Acadie, 1978.

Elliot, Elaine and Lee, Virginia. *Maritime Inns & Restaurants Cookbook.* Halifax: Formac PUblishing, 1990.

*Fry's Chocolate Cookbook: Gold Edition.* Cadbury's Beverages Canada, 1990.

*Good Friends Cookbook.* Compiled by Friends of Interim Place, Mississauga. Toronto: Key Porter Books, 1991.

*The Guide to Good Baking 90's style.* A supplement to The Five Roses Guide to Good Cooking. Montreal: Ogilvie Mills Limited, 1990.

*A Guide To Home Preserving.* Compiled by Laurie Reed Westover. Toronto: Bernardin of Canada, 1990.

*The Harrowsmith Salad Garden.* Camden East, Ont.: Camden House Publishing, 1992.

Hertzberg, Deborah. *Cooking Above the Tree Tops at Kilima.* Victoria, B.C., 1990.

Howard, Margaret and MacDonald, Helen Bishop. *Eat Well, Live Well.* Compiled for Canadian Dietetic Association. Toronto: Macmillan of Canada, 1990.

Hrechuk, Irene and Zasada, Verna. *Grandma's Touch.* Edmonton: Centax, 1990.

*Impossible Pie.* Compiled by Lucy Waverman. The Hospital for Sick Children Capital Campaign. Toronto: The Printing House Ltd., 1990.

*Just for You: Favourite Recipes from Canada's Top Cooks.* Compiled for the Women's Legal, Education and Action Fund (LEAF). Toronto: Macmillan of Canada, 1992.

Lindsay, Anne. *Lighthearted Everyday Cooking.* Toronto: Macmillan of Canada, 1991.

McCrorie, Brad. *Fresh From the Market.* Toronto: Doubleday Canada, 1991.

*Meech Lake Soup: A Collection of Parliamentary Recipes.* Charity fundraiser compiled by the Parliamentary Spouses Association, Ottawa, 1990.

Meraglia, Cosimina. *Giorgio's Authentic Italian Cook Book.* Yellowknife, N.W.T.: Giorgio's Restaurant Ltd., 1990.

Mercer, Barbara. *A Week at Galecliff.* St. John's, Nfld.: Breakwater, 1990.

*Milk's Microwave Cookbook.* Compiled by Barb Holland. Ontario Milk Marketing Board, 1991.

Mouzar, Mary and Uhlman, Joanne. *Kiss The Cook Who Microwaves* Series. Halifax: Periwinkle Publishing, 1990.

Murray, Rose. *Rose Murray's Comfortable Kitchen Cookbook*. Toronto: McGraw-Hill Ryerson, 1991.

*New Brunswick Pictorial Cookbook*. Photographs by Sherman Hines. Recipes compiled by Margaret Jones. Halifax: Nimbus Publishing, 1991.

*Newfoundland Pictorial Cookbook*. Photographs by Sherman Hines. Recipes by Al Clouston. Halifax: Nimbus Publishing, 1990.

Oliver, Margo. *Good Food For One*. North Vancouver, B.C.: Self-Counsel Press, 1990.

Paré, Jean. *Company's Coming: Lunches* and *Pies*. Edmonton: Company's Coming Publishing Ltd., 1992.

Reesor, Ruby. *Aunt Ruby's Recipes*. Markham, Ontario: Allspeed Copy Inc., 1990.

Richardson, Noël. *Summer Delights*. Vancouver: Whitecap Books, 1986 and 1991; *Winter Pleasures*, 1990.

Robinson, Kathleen, with Pete Luckett. *Pete Luckett's Complete Guide to Fresh Fruit & Vegetables*. Fredericton, N.B.: Goose Lane Editions, 1990.

Rosenberg, Monda. *The New Chatelaine Cookbook*. Toronto: Macmillan of Canada, 1992.

Schultz, Judy. *The Best of Seasons Menu Cookbook*. Red Deer, Alberta: Red Deer College Press, 1991.

Sharp, J.J. *Flavours of Prince Edward Island*. Halifax: Nimbus Publishing, 1990.

Spicer, Kay. *From Mom, With Love*. Toronto: Doubleday of Canada, 1990.

Stern, Bonnie. *Appetizers*. Toronto: Random House of Canada, 1990.

Stewart, Anita. *From Our Mothers' Kitchens*. Toronto: Random House of Canada, 1991.

Watson, Julie. *Seafood Menus for the Microwave*. Halifax: Nimbus Publishing, 1990; *Heart Smart Cooking on a Shoestring*. Toronto: Macmillan of Canada, 1991.

Waverman, Lucy. *Fast & Fresh Cookbook*. Toronto: McGraw-Hill Ryerson, 1991.

*What's Cooking at Goose Bay*. Compiled by the staff at the Royal Bank of Canada, Happy Valley and Goose Bay, Labrador, 1990.

*Yukon Order of Pioneers Ladies Auxiliary Cookbook*. Whitehorse, 1991.

# *Publisher's Acknowledgements*

*The cookbooks in the Cookbook Samplers have been photographed with the permission of the following:*

p. 11
*Blue Ribbon Cook Book,* 1905. Blue Ribbon Limited, Winnipeg. *Canada's Favorite Cook Book* by Annie R. Gregory, 1902. Bradley-Garretson Co., Ltd. and The Linscott Publishing Co., Brantford. *Culinary Landmarks,* 1909. Courtesy of St. Luke's Women's Auxiliary, Sault Ste. Marie. *Laurel Cook Book,* 1909. Laurel Mission Circle of St. John Presbyterian Church, Hamilton, Ontario. *Ogilvie's Book for a Cook,* 1905. Courtesy of Ogilvie Mills Ltd., Montreal. *Public School Household Science* by Mrs. J. Hoodless and Miss M.U. Watson, 1905. Copp Clark Pitman Ltd. *The Dominion Cook Book* by Anne Clarke, revised edition 1901. George J. McLeod Limited, Toronto. *The Hughes' Household Calendar Cookbook,* 1909. Geo. E. Hughes Apothecaries Hall, Charlottetown, Prince Edward Island. *The King's Daughters Cook Book,* 75th Anniversary Edition, compiled by Mrs. Robert Burns McMicking, Victoria, BC, 1979. Unusual House, Vancouver. *The New Cook Book: A Volume of Tried, Tested and Proven Recipes,* Revised Edition, by the Ladies of Toronto and Other Cities and Town, Edited by Grace E. Denison, 1905. Rose Publishing Co., Toronto. *The New Household Manual and Ladies Companion Embracing A Repository of Valuable Recipes,* 1901. R.A.H. Morrow, St. John, New Brunswick. *The Wheat City Cook Book,* The Ladies of the Methodist Church, Brandon, Manitoba, 1901.

p. 35
*A Calendar of Dinners* by Marion Harris Neil, Including the Story of Crisco, 1917. Courtesy of Procter and Gamble. *Cowan's Dainty Recipes,* 1918. Cowan Company Limited, Toronto. *Fish and How To Cook It,* 1914. Department of Naval Service, Ottawa, Reproduced with the permission of Supply and Services Canada, 1992. *Five Roses Cook Book,* 1915. Courtesy of Ogilvie Mills Ltd. *La cuisine raisonnée,* 1919 and 8th edition 1957, La Congrégation de Notre Dame. Courtesy of Éditions fides, Ville St. Laurent, Quebec. *Lillian Massey School Book of Recipes* edited by A.L. Laird and N.L. Pattison, 1917. Toronto. *Metropolitan Cook Book,* 1918. Courtesy of Metropolitan Life Insurance Company, Ottawa. *Moffat Cook Book,* 1915. Trademark of CANCO INCORPORATED. *Ogilvie's Book for a Cook,* 1916. Courtesy of Ogilvie Mills Ltd. *Purity Flour Cook Book,* 1917. Courtesy of Maple Leaf Foods. *Reliable Recipes,* 1919. Egg-O Baking Powder Co., Hamilton. *Robin Hood Cook Book,* 1915. Courtesy of Robin Hood Multifoods Ltd. *The Real Home-Keeper: A Perpetual Honeymoon for the Vancouver Bride,* 1913. Real Home-Keeper Publishing, Vancouver. *War Time Cook Book,* compiled by Duke of Wellington Chapter of The Imperial Order of the Daughters of the Empire, Sherbrooke, Quebec, c. 1910. Courtesy of The Imperial Order of the Daughters of the Empire, Toronto.

p. 57
*Canadian Cook Book* by Nellie Lyle Pattinson, The Ryerson Press, 1923. Courtesy of McGraw-Hill Ryerson Ltd., Whitby, Ontario. *Cheese and Ways to Serve It,* Kraft-Phenix Cheese Company, 1928. Courtesy of Kraft General Foods Canada Inc., Don Mills, Ontario. *Cookery Arts and Kitchen Management* by Anna Lee Scott, 1926. Courtesy of Maple Leaf Foods.

*Fleischmann's Recipes,* 1924. Courtesy of Specialty Brands, Toronto. *Jell-O At Home Everywhere,* 1922. The Genesee Pure Food Company of Canada, Bridgeburg, Ontario. Courtesy of Kraft General Foods Canada Inc., Don Mills, Ontario. *La bonne cuisine canadienne,* Ministère de la Voirie, Quebec, 1927. *Les secrets de la bonne cuisine* by Soeur Sainte-Marie Edith, Directrice de l'école ménagère, Congrégation de Notre Dame, Montreal, 1926. The Canadian Printing and Lithographing Company, Montreal. *Margaret Currie: Her Book* by Margaret Currie, The Montreal Star, 1924. Hunter Rose Co., Toronto. *McClary's Household Manual,* 1922. Trademark of CANCO IN-CORPORATED. *Moffat's Cookery Book,* 1926. Trademark of CANCO INCORPORATED. *National Sea Food Recipes* by the Women of the Maritime Provinces, 1923. National Fish Co. Ltd., Halifax. *Old Homestead Recipes,* 1920. Courtesy of Maple Leaf Foods. *Queen Anne Cook Book,* The Queen Anne Chapter IODE, Kitchener, Ontario, 1925. Courtesy of the Imperial Order of the Daughters of the Empire, Toronto. *Salad Secrets,* Keen's Mustard, 1928. Courtesy of RECKITT & COLMAN CANADA INC. *The Girl at Catelli's,* 1920. Used with the permission of The Borden Company Limited. *The Little Blue Books Home Series,* Department of Health, 1922. *The New Edwardsburg Recipe Book,* c. 1920. Courtesy of Best Foods Canada Inc. *The Unity Lodge Cook Book,* 1927. Tuxford, Saskatchewan. *The Westinghouse Refrigerator Book,* c. 1920. Courtesy of Westinghouse Canada, Hamilton. *When We Entertain* by Anna Lee Scott, 1915. Courtesy of Maple Leaf Foods. *The Home Cook Book,* 1923. Hunter, Rose and Company, Toronto, Ontario.

p. 80
*3 Meals a Day Recipe Review,* 2nd edition, by Jessie Read, The Evening Telegram, 1935. Courtesy of York University, Scott Library Special Collections, North York, Ontario. *Apple Secrets,* Compiled by Alice Stevens, 1931. Associated Growers of British Columbia Ltd., Vernon, B.C. *A Family Tradition – The Magic Baking Powder Cook Book,* c. 1930. Reproduced with the permission of Nabisco Brands Ltd, Toronto, Ontario, Canada. "NABISCO" ® and MAGIC ®Baking Powder are trade marks of Nabisco Brands Ltd, Toronto, Canada, © all rights reserved. *A New Way of Living,* 1932. Courtesy of Kellogg Canada Inc. *Baking Made Easy,* 1938. Courtesy of Robin Hood Multifoods Inc. *Canada's Prize Recipes,* 1930. Courtesy of Best Foods Canada Inc. *Davis Dainty Dishes,* Davis Gelatine, 1939. Courtesy of Davis Germantown (Canada) Inc. *Delectable Dishes,* 1936. St. George Church, Montreal. *Maple Leaf Cooking School,* directed by Anna Lee Scott, 1932. Courtesy of Maple Leaf Foods. *Mrs. Flynn's Cookbook* compiled by Mrs. Katherine C. Lewis Flynn, 1931. Published by the Ladies of St. Elizabeth's Aid Society of St. Vincent's Orphanage, Charlottetown, P.E.I. Courtesy of Prince Edward Island Museum and Heritage Foundation, Charlottetown. *Tasty Meals for Every Day,* 1933. Courtesy of Maple Leaf Foods. *The Maple Leaf Canadian Recipe Book,* The Department of Trade & Commerce, c. 1930. Reproduced with the permission of the Ministry of Supply and Services, Canada, 1992. *The Purity Cook Book,* 1932. Courtesy of Maple Leaf Foods. *Vincent Galleries Book of Cookery* compiled and edited by Florence Elizabeth Stewart and Gretchen Day Ross, 1936. Vancouver. *Watkins Cook Book,* 1935. The J.R. Watkins Co., Montreal.

p. 103

*51 Ways to a Man's Heart* by Anna Lee Scott, c. 1940. Courtesy of Maple Leaf Foods. *Blossom of Canada Home Tested Recipes*, 1945. Courtesy of Maple Leaf Foods. *Borden's Eagle Brand Magic Recipes*, 1946. Used with the permission of The Borden Company Limited. *Campbell's Flour Home Tested Recipes*, 1945. Courtesy of Maple Leaf Foods. *Canadian Cook Book for British Brides*, Women's Voluntary Services Division, Department of National War Services, 1945. Courtesy Department of National Defense. *Carnation Cook Book* by Mary Blake, 1943. Courtesy of Nestlé Canada Inc. *Edith Adams 11th Annual Cookbook*, 1944. Courtesy of the Vancouver Sun. *From Market to Table* by Marie Holmes, 1940. Courtesy of Marjorie Flint. *How to Eat Well Though Rationed* by Josephine Gibson, 1943. Vital Publications, Toronto. *I Like Your Crust, One Good Cook Tells Another*, and *You Too*, c. 1940. Jewel Shortening. *Presto Cooker Recipe Book*, 1948. Courtesy of Regal Ware Canada Inc., Orangeville, Ontario. *Robin Hood Prize Winning Recipes* Selected by Rita Martin, 1947. Courtesy of Robin Hood Multifoods Inc. *Rogers' Golden Syrup Recipe Book*, c. 1940. Courtesy of B.C. Sugar Refining Co. Ltd., Vancouver. *Sugar Savers*, 1947. Agriculture Canada, reproduced with the permission of the Minister of Supply and Services Canada, 1992. *The Black Whale Cook Book*, compiled by Mrs. Ethel Renouf, 1948. Gaspé County, Quebec. *The Cook's Tour to the Realm of Cakes* by Anna Lee Scott, c. 1940. Courtesy of Maple Leaf Foods. *The Purity Cook Book*, 2nd revision, 1945. Courtesy of Maple Leaf Foods. *War Time Recipes*, Fort Anne Chapter I.O.D.E., c. 1940. Courtesy of Imperial Order of the Daughters of the Empire, Toronto.

p. 126

*British Columbia Women's Institutes Centennial Cook Book*, 1958. Evergreen Press Limited, Vancouver. *Buckskin Cookery*, A Souvenir Cookbook of pioneer recipes donated by Old Timers and Natives of B.C., 1957. Gwen Lewis, Quesnel, B.C. *Canadian Fish Cook Book*, Department of Fisheries, 1959. Reproduced with permission of the Minister of Supply and Services Canada, 1992. *Cooking the Co-op Way*, published by the Manitoba Women's Guild in conjunction with Federated Co-operatives, 1959. Courtesy of Federated Co-operatives, Manitoba. *Coronation Cook Book*, compiled by the Ladies of St. Matthew's, 1953. Courtesy of the Council of St. Matthew's Church, Kitchener. *Dutch Oven*, compiled by the Ladies Auxiliary of The Lunenburg Hospital Society, 1953. Lunenburg, Nova Scotia. *Farm Women's Union of Alberta Cook Book*, 1956. Edmonton. *Favourite Recipes compiled by The Woman's Association of Bridge Street United Church*, 1959. Courtesy of Bridge Street United Church Women, Belleville, Ontario. *Favorite Recipes from the United Nations*, 2nd edition, 1959. Courtesy of Robin Hood Multifoods Inc. *From Ottawa Kitchens*, Recipes of Ottawa Hostesses, 1954. Courtesy of Save The Children Canada, Ottawa. *From Saskatchewan Homemakers' Kitchens* compiled by Homemakers' Clubs, 1955. *Fun Fare*, c. 1950. Courtesy of Maple Leaf Foods. *Janet Peters' Personal Cookbook from the pages of Canadian Homes and Gardens*, 1956. Courtesy of Canadian Homes and Gardens © Maclean Hunter Ltd. *Meeting Over Tea*, c. 1950. Courtesy of The Tea Council, Toronto. *New Brunswick Recipes*, 1958. Courtesy of New Brunswick Home Economics Association. *The New Purity Cook Book*, 4th edition, 1959. Courtesy of Maple Leaf Foods. *Traditional Ukrainian Cookery* by Savella Stechishin, 1957. Copyright Trident Press Ltd., Winnipeg. *We Can Cook Too!* compiled by the Montreal Branch of the Canadian Women's Press Club, 1956.

p. 149

*A Guide to Good Cooking with Five Roses Flour,* 20th Edition, 1962. Courtesy of Ogilvie Mills Ltd. *A Treasury of Nova Scotia Heirloom Recipes* compiled by Florence M. Hilchey, 1967. Reprinted with the Permission of the Nova Scotia Department of Government Services, Halifax. *Blue Flame Food Magic*, c. 1960. United Gas Company. *Centennial Cook Book, Canada's Favourites* compiled by the Federal Women's Committee of the New Democratic Party, 1967. Courtesy of New Democratic Party, Ottawa. *Family Heirlooms* by Trina Vineberg, 1965. Used by permission of the publishers, McClelland & Stewart, Toronto. *Fare Exchange* by Dorothy Allen-Gray, 1963. Kingswood House. *Food Fun – The Step by Step Cook Book for Boys and Girls* edited by Glenora Pearce, 1963. Courtesy of Federated Co-operatives, Manitoba. *Food that Really Schmecks* by Edna Staebler. Used by permission of the Canadian Publishers, McClelland & Stewart, Toronto. *Helen Gagen's Summer Foods*, The Telegram, c. 1960. Courtesy of York University, Scott Library Special Collections, North York, Ontario. *Margo Oliver's Weekend Magazine Cook Book*, 1967. Courtesy of Margo Oliver. *Muriel Wilson's Colonist Cook Book*, 1963. Courtesy of the Times Colonist, Victoria, B.C. *Saskatchewan Sportsman's Gourmet Guide* by Henrietta Goplen, 1968. Courtesy of Douglas & McIntyre, Vancouver. *The Art of Home Baking*, 1964. Courtesy of Maple Leaf Foods. *The Northern Cook Book* by Eleanor A. Ellis, 1967, revised edition 1979. *Traditional Macedonian Recipes*, 1969. Ladies Auxiliary of the Macedonian Patriotic Organization, Toronto.

p. 173

*A Collage of Canadian Cooking* , 1979. Courtesy of the Canadian Home Economics Association. *Canadian Mennonite Cookbook*, 1973. Reprinted with the Permission of Stoddart Publishing Co. Ltd., Don Mills, Ontario. *Classic Canadian Cooking* by Elizabeth Baird, 1974. Used with the Permission of James Lorimer & Company Ltd., Publishers, Toronto and Halifax. *Fat-Back and Molasses* by Ivan F. Jesperson, 1974. St. John's, Newfoundland. *Helen Gougeon's ORIGINAL CANADIAN COOK-BOOK* © 1975 Helen Gougeon Schull, published by Tundra Books, Montreal. *La Cuisine de Monqiue Chevrier* by Monique Chevrier, 1973. Éditions Mirabel, Montreal. *Madame Benoit Cooks at Home* by Madame Benoit, 1978. Courtesy of Bernard Benoit. *Northern Kitchen* compiled by Women's Auxiliary, Chapel of the Good Shepherd, Fort Churchill and The Ladies Aid, St. Paul's Anglican Mission, Churchill, Manitoba, 1973. *Out of Old Nova Scotia Kitchens* by Marie Nightingale, 1971. Reprinted with permission of Nimbus Publishing, Halifax, Nova Scotia. *The Best of Bridge*, 1976. Reprinted with the permission of Centax Books and Distribution, Regina. *The Chatelaine Cookbook* by Elaine Collett, revised edition, 1973. Courtesy Chatelaine © Maclean Hunter Ltd. *The Complete Gas Barbecue Cookbook* by Jo-Anne Bennett. Courtesy of General Store Publishing, Burnstown Ontario. *The Gourmet's Canada* by Sondra Gotlieb, 1972. *The Mary Moore Cookbook* by Mary Moore, 1978. *Time-Honoured Recipes of the Canadian West*, 1979. Courtesy of Nabob Foods Limited, Vancouver. *Western Favourites*, 1979. Courtesy of Canadian Western Natural Gas Company Limited, Calgary.

p. 196

*A Taste of Chinatown* by Joie Warner, 1989. Used with permission of Little, Brown & Company, Toronto. *Across The Table* by Cynthia Wine, 1985. Published by Prentice Hall Canada, Scarborough, Ontario. *Choice Cooking* by the Canadian Diabetes Association, 1987. Reprinted with the permission of NC Press, Toronto. *Come 'N Get It* by Bunny Barss, 1983.

Courtesy of Douglas & McIntyre, Vancouver. *Company's Coming, 150 Delicious Squares* by Jean Paré, 1981. Used with the permission of Company's Coming Publishing Limited, Vermillion, Alberta. *Cooking Collections, Canadian Feasts from Land and Sea* by Federated Women's Institutes of Canada, 1988. Reprinted with the permission of Centax Books and Distribution, Regina. *Cuisine de Québec* by the Institute de Tourisme et d'Hôtellerie du Québec, 1985. Les Editions La Presse Inc., Montreal. *Desserts* by Bonnie Stern, 1988. Reprinted with permission of Random House, Toronto. *Favourite Recipes from Old Prince Edward Island Kitchens* by Julie V. Watson, 1986. Courtesy of Hounslow Press and photograph courtesy of Stanhope Beach Lodge, G. Auld. *Georgian Bay Gourmet Summer Entertaining* by Anne Connell, Helen Decarli (Graham), Mary Hunt and Jean Leavens, 1983. Courtesy of the authors. *Let's Break Bread Together*, 1984. Courtesy of United Church in Meadowood, Winnipeg, Manitoba. *Lucy Waverman's Seasonal Canadian Cookbook*, by Lucy Waverman. Copyright 1989 by Lucy Waverman. Cover design by Scott Richardson and Cover Illustrations by Catherine Chafe. Published by HarperCollins Publishers Ltd., Toronto. *Smart Cooking* by Anne Lindsay, 1986. Macmillan Canada. *Spuds! Dulse! Fiddleheads!* by Judith Comfort, 1986. Reprinted with permission of Nimbus Publishing, Halifax, Nova Scotia. *The Canadian Living Cookbook* by Carol Ferguson and the Food Writers of Canadian Living, 1987. Courtesy of Canadian Living and photographer Fred Bird. *THE CANLIT FOODBOOK* compiled by Margaret Atwood. Copyright 1987 by The Writer's Development Trust. Cover design by The Dragon's Eye Press. First published in 1987 by Totem Books, a division of Collins Publishers Ltd. *The Farmers' Market Cookbook* by Jo Marie Powers and Anita Stewart, 1984. Reprinted with the Permission of Stoddart Publishing Co. Ltd., Don Mills, Ontario. *The Gathering: The Rural and Native Heritage Cookbook*, 1985. Courtesy of Lovesick Lake Native Women's Association. *The Harrowsmith Cookbook, Volume 1* by the Editors and Readers of Harrowsmith Magazine, 1981. Courtesy of Roger Hill, Photographer, Toronto. *The Homemaker's Magazine Cookbook* by the Food Editors of Homemaker's, edited by Thelma Dickman, 1986. Courtesy of Homemaker's Magazine – Telemedia Procom Inc. *The Recipes Only Cookbook* by Carroll Allen and the Food Writers of Recipes Only Magazine, 1989. Courtesy of Homemaker's Magazine – Telemedia Procom Inc. *The Western Living Cookbook* by Eileen Dwillies, 1987. Courtesy of Eileen Dwillies.

p. 222
*A Taste of Acadie* by Marielle Cormier-Boudreau and Melvin Gallant, 1991. Courtesy of Goose Lane Editions Ltd., Fredericton, New Brunswick. *A Taste of Quebec* by Julian Armstrong, 1990. Macmillan Canada. *Canadian Living's Country Cooking* by Elizabeth Baird and the Food Writers of Canadian Living, 1991. Courtesy of Canadian Living and photographer Fred Bird. *Eat Well, Live Well* by Margaret Howard and Helen Bishop MacDonald, 1990. Macmillan Canada. *From Mom, With Love* by Kay Spicer, 1990. Courtesy of Doubleday Canada Ltd. *Impossible Pie*: A Project for the Hospital for Sick Children Capital Campaign compiled by Lucy Waverman, 1990. A cookbook developed by The Printing House Ltd. to raise funds for the cardiology quadrant at The Hospital for Sick Children. A proud Canadian project. *Lighthearted Everyday Cooking* by Anne Lindsay, 1991. Macmillan Canada. *Milk's Microwave Cookbook* compiled by Barb Holland, 1991. Courtesy of Ontario Milk Marketing Board. *Rose Murray's Comfortable Kitchen Cookbook* by Rose Murray, 1991. Produced by B & E Publications Inc. for McGraw-Hill Ryerson Limited. *The Best of Seasons Menu Cookbook* by Judy Schultz, 1991. Title © Judy Schultz, Photograph by Stephe Tate © Stephe Tate, Darklight Studios. *The Five Roses Complete Guide to Good Cooking*, 26th Edition, 1989, and *The Guide to Good Baking 90's Style*, 1990. Courtesy of Ogilvie Mills Ltd., Montreal. *What's Cooking At Goose Bay* compiled by the staff at The Royal Bank of Canada, Happy Valley and Goose Bay, Labrador, 1990. Courtesy of The Royal Bank of Canada, Happy Valley, Labrador. *Yukon Order of Pioneers Ladies Auxiliary Cookbook*, Whitehorse, 1991.

Excerpts have been reprinted from previously published material with the permission of the following:

p. 4 and p. 7 Barss, Beulah (Bunny), *Come 'n Get It* (1983). Courtesy of the publishers, Douglas & McIntyre, Vancouver. p. 4 Berton, Laura Beatrice (1961). Used by permission of the Canadian publishers, McClelland & Stewart, Toronto. p. 5 Broadfoot, Barry, *The Pioneer Years* (1983). Courtesy of Doubleday Canada. p. 5 Silverman, Eliane Leslau, *The Last Best West*. Courtesy of Eliane Leslau Silverman. p. 5 Montgomery, Lucy Maud, *Anne of the Island* (1968). Used by permission of the Canadian publishers, McClelland & Stewart, Toronto. p. 6 Duncan, Sara Jeannette, *The Imperialist*. Used by permission of the Canadian publishers, McClelland & Stewart, Toronto. p. 8 Murray, Rose, *The Christmas Cookbook*, published by James Lorimer & Company, Toronto and Halifax. p. 28 Cookson, Joseph, Huntsville in 1916 as appeared in The Muskoka Sun, July 26, 1990. p. 28 McClung, Nellie, *The Stream Runs Fast*. Courtesy of her grand-daughter, Nellie McClung. p. 30 Benoit, Jehane, *Madame Benoit Cooks At Home*. Courtesy of Bernard Benoit. p. 31 White, Howard, *Raincoast Chronicles*. Courtesy of Howard White and Harbour Publishing. p. 50 Leighton, Douglas, *A Taste of Banff*. Courtesy of Douglas Leighton. p. 50 Scargall, Jeanne, *The Canadian Homestead Cookbook* (1980). Courtesy of Jeanne Scargall. p. 52 Farmer, Fanny Merritt, *The Boston Cooking School Cook Book*. Used by permission of the Canadian publishers, McClelland & Stewart, Toronto. p. 52 Speechly, Margaret M., *The Country Homemaker*, published by The Grain Grower's Guide. Courtesy of The Country Guide. p. 53 Alberta Power Limited, *Diamond Dishes*. Courtesy of Alberta Power Limited. p. 72 Collins, Robert, *Butter Down The Well* (1984). Courtesy of the publishers, Douglas & McIntyre, Vancouver. p. 74 Millar, Nancy, *Home on the Range*. Courtesy of Nancy Millar. p. 75 Conrad, Laidlaw and Smith, *No Place Like Home*, published by James Lorimer & Company, Toronto and Halifax. p. 75 Murray Gill, Janice, *Nova Scotia Down-Home Cooking*. Courtesy of Janice Murray Gill. p. 96 T. Eaton

Company Limited, advertisement in *The Victory Cookbook*. Courtesy of The T. Eaton Company Limited. p. 97 Gamester, George, newspaper column as appeared in The Toronto Star, Courtesy of Toronto Star Syndicate. May 2, 1990. p. 99 Porter, Helen, *Below The Bridge*, © Helen Porter. Published by Breakwater. p. 118 Wilson, Muriel, *The Colonist Cookbook*. Courtesy of the Colonist/Victoria. p. 120 Gzowski, Peter, *The Morningside Papers*. Used by permission of the Canadian publishers, McClelland & Stewart, Toronto. p. 142 Berton, Pierre and Janet. Used by permission of the Canadian publishers, McClelland & Stewart, Toronto. p. 144 Staebler, Edna, *Food That Really Schmecks*. Used by permission of the Canadian publishers, McClelland & Stewart, Toronto. p. 146 Waverman, Lucy, newspaper column as appeared in Toronto Sun, April 25, 1991. Courtesy of Canada Wide Features Service. p. 166 Gotlieb, Sandra, *The Gourmet's Canada*, 1972. p. 167 Baird, Elizabeth, *Classic Canadian Cooking*, published by James Lorimer & Company, Toronto and Halifax. p. 169 Allen, Carroll, This Bountiful Land as appeared in Homemaker's Magazine. Courtesy of Homemaker's Magazine. p. 172 Wine, Cynthia, Status Food as appeared in Homemaker's Magazine, April, 1982. Courtesy of

Homemaker's Magazine. p. 188 Kane, Marion, How We Ate in the Eighties (Dec. 27, 1989). Courtesy of Marion Kane and The Toronto Star. p. 190 Wine, Cynthia, *Across The Table*. Prentice Hall Canada Inc. p. 191 Schultz, Judy, "A Taste of Five Cities." Courtesy of Judy Schultz. p. 212 Baker Cowan, Bonnie, editorial column as appeared in Canadian Living, February 1991. Courtesy of Canadian Living. p. 214 Kates, Joanne, article as appeared in The Globe & Mail Toronto magazine. Courtesy of Joanne Kates. p. 214 White, Jim. Courtesy of Jim White and the Toronto Star. p. 215 Collacott, Pam, as appeared in article Today's Kids Are Adept at Using Microwave Ovens. by Judy Creighton. Courtesy of The Canadian Press. p. 215 Rosenberg, Monda, article as appeared in Chatelaine. Courtesy Chatelaine magazine © Maclean Hunter Ltd. p. 215 McCallum, Janet, as appeared in article Yuppies Turning Into Cheapies in The Toronto Star, February 27, 1992. Courtesty of Toronto Star Syndicate. p. 221 Wiseman, Henry, as appeared in newspaper column in The Toronto Star, Courtesy of Toronto Star Syndicate. September 9, 1989. p. 221 Suzuki, David, newspaper column as appeared in The Toronto Star. Courtesy of Toronto Star Syndicate. January 20, 1991.

# Recipe Index

Recipe names in roman type indicate complete recipes. *Recipe names and page numbers in italics indicate references only.*

• JAMIE KENNEDY • PAUL KING • JUDI KINGRY • DAVID KINGSMILL • BETTY KIRBY • PAULINE KLOSEVYCH • DINAH KOO • ALICE KRUEGER • BONNIE LACROIX • ROSE LACROIX • ANNIE L. LAIRD • LOUISE LAMBERT-LAGACE • ANITA LANDRY • EUSTELLE LANGDON • JANE LANGDON • YOLANDE LANGUIRAND • LUCETTE LAPOINTE • SUSANNE LAPOINTE • ARLENE STACEY LAPPIN • JULIETTE LASSONDE • BARBARA J. LAUER • IRENE LEAVITT • EVELYN LEBLANC • SUZANNE LECLERC • SUSAN LEE • GWEN LESLIE • CLAUDETTE LEVESQUE • GRACE LEWIS • GWEN LEWIS • ANNE LINDSAY • ANN McCOLL LINDSAY • MARILYN LINTON • LISBETH LODGE • MARTHA LOGAN • BARBARA LOGSDAIL • LILLIAN LOUGHTON • SARAH LOVELL • NICK LUCIANO • PETE LUCKETT • ANNE LUKIN • ISOBEL MacARTHUR • BIRTHE MARIE MACDONALD • HELEN BISHOP MACDONALD • KATE MACDONALD (BUTLER) • LINDA MACDONALD • MARION MACDONALD • SUSAN MACDONALD • MARGARET MACDONNELL • MARGARET MACFARLANE • BEA MACGUIRE • FRANCES MACILQUHAM • HELEN MACKERCHER • JOAN MACKIE • ROSEMARY MACLEAN • MRS. AYLMER MACPHERSON • JAN MAIN • MICHELLE MARCOTTE • ETHEL MARLISS • RITA MARTIN • VIRGINIA MARTIN • LOUISE MARTINEAU • MAY MASKOW • LILLIAN MASSEY • RHONDA MAY • GRACE MAYERS • LILLIAN McCONNELL • MARGARET McCREADY • BRUCE McDONALD • CAROLYN McDONELL • SHEILA McDOUGALL • ANNE McEACHERON • PEARL McGONIGAL • MARY McGRATH • JANE McKAY-NESBITT • JUDY McKINNON • JENNIFER McLAGAN • BARBARA McLAREN • MRS. ROBERT BURNS McMICKING • BILL McNEIL • BARBARA McQUADE • ROXANNE McQUILKIN • CAREN McSHERRY-VALAGAO • VICKI McTAGGART • MARG MEIKLE • SUSAN MENDELSON • UMBERTO MENGHI • ANN MERLING • VIVIAN MERRILL • ANNA MEYER • BERNARD MEYER • BARBARA MIACHIKA • NANCY MILLAR • BEA MILLER • SHIRLEY MOASE • BETH MOFFATT • MICHELINE MONGRAIN-DONTIGNY • PHILIPPE MONSARRET • KERRY MOORE • LOUISE MOORE • MARY MOORE • GORDON MORASH • GLENYS MORGAN • HELEN MORNINGSTAR • NORMA MORRIS • DOREEN MORRISON • GWENNA MOSS • SCOTT MOWBRAY • CONNIE MURPHY • ROSE MURRAY • JEAN MUTCH • MARGARET MYER • WENDY NEALE • MARION HARRIS NEIL • HELEN NEILSON • ANNE NESBITT • SHIRLEY NEWHOOK • LENORE NEWMAN • SUSAN NEWSON • DAVID NICHOL • MARIE NIGHTINGALE • ANGELA NILSON • EILEEN NORMAN • VIRGINIA NORRIS • GAIL AND JEAN NORTON • CATHY O'BRIEN • EMMIE ODDIE • JEAN ODDIE • MARGO OLIVER • MARILYN O'REILLY • ELLEN O'RILEY • BERTHA G. OXNER • MARIE PACE • ODILE PANAT-RAYMOND • JEAN PARÉ • EDNA W. PARK • KAYE PARKER • JOYCE PARSLOW • MABEL PATRICK • JEAN PATTERSON • TRUDY PATTERSON • NELLIE LYLE PATTINSON • GLENORA PEARCE • JOYCE PEARSON • JEAN PECK • SHEILA PECK • LAURA PEPPER • JAN PESKETT • JANET PETERS • L.B. PETT • MARGARET PETTILLO • SINCLAIR PHILIP • BERYL PLUMTRE • KITTY POPE • MARGARET POPE • ETHEL POST